Bollywood Cinema

Bollywood Cinema
TEMPLES OF DESIRE

VIJAY MISHRA

ROUTLEDGE NEW YORK AND LONDON

Published in 2002 by
Routledge
29 West 35th Street
New York, NY 10001

Published in Great Britain by
Routledge
11 New Fetter Lane
London EC4P 4EE

Routledge is an imprint of the Taylor & Francis Group.

Printed on acid-free, 250-year-life paper.
Manufactured in the United States of America.

10 9 8 7 6 5 4 3 2

Library of Congress Cataloging-in-Publication Data

Mishra, Vijay.
    Bollywood cinema: temples of desire / Vijay Mishra.
        p. cm.
    ISBN 0-4159-3014-6 (alk. paper) – ISBN 0-4159-3015-4 (pbk.)
    Includes bibliographical references and index.
        1. Motion pictures—India. I. Title.

PN1993.5.I8 M46 2001
    791.43'0954—dc21   2001019672

For my daughter, Paras

> That time is past,
> And all its aching joys are now no more
> And all its dizzy raptures.
> > *Wordsworth*

> It is hard to forget
> Those once forgotten days,
> Days not meant to return—
> Why does the heart recall them?

> If days were doves,
> I would have caged them,
> Caressed and cradled them,
> Fed them on pearls of love,
> Clasped them to my breast.
> > *Shailendra*

> For a thousand years unseen
> The narcissus bemoans its fate;
> Rarely is one born
> With passion eternal, pain unending.
> > *Hazrat Jaipuri (attr.)*

Contents

Preface

I began writing this preface in the library of the National Film Archive of India. The library is in fact no more than a reading room, solidly built with a central pillar. Around the long reading tables a few students of Indian cinema pore over old newspapers and examine photographs of films. The central catalogue of print material is perhaps more useful as a sign of the amount of material that can no longer be retrieved. Although current issues of Indian periodicals are readily available, back issues of journals, books, and many key films are difficult to trace even when they do exist in the stacks. Despite these shortcomings, it is the only reading room in the world that can take you back to old Indian film periodicals and fanzines. Enthusiastic librarians bring copies of magazines from the stacks if they can locate them. Without air-conditioning, the midday heat, even in the month of December, can become unbearable. Books as well as humans begin to discolor, and many of the old magazines have deteriorated beyond repair. As I brood over this preface I recall something an Indologist (possibly Heinrich Zimmer) once wrote. During a research trip to India he observed that very often we begin to understand ourselves only after we have examined another culture in some detail. I think he elaborated this pithy observation through a parable about an old man who went afar looking for gold only to discover, upon his return, that the gold lay hidden under the floor of his own kitchen. The narrative of search and discovery hit me with uncanny force in this library as I rummaged for information on Bombay Cinema. Unlike Zimmer, I came to India not as a total outsider. I grew up in the colonies, but belong, racially and as Hindu, to India. I am a descendant of illiterate Indian indentured laborers who left the plains of North India in the last quarter of the nineteenth century to work on the sugar plantations of Fiji. Although they constituted a microcosm of India in terms of linguistic, religious, and caste divisions, they were nevertheless basically peasant in origin and working class in their social attitudes. In Fiji this fragment society constructed a largely mythical—some would say illusory—India which had little basis in fact. My own India had grown through the myths of these indentured laborers, and like all mythical relationships, mine too had an implicit capacity to distort and magnify. Yet these myths or, more accurately, ideologies, since they were imaginary systems of belief, framed our ambivalent relationship to Mother India. From around 1930 onward, however, these myths of the mind began to be mediated through their projection onto the visual. In an uncanny fashion, cinema reinforced the Fiji Indian myths of an ancient land still basking in its epic glory. At the same time spectatorial fascination with the newfound power of the visual, what Fredric Jameson has called the essentially pornographic fascination that the mind has with cinema, triggered a desire for India in ways that radically transformed what until then had existed only as the fantastic clichés of our forefathers.

I came to India to do archival research and to write about Bombay Cinema as a scholarly object of knowledge. Trained as a literary critic at an ancient English university, I felt that only scholarly detachment could lead to a book that would have any respectability. But as I began to write my notes in a friend's flat in Colaba, Bombay, I suddenly realized how correct the Indologist and Fredric Jameson in fact were. I had come to India in search of the pot of gold only to find that that pot had been buried deep in my unconscious. When I saw the old films again in the Pune Film Archive, I realized that the joy of cinema was essentially sensual, stored up in the "bodily synapses" and that what I was analyzing was not so much the films themselves as repeating the original moment, the earlier gaze, of the subject, myself, viewing films. The film history I had come to construct in Pune was already there in the muscles and sinews of my body. In the end whatever I wrote will have to be framed in the experience of diaspora. Imagine my surprise when among the dun-colored and often decaying film journals in the archives I chanced upon a very early essay titled "Indian Films in Fiji Islands" published in the *Indian Cinema Annual of 1933*. The essay was written by a certain S. Pratap of Suva, Fiji. I had suddenly found a way in which I could write a narrative about myself in this preface. Like Marlow when he encountered Towser or Towson's book on seamanship (a battered copy lovingly restitched by a Russian captain), I was fascinated by this chance discovery and, more important, by the diaspora's intervention into the discourse of film criticism.

Here in front of my very eyes was an account of the beginnings of the reception of Indian films in Fiji of which, in one way, I too had been a part. The notes were sketchy, barely two pages long, but I could reconstruct an entire narrative from them. S. Pratap tells us that *Anarkali* (1928), a silent film version of what was to become a very popular film narrative, was the first film shown in the capital, Suva, in a theater owned by B. Ram Singh, founder of the Indian Picture Show Company. It was followed by *Madhuri* (1928), another silent feature film. The first talkie shown, probably in 1932, was *Veer Abhimanyu* (Valiant Abhimanyu, 1931). When the largest theater in Fiji, the Lilac, was completed in 1932, *Ayodhya Ka Raja* (The king of Ayodhya, 1932) was shown to a packed house. Such was its popularity that the film was screened twice in the same night. By 1933 there were seven cinema houses in Fiji, three (the Lilac, the Century, and the Regal) in Suva. In the same year an Indian Film Corporation had been established by Baejnath Gaji with the explicit aim of importing high-quality films from India. At the time of writing, Pratap notes that films such as *Meri Jan* (?), *Gul Bakavali* (1932), *Maya Bazar* (The bazaar of illusion, 1932), and *Zarina* (1932) had been screened. Although rental charges for films remained relatively high, the one hundred and thirty thousand Fiji Indians embraced Bombay Cinema with enthusiasm and indirectly subsidized distributors so that they could participate in cinematic moments that confirmed their own dreams about India.

As I read the above account with its matter-of-fact style and undercontextualized information, I began to understand why later versions or repeats of these films were so popular in Fiji. Filmistan's *Anarkali* (1953) was shown in my small town theater (the Empire, built in Nausori in 1951) in the early 1950s to huge audiences. *Veer Abhimanyu* was bought by one of the distributors and shown in theaters well into the '50s. Subsequent versions of *Gul Bakavali* (1947, 1956, 1963) were all extremely popular. But it was clearly *Ayodhya Ka Raja* that set the scene for the success of mythological films. Perhaps we saw our own lives in Fiji in terms of Rama's banishment and retrospectively glorified *rām rājya*, the Kingdom of Rama. There was something oddly millenarian in our outlook in that films reinforced the possibilities of a glorious past no longer available to us in the complex politics of colonial Fiji. Hence the many Rama films—*Ram Rajya* (1943), *Rambaun* (Rama's arrow, 1948), *Sampoorna Ramayana* (The extant *Rāmāyaṇa*, 1961) and so on—were enormously popular with Fiji Indians. By the time I began to see films mythologicals were very much on the ascendant. But in the early 1950s two other forms began to take hold of our imagination. The first were the stunt films. The master of this form was Homi Wadia, whose *Hind Kesari*

(The lion of India, 1935) broke all previous records in Fiji. It was a remake of any number of Hollywood stunt films (*Zorro*, for instance) in which the seemingly idiotic hero is, by night, the masked bandit and lover extraordinaire. Wadia's many stunt films as well as his Scheherazade-inspired Arabian Night tales—*Aladin* (1952), *Alibaba* (1954), *Hatimtai* (1956)—made up the first group of films that I saw. The second group centered on melody and song and may be remembered through the names of stars. So I recall films that featured Raj Kapoor—*Aag* (Desire, 1948), *Barsaat* (Monsoon, 1949), *Baware Nain* (Romantic gaze, 1950), *Awara* (The vagabond, 1951), *Aah* (Sighs from the heart, 1953), *Shree 420* (Mr. 420, 1955)—or Dilip Kumar—*Mela* (The fair, 1948), *Andaz* (Style, 1949), *Babul* (Childhood home, 1950), *Deedar* (Vision, 1951), *Aan* (Vow, 1952), *Amar* (Forever, 1954)—or Bharat Bhushan—*Baiju Bawra* (1952). It was later—toward the end of the 1950s—that I became aware of Guru Dutt, whose films changed my entire outlook on Indian popular cinema. Non-Hindi or non-Bombay films hardly ever reached Fiji. There were rare screenings of a Gujarati film or a Tamil film, but since every Indian in Fiji speaks Fiji Hindi (and understands standard Hindi) the need for Indian regional cinema never really arose.

When I left for New Zealand in 1964, the first continuous phase of my encounter with Bombay cinema came to an end. After that I returned to Fiji only twice for any significant length of time—during 1968–69 and again during 1972–73—and on those visits I managed to catch up with the films I had missed. My return to Fiji in 1972–73 coincided with what was to become one of the most significant shifts in the construction of the star hero in Bombay Cinema—that from Rajesh Khanna to Amitabh Bachchan. After that I watched Bombay Cinema on videocassettes or in small university halls where diasporic Indians screened films, almost invariably for nostalgic purposes. During all these phases, and especially during the heyday of the 1950s and the early 1960s, the knowledge which came to me took the form of anecdotal information about stars. In fact the potted summary that I can make from memory at this juncture is really about stars who dominated Bombay Cinema at any given time. In this regard my earliest memories are those of my maternal uncle recalling the likes of Master Vithal, a professional wrestler with some of the skills of Douglas Fairbanks Jr., the Billimoria brothers (Dinshaw and Eddie), Master Nissar (the early singer-actor), and Jairaj. Except for Jairaj, who survived into the early '50s, I have no recollection of them. And then there was a second phase of actors about whom we heard a lot more. They were K. L. Saigal and Ashok Kumar. Saigal's big early hits were *Chandidas* (1934) and *Devdas* (1935) and I think my uncle never stopped comparing all subsequent actors and singers to Saigal. I saw *Devdas* in the National Film Archives of Pune and was struck by the high quality of the production. In Fiji, however, the Saturday night Hindi program on national radio (the Fiji Broadcasting Commission) constantly played Saigal songs and always referred to him as *saṅgīt samrāṭh* (the king of music). Not surprisingly, I grew up with Saigal. When Mukesh sang "dil jaltā hai to jalne de" (When the heart burns, let it do so) for the film *Pahali Nazar* (The first encounter, 1945) we immediately knew that he was intervening into a style of singing made famous by Saigal. Saigal was perhaps the first real superstar, not particularly good looking, nor especially gifted as an actor, but he could sing, and in a style that has remained unique. When he died suddenly in 1947, still at his peak, even remote Fiji mourned collectively. Back in India the Indian Muslim Congress canceled its daily meeting in Bombay. The other name that I associate with the period is Ashok Kumar, the very antithesis of the impulsive hero Saigal, who began with Himansu Rai's *Jeewan Naiya* (The boat of life, 1936) and *Achhut Kanya* (The untouchable girl, 1936). His finest film was possibly *Kismet* (Fate, 1943), which I saw afterward. He remained an important actor well into the late 1950s but eschewed romantic roles and, in later years, invariably co-starred with Nalini Jaywant. After the '50s he took on decidedly older roles. Others I recall are Surendra, the actor and singer of *Anmol Ghadi* (A priceless watch, 1946) and immediate precursor of Dilip Kumar; Shyam, who died on the sets of *Shabistan* (1951); Motilal, who acted in *Mr. Sampat* (1952), a film based on an R. K. Narayan novel; Pahari Sanyal and Prithviraj Kapoor, the latter in films such as *Nal Damayanti* (1945) and *Vikramaditya* (1945).

In the 1950s, the star system was totally dominated by three names: Dilip Kumar, Dev Anand, and Raj Kapoor. I saw Dilip Kumar's huge hit *Milan* (The meeting, 1946) as well as Raj Kapoor's *Aag* (1949) when they were shown again in the theaters in Fiji in the early '50s. Though his first film was *Hum Ek Hain* (All for one, 1946), my memory of Dev Anand begins with *Taxi Driver* (1954). Among them they divided three heroic types: Dilip Kumar, arguably the finest actor of Bombay Cinema, played the role of the tragic hero who would rather lose his love than his duty to his friend; Raj Kapoor was a romantic tramp who, like Chaplin, displayed strong melodramatic characteristics; Dev Anand was the consummate urban hero, a kind of a postcolonial dandy, keeping up with whatever was the current aspiration of the Indian middle classes. However, such was the domination of these actors that there were few hits in which they didn't have leading roles. Some actors broke past the hegemony of the Dilip Kumar—Dev Anand—Raj Kapoor triumvirate. Kishore Kumar starred in *Chalti Ka Naam Gadi* (That which goes is life, 1958), probably the best comedy made in that genre; Bharat Bhushan in *Baiju Bawra* (1952), again one of the very finest of all musicals, and Shammi Kapoor in *Dil Deke Dekho* (Give your heart away, 1959) which began the tradition of the hero as dancer and consummate imitator of Western rock stars, notably Elvis Presley. There were others who made massive inroads in one way or another: Balraj Sahni, with his extraordinary performance in *Do Bigha Zamin* (1953), and Suni Dutt, Raaj Kumar, and Rajendra Kumar, who between them combined social issues with melodramatic romance (*Sadhna* [1958], *Dil Ek Mandir* [The heart is a temple, 1963]). In the 1960s many others came into their own—Dharmendra (a very natural actor with diverse skills), Manoj Kumar, Shashi Kapoor, Jeetendra, Waheeda Rehman, Vijayanthimala—but in a sense they were never able to displace totally the star status of the original triumvirate of Dilip Kumar, Raj Kapoor, and Dev Anand.

The dislodging of the triumvirate came rather dramatically. That moment occurred with the arrival of Rajesh Khanna in Shakti Samanta's *Aradhana* (1969). He sang the song "mere sapnoṁ kī rānī phir ayegī tū" (When will you come again the queen of my dreams) that brought not only a relatively new voice (that of playback singer Kishore Kumar who had been singing for years but had been overshadowed by the great singers like Mukesh and Mohammed Rafi) but a whole new style for the repackaged romantic, *becārā* hero. Rajesh Khanna has received the rare accolade of being the first superstar, larger than even Dilip Kumar. *Anand* (1970), directed by Hrishikesh Mukherji and dedicated to both Raj Kapoor and the city of Bombay, demonstrated the immense melodramatic capacities of Rajesh Khanna. The story of the dying cancer patient was the perfect narrative for the expression of the *becārā* complex for which he became famous. Rajesh Khanna's rise was meteoric, his fall equally so. Within four years (by 1972) Rajesh Khanna was on the wane. His marriage, a year later, to Dimple Kapadia and his prima donna temperament (demanding that he be given the best lines, for instance) didn't help either. But the pent-up feelings of the cinematic hero, artificially created by the industry, exploded in the figure of Amitabh Bachchan in *Zanjeer* (1973). After that the nature of the hero began to be defined in terms of the angry hero in rebellion, more in tune with a slum aesthetics than with the staid expectations of the middle class. The old staple of laid-back melodrama composed of comic interludes, romance, romantic songs gave way to the idea of the hero in total control of his destiny. Here was a composite film personality that combined heroic Rama with the antiheroic Karna and the stoic Yuddhishthira. Bachchan in many ways brought the tradition of the classic Bombay triumvirate (Dilip

Kumar, Raj Kapoor, Dev Anand) to an end as he combined in his own cinema personality all the characteristics for which the 1950s triumvirate were famous: quiet melancholy, comic self-reflection, and urbanity. Despite a serious accident during the shooting of the film *Coolie* (1983) and a stint as a parliamentarian, Amitabh Bachchan has been the superstar extraordinaire of Bombay Cinema. In retrospect it is clear that no previous star, not even K. L. Saigal or Dilip Kumar or Rajesh Khanna, ever reached the heights of Amitabh Bachchan. Yet like the earlier triumvirate, Amitabh Bachchan did not let others flourish, though one must mention Rishi Kapoor, Vinod Khanna, Mithun Chakraborty, and Anil Kapoor, actors who did, in a few films, reach star status. The fanzines called Amitabh Bachchan number one (*numero uno*) for years. But age finally caught up with him too. Despite the success of *Hum* (The collective, 1991), the 1990s and beyond belonged to the younger generation, the likes of Aamir Khan, Salman Khan, Sunny Deol, Sanjay Dutt, Akshay Khanna, Govinda, Hrithik Roshan, and above all Shah Rukh Khan, an actor who combines the aggressiveness of Amitabh Bachchan with the quiet detachment of Dilip Kumar and, most important, is the first Indian star to play some of his best roles in Bombay's own version of films about the Indian diaspora.

Even as I make these celebratory remarks, the absence of female stars in them must be explained. One of the parallel source texts for the construction of the filmic hero—the fanzines—do not give us a female star syntagma. In the November 1990 issue of *Filmfare* there is a section titled "Stargraphs" in which women are mentioned simply as names opposite whom the male stars acted. Despite the relegation of women to a footnote, it is possible to construct a female "stargraph." At the head of this list must surely be Devika Rani, best known for her portrayal of the untouchable girl in *Achhut Kanya*. Sulochana (Ruby Myers) may be mentioned in the same breath. Later one would add the names of Noor Jehan and Suraiya, who together created the massive hit *Anmol Ghadi*. In the 1950s the great female star was undoubtedly Nargis who was largely responsible for Raj Kapoor's string of successes, *Aag, Barsaat, Awara, Aah, Shree 420*. Of course, her portrayal of the mother in Mehboob Khan's *Mother India* remains one of the great moments of Indian cinema. Others who reached star status included Madhubala, Meena Kumari, and Bina Rai in the 1950s, and Waheeda Rehman, Vijayanthimala, and Nutan, a gifted star, in the later '50s and early '60s. The only women who reached that status in the '70s and '80s is Rekha, though Hema Malini certainly has had a large following. It is clear that Sridevi has achieved stardom more recently, and Madhuri Dixit, Kajol, Karishma Kapoor, and Aishwarya Rai dominated the 1990s and the turn of the millennium. Bombay Cinema has extensive texts about these

female actors, many salacious and unreliable but central nevertheless to the
way in which their screen personae were created. The highly suggestive lives of
the mothers of Meena Kumari and Nargis invaded those of their daughters,
and their screen personalities were often constructed by spectators in terms of
their prefilmic lives. Other relationships, some true, others purely fictitious,
such as those of Dharmendra and Meena Kumari or Dharmendra (yet again)
and Hema Malini or, going further back, Raj Kapoor and Nargis, and Motilal
and Shobhna Samarth, provide important stories in any examination of the
Bollywood film as a popular art form.

This personal narrative, however, is incomplete because the genre (with
its mix of epic, romance, and melodrama) also required, at some point, the
development of the villain. My first memories of villains are B. M. Vyas in
Homi Wadia's Arabian Nights fantasies and curiously as the demon Ravana
in Wadia's *Sampoorna Ramayana*, K. N. Singh in *Awara,* and Sapru in *Samrat*
(The emperor, 1954). I can recall other villains as well, notably Jeevan,
Murad, Tiwari, Hiralal, and Jayant. They were constructed rather crudely and
invited a "hiss the villain" response from the audience. One feature of the villain (unless he was an antihero, which was rare) was that he had no redeeming qualities whatsoever and had to be killed off or imprisoned or sentenced
to death. This construction of the villain has remained largely unchanged,
though in recent years audiences have begun to respond to villains very differently. It may well be that the ambivalent nature of the hero portrayed by
Amitabh Bachchan finally brought to an end the basic polarity between hero
and villain. The villain, as *Indian Today* (November 30, 1988) observed, is in
fact no longer despised. A "good" villain has become quite important to commercial cinema. Ever since the enormous success of Amjad Khan (son of the
earlier hero/villain Jayant) as Gabbar Singh in *Sholay* (Flames, 1975) (his one-
liners gripped the popular imagination), villains have become more and more
sophisticated, "polished, erotically attractive, modern and in full control of
[themselves]" (Nandy 1998: 9). They have been given better lines and have
attracted people who may have otherwise stayed away from the role of a villain. A case in point is Pran, who perfected the character of villains in the late
1950s and 1960s. Then came *Upkar* (Good deeds, 1967) in which he changed
his role and played, after a long break, the role of a decent man. Toward the
end of the 1980s, however, he returned to being a villain because the roles had
become more exciting. Script writers such as Javed Akhtar concede that the
lines given to villains are better than those for heroes. Of the recent crop of
villains the most exciting ones are Amrish Puri (who also played Mola Ram
in Spielberg's *Indiana Jones and the Temple of Doom*), Prem Chopra, and

Gulshan Grover (Pran's son). In the 1970s Ajit, the swashbuckling hero of the
1950s and the iconoclast unbeliever of *Nastik* (The atheist, 1954), added a
new dimension to villainy with his one-liners such as "is ko hamlet vālā poison de do jis se vo to be se not to be ho jayegā" (Give him Hamlet's poison
so that he may move from being "to be" to "not to be"), "is ko liquid oxygen
meṁ ḍubā do liquid ise jīne nahīṁ degā aur oxygen ise marne nahīṁ degā"
(Drop him into liquid oxygen: liquid won't let him live and oxygen won't let
him die). Another line is from Prem Chopra: "maiṁ vo bal hūṁ jo patthar
ko kāṁc se toṛtā hai" (I'm that power which breaks stone with glass). Some
of these lines were brilliantly satirized by Naseeruddin Shah in Kaizad
Gustad's *Bombay Boys* (1998) originally made in English but dubbed into
four Indian languages. The villain—often a smuggler or terrorist—now occupies a larger space in the films. His range is greater (though his end remains
predictable), and he is represented (through clothes, gesture, voice) as a more
cosmopolitan amalgam of other filmic villains around the world. It is not
unusual for Amrish Puri to combine the figure of a Hindu sadhu, Mad Max,
and a futuristic villain straight out of a Hollywood science fiction. In someone like Anupam Kher (in *Mast Kalander* [1991] for example), the villain
even begins to give dark hints of his gay background. Though the villains of
the 1950s were thoroughly bad—for example, the villains of *Dil Deke Dekho*
(1959) and *Tumsa Nahin Dekha* (No one like you, 1957) were Westernized,
clubgoing baddies, and in *Madhumati* (1958) the villain was a rapist zamin-
dar—the movies of the 1990s in particular rendered the villain more ironically. In some instances it is the villain around whom a political critique of
the nation is centered. As if to underline the growing significance of villians,
Filmfare Awards now include an award for "Best Performance in a Villainous
Role," which in 2000 went to Sunil Shetty (*Filmfare,* April 2001).

Against the growing complexity of the male villain, the female villain has
remained quite static. She is depicted invariably either as a vamp or a Kaikeyi
figure who would fight for the rights of her own son at any cost and against
the common social good. There is also the subvillain who is the avatar of the
scheming Manthra, the evil adviser of Queen Kaikeyi. Her role, in many
ways perfected by Lalita Pawar, was to feed lies and invectives to otherwise
honorable family women. More recently, however, the female as the revenger
is showing potential signs of appropriating some of the characteristics of the
villain. The epic tradition from which we draw our Kaikeyi and Manthra
archetypes, however, do not have a full-fledged female villain along the lines
of a Ravana or a Duryodhana, which probably explains the lack of complexity of the female villain.

One would expect a genre as large as Bombay Cinema to have produced critical studies commensurable to its size. And given that the Indian diaspora—a large target audience of the form—consumes this genre feverishly, the genre should have been an important cultural object for diaspora scholars. The bibliography, however, shows critical or scholarly investment inversely proportional to its size. Not until quite recently has Bombay Cinema begun to receive attention as an object of serious critical scholarship. But even so, far fewer book-length studies of this cinema exist in the West than, say, books about Japanese or Chinese cinema. With the singular exception of Satyajit Ray, no Indian auteur has been the subject of comprehensive critical monographs of any real theoretical sophistication. There have been a few studies, a work in Marathi and two in English on Guru Dutt, a book or two on Raj Kapoor, but nothing more. There may be a number of reasons for this. The first is that influential Indian critics such as Chidananda Das Gupta (a founding member of the Calcutta Film Society) have divided Indian cinema into two almost irreconcilable parts: an art cinema meant for the self-conscious transnational aesthete (and therefore eminently suitable for critical analysis) and a popular variety (a lower form and therefore not an art object) meant for the general population and the diaspora. The second is that the latter, the popular, had not been theorized, again until quite recently, in ways that would make it a critically significant cultural Indian form. Like much else in contemporary Indian culture there is also a colonial residue here that we need to remember. The Cinematograph Acts of 1918 and 1919 and the establishment of the Indian Cinematograph Committee of Inquiry in 1927 were informed by an emphatic definition of cinema as pure entertainment without any social (and even artistic) significance. These assumptions about cinema made their way into postcolonial India's Cinematograph (Amendment) Act of 1973, too. The detritus of colonial history explains the tensions that continue to exist between the film industry and the various Indian ministries of culture.

There is no simple theory of Bombay (Bollywood) Cinema. In this book I have taken the position that any theorization must address both material features (the political economy of the form) as well as reception and aesthetic judgment. In fact the book is primarily about judgment and analysis of selected texts from the Bombay Cinema as one interconnected, heterogeneous genre to which I have given the term *grande syntagmatique* (after Metz). The immense complexity of the genre, indeed its novel-like flexibility, means that embedded in the form are texts of extraordinary variety. The form may indeed be discussed as instantiations of aesthetic engagements with the historical growth of the nation-state, as appropriations of the pan-Indian epic and folk traditions by a mechanically reproduced form, and even as representations of styles of singing and acting (the song text, the actor text). There is also an entire history of reception (in terms of class, gender, and so on) through which this filmic practice may be defined. Yet despite the controlling conventions of any self-assured and dominant/dominating genre on the ascendant, the form has developed ways of bypassing its own inherently imperialistic discourses. Here the voices of women and the underprivileged generally require urgent attention. One senses that women do not want to be represented simply as voyeuristic objects for the male gaze or as composite Other, wife, or lover figures. Indeed it is precisely the struggle within the form itself for the release of alternative voices that emancipates the Bombay film from accusations of parasitism, low cultural form, absence of political awareness, and so on, so often directed against it. As Ashish Rajadhyaksha has observed, "The irony being, of course, that it is commercial cinema, drawing confidently from the Indian performing arts and the energy of their musical and melodramatic range, which possesses the greater vitality" (1985b: 106). In a film such as *Naseeb* (Destiny, 1997), the disruption takes the form of a woman being given enough space to voice the need for freedom and control of her body. Pooja (Mamta Kulkarni) declares her love and fidelity to her husband Deepak (Rahul Roy) in front of her erstwhile lover Krishna (Govinda) directly: "har yug mem sītā kī agnī parikṣā nahīṁ hotī" (Sita does not have to undergo the ritual of fire in every age). Of course, the afflicted lover must shoot himself against the backdrop of a temple, which is not an uncommon way in which a disturbance in the cultural order is contained in this cinematic form. But not before an ideological counterstatement has been made. In Aamir Khan's recent film *Lagaan* (Land tax, 2001), the ideological counterstatement involves the use of cricket to critique the colonial past. The game of cricket—the great sporting legacy of the British to India and, after Bollywood Cinema, India's most conspicuous cultural past time—is used in this film as a field of battle (and ideological struggle) between the British (a relatively homogeneous group) and the Indian (a motley of castes and religions). In most other filmic texts, celebratory moments of colonial experience from the point of view of the colonized took the form of recognizable anti-colonial acts (strikes, protest march, epic sacrifice by a group or an individual). In this film the moment is framed as a sly mimicry of an imperial game where the subaltern (with the help of a complicit white woman, who also happens to be the commanding officer's sister) initially imagine cricket to be no more than their own *gollī daṇḍā* (a well-known rustic game) and then begin to recognize its complex rules and power. Cricket is the modernist *gollī daṇḍā* that the peasant masters; but unlike *gollī daṇḍā* which is essentially a past time, it may be the center of wagers and sites where matters of imperial significance are decided upon in a gentlemanly fashion. The interesting thing about the match in *Lagaan* is that the subaltern side wins but not before, as is the norm in Bollywood Cinema, divine intercession is   prayed for the night before the final day of the match.

The Bombay film, in its distinctly "Mumbai-ishtyle," as the current leading star Shah Rukh Khan has called it (*Times of India,* January 24, 1999: 6), is the preeminent art form of modern India and acknowledged as such in Baz Luhrmann's tribute to it in *Moulin Rouge.* It requires special skills of interpretation and a thoroughgoing knowledge of Indian culture. To expand upon the pleasures of Bombay Cinema (from within both homeland and diasporic cultural specificities) I will examine in this book key texts that established the form in the 1930s and early 1940s and then use the poetics of melodrama to establish and refine its broad characteristics. This would also take me to the ways in which colonial literary discourses (sentimentality, gothic romance, realism) were appropriated by cinema in India, and the ways in which the all-pervasive trope of the Mother is handled in the seminal text of this genre, *Mother India,* where the Nehru ideal of "*Bhārat Mātā,* Mother India" is offered as a composite, secular India against, one could argue, the originary moment of the sacred nation as a politic based on the myth of the dismemberment of the goddess Sati, Lord Shiva's first wife. In this myth Sati is systematically sliced off by Lord Vishnu to prevent cosmic disruptions that were underway as Shiva danced inconsolably with the dead body of his wife. Wherever pieces of the body fell, a sacred site was established and these sacred sites, created out of a body dismembered, constitute one version of the sanctity of the Indian nation-state. I will look at the 1950s and 1960s (which many consider the high period of Bombay Cinema) through an examination of two auteurs: Raj Kapoor and Guru Dutt. The 1970s and early 1980s will be handled through the theme of the actor as parallel text where I examine the star persona of Amitabh Bachchan. My ongoing claims about Bombay Cinema as a *grande syntagmatique* will be discussed through the segmentation of two films separated by twenty-five years: *Baiju Bawra* (1952) and *Amar Akbar Anthony* (1977). The late 1980s and the 1990s will be discussed through chapters on the relationship between fundamentalism and the popular and on the relationship between Bombay Cinema and the burgeoning Indian diaspora.

A large number of films I examine in this book were seen in the Empire and Regent theaters, Nausori, in the company of my cousin Arjun, my uncles Ram Mishra and Shiu Mishra, my sister, Shiro Shankar, my school-mates Saizad Ali, Deo Narayan, Sarwesh ("Tomato") Thakur, Mohammed Shafique, Chatu (Clarence) Nair, Ashish, Raymond Surujpal, Bal Krishna, Kamal Robert, and, above all, my brother, Hirday Mishra, with whom I have shared some of my most intense joys of Hindi cinema, including watching the original version of Raj Kapoor's *Aah* (Sighs of the heart, 1953). The viewing of these films would not have been possible without the weekly supply of 2 shillings from my mother and late father to support my indulgence. Without that quiet and unquestioning support, which can only come from parents, there would have been no filmic archive to begin with, and no book. My wonderful primary school teacher, Mr. Shiu Prasad, reminded me even then that the great tradition of (female) film singing survived in Geeta Dutt and not in the impossibly saccharine notes of Lata Mangeshkar. In my mature years a less innocent viewing was made possible in the incomparable company of my extraordinary friends Krishna Datt and Sachi Reddy. In the margins of this book lurk the contributions they made as first readers of this cinema. But there is one person who was much older than me but who opened my eyes to the possibilities of film criticism as narrative at the tender age of 13. This man was Silas Singh, who taught me the discipline of actually constructing basic narrative structures into which the various films might be slotted. With this aid I constructed, even then, a number of narrative paradigms against which I always measured the films I saw. That discipline allowed me to remember the narratives of a considerable number of films. Even in this book, many of my narrative reconstructions go back to my first encounter with these films. I last saw Silas Singh in 1962 as he came in a taxi to our Dilkusha home in Nausori to say farewell. He had won an East-West Center scholarship to read toward a degree in education. As he shook my hand he said, "has has ke bahārem bhī śabnam ko rulātem haim" (Haughtily the winds of spring trouble the morning dew), lines from one of Talat Mehmood's *ghazals* (love songs). That was his cryptic way of reminding me of the years we had spent together discussing Hindi films and the power of metaphor.

The writing of this book, a book so very close to my heart, was made possible through a research grant from Murdoch University, which took me to Bombay and Pune on a number of occasions. The award of a large grant by the Australia Research Council during 1995–96 provided me with opportunities to extend my research into cinema and the diaspora. My cultural studies colleagues at Murdoch University, in particular Tom O'Regan and Krishna Sen, gave me ample opportunities to share my ideas with their film and media students. At the National Film Archive, Pune, Mr. P. K. Nair, its sometime director, made the resources of the library available to me at very short notice. I must also thank Gayatri Chatterjee of the Pune Film and Television Institute for introducing me to the latest variety of Hindi movies. The staff of the library in the National Film Archive and Murdoch University have been extremely helpful. The stills used in this book are reproduced with the permission of the National Film Archive of India, Sanjay Leela Bhansali (Bhansali Productions), Aziz Mirza (Dreamz Unlimited), Aditya Chopra (Yash Raj Films), and Praveen Nischol (Daasa Movies). Sunil Dutt and Dev Anand found time in their very busy schedules to speak to me. In Bombay my friends Sarla Sujan and Leela Advani not only made a Colaba flat and rooms in the Radio Club available for my use but also introduced me to Bombay, "that super-epic motion picture of a city" of Salman Rushdie. Amrit Gangar enthusiastically introduced me to the Bombay cultural scene on my most recent visit to India and has continued to provide me with invaluable information about Bollywood. Veena Sarna of Dreamz Unlimited made me very much at home with her complimentary words about my Urdu and Sanskritized Hindi.

Clearly one cannot rely on memory alone to write a book on cinema. Apart from films seen in the National Film Archive, Pune, many others were borrowed from friends in Perth. I would like to thank them for their help. Dr. S. T. Arasu and Dr. Krishna Somers provided me with back issues of Indian weeklies and bi-monthlies that they had collected over many years. Wimal Dissanayake, an important figure in bringing Bombay Cinema to the attention of American film critics, encouraged me to complete the manuscript.

The book owes an immense intellectual debt to Rosie Thomas and to the many wonderful contributors to the *Journal of Arts and Ideas*. I can't do full justice to the articles in all the issues of this journal, nor to all the contributors to it, but it would be remiss of me if I didn't single out the essays by Anuradha Kapur, Geeta Kapur, M. Madhava Prasad, Ashish Rajadhyaksha, and S. V. Srinivas. I have drawn enormous encouragement from critical discussions about Bombay Cinema I've had with Peter Jeffery, Sujit and Meenakshi Mukherjee, Stephen Slemon, Brian Shoesmith, Sanjay Srivastava, and Harish Trivedi. I thank Heather Meek for laboriously typing and editing the manuscript. I am grateful to Jo-Ann Wallace, chair of the University of Alberta English Department, and Kateryna Longley, dean of the Division of Social Sciences, Humanities, and Education, Murdoch University, for granting me leave to attend various film events and conferences. Mridula

Chakraborty, Shazia Rahman, Nicole Schiele, and Sangeeta Nadkarni, my sometime postgraduate students, opened up areas that come only to young critical minds. I thank Bill Germano, Damian Treffs, and the anonymous readers at Routledge for their encouraging words. My thanks also go to the editorial staff at Routledge for their exemplary reading and editing of the manuscript. My children, Rohan and Paras, have always been my most forthright critics and I thank them for prodding me along. Finally, the book owes its inspiration to my wife, Nalini, who encouraged me to write about Bombay Cinema as the decisive moment in the Indian encounter with modernity. A Bombay film buff with an amazing capacity for recall, she has been responsible for correcting many matters of detail and interpretation. I also thank her for silently suffering my long absences from home, and for her understanding. The errors that remain in the book are, of course, my own responsibility.

The book is dedicated to my daughter, Paras Rowena Nalini, who has read it as her father's autobiographical fragment. Herself a writer of great style and vivacity, I regret that this, a father's gift to his daughter, is not quite up to her severe academic standards.

Vijay Mishra
Pune—Edmonton—Perth

A Note on Transliteration

Titles of Indian films have been given in the Indian film industry's own style of transliteration. Hence *Barsaat* and not *Barsāt*. Quotations from Indian languages (Sanskrit, Hindi, Urdu) have, however, been transliterated in the standard manner. These quotations also include citations of songs and dialogues. Names of characters in films and in the literary corpus as well as names of authors have been given in their romanized equivalents. Hence Krishna and Rama, not Kṛṣṇa and Rāma. Titles of all films have been translated into English except where the titles are proper names such as *Anarkali*, *Devdas*, and so on. A number of relatively common words such as rasa, dharma, bhakti, maya, moksha have been written in their familiar forms and without diacritical marks. Although Bombay is now called Mumbai (and correctly so), for obvious historical reasons I have kept the colonial name and spelling of the city.

Chapter One

INVENTING BOMBAY CINEMA

Cinemas, one Indian film critic has surmised, are "the temples of modern India" (Das Gupta 1988: 130). They are designed to seduce: monumental spaces gleam with light and color, vestibules are plastered with posters of gods and goddesses, red carpets exude desire and wantonness. Devotees come in huge numbers to worship, "to take *darśana*," at the shrine of the new image, the oneiric image that will create their new gods and even their new beliefs. In an act of sly complicity (between those who control the mode of production and those who consume the finished product), the screen projects the increasingly reward-seeking desires of the Indian lumpen-proletariat. Where once, it seems, cinematic desire was a collective middle-class desire, deflected onto a larger nationalist program, it is now the aggressive desire of phantasmal self-projection, with the nation as only one of many objectives of the desiring machine. In this aggressive self-projection and demand for reciprocity, in the suturing of image and spectator, may be discovered the impetus of my metaphor of Bombay Cinema as temples of desire.

The massive size of Indian cinema is obvious from the statistics: eight hundred films a year shown in more than thirteen thousand predominantly urban cinemas, viewed by an average of 11 million people each day, and exported to about a hundred countries. Between 1913 (when Dhundhiraj Govind (Dadasaheb) Phalke produced *Raja Harishchandra*, the first Indian film) and 1981 more than fifteen thousand feature films had been produced in India. Almost as many films have been produced since 1981. By 1983 it was India's sixth-largest industry, grossing around $600 million annually and employing some three hundred thousand workers. But the form is much more than these figures show. Its value as cultural capital has to be seen in the way in which this "Epico-Mythico-Tragico-Comico-Super-Sexy-High-Masala-Art" (Rushdie 1995: 148–49) has invaded all aspects of popular culture, from traditional folk performances to video clips, CDs, and cassettes. Its formulaic structure as well as its technical know-how (practice) are used to produce televisual films including soap operas and mythologies. As well, the industry has spawned countless fan magazines feverishly consumed by an ever-widening community of national and diasporic readers. Even in the burgeoning area of television, both local and cable, the impact of cinema is pervasive. Pendakur and Subramanyam, two experts on the political economy of Indian cinema, make this point explicitly when, referring to India's most popular satellite channel, Zee TV, they note that the "influence of the film world is omnipresent" (Pendakur and Subramanyam 1996: 68). In two areas this impact has been particularly obvious. On MTV's top twenty countdown, song-and-dance sequences are all taken from Bombay Cinema, which, in turn, has responded to this demand by incorporating stage-managed "autonomous" song-and-dance sequences in its filmic design. In recent films these sequences have either been an elaborate stage act (which can be transferred easily to the live stage in concert halls) or filmed in exotic locales in India or overseas. On cable TV, which began to reach "an awesome 8,000,000 homes by mid-1994" (Poduval 1999: 111), some of the most popular shows (*Sunhere Pal, Ole Ole,* and *Cinema Cinema*) deal with commercial cinema. The second area relates to serials produced for TV. In the relatively short history of Doordarshan (the national TV network introduced in 1959 and dramatically expanded only in the early '80s when India hosted the Asian Games), the two most successful serials ever produced have been the *Rāmāyaṇa* and the *Mahābhārata*. Both of these were produced by Bombay filmmakers: the first by Ramanand Sagar (a not altogether successful film producer who is nevertheless remembered for scripting Raj Kapoor's *Barsaat*), the second by B. R. Chopra (a household name in Bombay Cinema). But even as the serials redefined the hitherto staid and antimodern thinking of Doordarshan, they also signaled the end of Doordarshan's domination. Since January 1991 when Satellite Broadcasting began from Hong Kong on Star TV (Satellite Transmission of Asian Region TV), the media scene in India has undergone a radical change. In the 1998 financial year, Zee Television, for instance, had grossed 475 crore rupees ($115 million). In the same period Doordarshan's income dropped by 14 percent and continues to slide (*Times of India,* January 24, 1999: 6). The aggressive programming on the part of the other independent TV stations—Sony Entertainment, Star TV (now part of Rupert Murdoch's media empire), and Star Plus, producer of the phenomenally successful *Kaun Banega Crorepati* (Who wants to be a millionaire?) and likely buyer of BBC1's *Yes Minister/Yes Prime Minister* series—have also dented the hitherto unchallenged supremacy of the national television. Insofar as Zee TV is concerned, during 1998 it showed 25 percent of the top fifty TV serials. Cutthroat competition, especially in the cities where "the superior quality of transmissions" and the slick programs of Star, Zee, Sony, and others are "luring audiences away from the national television" (Prasad 1999: 125), led P. C. Lahiri, the corporate director of Zee TV, to make the following cynical observation:

> Doordarshan, which used to be a profit-making enterprise for the government, is turning out to be another white elephant. With the government turning a blind eye to PBC, will Doordarshan end up with zero earnings and zero viewership? (*Times of India,* January 24, 1999: 6)

The phenomenal success of cable and satellite TV in India (and in the diaspora) has also meant that the erstwhile hegemony of film as the primary medium of entertainment has been somewhat eroded. Nevertheless, the evidence suggests that in real terms the number of viewers have not declined and the film industry has very successfully intervened into television programs. So although we need to address the general question of the proliferation of visual media in India (which is why references to TV and cable networking must be kept in mind throughout this book), cinema remains the cultural dominant of India, its "sole model of national unity" (Chakravarty 1993: 310) and the dominant "simulacral realm of mass culture" through which "all political struggle [in the postmodern era]" must necessarily pass (Shohat and Stam 1994: 6). It is on these assumptions that I want to proceed.

In the context of Indian commercial cinema generally Hindi cinema or Bombay (Bollywood) Cinema is the largest player. It is also the model for popular regional cinema and is in this respect closer to being an all-India cinema. Although there is something rather artificial about the culture that Bombay Cinema constructs—a culture that is built around a (male) North Indian Hindi-speaking subject—it does give rise to the possibilities of a "shared experience" that may, if we wish to extend the argument further, make "the people produce itself continually as national community" (Balibar and Wallerstein 1991: 93) or transform them into the "abstract 'national' subject" (Rajadhyaksha 1999: 137). As the "major shaper of an emerging, pan-Indian popular culture" (Kakar 1990: 26) and subjectivity, Bombay Cinema seems to have transcended class and even linguistic difference by emphatically stressing "the myths on which the Indian social order survives in spite of changes" (Raina 1986: 131). The structure of the film is therefore designed to accommodate deep fantasies belonging to an extraordinarily varied group of people, from illiterate workers to sophisticated urbanites. A key binary that has been detected by almost all commentators of this form is the modernity/tradition binary. Modernity is disavowed even as it is endorsed; tradition is avowed even as it is rejected. M. Madhava Prasad (1998: 9) sees this as the classic instance of Marx's metaphor of the *camera obscura,* which he used to "define ideology as the inverted representation of real social relations." The contradiction implicit in any ideological formation highlights tensions in the culture itself; in the case of Bombay Cinema, although the narrative form locates itself in tradition, textual ideology is firmly grounded in modernity. The contradiction gradually gets internalized by the implied spectator and is one of the key elements that governs its filmic representationalism. To think through the question of the "intelligibility" of the form, I want to reprise some mediating forms and principles that have a direct bearing on this cinema. I refer to these mediators as epic intertexts, theatrical form, frontality, the art of Raja Ravi Varma, the foundational semiotics of the cinema of Phalke and the heterogeneous form of Indian cinematic production. My indebtedness to the work of Geeta Kapur, Anuradha Kapur, Ashish Rajadyaksha, and M. Madhava Prasad will be evident as I proceed.

THE SYSTEM AND ITS MEDIATORS

"The epics and myths of the country," wrote Chidananda Das Gupta, "would seem to present the most widely acceptable base for the artistic development of the Indian cinema" (quoted in Chakravarty 1993: 125). My aim in declaring the pan-Indian epics, the *Mahābhārata* and the *Rāmāyaṇa,* as crucial cultural intertexts is not based on a crude theory of structural homology or even structural displacement. My interest is more with powerful texts that are "founders of discursivity" (Foucault 1980: 154). What Foucault had in mind was a theory of decisive or foundational texts that get endlessly rewritten, though not necessarily endorsed. They are critiqued, their values challenged, their structures destabilized, even parodied, but they remain foundational nevertheless. Foucault refers to Marx and Freud as the key modern founders of Western discursivity. In Indian culture that position is singularly held by the epic texts, whose rules of discursivity invade principles that govern the formation of the Bombay film. In other words, the narrative functions and discourses of the precursor epic texts are enabling conventions as well as a repository of shared information (or knowledge). These texts are marked by generic capaciousness and lack of closure, by the interweaving of relatively autonomous fragments within the main narrative structure and by "unresolved, indeed unresolvable ambivalence" (Shulman 1985: 110). The literary evidence everywhere demonstrates a delight in mixed forms, a kind of restless generic permutation—"what is not here is nowhere else to be found" (yad nā iha asti nā tat kvacit) claims the *Mahābhārata,* and the minstrels in the *Rāmāyaṇa* of Valmiki declare that their epic "is replete with all the poetic sentiments: the humorous, the erotic, the piteous, the wrathful, the heroic, the terrifying, the loathsome, and the rest" (1984: *sarga* 4, *śloka* 8). Something else needs to be stressed: these are not just secular texts of culture; they are texts of *darśana,* of religious homage, as well as texts that function as metatexts of tradition and dharmik values. In them are contained those absolute values by which tradition can be maintained even as modernity is endorsed. In the realm of the popular, dharma is rarely if ever distorted so that in the end Govinda, the antihero in *Shikari* (The prowler, 2000), is presented as someone whose turn to barbarism arose because his own dharmik order (his father was a priest) had been so cruelly destroyed by the feudal order. The relay through dharma-adharma-dharma allows for transgressive eruptions to take place from within so that the unspeakable, the anti-dharmik, may be articulated. Hence pleasures of transgression are entertained as the spectator identifies with any number of ideologically unstable elements with the foreknowledge that the order will be reestablished. The full disruptive potential of the great epic, which ends in an apocalyptic vision of ends, thus exists only as a trace in the genre.

Three concepts—epic genealogy, the persistence of dharmik codes and the power of the renouncer—are key legacies of the epic precursor texts. The theme of genealogical purity and banishment (in the epics heroes are periodically banished) surfaces in Raj Kapoor's influential film *Awara* (The vagabond, 1951), where two patterns may be detected. A wife is banished by her wealthy lawyer husband because she was kidnapped by a gang of thugs. The same lawyer, later in life, refuses to acknowledge his son as his own. The relay through which parental recognition is finally endorsed allows important ideological concerns about morality and modernity to be raised. But there can be no ultimate concession to genealogical purity without first addressing dharmik principles. In *Main Tulsi Tere Aagan Ki* (I'm the holy basil of your garden, 1978) it is the genealogically impure half brother (whose mother was a prostitute) who finally saves the family name from disgrace. But in films like this the half brother's goodness is ontologically given—his mother was not a prostitute after all, as mothers rarely are. Any number of films—*Ram*

Teri Ganga Maili (Rama your Ganges is dirty, 1985), *Koyla* (Burning coal, 1998), and so on—could be added here.

Apart from genealogy and the overriding principle of dharma, the epic intertexts also introduce the figure of the renouncer whose *tapas* (severe austerities) can challenge the power of the gods themselves. In the epics Bhishma and Ravana attain godly strengths through their vows of renunciation and the practice of *tapas*. At the level of the social the renouncer becomes something of a free-floating signifier whose independence from the social allows him enormous freedom of action. In many ways the Amitabh Bachchan figure in *Zanjeer* (The chain, 1973), who combined the renouncer ethic with that of the revenger, is an excellent example of how these themes can be put to dramatic use. More immediately, however, it is important to note how it is the renouncer rather than the man-in-the-world (Louis Dumont's terms for the essentialist opposition of *nivṛtti* and *pravṛtti* in Indian culture) who is of greater interest to the form of Bombay Cinema. Two fundamental character types may be located here as well. The first is the hero in *vipralambha*, the hero estranged from his lover or detached from the world. A summary of key popular Bombay actors of the past fifty or so years makes this point self-evident. So Dilip Kumar blinds himself when sight does not lead to reciprocal recognition from Nargis in *Deedar* (Vision, 1951). Both Raj Kapoor in *Mera Naam Joker* (The joker, 1970) and Dev Anand in *Bambai Ka Babu* (A gentleman from Bombay, 1960) lose the women they love. In *Sangam* (The confluence, 1964) the renouncer is Rajendra Kumar, the hero's friend with a barely disguised homoerotic feeling toward Raj Kapoor, and an actor whose periodic deaths on the screen killed off voyeuristic pleasure in one's objects of love (M. Madhava Prasad 1998: 79–87). A later matinee idol, Rajesh Khanna, was, for a while, continually in a state of *vipralambha* (*Amar Prem, Amardeep,* etc.) and Amitabh Bachchan too in an interesting movie like *Silsila* (Continuity, 1981) sacrifices his love for duty. The preeminent actor of the 1990s, Shah Rukh Khan (an actor who has a fine sense of the "composite" tradition of Bombay actors), adopts the role of the lover-in-estrangement as well. In a film such as *Kabhi Haan Kabhi Naa* (Sometimes yes, sometimes no, 1996) this is certainly the case although in at least three other Shah Rukh Khan films—*Deewana* (Hopelessly in love, 1992), *Raju Ban Gaya Gentleman* (Gentleman Raju, 1997), and *Mohabbatein* (Varieties of love, 2000)—a high level of estrangement from the world frames the mood of the hero. To use a phrase I alluded to in my preface, we can call this the *becārā* complex, the complex of self-pity that produces the condition of the melancholic hero. The hero in *vipralambha*—the condition of the sentimentalist—is also the figure around whom the denial of materialism is enacted. But here too there is a massive ambiguity. Whereas a film's mise-en-scènes provide us with images of a well-to-do middle-class lifestyle, its verbal texture, its speech acts, are framed around an abrogation of the material. This contradiction says something about spectatorial subjectivity and how material props may be read as rewards for the ethical, renunciatory life.

The second figure is the Mother, whose representation in Bombay films (unlike that in the epics, where she has been more ambiguously constructed) is a semantic and structural invariant. The filmic Mother often renounces everything for the sake of her husband or son. Conversely, however, when a Mother renounces her own son (which is rare) or her husband (which is rarer still—after all a wife is called a *dharmapatnī,* the wife of dharma) the sheer emotional weight of her act is enormous. So Kunti's plea to her firstborn, Karna, for the lives of her five legitimate sons in the *Mahābhārata* also implies an act of monumental renunciation because Karna must die as a consequence. Similarly, Nargis must shoot her son Birju (Sunil Dutt) in *Mother India* because her son had subverted codes that transcend filial obligations, codes indeed of dharma itself. The moment she shoots her son dead, she is canonized, she becomes a supermother, that terrible renouncer who is at once Mother and avenging goddess Kali/Durga. The exposition of dominant character types does not, of course, mean that at the level of filmic practice characterization linked to a local cultural valency reflects an Indian distinctiveness or exclusivity against the self-centered, narrowly pragmatic, and unidirectional character of the Hollywood hero (Vasudevan 1989: 31).

Occasionally one comes across a film such as *Arth* (Substance, 1983) that proposes to replace the concept of Mother with the more radical category of Woman, or films such as *Jogan* (1950) and *Kanhaiya* (1959) in which the renouncer (as the Lord's "bride") has to choose between corporeal sexual desire and desire sublimated as intense love of God within the semantics of *bhakti.* In the dramatization of women in the epics, however, both Satyavati and Kunti are women first and mothers only subsequently. In some very recent films such as *Hum Aap Ke Hain Kaun* (Who am I to you? 1994) and *Kuch Kuch Hota Hai* (Sometimes things do happen, 1998) a certain *jouissance* returns to the portrayal of the mother but it remains subdued and predictable. Against this, other films such as *Khalnayak* (The antihero, 1993) and *Soldier* (1998) have constructed the suffering mother as a traumatized figure (played by Raakhee), alternating between wholesome emotions of self-sacrifice and frighteningly neurotic compulsion toward revenge. If Nargis was the sacrificial Mother, Raakhee is the postmodern black-sari-clad demotic/demonic Mother figure.

The selection of renouncer-hero in estrangement and of the Mother figure does not mean that they are the only character types we need to consider. Four others—the heroine, the villain, the *vidūṣaka* (the buffoon or the courtly fool), and the double (the device of "splitting" a character)—are extremely important, too. In a film such as *Kanoon* (The law, 1960) the device of the double is the only way in which an absolute threat to the law—the possibility that the judge himself is the killer—can be resolved. I have not addressed the other character types, significant as they are, largely because my concern has been in trying to map out the ideal of the renouncer onto two character archetypes.

The above themes from the epic pretexts undergo further mediation. Two crucial mediations need to be addressed here: first, the various folk plays and theaters that used material from the epics; second, the pictorial transformations that appeared, as lithographic prints (later as calendar art), in people's homes. These also established stylistic forms that cinema adopted as part of its system. In her brilliant work on Parsi mythological drama at the turn of the twentieth century (and immediately preceding Phalke) Anuradha Kapur has shown how Parsi theater merged local idioms with received colonial forms. I shall come to these alternative colonial forms with reference to melodrama later; it is sufficient at this juncture to extend Anuradha Kapur's research to explain an important form of mediation between the filmic and the mythical. Kapur herself had noted in parenthesis: "it is significant that early cinema companies were formed by Parsi theatre managers who attempted to translate their stage successes onto celluloid" (1993: 90–91). The Parsis of India, it must be said, were a thoroughly colonial lot and perhaps colonialism's best hybrid Other and mimics. Given their numerically marginalized status in India, they were more likely to be complicit in the project of imperialism. But in matters of creative hybridity their contribution to Bombay culture was enormous. To theater they brought forms chosen eclectically but vigorously. Localized narratives drawn from the epics would be combined with music and mise-en-scènes that reflected both the traditional (the bucolic, the pastoral) as well as the modern (the urban street). The Grant Road Theatre (opened in 1846) is where Parsi companies began to perform in earnest after years of performances at various makeshift sites. Productions in this theater were marked by great verve and experimentation, enthusiasm for the form, and generally creative eclecticism. Various companies performed the standard fare of English classics (Shakespeare and Sheridan were high on the list), but also Indian high cultural texts such as Kalidasa, autonomous narratives from the epics (Radheshyam's *Vīr Abhimanyu* for instance), and Persian *mathnavīs* such as *Lailā-Majnūn*. But what is of significance beyond the fact that when cinema came to India, Parsi theater provided it with a ready-made repertoire of narratives, themes, and dialogues is the manner in which Parsi theater creatively combined its borrowings. What it created may be seen as a unique theater genre where *Nautaṅkī, Raslīlā,* and *Rāmlīlā* as well as various musical and speech styles came together. To borrow a phrase that Anuradha Kapur uses with reference to Radheshyam's plays, we can say that Parsi theater "eclecticism was as much a refiguration as a modernizing impulse" that paved the way for cinema in India (1993: 91).

Apart from the formal question of narrative mediation—Parsi theater supplying cinema with ready-to-use narratives—two crucial framing devices need to be noted. The first is the legacy of the British proscenium arch theaters that came to India and formed the basis of Parsi theater. The proscenium arch, with its formal properties of stage division and the creation of a fourth (invisible) wall between the spectator and the actor, the stage and the seating, began a new "vocabulary" for the stage since the "stage relations set up in the proscenium arch were radically different from those of open staging" that had existed in "pre-colonial and early colonial India" (A. Kapur 1993: 88). The spectator as a part of a group in an auditorium faced the proscenium arch stage in a virtually identical manner. Except for the angle of vision, each spectator had the same erotic or voyeuristic relation with the actor. But since the space in front of the stage divided spectator from actor, there was no lived reciprocity of gaze, only a formal one (which grew out of the necessity of intersubjective spectator-actor binding). This takes me to the second framing device, which also grew out of the spatial conditions of the proscenium theater. This is the "frontality of the performer vis-à-vis the spectator" (92), in which an unspoken compact between the performer and the spectator in the colonial space of the proscenium theater creates an erotic economy of the look and the counterlook. This complicit economy will continue to govern Bombay Cinema. In Parsi theater itself, however, dramatic performances that had their origins in anything but the space of a proscenium theater broke past the laws of frontality. The use of the twice told tale, where events appeared to have happened before the scene being enacted and would happen outside the frame of the theater, was one such device. The use of direct communion with the audience in a self-conscious display of the self as well as departures from the letter of the script were other devices. A recent performance of the Hindi version of Vijay Tendulkar's *Añjī* at the Nehru Centre, Bombay (September 2000), had a *sūtradhār* ("director," played by

Dinesh Thakur) as actor internal to the text who departed from the text to chastise the audience for coming in late. The use of the musical style of *thumrī* again connected this play with the tradition of Parsi theater where the limitations of the proscenium theater and the binding of frontality is undercut by the fuller musical traditions of *thumrī, dādrā, hori,* and *ghazal.* Kapur points out how these musical forms were more than just pure song. Unlike the high Mughal *khayāl* tradition of economical use of words, the musical traditions used by Parsi theater (and Bombay Cinema) required the body to enact the words sung.

I have attempted to make a more direct connection between Parsi theater and the system of Bombay Cinema than Kapur (whose brief in her essay was not quite about mediations between one semiotic system and another), but her insights can certainly lead to the conjunctions I have outlined. If, however, full frontality and the spectator-actor dynamics of the proscenium arch were factors that affected cinema (the credit stills alongside Madhuri Dixit and Salman Khan directly singing to the audience in *Hum Aap Ke Hain Kaun* is a classic late example), the manner in which the body was constructed—the body's pose, its mise-en-scènes—may be partly traced back to the art of the painter Raja Ravi Varma (1848–1906). Although Varma clearly owed much to British colonial painters, it is clear from any viewing of the Varma paintings (such as those collected in the National Gallery of Modern Art, Delhi) that he was not in the game of constructing for the Indian citizen an absent history of the nation, as Thomas Hickey, Arthur William Davis, Francesco Renaldi, Robert Home, George Place, James Wales, and George Chinnery, colonial painters all, tried to do. For Varma, whom Rajadhyaksha has called "the direct cultural predecessor to Phalke" (1987: 61), it was a matter of indigenizing both the material (oil, the easel format, what Geeta Kapur has said was as much a matter of "the struggle of a native to gain the source of the master's superior knowledge" [1989: 60]) and the point of view of the dominant colonial painters mentioned above. Here the reclaiming of one's history is not unlike the nationalist proposition of Bombay Cinema generally where also an imperialist mode of production is harnessed, finally, toward specifically nationalist goals. In the exemplary instance of Bimal Roy's *Bandini* (The caged, 1963), an anticolonial struggle in the mid-1930s acts as a moral reminder of the need for sacrifice in the wake of the India-China War. Like the colonial antecedents, Varma too enacts heroic moments in the nation's history. Often these are mythical moments drawn from our first precursor texts as a counterpoint to, say, Robert Home's *Lord Cornwallis Receiving the Sons of Tipu Sultan As Hostages*

(c. 1793–94). Varma's *Krishna Liberating His Parents* (1905), and *Victory of Indrajit* (1905) may be included here. But even where the target texts are not as direct we find a mode of representation that establishes very much an Indian aesthetic. We may compare James Wales's *Beebee Amber Kooer* (1792) with Varma's undated *Portrait of a Lady* in the National Gallery of Modern Art, Delhi. Both these texts can be readily superimposed upon each other. But whereas the Wales text provides a painter's look that is both orientalist and largely detached, Varma's *Lady* is the look of the painter himself engrossed in the effort made by the woman in the picture to actually pose for the painting. Varma's art acknowledges its colonial origins but then defiantly introduces discordant Indian colors to make a statement about the representational acts of the painter as native informant. The gaudiness captured here, what Geeta Kapur has referred to as "the simulation of substances . . . flesh, cloth, jewels . . . "(1989: 60) is self-conscious sly mimicry and nonplussed insouciance. As in the case of cinema, Western techniques are means by which a precolonial golden past may be invoked and then reworked into the national project.

Although one would be hard-pressed to locate the examples of Parsi theater and Varma's paintings in the tradition of high realist European aesthetics, it is clear that a move toward naturalism had created at least a sense of what was there to be represented realistically. Or put slightly differently, there was a growing sense of what could be collected around a subject so as to bring out the subject's larger context. Ravi Varma didn't simply provide the props by which a body may be naturalistically framed (jewelry, heavy drapes, period furniture); he attempted to rewrite—to "re-vision"—Indian civilization for his contemporaries (G. Kapur 1989: 65) even as he created a staged vision within the constrained semiotics of the received proscenium arch theater, and played to the artistic needs of a growing, sycophantic post–Indian Mutiny middle class (Nandakumar 1995). For the great form of mechanical reproduction, cinema, Varma's art is one of its more tangible antecedents. Rajadhyaksha writes that Varma's "impact on what we can today call industrial art remains massive." He adds, "From calendars to posters, to the design and packaging of small-scale indigenous consumer products, to street-corner art including cheap film posters, we see this impact" (1987: 61).

When we move to the founding father of Indian cinema, Dadasaheb Phalke, we need to be conscious of the ways in which the epic and mythic traditions had been harnessed toward seemingly realist forms of representation. In the hands of Varma the past is repackaged and reproduced. Many of his paintings were mass produced as oleographs for the burgeoning middle-

Raj Kapoor and Premnath in Raj Kapoor's *Aag*, 1948. A collage of looks broken by the indigenous gaze of the woman in a Raja Ravi Varma-type painting. Publicity Still Kamat Foto Flash.

class market (Rajadhyaksha 1987: 63), which also meant wider exposure of his work. More significantly Varma introduced a consciousness about Indian ways of representing scenes and characters from the epic and mythic texts. With Phalke's *Raja Harishchandra* (1913), India's first feature film, three things came to a head simultaneously: the internal struggle among cultural forms for artistic preeminence, the political relevance of art, and how to combine the static Indian images of Varma's art into moving images. The first (the struggle for preeminence) may be considered in transcendental terms as a debate about what constitutes the best form of cultural representation; the second (political relevance) in distinctly localized terms as what best defines the historical moment of the nation-state (and indeed what it is to begin with). In Phalke the various strands that I have outlined (the immediate as well as timeless precursors, the *śruti* (heard) as well as *smṛti* (remembered) texts of culture) flow into one another. As Rajadhyaksha has noted: "(Film) had to cohere and find a dynamic logic for the several movements that converged to produce its images" (1987: 65). Film, of course, deflects these debates because at its moment of inception (and for a long period afterward) it was not seen as challenging the other great arts of painting, music, or literature, or as having the same political impact. It also had to recapture, as an "unauthored form," the dynamic tradition of the oral teller of tales that the bourgeois novel had so seriously challenged. So with Phalke's films a political aesthetic emerges that makes the tradition alive and connects it with the nascent independence movement as well. Phalke was proud to declare that his films were *swadeshi*, or home-grown both in their content as well as in their mode of production since the entire production process was in the hands of Indians. "My films are Swadeshi in the sense that the capital, ownership, employees and stories are all Swadeshi," Phalke had said (quoted in Rajahyaksha 1996b: 398). If we add to this the intrinsically democratic form of its reception—the screen is collectively gazed upon—we begin to sense the value of Walter Benjamin's well-known pronouncement of the political value of an anti-auratic art form, an art form that advanced a nonfascist theory of art and that liquidated the "traditional value of the cultural heritage" (Benjamin 1973: 223). With Phalke, Benjamin's central thesis—"instead of being based on ritual, (film) begins to be based on another practice—politics" (226)—begins to take shape in the localized context of colonial India. Like Benjamin, Phalke clearly saw cinema as a means of blasting open ideology, as a means of releasing culture from its bondage to cult, aura, and ritual. In political terms, cinema is seen as being as intrinsically antifascist as its technology of reproduction and its mass reception (something that even Varma's oleographs or the rich theatrical traditions of Marathi drama upon which Phalke drew for inspiration could not achieve) and releases art from precisely those bonds of authority that underpin fascist thinking.

The foregoing received traditions or controlling influences led quite naturally to a heterogeneous mode of production and the creation of a filmic genre that was marked by a loosely defined notion of form. Ashish Rajadhyaksha has called the dominant form epic melodrama and M. Madhava Prasad, varying this concept slightly, has called the dominant form of the 1950s and 1960s (for many the period when Bombay Cinema reached its high point) the feudal family romance. The Indian Film Censorship Board uses the word "social" to designate the dominant genre of Indian films generally. In 1988, for instance, 537 films were classified as "social." In my reading I would want to claim that Bombay Cinema is itself a genre that is primarily a sentimental melodramatic romance. I would want to claim, further, that it is a grand syntagm (*grande syntagmatique*) that functions as one heterogeneous text under the sign of a transcendental dharmik principle. It is for this reason that the form is so patently "synchronic" in the sense that anyone familiar with the syntagm can enter into this cinema at any point and pick up its narrative. Two things come together here: the first is the pervasiveness of a capacious or encyclopedic form; the second a textual capacity to elicit a wide variety of responses from the audience. These responses remain linked to a thoroughly nativist aesthetics of *rasa*. To a large extent the open-ended definition of the form I advance (identifiable as Bombay Cinema) grows out of the heterogeneous production practices that govern this form. As Madhava Prasad has pointed out (1998: 42–51), the Bombay film is manufactured out of "pre-fabricated parts" which have not necessarily grown out of a unified sense of the filmic script. Often the script is a loose idea that grows as the film is manufactured in parts—prerecorded songs and music, shootings undertaken in a haphazard fashion, concessions made to financiers who may well be (as the evidence increasingly suggests) powerful Bombay underworld figures such as Nazim Hassan Rizvi and Dawood Ibrahim (now operating from Karachi). A recent report shows that Rizvi may well have "used threats to persuade other film-makers to shift their release dates to give his movies a clean run at the box office, as well as pressuring stars (like Hrithik Roshan) to take part in his works" (*Australian,* December 18, 2000: 6). The end product thus carries the marks of its mode of production as well as the ideology of its financiers. But because the procedure (the manner in which the various components are brought together) itself becomes thoroughly systemic (like the serialized novel which is then transformed into book), the method of manufacture is an important component of the form and is therefore naturalized.

A transcendental principle of dharma (the ultimate Hindu Law), a decentered notion of genre, and a mode of heterogeneous manufacture combine to create the sentimental melodramatic romance that is Bombay Cinema. The flexibility of the genre makes for the notion of dharma to be transgressed in a regulated manner, as irruptions in the text, as presentiments of alternative (and even superior) critiques, rather than as the construction of a radically new world order. Suggestively, Bombay Cinema interprets to the point of change but never changes the ethical order itself. It must be said that the form has had to adjust to shifts in audience from predominantly middle-class, urban spectators to urban slum dwellers. The shift has also meant that Bombay Cinema has had to rework dharma through structural binaries that require minimal interpretive skills. Indeed as popular cinema has moved from colonial to postcolonial India its narratives and themes have become much more accessible, more direct, less ambiguous. One senses this if one looks at two films of the early 1950s—*Awara* (1951) and *Do Bigha Zamin* (Two acres of land, 1953)—in which questions of power, privilege, and caste are rendered somewhat ambiguously—and two films of the 1960s—*Jis Desh Men Ganga Behti Hai* (Where flows the Ganges, 1960) and *Upkar* (Good deeds,

1967), in which utopian national narratives are located within the primitive binary of Western Evil and Oriental Goodness. This binary representationalism is true even of more sophisticated films such as *Sujata* (The well-born, 1959) as well. Dharma is then pragmatically recast as a nationalist ethos of which the Bombay Cinema (and Indian popular cinema generally) is a crucial cultural source. But it also has a strong private motive because in making the essential conflict a dharmik one, the forms of resolution become quite naturally pre-textual and hence, in a curious way, a justification for the film industry's own existence: the film too, finally, has a matrix enshrined in all Indian texts, and is, therefore, morally beyond reproach. Dharma then is both the larger narrative, an organizing principle, and a screen that hides the blatant inconsistencies inherent at all levels in the filmic text. It also hides the very processes of monopoly and exploitation that produce the text. The illusory unity of the text achieved sometimes through an excessive demonstration of the grammar of dharma (as in *Swami* [1977] or in *Sadhna* [1958]) is no more than a systematic ploy aimed at deflecting the exploitative nature of the economic and social orders. These are the features that Indian "middle (brow) cinema" such as *Arth* and *Aadharshila* (Foundation stone, 1982) propose to deconstruct. But, as always, deconstructive moments are continually being reincorporated back into this massive grand syntagm, back into Bombay Cinema as generic form. In this respect *Arth* does not offer a new syntax for the female body, which, in the film, continues to be constructed through the idioms of Bollywood cinema. The alternative syntax based on staggered, discontinuous camera shots, on unhinging the woman's body from the central space of the filmic frame, on deflecting the gaze, and so on, are not part of *Arth*'s cinematic machinery. There is nothing here of that "counter-cinema" that we associate with someone like Jean-Luc Goddard (Wollen 1982), with which an alternative filmic epistemology may be advanced.

ESTABLISHING THE GENRE

Key paradigmatic features of the genre of Bombay Cinema, such as the ongoing conflict between tradition and modernity within a nationalist project, get established in the films of the 1930s and the early 1940s. As a preamble to my reading of a selection of films from the period, I want to begin with Ashis Nandy's discussion of mass culture, the Indian urban middle classes, and the role of popular cinema as the successor to a pan-Indian cultural ethos (1995: 196–236). Bombay Cinema, in Nandy's argument, is "mass culture" or "popular mass culture," not popular culture per se. This mass culture has, in recent times, exhibited many features of low Western forms in place of an earlier deference to high Western culture and its canonical artistic forms that we find in representative texts of the 1930s and 1940s such as *Aadmi, President, Devdas,* and *Kismet.* These films situate themselves in the midst of debates between tradition and modernity; they carry a consciousness about folk and classical art forms, and they suggestively include India's regional variations. On the other hand films such as *Zanjeer* (1973) and *Coolie* (1983) show little theoretical self-consciousness about this complex heritage but a greater degree of self-assurance and transnationalism. In one respect this may be a leveling process or even a process of democratization or globalization on the part of a much more self-assured cinema. However, even as it becomes global, Bombay Cinema can address the issue of a political or social critique only by trans-forming the critique itself into allegorical oppositions between good and bad, sanctity and scandal, dharma and adharma, indeed into a Manichean world order. And it is through the shifting of the sign from social practice to absolute, perennial (Hindu) values that mass cinema keeps faith with its epic and puranic traditions. In the process, though, traditions themselves cease to have that organic connection with art (here cinema) that one finds in folk and popular theater. Nandy very correctly points out that this leads to an "instrumental view of cultural traditions and world views" and to a mode of representation that generalizes and externalizes so that there is little room for an examination of the psychology of motivation, guilt, sexuality, and so on (1995: 204). From another reading this may also be the contramodern ele-ment of Bombay Cinema that people, including the Indian diaspora, find so very interesting—that indeed Indian cinema does not take the complete Western path of modernity, of what the Iranian secular leftist Jalal Al-e Ahmad referred to as westoxification (*gharbzadegi*). In an India where moder-nity is no longer something that "belongs" to a specific group and is the "con-dition" of the state, "a critique of modernity from the point of view of 'eternal India'" is most clearly found in the trans-Indian and universalist agenda of commercial cinema. In this respect Bombay Cinema has taken the agenda of high art and made it into its own but without mimicking the laws that gov-erned the production of that art form. Instead it objectifies the modern but strips it of any moral value. The kind of cinematic specularity that gets endorsed is not spectatorial identification with the modern as such but the modern inscribed within dharmik registers that have a time-immemorial force: the modern hero doubles up as the premodern hero from the nation's epic past. This presencing of history and culture through the nation's meta-texts has a much longer history. If we stay with the Nandy thesis, early

Bombay Cinema was a decidedly ideological form (insofar as its internal dynamics and audience expectations are concerned) and addressed a self-conscious nationalist drive toward modernity even as these early films established the generic parameters within which Bombay Cinema continues to operate. How far this is true is what we need to address next.

In the 1930s and 1940s the big studios—Bombay Talkies, Ranjit Movietone, and Imperial Film Company—adopted specific cinematic practices to mediate cinema and Indian realities. Referring in particular to cinematic mise-en-scènes, the noted critic Bikram Singh observed: "Everything out there in the real world—be it a house, a piece of furniture, a stretch of street, a court-room or a prison, must be reshaped, sandpapered, painted and varnished before it becomes a part of a film" (1983: 30). The tropes of the modern—house, street, furniture, courtroom—are in one sense "tamed" along the lines of Hollywood cinema. But with a difference. In the case of Bombay Cinema the narrative discourses in which the representation took shape had less to do with the tradition of realism and the texts celebrated by F. R. Leavis and the neo-traditionalists who wrote for his journal *Scrutiny* than to its aberrant form in melodrama and gothic sentimentalism.

The conscious adoption of this tradition (which by all accounts was the popular English/European tradition of Henry Mackenzie's *The Man of Feeling* [1771] and Goethe's *Werther* [1774]) led to a corresponding devaluation of the realist in favor of the pastoral-sentimental. This is not to say that a significant body of realist texts do not exist. *Dharti Ke Lal* (Children of the earth, 1946), *Do Bigha Zamin* (Two acres of land, 1953), *Jagte Raho* (Stay awake! 1956), *Kaagaz Ke Phool* (Paper flowers, 1959), and the exemplary texts discussed later in this chapter are not insignificant realist texts. Even so, filmmakers such as Shyam Benegal and Kumar Shahani have continued to read the form as profoundly unsatisfying, alienating, and even emasculating. Parting company from the tradition of novelistic realism, Bombay Cinema is seen by them as a self-consciously ideological form, "a pure dream, empty and vain," alienated from the "concrete history of concrete material individuals materially producing their existence" (Althusser 1984: 34). Both Benegal and Shahani have spoken about the need for "antiforms" (Shahani 1986: 101) such as Shahani's own *Maya Darpan* (The mirror of illusion, 1972) and Mani Kaul's *Duvidha* (Confusion, 1979). However, I would want to stress that behind these deconstructive texts stand a massive canon which took firm shape in Himansu Rai's *Achhut Kanya* (The untouchable girl, 1936) and related texts of the period. To grasp Bombay Cinema as "ideological form" I want to begin with *Achhut Kanya* as an exemplary text that established the genre, followed by a reading of four other key texts of the period between 1935 and 1943: *Devdas, Aadmi, President,* and *Kismet.*

After a string of basically orientalist films (*The Light of Asia, Shiraz, A Throw of Dice, Karma*), Himansu Rai, with Devika Rani, established Bombay Talkies, keeping Franz Osten of the Emelka Film Company in Munich as their director. "It was Rai's Bombay Talkie, output in the 1930's," wrote Ashish Rajadhyaksha, "which defined, stylistically, the Hindi film industry, creating the Hollywood-style star system and the song-dance entertainer" (1986: 50–51). There were more direct borrowings of cinematographic practices from Hollywood as well: the long shot, the reverse shot, the point-of-view shot, montage, and indeed much of the camera work that now constitutes the staple of both Bombay and Hollywood cinematic narration. Himansu Rai's first important film, *Achhut Kanya* (The untouchable girl, 1936), is, however, important also for two other kinds of historical negotiations. The first is the use of the metaphysical tradition to explain or resolve the historical moment. The second is the use of a nationalist agenda as part of the ideology of the aesthetic. The unseen, uncited figure that looms large is Mahatma Gandhi, who had effectively glamorized the figure of the ascetic renouncer, and had grafted social action onto new symbolic alignments and associations. Nowhere is the latter more obvious than in the reconstitution of the untouchable as Harijan. While this gesture made no difference to the real relations between castes in India, it did mean that the Harijan could be incorporated into the larger narrative of anticolonial struggle. The rhetoric of Indian nationalism was thus predicated upon a representation of an India no longer cursed by the reality of untouchability. But like much else in the Mahatma's own teaching, the fight against untouchability was presented not in material but in dharmik terms: how one got the original dharma right and not how one restituted the absolute Other outsider back into a caste-ridden system. In the hands of Himansu Rai, cinema functioned as a compensatory form as it shifted the sign of the untouchable from social reality to romance but without losing sight of the dharmik ideal. Which is why it is not uncommon to find readings of *Achhut Kanya* in the popular film periodicals as "a typical and tragic story of a Harijan girl's unrequited love for a Brahmin youth."

A film that dealt with prohibited love between the twice-born caste and the casteless was a radical undertaking because the quest for a casteless Indian society was a redemptive dream of the nation in the making. But a social agenda of such revolutionary rigor would have required an aesthetic well beyond the capacities of popular cinema. So the narrative had to be presented as a memorially reconstructed story in the text, and presented furthermore by

Ashok Kumar and Devika Rani in Himansu Rai's *Achhut Kanya*, 1936. Broaching untouchability. Courtesy National Film Archive of India.

the "transsocial" figure of the renouncer-fakir. The first listeners of the tale—a couple with their own marital problems—are thus inscribed "spectators" who take *darśana* (a privileged look endorsed by a higher authority but also an act of philosophical critique) at the shrine of the untouchable woman on our behalf. At the end of the tale our world, the world here and now, is remarkably undisturbed as the narrative frame—like the frames of the Indian gothic discussed in the next chapter—diminishes authorial responsibility by significantly distancing the viewer/reader from the text and transforming the life of the "untouchable girl" into a literary event. What has happened to the radical principle of granting full subjectivity to the *achūt kanyā*? In the real world, there is no untouchable subject who can claim total freedom since he or she is defined in terms of the power and gaze of the established castes. In that very definition, however, there is the possibility of radical struggle along Hegelian lines. Withholding freedom from the untouchable inducts, in that very social act, the possibility of displacement and emulation (of the master). In Himansu Rai's film, the representation of the untouchable through the star figure of Devika Rani cancels out the possibilities of the Hegelian master-slave dialectic. In *Achhut Kanya* the viewer in fact identifies, voyeuristically, with the star and removes the politics of the subaltern untouchable completely from the text. Cinema confronts a radical opposition (Brahmin-untouchable) and an essential social fact of Indian modernity but deflects its dramatic consequences. Although it was claimed that "millions all over the country shed tears of sympathy for the beautiful Harijan girl who gave her life at the altar of religious bigotry and human intrigue" (Garga 1984: 97), it is unlikely that the outpouring of sympathy led to any improvement in the lives of Indian untouchables. Instead, *Achhut Kanya* is concerned with the projection of an unproblematic liberal humanist worldview (couched in melodramatic excess) in which the metatext of dharma finally triumphs. As Ashis Nandy observed, Bombay Cinema keeps faith with its absolutist traditions, unlike folk and popular theater, which always had a more transformative political potential. Although intercaste marriage takes place when Bimal Roy returned to the theme of caste and untouchability in *Sujata* (The well-born, 1959), the highly cultured star quality of Nutan once again canceled out the "horror" of miscegenation between the upper-caste Adhir (Sunil Dutt) and the untouchable Sujata (Nutan). In that film, a controlled transgression becomes a sign of the form, and the deployment of the song-text a means of coding, extradiegetically, the radical agenda of the title. In *Achhut Kanya* that agenda is already becoming thoroughly systemic as the husband who had planned to kill his wife for infidelity emerges reformed upon listening to the fakir's tale, and the audience is left with the redemptive strains of the devotional song "hari base sakal saṃsāra" (The Lord dwells everywhere). The untouchable is finally incidental to the triumph of the form which subsequently becomes eminently iterable. Other disadvantaged classes or professional types—the peasant, the prostitute, the single mother, the widow, the saint, those wrongfully condemned by the justice system—will enter the formulaic world established by *Achhut Kanya*, extending its themes, displacing its main characters but leaving the form itself intact.

By 1940 three other directors had joined Himansu Rai to make their contributions to the establishment of Bombay Cinema as a genre. Two came from Calcutta; the third was a Marathi with strong links with both Poona and Bombay. These three, P. C. Barua, Nitin Bose, and V. Shantaram, collectively established the broad parameters within which serious Bombay Cinema was to function. Their significance was noted as early as 1940 by K. A. Abbas, a founding member of the Indian People's Theatre Association (IPTA), who wrote a critique on their contrasting styles (1940: 52–56). First, argued Abbas, there is Barua, the aristocratic director from Calcutta, who constructs the figure of the tragic hero moved by the agony of unrequited love in *Devdas*. Second, there is the technical mastery of Nitin Bose's opening shots of *President*. In these shots, the camera focuses on a clock on the wall as it chimes the half-hour, then moves to the swing door, which is rend apart, like a curtain, with the entry of the figure of a woman. "Try to shoot this scene in any other way and its lack of realism would be exposed," comments Abbas (54). At the end of the film, when the female president's mind has become seriously unbalanced, Nitin Bose gives in quick succession a number of quite haphazard shots of the empty room. Finally, there is Shantaram, whose *Aadmi* acts as a counterpoint to Barua's gloomy conception of the tragic hero. In fact Shantaram parts company with Barua (and with Himansu Rai) by emphasizing the continuity of life and the larger moral and social responsibilities of the individual in society. Love and romance can drain a person's energies and distort his or her reading of reality. To change the social order one needs a clear-headed comparative sense, combined with an ability to weigh issues, to reason and analyze one's initial, emotional, responses. "Where Barua is vague, Shantaram is definite; where Barua seeks to portray life as *he* sees it, Shantaram goes further and shows how it should be lived" (55), writes Abbas. Shantaram is "conscious of the economic realities of life" and realizes what it is like to be poor. Only the economically self-sufficient, says Abbas, can have the luxury of a Devdas moving from one station to another in a first-class carriage.

I have used Abbas strategically to introduce three texts which, together with a fourth text, *Kismet*, I now will examine at some length. Breaking chronology, I shall begin with Shantaram's *Aadmi* (Man).

Shantaram's *Aadmi* was released in Central Cinema, Bombay, on September 9, 1939. As the acerbic editor of *Filmindia*, Baburao Patel, wrote in an extended review of the film (1940: 37–40), *Aadmi* was loosely based on Robert Sherwood's *Waterloo Bridge*, which was first made into a movie by Universal Pictures in 1931. (MGM made another version with Mervyn LeRoy, producer of *The Wizard of Oz*, as director in 1940.) In Shantaram's version, policeman Moti (Sahu Modak) meets a singing prostitute, Kesar (Shanta Hublikar) during a police raid on call-girl premises. They fall in love. The hero takes the girl to his mother. Upon seeing the mother's piety, Kesar runs away, helped by Mannu, the hotel tea-boy. Pursued by her old pimp and caretaker, she retaliates by killing him. She is imprisoned for life. The hero, Moti, wishes to end his life but is dissuaded by Kesar from doing so.

Although Patel traced correspondences between Shantaram's film and its Hollywood prototype, what he defended extensively was the film's social realism (and its activist, regenerative possibilities couched in an antidrink, antisuicide manifesto). Much of the realism should be credited to Shantaram's art director, Sheikh Fattelal, whose sets emphasized the cheap lanes of the redlight districts of the cities in India. Fattelal also placed the camera close to the characters so that their expressions might be more clearly seen. It is his camera work rather than the film's semantic content that is the most powerful feature of the film. With Vishnu Govind Damle, Fattelal had directed *Sant Tukaram* some three years before *Aadmi*. There he established the use of sparse background to accentuate the finely etched features of the actors. It is in that general compositional style of Damle-Fattelal films that one would situate *Aadmi* cinematically. Its opening shot of a police raid signified by the stomping of feet before a torch shows the face of a woman is a characteristic Damle-Fattelal sequence. *Aadmi* thus foregrounds its technique as the camera becomes a self-conscious viewing eye. It is a form of montage linking "movement images" (1986: 30), to use Gilles Deleuze's useful term, which is used to signify a particular temporal order. The policeman Moti's number, 255, will be etched out with the aid of a candle by Kesar the prostitute; it will be wiped off toward the end with a brush when Kesar disappears. When Moti brings Kesar home so that the mother may bless her, the double narrative—the lovers' knowledge of Moti's mother's lack of knowledge of Kesar's background—is enacted through shots that intercut their gazes with shots of the mother's idol of a female deity with flowers in both hands. These scenes around the deity are shot with nondiegetic lights, flickering hurricane lamps, or candle. Every time Moti comes to visit Kesar she makes a mark on the wall. Over a period of time these vertical strokes cover a section of the wall and begin to look like prison bars. The symbology here is simple, but they situate the condition of the "freed" prostitute who now sits in a "respectable" room, waiting for a job, and who has a lover who can visit her only in the cover of the night: "In the evening, when it is dark," says Moti to Kesar. Clearly *Aadmi* cannot opt for the romantic solution of a later film such as *Sadhna* (1958), where the hero marries the prostitute after she had gone through ritualistic cleansing around a fire, accompanied by chants from holy texts. What Shantaram must pursue is the whole question of whether there are regenerative possibilities in this world, without of course losing the popular basis of the form. Hence the well-known parody of a song from *Achhut Kanya* is both a comic interlude and a history of Bombay Cinema to date. In this antiromance ("Life's for Living" is the English subtitle of *Aadmi*), Moti and Kesar chance upon a love scene that is being shot. The hero of that romance recites these cliché-ridden lines:

> Beloved in this world there are only you and me
> Even the cuckoo speaks of our love . . .

The Anglo-Indian heroine has considerable difficulty in getting her lines right as she continues to speak with a distressing Anglo-Indian accent. The filmic discourse on love, which is endlessly reprised, is now repeated by Moti and Kesar, who break out into a song of their own that consciously plays on the scene being clumsily enacted before them and connects, parodistically, with K. L. Saigal's hit, "prem nagar meṁ banāūṁgāṁ ghar maiṁ" (In the city of love I will build my mansion). Impressed by the performance of the newcomers, the director offers Kesar the heroine's role, but she walks off, laughing. Piqued, the original Anglo-Indian heroine also walks off the set, furiously dismantling the sari that she had draped over her skirt. While the target of Shantaram's satire was the way in which *Achhut Kanya*'s social realism is destroyed by the triumph of romance and the use of an Anglo-Indian body (Devika Rani) for the "authentic" Indian, Shantaram nevertheless quietly colludes with the form. Looked at another way, even as the genre is being deconstructed (albeit only in terms of its sentimental song-text) the centrality of the song syntagm and the song situation is reinforced.

Sheikh Fattelal's camera work is evident once again toward the end of the film when Kesar refuses to hoodwink Moti's pious mother by presenting herself as other than she is, and she departs, leaving Moti to go out looking for her. Shantaram gives us a number of dramatic intercuts between Moti's agitated walk (the camera again focuses on his shoes), the furious sound and picture of a waterfall, and Kesar's struggle to escape. When Kesar is caught for killing her former procurer and pimp the camera lingers on Moti's shoes, which had been made for him by Kesar. Wishing to kill herself, Kesar leaves a message behind for Moti through the trusted tea-boy: "prem ke liye duniyā nā choṛnā" (Do not leave the world because of love). As Moti walks out, the camera once again emphasizes his shoes, which is in fact the last shot of the film proper. The film had begun with a conundrum of sounds created by the rush of footsteps and shoes. It ends with a single image of a pair of shoes, recalling Van Gogh's well-known painting of peasant shoes, *A Pair of Boots*. Where Barua's *Devdas* had emphasized symbolic self-immolation in the Hindu ritual of fire, *Aadmi* stresses the labor of work needed to keep humankind going. Action, through the symbology of shoes, triumphs over renunciation through love, *pravṛtti* (living in the world) over *nivṛtti* (renunciation).

If Prabhat Theatres in Poona led the way with socially oriented films, New Theatres in Calcutta continued to work in the romantic hero tradition of *Devdas*. Unlike Prabhat Theatres and, generally, the Marathi tradition of strong radical films with anticolonial messages in their margins, New Theatres' brand of filmic representation was locked in the received generic typologies of sentimentalism and romance. The film that I wish to examine now is Nitin Bose's *President* (1939). I have already referred to Abbas's recog-

Sahu Modak Shanta Hublikar in V. Shantaram's *Aadmi*, 1939. Illicit love between police-man and prostitute. Courtesy National Film Archive of India.

nition of Bose's camera work. I want to quickly examine the idea of factory work, the iconic figure of the singer-hero Saigal, and the reversal of gender roles in the figure of a strong-willed woman president of a cotton mill, Shrimati Prabhabati (Kamlesh Kumari). The cotton mill is both a signifier of the new capital which came with the colonizer as well as a statement about the extent to which primary produce (like cotton and jute in Bengal) could now be processed in the local metropolis. Originally, of course, Indian products simply fed the cotton mills of Manchester. Yet this powerful critique remains in the margins of the text as romance is foregrounded. Enter the figure of K. L. Saigal, the singing star, into the lives of the initially asexual president and her sister, Sheila, an energetic young girl. The discourse of love is then projected through both dialogue and songs such as "nā koī prem kā rog lagāye" (Let no one inflame the sickness of love) and "prem kā hai is jag meṁ bāt nirālā" (The subject of love is intriguing in this world).

When the president recognizes that Prakash (Saigal) loves Sheila rather than her despite her gift of accelerated promotion in the factory for Prakash, she finds it much more difficult to come to terms with the reality. Her mind gradually gives way, her language becomes more and more fragmented, until finally she goes mad and dies. Before that tragedy occurs, there is union agitation for better work conditions that may be connected metonymically, not organically, with the larger anticolonial struggles—salt march, industrial strikes, noncooperation—taking place in India. Meanwhile the president's own world disintegrates. A hard-headed woman who had run a cotton mill by herself finally succumbs to the agonies of the heart. The stereotypical representation of woman here should not go unnoticed. *President*, the film, finally writes off the woman president whose emotions are far too strong to keep her intact in moments of crisis. At the end, the president leaves Prakash (who has been hit by a mill agitator) in the hands of Sheila and walks toward the conference table as the camera repeats the moment with which the film had begun. She walks around the table. The background is stark black and white, the walls are bare, the light throws shadows as she says "I'll have to go" and thinks that her car is coming. She hears footsteps and falls down dead. The suicidal act, in one sense, becomes the act of heroism through renunciation. But not before—and this again is a systemic feature of the form—the film had introduced the professional middle-class woman who will emerge later in the avatars of lawyer (*Awara*), doctor (*Amar Akbar Anthony*), teacher (*Shree 420*), policewoman (*Khalnayak*), businesswoman, and so on.

Chronologically *Devdas* (1935), the Hindi version of the Bengali original based on Saratchandra Chatterjee's highly sentimental novel of that name, should be placed at the head of this section, before *Achhut Kanya* (1936), in fact. I come to *Devdas* now because that film established the dominance of a particular aesthetic—that of the sentimental lover—in Indian cinema generally. This aesthetic, phenomenologically, may be connected with the rasa of *karuṇa*, of pity, one of the two dominant Sanskrit *rasa*s. Since *rasa* is a theory of reception, and is realized through a transactive relationship between "what is staged and the spectator" (Heckel 1989: 37), it requires a silent collusion, a dialogue (*saṁvāda*) between spectator and object as well. In this dialogic relay *karuṇa* became a *rasa* of emotional intensity with the greatest transactive pull. The deployment of the form is, however, not simply a "local" matter since the crucial intertext of Saratchandra Chatterjee's novel was not any Indian text but Goethe's great sentimental novel of *Weltschmerz* (unease with the world) and *Ichschmerz* (unease with the self), *Werther*. All later versions of the theme—*Aah* (Sighs of the heart, 1953—the original version), *Nazrana* (A gift of love, 1961), *Bambai Ka Babu* (The gentleman of Bombay, 1960)—echo the sentimentalist discourse of *Devdas*. When released in 1935, *Devdas* turned out to be a great success. The *Bombay Chronicle* observed: "Reports from the ten cities in every part of India where New Theatres' now famous classic *Devdas* is being shown are unanimous that this brilliant picture is the highest peak of screen achievement" (*Movie*, September 1983: 98).

Like Bose, Shantaram, and Rai before him, Pramathesh Chandra Barua (1903–51) too is enthralled by the iconic nature of the filmic sign. The first shots of *Devdas* show a slender woman walking off somewhat mysteriously toward a hedge of flowers with a pooja vessel in her hand, gently swaying from side to side. As she walks out of the camera our attention is drawn away from the visual to the auditory as we hear Saigal singing from beneath a tree, "bālam āye baso more man mem" (Come, my beloved, and dwell in my mind). The camera fetishizes beauty and mystery, the movement and the look, and captures an impending tragedy. What we see here beyond the effects of the shots (which Abbas had recognized as well) is the manipulation of Saigal's voice as it works in conjunction with a realist aesthetic. (Abbar, who was a member of the Communist Party–affiliated Indian People's Theatre Association [IPTA], was especially sensitive to this.) We hear the voice before we see his face; and he is able to break his song into segments so that the dialogue interlaces the song itself. Saigal had come to New Theatres in 1932 with his first film, *Mohabat Ke Ansu* (The tears of love, 1932), but it wasn't until his portrayal of a saint-singer in *Chandidas* (1934) in which he carved for himself the distinctive role of the singer-actor that led to the writing of scripts around his singing ability. *Devdas* is no exception, and the opening shots actually emphasize the importance of song in the film. (The popular fanzine *Star and Style* (May 30, 1969) referred to Barua's treatment of the tragic theme as marking also the beginning of a particular kind of film song.) This dominant established, the narrative of *Devdas* is then represented through three further cuts in which Devdas is seen with his father, mother, and brother, respectively. The fifth cut takes us back to Parbati, who, as in the first scene, asks Devdas if it were true that he is going away. The next image is of an itinerant blind singer (K. C. Dey) singing: "mat bhūl musāfir tujhe jānā hī paṛegā" (Don't forget, stranger, one day you'll have to go) where the simple departure to the metropolis is transformed into a background song. The romance, the song, and now the figure of the itinerant singer gradually establish some of the key norms of Bombay Cinema.

Apart from the use of these opening filmic cuts to establish the major mise-en-scènes (except the train and the courtesan's *koṭhā*, which come later), another memorable shot occurs when, rejected by his family as well and without any money, Devdas is found drunk on the footpath by Chandramukhi, the prostitute. In this shot of Chandramukhi getting off the horse cart to take Devdas away, the camera is placed behind the wheel of the cart so that the eye sees the movement of Chandramukhi toward Devdas and their return to the horse cart through a frame that is crossed by the spokes of the wheel.

K. L. Saigal and Jamna in P. C. Barua's *Devdas*, 1935. Love explodes into song. Courtesy National Film Archive of India.

There is clearly a prescient narrative of time (through the wheel) suggested here. But the zigzag lines on the screen also suggest the dangers of the wheel-of-time theory of history, because that theory will finally deny heroic resistance.

True, many of the themes in *Devdas* are not new, but there had not been a film in which they had been pushed to such ambiguous extremes. Let me take them up with reference to six orders: the order of marriage; the order of social decorum; the order of patriarchal power; the order of pleasure in the *koṭhā* (brothel); the order of symbolic violation; the order of the promise to return. The first of these, the order of marriage, works on caste containment (despite age disparity) and caste exclusion (despite age parity). In this order a filmic principle is established that leads to the marriage of the woman to someone at least twice her age. Parbati marries a man of 40 with a grown-up family. (The theme resurfaced most significantly in *Sharada* (1957) where Raj Kapoor is a quasi-Devdas character.) The second, the order of social decorum, establishes the conditions under which certain transgressive acts may be undertaken. In *Devdas* one of the most important moments of transgression takes place with reference to this order when Parbati enters Devdas's house in the middle of the night and is seen by the watchman. She had come, she says, to give herself to Devdas although her parents were against the marriage. At dawn he takes her home, denying Parbati her request. Two things come together: denial of desire on the part of the sentimental hero and refusal to contradict a patriarchal interdiction. The third order arises out of the latter observation. The fourth—pleasures in the *koṭhā* where the figure of the courtesan as alternative lover is introduced—is read as a perversion of desire and cause for return to Parbati. The fifth, the order of symbolic violation, occurs when Devdas strikes Parbati with a stick. Her forehead bleeds as she reminds Devdas of her wedding the following day. Having denied Parbati legitimate sexual pleasure, the sentimental hero now disfigures the object of love. The sixth, the promise to return, is framed in the space of the aimless train journey (and the two-day bullock-cart journey marked by song) that finally brings the sentimental hero to the door of his beloved. The train journey—an important sign of the modern in the film—and its codes of representation (cuts to names of numerous stations, shots of rail tracks, and the introduction of the figure of the companion) become thoroughly systemic in this cinema.

These themes, laid down in such an economical manner here, gain their power because of repetition. Scenes are duplicated but their content reversed: Devdas returns to Parbati and disfigures her; Parbati returns to Devdas to save him from drink but this time Devdas asks married Parbati to elope with him (which she refuses to do, although she speaks of him as her "soulmate"). In the end, however, the space of the home constrains her. When she is told that someone called Devdas had died, she runs toward the main gate saying, "I'm going to Devdas." Her stepson yells, "Mother is going to Devdas" and a voice is heard that she must be stopped. The main gates close, and she is trapped inside her own house. All we hear is the name "Devdas." The final shots are of the burning pyre, that severe symbol of Hindu death: K. C. Dey sings about death, the pallbearers stand alongside the pyre, the camera gives a close-up of the pyre burning furiously. The spectatorial desire here is for the oceanic sublime; the sentimentalist becomes the latest avatar of the renouncer in Indian society.

Barua's cameraman Bimal Roy did a remake of *Devdas* (with Suchitra Sen as Parbati and Dilip Kumar as Devdas) in 1955. Bimal Roy's earlier major work was *Do Bigha Zamin* (Two acres of land, 1953) in which a lone peasant's struggle against his landlord is presented as an allegory of the persistence of feudal structures even in postcolonial India. Unsurprisingly, the camera work in this *Devdas* is not very different from Barua's original. Bimal Roy continues to use montage and immediate cuts to juxtapose two moments so as to establish symbolic continuities between them. A shot of Paro (Parbati) getting into a horse cart on her way to her husband's house is immediately followed by Devdas getting off another horse cart. Paro's gaze in

Suchitra Sen and Dilip Kumar in Bimal Roy's *Devdas*, 1955. Moments before symbolic violation. Courtesy National Film Archive of India.

a mirror where she sees the wound inflicted on her forehead by Devdas is again followed by a shot of Devdas in a room in Calcutta with his friend Chunnilal (Motilal). Bimal Roy thus uses image to make suggestive connections between one cinematic moment and another. Montage and juxtaposition (the latter sometimes linguistic, as when a word such as "jewelry" is used by another to establish continuity between one event and another or between one image and another) remain dominant. If anything, Bimal Roy's cinematic fidelity to the earlier text verges on adulation: after all the film is dedicated to both P. C. Barua and K. L. Saigal. Twenty years on and the power of cinematic fidelity is so strong that except for the nondiegetic elements of song there is little sign here of ideological shifts that have occurred in India itself. The compulsion to repeat demonstrated the continuing allure of *Devdas* as an intrinsically useful form.

If Bimal Roy's 1955 version paid slavish homage to the original, it seems highly unlikely that the next full reprise of this text will do so. Sanjay Leela Bhansali, who has signed up Shah Rukh Khan to play Devdas, Aishwarya Rai to play Parbati, and Madhuri Dixit to play the courtesan Chandramukhi, has already declared:

> Even though it (*Devdas*) will be a period piece set in the '30s, we will have to add a contemporary flavour to it. [*Devdas*] is a love story—a great one at that. *Amanush,*

Muqaddar Ka Sikander and so many others have been versions of *Devdas* and were immensely successful. Quality literature is always relevant, never time bound. (*Hindustan Times*, City Section, August 29, 2000: 1)

The Barua and Bimal Roy (and the likely Bhansali) *Devdas* texts constitute a single interconnected text. From our vantage point, to read one is to read the other. The *Filmfare* review of *Devdas* (April 27, 1956: 21) made precisely this point but was quick to add, somewhat absurdly, that the insistence on caste differences in the Bimal Roy version is no longer significant as the "prejudices of caste are rapidly becoming a thing of the past" because the Indian constitution gives everyone equal rights.

Himansu Rai, P. C. Barua, V. Shantaram, Nitin Bose, and Bimal Roy were not making art films—they did not lay down, as Ashis Nandy observes, "the basis for future directors of art films" (1995: 203). They were makers of popular films for a primarily urban, middle-class Indian audience. They reproduced works of art in an age of mechanical reproduction, embraced modernity without either overtly critiquing it or being dragged into its high forms, and they used cinematic techniques without any real self-consciousness about differences between "artistic" and "nonartistic" filmic practice. But by the very nature of its reception, the form they produced was a popular form, not the present-day "mass" form in Nandy's terms. The "massification" of cinema, however, goes further back than Nandy concedes, and the key text in this process was *Kismet* (Fate, 1943), a film that brought the tradition from *Achhut Kanya* to *Aadmi* to a close but at the same time opened up the genre for its use and abuse in post-independence India.

In 1970, *Kismet* held the record as the longest running hit of Indian Cinema (*Star and Style*, February 6, 1970: 19). Some years later, in 1983, when *Kismet* was shown on London's Channel 4 Television during its highly acclaimed season of Indian cinema, it was introduced rather blandly as "a classic version of the return of the prodigal son." In broad outline the narrative of this film is certainly about the final return of the hero Shekhar (Ashok Kumar) to his father's household, which he had dramatically left as a young child over the issue of who his real mother was. The young Madan becomes Shekhar the professional pickpocket, a new heroic figure in cinema, who will resurface as Raj in *Awara* (1951) and will be transformed further as the Amitabh Bachchan figure in late capitalist India. The reestablishment of the lost order of family romance occurs via a locket which generates, as in Dickens's *Oliver Twist*, a chain of signifying events that finally returns the hero to his rightful parents.

The design of *Kismet* is an extension of the possibilities of the form as it achieved its stylistic definition in *Achhut Kanya*. In the hands of Gyan Mukherji, the screenplay writer and director, and Anil Biswas, the music director, the rough edges of the *Achhut Kanya* archetype are smoothed over, the songs refined, and the star system firmly entrenched. But *Kismet* wishes to be more than just an Indian picaresque. This is 1943, and there is immense agitation in India. The Cripps Mission has failed to resolve deep-seated divisions between the Muslim League and the National Congress. There are riots in Poona, and a famine in Bengal the likes of which India had not seen for sixty years. The Mahatma has adopted fasting as a political tool; Jinnah is resolute in his demand for Pakistan. The British are at war; the Japanese bombard Vizagapatam in April 1942. The Quit India campaign is matched only by a communal deadlock. But some people are also getting rich, as pointed out in the popular fanzine *Star and Style* (February 6, 1970: 19):

> [*Kismet*] owes its amazing, unexpected success to the time in which it was made. The War period had produced a climate for quick riches and success in certain trades. For the go-getters, the people on the move, luck (kismet) was the password. The dream of rags-to-riches was frequently becoming a reality for those who could venture and dare. And "kismet" was the handy word to explain away such quick success. No wonder that the film using this title as well as this spirit in its contents became such a resounding success.

The film combines the newfound wealth of an emergent bourgeoisie with the necessity of the anticolonial struggle. Despite strong colonial censorship, the political is imbricated in the diegesis of the text. Two instances will suffice as examples. In the first, political eruption takes the form of the cry of the newspaper boy who screams "Hitler's air attack, a necklace stolen, buy *Zamana*." The second political slippage is through the parallel narrative of the song. Indeed the political syntax of *Kismet* is to be found in a song sung twice in the film.

The hero, Shekhar, takes Rani's father (from whom he had stolen a valuable gold watch) to the theater to see Rani perform (Muslim Mumtaz had become Mumtaz Shanti the star). As the curtain parts, we see groups of people in military uniform playing chorus to Rani's song. In the background is a large map of prepartition British India in front of which, toward the end of the song sequence, Rani stands on crutches in the guise of the Hindu goddess Durga. To the accompaniment of a military musical score, we hear the opening lines of a patriotic song:

> From the heights of the Himalayas
> We've thrown down the gauntlet today.
> Give way, give way, you people of the world
> For Hindustan is ours.

Since Rani occupies center stage against the backdrop of the map of India, her presence as crippled heroine signifies perhaps the rape of India herself under imperialism. There are no radical gestures on her part because only symbolic platitudes can get around interwar censorship of antigovernment rhetoric. However, the nationalist slogan—Quit India—is clearly foregrounded but only on stage, as a prop in a performance framed by the seemingly innocuous genre of romance. So although outwardly the narrative proper has nothing to do with politics, verses are repeated by the chorus wearing regional costumes to underline India's collective outrage against the British. The political, the romantic, the devotional coexist side by side in *Kismet* within a genre (as Bombay Cinema) where the form always triumphs over ideology. Free Shekhar releases a dove in the air; a benign police inspector signals the new dharma.

The films discussed above—from *Achhut Kanya* to *Kismet* (chronologically from *Devdas* to *Kismet*)—I argue establish a particular mode of filmic representation that will become codified in Bombay Cinema. In the films that establish this genre we see the Indian mind taking hold of one of the great achievements of modernity and transforming it into a thoroughly local form. But even as the form triumphs and metatextual absolutisms continue to frame its ideology (Bombay Cinema is an allegory of the nation in the making), it begins to rethink its own connections with history (in a peculiarly hybrid, postcolonial fashion), as well as its own coercive or deconstructive capacities. Although the reception of any cultural object is linked to gender, class, linguistic and racial difference, indeed to everything by which the reader/spectator may be defined, at the formal level Bombay Cinema is a genre (a single text, a *grande syntagmatique* to reinflect slightly Christian Metz's use of the term) that works through predictable forms (music, dance, song, dialogue) and production practices (staged entry and departures, jump cuts, close-ups) aimed at an intersubjective reception in which the viewer is complicit with the object of contemplation. Govind Nihalani's defense of his film *Thakshak* (The serpent, 1999) referred to four characteristics of this cinema that stand out: star quality, music, story, and moral to which a certain *andāz* or "style," he said, should be added (ATN Canada, October 1999). The characteristics that Nihalani refers to were established more than sixty years before in the films discussed in the second half of this chapter. Does predictability, however, exhaust the form, naturalize it to the extent that it takes away from art its radical possibilities? Can temples of desire ("cinema cinema sab kā hai sapnā" [cinema, cinema, it is everyone's dream] the Bollywood lyricist and dialogue writer Javed Akhtar declares) take away from spectators their critical faculty? Are all cinema halls to be called Abhilash Talkies ("talkies of desire, of *kāma*"), the name given to the cinema house in Arundhati Roy's *The God of Small Things*? One of the things that worried Walter Benjamin was the dangers of a nonrevolutionary art, an art meant only for contemplation/concentration (auratic art) and not for "distraction" (*Zerstreuung*) or estrangement. Benjamin referred to film as a radical form of mechanical reproduction that politicized art and drew attention to the social. Films might be used for fascist ends, but their modes of production and reception (the film as the product of many hands) are fragmented enough to destabilize the seeming unity of the text, and blast open its ideological constraints. Montage, for instance, strips objects of their aura, and this technique of the juxtaposition of dissimilarities becomes, for Benjamin, a major principle of the radical nature of filmic production. Are there possibilities of a revolutionary countercinema in Bombay Cinema as well? Or even a rejection of Bombay Cinema outright, as so forthrightly expressed by the tribals in Andrzej Fidyk's documentary *Battu's Bioscope*? Although it is true that the form's dominant Hindu nationalist ideology would remain intact in the genre, the great strength of Bombay Cinema, like that of the dominant literary genre of modernity—the bourgeois novel—will always lie in its capacity to carry deconstructive or transgressive moments or "regulated transgressions" (Žižek 1997a: 27) in its interstices, which is why the Bombay film can endorse the dharmik order even as it accommodates the modern and transgresses that order.

Chapter Two

MELODRAMATIC STAGING

In an interview with Janet Bergstrom, Raymond Bellour remarked that "the classical American cinema continued in the 20th century the great tradition of the 19th century European novel" (Penley 1988: 188). The continuation, however, is not a matter of staying sincere to the highly diversified nature of the form; nor is it to be confused with André Bazin's observation that in the hands of a medium-conscious director such as Rossellini, the aesthetic of (Italian) cinema is "simply the equivalent of the American novel" (Bazin 1971: 2.39). Instead, in the hands of Hollywood the novel went through a leveling process, the form was stripped of its heterogeneity and homogenized. But something else happened there as well: Hollywood cinema reorganized the received [reductive] realist narrative according to the structural universal of the Oedipal scenario. In this reorganization, what got enacted was the displacement of desire for the mother onto another woman without completely bypassing, symbolically, the overhanging threat of castration. While Bellour's argument could be applied to Bombay Cinema, what we have detected thus far is that any discursive historicization of Bombay Cinema needs to take into account two different traditions: a series of localized mediations and the melodramatic novel of the colonizer. To reprise my point, in Bombay Cinema (which began as a colonial form) one of the great borrowed literary forms has been melodrama. The expressive possibilities of this mode, I argue, are taken up in a highly localized manner by Bombay Cinema where "[melodramatic] pathos is [almost] everything" (Kakar 1981: 33) and which is "tendentially capable of being described as melodramatic" (Prasad 1998: 57).

If for Bellour, and Fredric Jameson, the realist novel stands behind Hollywood cinema, it must be said that for Indian cinema the realist novel, though decisive, was one among many defining antecedents. Apart from the impact of the local—from *Nautankī* to Tamasha and, especially, Parsi theater—Western genres were filtered through what one senses is the immensely pervasive influence of Romanticism on the Indian educated imagination. The upshot of this influence was the consumption of texts that carried with them some of the undercurrents of Romantic sentimentality. There is nothing specifically Indian or particularly new about the valorization of that sentimentality. It surfaced in Byron's praise of Walpole's *The Mysterious Mother* and of Dryden's plays. This mediation of the realist through the underside of Romanticism—sentimentalism—foreshadows the mediation of the received tradition of the novel on the part of the Indian colonial by what I have called, after Rey Chow (1995: 170), "melodramatic staging." Here one needs to recall that in this staging, the texts—the filmic texts—did not defer to any one specific ideal of melodrama, but rather to a mixed discursive form that carried with it strong elements of sentimentalism, characterological binarism (the absolutist triad of father, mother, and child), the use of the tableau, and so on. The point is that there is no exact match between an Indian film and a Western melodrama. What happens is that melodramatic features are selectively used to stage any number of quite serious and in themselves nonmelodramatic moments. For instance, epics need not be melodrama; but Indian film epics invariably are, because melodrama in this cinema is not simply a genre, it is collectively representation, narrative structure, and a "mode of cultural production/assimilation" (Rajadhyaksha 1993: 59). More significantly, as Rajadhyaksha has noted, "The [Bombay] film melodrama . . . acquired the status of the privileged form of representation of an industrialized, modernizing nation-state, and the means by which the key hegemonies informing the post-war and post-Swadeshi idea of a 'national' culture were repressed" (1966b: 408–409). And so even mythologicals and devotionals (to use the Indian Censorship Board's own classificatory system) are staged melodramatically. The only form that arguably escapes from this staging is the stunt film, especially those made by the master stunt director Homi Wadia. How do we explain these local variants?

Before addressing this question, I want to pause here and rethink melodrama and its appropriation by Indian readers in particular. The historical moment of melodrama (literally, "a play with music") was the late eighteenth century, when it was a theatrical performance with song and music. Although French melodrama with its "transclass" coding and democratic style has closer parallels with Bombay Cinema, it is English melodrama (a decidedly

lower-class entertainment but, unlike the realist novel, not necessarily revolutionary) that is its immediate antecedent. Nevertheless what Peter Brooks
says about French melodrama is worth noting because of its analytical value.
Writes Brooks (1982: ix):

> [Melodrama] seemed to describe, as no other word quite did, the mode of their
> dramatizations, especially the extravagance of certain representations, and the
> intensity of moral claims impinging on their characters' consciousness. Within an
> apparent context of "realism" and the ordinary, they seemed in fact to be staging a
> heightened and hyperbolic drama, making reference to pure and polar concepts of
> darkness and light, salvation and damnation.

During the French Revolution, melodrama picked up a Jacobin flavor and was
identified, in part, as a people's theater. At the turn of the nineteenth century
it became the dominant form of English theater and incorporated into its form
features of pantomime, dumb show, and other vignettes. In one sense its spectacle and emotion-based form parted company with the realist representationalism of both the earlier drama and the novel, and with romance. Thematically,
too, the emphasis shifted from discoveries of the self and its restitution into a
familial or moral order to an emphasis on real or imagined loss with imprisonment the likely fate of the hero. The significant thing about melodrama is that
the idea of "loss" is staged melodramatically, not tragically and even morality is
sentimentalized. Reflecting this convention, the melodramatic hero of Bombay
Cinema is given an appropriate *becārā* discourse before the loss is represented.
In this sense, seemingly heroic moments of sacrifice—Dilip Kumar's in *Gunga
Jamna,* Sunil Dutt's in *Mother India,* Amitabh Bachchan's in *Deewar* (The wall,
1975) or even Hrithik Roshan's in *Fiza* (2000)—are framed within a melodramatic register. Writing about Dilip Kumar, Akbar S. Ahmed states, "Dilip
became the most famous melodramatic expression of the tragic strain of fatalistic philosophy in South Asian Society" (1992: 303). In these films—films
centered on themes of social misfortune—the individual as an ethical subject
(with humane, democratic values) either loses out completely or is integrated
back into the system, and stands for it. The eruptions around the figure of the
hero are complicated further when it comes to the figure of a woman whose
explosive or transgressive sexuality has to be contained by the social order. In
this respect, as we have seen, the figure of the woman is both a constitutive element of the Oedipal structure (upon whom desire has to be deflected) and a
danger to patriarchal control of woman's sexuality.

To take another leaf out of Peter Brooks's important study, melodrama
comes into being when bourgeois individuality finally breaks away from the

shackles of a feudal economy. Brooks's location of the break in the events surrounding the French Revolution is *the* classic theory of the genesis of melodrama, but his argument also connects the bourgeois individual with the bourgeois body, which is then represented, in melodrama, as an hystericized body. In a later essay (1994: 11–24), Brooks examines the transgressive power of a female body—here that of Charlotte Corday—that leaves its wound, its lethal mark, on the chest of the dead Marat. In Jacques-Louis David's memorable painting (*Marat assassiné*) Charlotte Corday's letter can be deciphered: "Il suffit que je sois bien malheureuse pour avoir droit à votre bienveillance" (The simple fact of my misfortune is my claim to your benevolence). Brooks makes the point that this sentence is "typical of those spoken by the virtuous characters in melodrama" although the genre had not been christened as such in 1793. In David's painting and in revolutionary melodramas generally, suggests Brooks, we detect the origins of "an aesthetics of embodiment" (1994: 17). This is a good point at which to pause and follow up the significance of the body as a sign. In the context of Indian popular cinema two things strike us immediately. The first is the body as a marker of character or discourse: the body need not speak, it speaks of itself. The second is the significance of a mark on the body (scar, birth defect) or an emblem associated with the body (necklace, ring) in the narrative of "discovering." Sometimes there is also a genetic association. Rita, as the lawyer in *Awara*, asks Judge Raghunath whether Raj (his son) doesn't have the same look, the same temperament, as he himself. And as we have already seen with reference to *Kismet*, the necklace or locket is used in many films as a means of reinscribing a person in the genealogical order. The melodramatic recognition scene—often presented as a tableau—is based on the recognition (and legitimation) of the correct signs against those evil signs to be excluded from the moral universe of the film. In this respect the body's capacity to "act out" to the point of "extremity" (through gesture, through utterances of shock and recognition) gets around the law of repression that stipulates that violation should not be given full semantic force. Not surprisingly, the villain's body is excruciatingly pummeled by the hero while the virtuous woman's body is probed to the point of violation before she is rescued. In this sense the melodramatic body is the site where the lifting of repression takes place and the socially or morally disavowed (censored) is momentarily avowed or scripted back into the alternative (but real) narrative of the text. Meaning, as Brooks remarks, is enacted on the body itself, which, of course, would suggest that the body is always, implicitly, in the process of being hystericized and encapsulated in a narrative of impossible or unrealizable desire.

In spite of the received tradition of melodrama and its availability, Indian filmic melodrama is not identical with any single melodramatic tableaux; nor is it the melodrama of the "hiss the villain" variety. There is something unabashedly local here, as key elements of melodrama (binary characterizations, coincidences, the use of the tableaux, excess of feeling that ends up trivializing emotion) are selectively adapted. In some instances, classic realist texts are melancholically rendered, as are *Jane Eyre* in *Sangdil* (Against love, 1952) and *Wuthering Heights* in *Dil Diya Dard Liya* (The pains of love, 1966). Melodrama acts like a glue that connects discrete texts and generic registers (from realistic to the comic carnivalesque) together. For the (Indian) spectator ideology itself—of family, gender, or power—finds a space for its articulation through melodrama. "Staging melodrama," of course, does not mean that one opposes some form of realist truth against melodramatic excess. Melodrama of the Bombay Cinema variety represents cultural truths of a metatextual kind—truths that bind eternal laws together—and not truths of a representational (lifelike) kind. But this is not to say that Bombay films do not carry alternative moments, worldviews, in their very design, nor indeed through the cinematic image—a gaze that denies spectatorial complicity, a gaze that locates its object away from the spectators, and so on. In this sense, melodramatic staging has a modernist edge to it because it both brings the dramatic into the novelistic and challenges what Fredric Jameson has called the universalizing code of realism (1990: 169), and what André Bazin, the great theorist of filmic realism, has called the codes of black-and-white photography. Melodrama forces us to take seriously the claim of many Bombay directors: "Why should the codes of realism dictate our choice of representational codes?" Indeed, to the various established forms of filmic realism—the modernist experimental, the documentary, the photographic, and the "composite" Hollywood—we could add Bombay "cinematic realism" as another category. To examine these further, I want to look at the manner in which elements of the epic form (denied by Raymond Bellour in favor of the classic realist text) are melodramatically staged in Bombay Cinema. To do this I will look, at two ways of staging India's great foundational text, the *Mahābhārata,* and an instance of the use of the realist novel by Bombay Cinema. This will be followed by a look at the more obviously melodramatic Indian gothic.

THE EPIC AND THE NOVEL

Some cultural texts do become foundational; by any definition the *Mahābhārata* (hereinafter *Mbh*) is one such text. In Indian culture the *Mbh* has been continually rewritten, with genres as varied as the Puranas, drama (both classical and modern), medieval romance, the Indian bourgeois novel, and finally the Indian film all retrieving the rules of their formation from it. There may be something so dreadfully imperialistic about this text that, in a moment of willful generalization or enthusiasm, one may even claim that all Indian literary, filmic, and theatrical texts rewrite the *Mbh*. Yet this very foundational text is a living form which is transmitted and consumed in a variety of ways. In this section I want to examine this text and look, in particular, at two modes of its staging. For the first mode, I use Peter Brook's stage and televisual text; for the second, I look at Bombay Cinema's rendition of the epic.

The *Mbh* itself reached its final form probably around the second century C.E. Its *terminus ante quem* is generally placed around the seventh and sixth centuries B.C.E., making its early versions (which are only a matter of conjecture) almost contemporary with Homer. Throughout its long history, this vast, heterogeneous text of one hundred thousand verses (or *ślokas*), absorbed a large number of quite divergent narratives—anecdotal and fantastic, as well as historical and theological. Hindu tradition states repeatedly, though probably never categorically, that the signature of one Krishna Dvaipayana Vyasa can be seen in an entire series of texts framed by the Vedas at one extreme and the Puranas at another. It is, however, in the *Mbh*, and especially in the Vulgate, that we are given an extensive account of Vyasa's role in the composition of a text with the help of the scribal services of Ganesha. Such fantastic accounts of writing led the German Indologist Herman Oldenberg to claim almost a century ago that though the *Mbh* began as a simple epic narrative, "it became, in course of centuries, the most monstrous chaos" (quoted in Mishra 1991: 195). From this "chaos" (which existed only in Oldenberg's mind), redactors and readers distilled texts (or narrative fragments) to suit their specific needs. One of its best-known sections, the *Bhagavadgītā*, quickly became a text in its own right, and was read as a self-contained poem about self and liberation, relatively independent of the *Mbh*. But texts undergo a very different kind of transformation in India. Since the original has no auratic status as such, a text is always what it is at a given moment in history. Consequently, the Indian hermeneutical and exegetical traditions never tried to reconstruct the original, but instead allowed the popular imagination to add to the *Mbh* and "translate" it into a didactic text of quite bewildering complexity but with strong religious appeal or dimension. In this respect, it could be argued, and persuasively I think, that Bombay Cinema (and its great father figure Dadasaheb Phalke) understood the essence of the epic tradition much better than the Indologists. It is at once an informant of Indian culture as well as a spectacularly successful case of ideo-logical transmission.

This transformation—the "sanctification" and consequent canonization of a text—must be placed in the context of what constitutes literary/religious value in Indian society and how texts are continuously read/reread and relayed. One begins, first, with an understanding of the larger context of oral reception and transmission of the epic from mother to child. Although told in fragments, a complete *Mbh* text is handed down over the years. Every Hindu child receives it and knows its genealogy by heart. Second, the *Mbh* text exists through folk, theatrical, and filmic representations. Finally, the *Mbh* is a global (as well as local) text-in-translation, a book that is read both in Indian vernaculars and in major world languages. Here, depending upon the culture of the receptor language, the *Mbh* becomes an extraordinarily var-ied and unstable text, from the popular nationalist translation of Rajagopachari to the incomplete Chicago translation of the great Sanskritist J. A. B. van Buitenen. The sense of finality implied in the third *Mbh* text is premature since there is now a fourth text, Peter Brook's monumental stage and television version of the *Mbh*. Brook's "performative" texts have been artistic events of such epic proportions that they need to be given some crit-ical space in any study of Indian culture that invokes the great epic. When we return to the ten-hour theatrical version (as performed at the Boya quarry in Perth, for instance) we sense Brook's understanding of the epic's propensity to destabilize, distort, and confuse the basic categories of good and evil, fate and free will. Brook, however, maintains that in "jumbling" these terms, the epic finally releases them from their historical accretions so that the words, bare, precise, pristine—as a dictionary entry, so to speak—look back at us. In this version the *Mbh* is used to revolutionize theater itself, and to reassert it as spectacle, a role so dramatically wrenched from it by film, that alarmingly antiauratic product of mechanical reproduction. Yet precisely because of its downplaying of aura and the sanctity of the original text, film becomes an important force in Brook's own production. It is film (and filmic techniques of representation, though without the camera) that is the mediating principle in Peter Brook's theatrical version of the *Mbh*.

In this version we return to the *Mbh* as spectacle, as performance, which remains deeply ambivalent about its political implications and about the pos-sibility of order. It must be added, however, that Brook's spectacular ten-hour version of the *Mbh* was based on Jean-Claude Carrière's dramatic recon-struction of the epic in which the narrative self is constructed in a highly postmodern fashion. Vyasa as writer becomes the most important character in the epic as a consequence. Others question him about his intentions: "Why have you created us if you are going to kill us sooner or later?" or "Are you still in charge of the plot since noble kings are also dying?" Since Vyasa has also invented Krishna we get interesting reversals whose logic comes straight out of the helixlike structure of Hindu thought. "Vyasa, which one of us has invented the other? . . . What role have you in store for me now?" are the kinds of questions Krishna asks. Not surprisingly, he gets the predictable reply, "You know well." The varying writer positions are either remarkably postmodern or signify an underlying tendency in Indian culture toward the dispersal of authority so that all that remains is a con-gealed longing for a mysterious unity and not a central, controlling autho-rial voice or presence. It is for this reason that the absence of a fully articulated (and personally accountable) tragic sense in Indian literature and film is not unusual. Perhaps only once, in the markedly uncomfortable figure of Karna, the antihero of the *Mbh*, do we come across a character whose moral universe locks itself into meaning, and whose reading of dharma is not in terms of the eternal law but through personal morality and responsibility. Of all the characters in the *Mbh* (Krishna included), Karna alone keeps his word throughout.

Where Peter Brook emphasized the extent to which the great epic fore-shadowed narrative techniques we would normally associate with late moder-nity, Indian filmic transformations of the great epic, including the Doordarshan TV serialization, have been less interested in this. The reason has been foreshadowed in this chapter through my reference to the impor-tance of melodramatic staging. Many of the elements of this staging—speak-ing the unspeakable ("I renounce my father!"), presencing the body as the signifier of the moral order, "the impossibility of conceiving sacralization other than in personal terms" (Brooks 1982: 16), representing a Manichean worldview through extravagant expressions of good and evil, virtue and vil-lainy, and so on—are already present in the epics. What is different is their "acting out," their embodiment in a melodramatic semiotic. If we now return to the 1965 Bombay version of the epic (*Mahabharat*), we get a text that shifts quite radically from writing as a heterogeneous practice with multiple points of view to an essentially monological representation of a world gener-ated by the laws of Krishna, the cosmic author. The *Mbh* as epic is now replaced, quite radically, by the *Mbh* as a religious text as transmitted by a particular Hindu view of the world and rendered melodramatically. In the end the highly complex narrative of the *Mbh* is stripped of its contradictions and becomes, instead, an affirmation of a dharmik world order that Krishna endorses. Since the laws of karma and dharma originate in him, the film now becomes a replay of universal principles, which are then reinforced through the filmic device of the song: melodrama, one remembers, originally meant "drama accompanied by music" (Brooks 1982: 14). The spectator therefore identifies with Krishna as the cosmic author or puppeteer who manipulates a narrative that is already known to him. This Krishna is, however, not the hero of the old epic, he is in fact already vested with characteristics he has acquired in the post-epic era: the cowherd stealer of butter, the lover of Radha, the pastoral swain and flute player, and so on. In this respect this is a very modern Krishna who is able to read the primal loss of traditional values—the epic confronts truth as crisis—through a pair of postcolonial Indian lens.

Beyond the inscription of a "contemporary" reading of Krishna back into the epic there is another kind of tacit understanding between the practice of the apparatus called Bombay Cinema and the spectators' knowledge of that material. Thus the "citation" of song-and-dance sequences, the foregounding of a conservative politics, the manipulation of stars, the glorification of a martial race in the context of the 1965 war with Pakistan, and a taste of what was to become the gradual Hinduization of the Indian body politic in later years (taken up in chapter 7 of this book)—all these are carefully inserted into the body of the filmic text. On top of this there is a clear reference to the *Mbh* as the text whose massive frames contain the essential book of the Hindus, the *Bhagavadgītā*, which is currently being transformed through the World Hindu Organization (the Vishva Hindu Parishad) as *the* canonical Hindu religious text. The film tells Hindus that they too have a book and that this book is the repository of all knowledge. Thus some ten minutes, or around 5 percent of film time, is set aside for the *Bhagavadgītā,* which is read unproblematically through the poetics of devotion and the principle of the necessity of (karmic) action. Since there is such a massive dose of devotional ideology thrown into the text, other devotional figures also invade it. Of special note is the figure of Hanuman, the classic Rama-bhakta and half brother of Bhima, who, of course, has such an important part to play in the *Rāmāyaṇa*. Since the *Rāmāyaṇa* text here is really the Hindi (Avadhi) version of Tulsidasa's *Rāmacaritamānasa*, it is interesting to note that so much of the discourses that we find in this later text are retrospectively inserted into the filmic *Mahabharat*. A notable instance of such discursive intrusion occurs in the context of the Draupadi *svayaṃvara*. When it becomes clear that no warrior has the necessary skills to perform the difficult feat of archery to win Draupadi's hand in marriage, her father says, "I am now convinced that my daughter will be a spinster for life." What he is paraphrasing is in fact straight out of the *Rāmacaritamānasa* of Tulsidasa: "likhā nā vidhi vaidehī bibāhū (For it is written that the daughter of Vaidya will remain unmarried). Two other features should be noted here. The first is the extent to which the film version is locked into the definitions of the popular in India. In other words, the spectator's own definition of cinema as the spectacle of the imaginary is never threatened by the intrinsically challenging nature of the background epic text. In the Pandavas's "Palace of Illusion" (a tableau mise-en-scène) we get ready examples of the modern, from television to song-and-dance sequences that are totally anachronistic. Clearly, at one level, whenever a film reads an event no longer contemporary with itself, it is by definition anachronistic: speech, background music, montage, and everything else besides mediate between the present and the past. The second feature that requires a gloss is again the positing of the *Bhagavadgītā*, in its quasi-monotheistic form, as the interpretive text for the rest of the *Mbh.* This is signaled by the isolation of the *Bhagavadgītā* in the theme song of the film: "jis ne dī bhārat ko gītā vo mahābhārat kathā" (I speak of the text that gave India the *Bhagavadgītā*). In the ten-minute *Bhagavadgītā* sequence the emphasis is on the idea of proper caste-propelled action. Arjuna, the Kshatriya, must therefore fight. But the extended and complex argument of the *Bhagavadgītā* proper is now rechaneled through Shakespeare's "Cowards die many times before their deaths, /The valiant never taste of death but once" (*Julius Caesar*, 1.2.33–34). A version of postcolonial packaging is at work here: sly mimicry, ironic reappropriation of master texts, and so on. The *Bhagavadgītā* is now reread through the high texts of imperialism and both, in the Bombay film, feed upon each other. When such quasi-parodistic refashioning takes place, the text itself becomes a strange amalgam of quite contradictory forces. For Bombay Cinema this is not unusual, and reflects the larger tradition that gave it shape.

Whereas the epic reached us in a completed generic form, the novel is a genre in the making. Its origins in bourgeois culture and its enormous plasticity allow materials from diverse discourses to be included within its overall form. This is more or less Mikhail Bakhtin's argument, which seems to me to be very appropriate in the context of the use of this form by the postcolonial Indian. "When the novel becomes the dominant genre, epistemology becomes the dominant discipline," Bakhtin had written (1981: 15). In the text (and film variant) that I want to examine next, R. K. Narayan's *The Guide*, what strikes me so forcefully is that an entire Hindu metanarrative of selfhood and dharma is now redefined or processed through a genre where questions of self are, inevitably, related to radically different notions of selfhood and being. For what the novel introduces is subjectivity linked to a socioeconomic order, ironizing the earlier metanarratives, and carving open domains of self not necessarily demonstrable through age-old essentialisms. It is possible, then, to see Narayan reading the self at two levels: the self as a grand metanarrative and the self as historically and socially constituted. Let us look at the metanarrative first. In this reading, the hero of the novel, Raju, would be defined as the self seeking *ātman*. The narrative is pre-given since the dharmik stages by which self-knowledge (*ātma-vidyā*) may be achieved are clearly laid down by the culture itself. We could then map out Raju's attachment to Rosie as a failure on the part of the self to distinguish between *saṃsāra*, the phenomenal world we inhabit, and the Real, which in this instance is not any socioeconomic base, or the Marxist "real," but the state of Brahman-consciousness that the *Bhagavadgītā* defines as the merging of the self into Krishna: "I am the rite, I am the sacrifice . . . " (ahaṃ kratur ahaṃ yajñah . . .), Krishna had said. The principle that governs *saṃsāra*, the world of illusion, is Maya, which is superimposed on the "body" of Rosie the dancer, the *nartakī*, whose finest dance is the snake dance. "She is a real snake woman," Raju's mother warns (1988: 136). Raju does not heed this warning and suffers as a consequence of his passion for the married dancing girl. His arrest for forgery (the ultimate sign of confusion of the self through writing as self-deception) occurs at precisely the moment Rosie performs her final item, the snake dance. What follows is imprisonment for two years. Release takes Raju to a remote village where despite himself he becomes a saint, sacrificing his life in the hope that the famine that has devastated the village will end. Raju, in this metaphysical reading of the novel, finally transcends the world of unreality and unites with Brahman. As S. Radhakrishnan's commentary on the *Bhagavadgītā* points out:

> Works are vain and bind us firmly to this unreal cosmic process (saṃsāra), the endless chain of cause and effect. Only the wisdom that the universal reality and the individual self are identical can bring us redemption. When this wisdom arises, the ego is dissolved, the wandering ceases and we have perfect joy and blessedness.
> (trans. Radhakrishnan 1963: 16–17)

At the second level, R. K. Narayan reads the metanarrative much more ironically since the subtext here is precisely the manner in which definitions of self are not so much governed by a grand metatext as by social and historical forces. Furthermore, it is the psychosocial complexity of the self, the person's caste, sexual, and gendered differences, that make the prescriptive application of a Brahmanical ideology (without any basis in the Real) impossible. For it soon becomes clear that Rosie's own past as a woman of the caste of temple dancers is a carefully developed theme that invites the metatext only to make her own departures from the norms of the metatext that much more marked. She defies the respectability offered her through marriage to an established archaeologist by having an illicit affair with Raju. And when Raju squanders her earnings in drinking and gambling, it is she who makes the break and leaves him, but not to return to Marco as the metatext might have prescribed. Of course in one version of the metatext she could never return to her husband's world anyway. Her decision to leave insinuates a growing radicalization of the female under way in Indian society. Similarly, Raju too may be inserted into quite specific social formations that would include the anxieties involved in earning a livelihood in India, the highly repressed nature of Indian sexuality, the attractiveness of the world of glamor so powerfully endorsed by Indian commercial cinema, and so on. Both the metatext and those forces that define the individual in a postcolonial capitalist world thus form the subject Raju. Yet the way in which Raju captures the imagination of Velan, the villager who reads even his confessional narratives as indicative of discourses that only enlightened individuals know, shows how in the culture the mantle of the Mahatma is thrust upon an individual despite the person's protestations. The ironic parallels with Gandhi (the Mahatma) are far too obvious to need further elaboration.

I have isolated two key concepts—definitions of the self in the novel and the power of the metatext—to demonstrate how the novel varies from the epic. In this sketchy account the emphasis has been on the processes of ironization of the self and the sociohistorical constructions of meaning. Where the epic locked itself into meaning, the novel opts for more open-ended possibilities. In the end, R. K. Narayan does not spell out the precise nature of Raju's spiritual achievement, leaving it ambiguous. What we must now see is the manner in which Bombay Cinema transforms the novel (as distinct from the epic). We must recall that our departure point, in the first instance, was classic American cinema and the underlying argument that this cinema works on realist fictions of the nineteenth century. It is absolutely salutary for us to now cite a specific instance of the transformation of a novel into Bombay Cinema.

Dev Anand's film version of *The Guide* was released in 1965, the same year in which *Mahabharat* was released. (Although directed by his brother Vijay Anand, Dev Anand, the star and producer of the film [through Navketan his production house], had such control over the film that I will refer to the film as Dev Anand's.) The film was made in both English and Hindi. The English version was directed by Tad Danielewski and scripted by

Pearl S. Buck (Vaidyanathan 1996: 91). I will be concerned only with the Hindi version. Called *Guide* (Hindi does not have the definite article), the film's definition of the heroic self is constructed out of two processes that are structural invariables in this filmic practice. The first of these processes deals with the manner in which extratextual apparatuses, notably the essays of gossip columnists in fanzines and established newspapers, project a particular image of the actor. Not uncommonly this projection is linked to the Indian definition of the heroic male as well as the Indian's projection of sexual fantasies upon an actor. The actor then acquires a charisma that locks him into expectations that in turn generate a particular character type on the screen. Even though the source text of Dev Anand's *Guide* is Narayan's ambiguous text, the film cannot be prized out of the glamorous definition of self-as-actor projected by Dev Anand for more than fifteen years prior to the making of *Guide*. Closely related to the first is a second process that requires cinematic heroes to play themselves in films so that their filmic presence will reproduce what the spectator expects of them. So point-of-view shots of Dev Anand are taken to accentuate his looks, his romanticism, and present him as a legitimate, unthreatening object of female desire. That men too adopt this position says something about the androgynous overlapping of male and female sexuality in India. The two interlocking processes are so overpowering that they combine to create the actor as a parallel text. Such profilmic constructions of the actor read back into the pan-Indian epic tradition now lead to very serious problems about realist representations: how does one act in character, and how does one shift the spectator's own regimes of reading? One of the reasons why I chose *Guide* is that its novelistic source will at least throw into relief the whole problematic of filmic representation of a realist text. As I have said before, the novel deftly undercuts the metatext of fixed unchanging values: Raju the guide is no saint, and his sacrifice probably does not change the lives of the villagers at all. One could argue that in the end even the drought does not break, as the language is self-consciously couched in the ironic final words of Kim in Rudyard Kipling's imperialist text.

Despite some extremely realistic scenes—notably the scenes dealing with the sudden arrival of Raju's uncle from the village and the mother's decision to leave the house—the film cannot transcend its own specific mode and implicitly sets up the not uncommon tension between the literary and the filmic in this cinematic system. This is especially true of the manner in which Raju's mother becomes the predictable *"filmi"* (a Hindi adjectival neologism of "film") mother and Rosie, finally, is indistinguishable from the star (Waheeda Rehman) who plays that role. Since continuity of a melodramatic kind must be maintained, both mother and mistress are made to return to the final scene of sainthood to be with the son and lover. The kinds of surplus value granted the mother or the constant mistress are again reinforced in the film. But so too are the confirmation of the final release and the experience of moksha ("enlightenment"). Even the gods are shamed by Raju's sacrifice, and there is thunderous downpour at the moment of his death. Release for Raju is also comfort for mother, mistress, and villagers: their happiness lies in the ultimate endorsement of selfless karma (the karma that seeks no self-gain) in the person of Raju. Narayan himself was less than amused by this filmic adaptation and objected both to the extravagant settings and to the changes made to the plot (Vaidyanathan 1996: 91–92). The simplicity of style and ironic point of view, both unusually strong in Narayan, were lost in this less than ambiguous and poorly rendered (in Narayan's aesthetic terms) film.

Yet the *ahaṃkāra*, the I-ness, which the novel had eschewed, surfaces in the filmic text through a direct iconographic equation of the hero, Raju/Dev Anand, with Krishna himself. The question is buttressed by the text of the *Bhagavadgītā* presented as a dialogue between the two selves of Raju as alternately Krishna and Arjuna. This is an interesting process since the dialogue itself tells us that *ahaṃkāra* (ego) must be denied. "Only the *ātman* is eternal, only I . . . you are *ahaṃkāra*, you must die," says the good angel in the hallucinatory sequence, constructed as much to revive for the spectator the romantic good looks of the hero Dev Anand as to underline the awkward metaphysics of the renouncer and the man-in-the-world. As a consequence of this conflation, the film fails to distance the two (I-ness and renunciation) and ends up endorsing *ahaṃkāra* (through the mechanics of the star personality) while at the same time denouncing it. As I have said, this contradiction arises from the demands of the star personality which must also occupy the heroic space that, in this case, really belongs to Krishna. The last words, again spoken by Raju's spiritual self ("Only I, only I") suggest that Raju/Dev Anand has unproblematically entered the bliss of Brahman. My worry here is not so much with the confirmation of the Hindu spiritual worldview as with the manner in which the star (Dev Anand) becomes the enlightened being. The ironic undercutting that marks the Raju of Narayan's novel is replaced by the star's attempt to redefine and rework his own history. Film, the product of mechanical reproduction (and technically anti-auratic), is deployed here to reduce a complex novelistic world to suit the star's own ideology.

Both *Mahabharat* and *Guide* thus transform two genres into Bombay Cinema's own predictable form. They are in fact commodified and repackaged so as to feed an imaginary desire for repetition and confirmation of the established world order on the part of the Indian spectator, male and female. We are no longer in the realm of form and genre; we enter the domain of ideology. And here, as we have seen before, it is an artificially constructed (and historically refined) worldview based on the Hindu law of dharma that always triumphs. But even high metaphysics—the domain of the absolute— gets staged melodramatically as this revisionist ideological system reinforces the essentialisms of the Hindu world order by fashioning its own authorized identities. In the domain of lived experience this "authorization" has even elided the differences between cinema and politics. The star becomes a political hero as well, as illustrated by the cases of MGR (M. G. Ramachandran) and NTR (Nandamuru Taraka Rama Rao), sometime chief ministers of Tamil Nadu and Andhra Pradesh, respectively, and the political careers of Jayalalitha and even Sunil Dutt, Amitabh Bachchan, Vijayanthimala, Rajesh Khanna, and Shatrughan Sinha. Their success reinforces the collapse of the sign and its referent: the star personality traduces and takes over real history.

THE INDIAN GOTHIC

A key Romantic (or more precisely pre- or even proto-Romantic) genre that needs to be factored into any theorization of melodrama and sentimentalism is the gothic. In literature the link between melodramatic modes and this genre is clear-cut. Some of its key practitioners were familiar with melodrama: Matthew Gregory Lewis, author of *The Monk* (1796), was well-known for his romantic melodramas, and Mary Shelley was clearly very impressed by Richard Brinsley Peake's melodramatic version of her novel *Frankenstein* (*Presumption*, 1823). The central themes of the gothic—the idea of claustral and confined space as the metaphor of the unconscious in the dark passages of the gothic castle, the terror that this space creates, the absence of transcendence, the threat of sexual violation, and so on—are worked through representational devices that use the compositional features of melodrama. The Indian gothic too uses the diegetic space of the mansion/castle as its central metaphor and as possible sites of sexual threat and confinement. Although we could explore the Indian gothic through these formal characteristics of the form, I want to suggest that the most productive way to enter into Indian gothic melodrama is to read the genre as a representation of the uncanny. In other words, the nature of dread that the supernatural moment gives rise to is related to a fear that is connected to the subject's unease with a space, a narrative, or an event that seems to be uncannily familiar. It is the "having being there before" feeling that is of value in my examination of the gothic here. Indian aesthetic theories do not have a fully developed theory either of the gothic or, more generally, of the supernatural. Rasa, a theory of reception little used in cinema theory, has only two kinds of aesthetic experience that may have some bearing on this literary mode. These are the *bhāva*s "fear" (*bhaya*) and "disgust" (*jugupsā*) and their corresponding rasas "fearful" (*bhayānaka*) and "horrific" (*bībhatsa*). This theory of aesthetic response was designed primarily for use in analyzing epic and dramaturgical texts, and it is easy to see how representative figures like the demon king Ravana would be framed with the aesthetic response of *bhayānaka* (fearful) in mind. However, since the rasas of both *bhayānaka* and *bībhatsa* are abstract qualities only, one cannot connect them directly to real psychological fears. They cannot be superimposed either upon the uncanny or upon feelings of horror. Moreover, the literary antecedent of the filmic gothic in Indian culture never underwent the kind of rupture occasioned by the moment of the gothic in Western literature. The challenge to realist modes of representation at the heart of the gothic never occurred because there was no realist hegemony to be challenged in the first instance. It is here that the interest in the gothic becomes both an instance of an intrinsic interest in a radically new form and symptomatic of the power of colonial discourses. If melodrama and sentimentalism fed into Indian filmic practice as an available discourse, then the gothic, which has its own history of sentimentalist and melodramatic appropriations, also brought with it a narrative that could be easily incorporated into Bombay Cinema. What clearly interested filmmakers was the capacity of the gothic to shock, to do precisely what Freud said the uncanny did to the ego, that is, bring it face to face with the return of its own repressed. Now the most powerful "repression," in terms of narrative diegesis, was the theory of rebirth, which had been part of Hindu thought from the very beginning. The self was eternal, it went through countless births until it attained the condition of Brahman through moksha. Since self-knowledge was Brahman-knowledge, the sages emphasized *nivṛtti*, renunciation, as a way to this self-knowledge and escape from the eternal recurrence of birth-death-rebirth ("nivṛtaṃ sevamanastu bhūtanyatyeti pañca vai" [he whose deeds lead to inaction, renunciation, transcends the five elements of this world], says the *Mānu Dharmaśāstra*). But the rest of us were locked into *pravṛtti*, action, as we lived in this world and were subject to the wheel of time and reincarnation. Because the narrative of reincarnation existed as a form of "eternal recurrence" it was possible to construct one's real or imagined past lives. The recall was not an occasion of dread, but simply an expression of the "real" conditions of human mortality in which the Hindu lived. What the gothic discourse did was make Indians aware of a past memory as something more than just a matter of simple recall. In turn reincarnation was a very real contribution to the general theory of the gothic. In other words, India presented the gothic with a narrative which its European form never had. In the latter, ghosts were the living dead, roaming restlessly in a twilight world because in life they had no peace, as in Charles Maturin's *Melmoth the Wanderer* (1820). Indian reincarnation now invests the supernatural with another history of its past and a memory of it in the new life. Recalling one's past life—and one that reworked the principle of the double—is thus an instance of an uncanny duplication, a mirroring of real, present history with an unreal past history whose authenticity is available only to the person who remembers. The colonized thus expand a genre of the colonizer and then internalize it into their own artistic domains. In this act of internalization, however, the epistemology of reincarnation is itself transformed as it is linked, in representational terms, to a filmic gothic that goes back to Friedrich Wilhelm Murnau's *Nosferatu* and to Fritz Lang. And Bombay Cinema—a defiantly plastic form—very quickly incorporated and indigenized that form as well. Not surprisingly the texts of what I call the Indian gothic were versions of recollections of one's past life. But their representation also brought to the Indian a "real" lived past as an act of consciousness. The structure of reincarnation always assumed that rebirth was related to one's karma in this world. As a Brahmanical ideology its direct aim was to ensure that the social order and one's position within it would be acceptable to the people. After all, one's birth in a lower caste, or as a dog, simply reflected the absence of good karma in one's previous life. Now Bombay Cinema strips reincarnation, in its gothic manifestation, of its karmic dimension. In the Indian gothic, reincarnation is an uncanny confrontation with one's past history structured, as in the English literary gothic, through the discourses of melodrama and sentimentality. In some ways Ann Radcliffe and Charles Maturin (the opening sections of the latter's *Melmoth the Wanderer*, in which a stormy night and wreck are followed by the history of the survivor, is repeated in *Udan Khatola*) are our crucial intertexts here.

There are three exemplary versions of this form in Bombay Cinema. The first is the simple recall, a retrospective narrative like *Udan Khatola* (The flying machine, 1955) in which an old man remembers his past in this world. In the end his lost love returns from death to take him away. The second are narratives in which one's prior life returns like a palimpsest. The classic narrative here is *Madhumati* (1958), though *Nadiya Ke Paar* (Beyond the river, 1948) was a less accomplished early prototype. A subgenre of the second type are films like *Mahal* (The mansion, 1949) in which the elements of the form are tantalizingly manipulated so as to keep a gothic reincarnation narrative at the forefront until the very end, when the text retreats into realism. A third version is a kind of a gothic whodunit where gothic mise-en-scènes and nondiegetic (gothic) music set up generic expectations of the uncanny. The classic instance of this form is *Bees Saal Baad* (Twenty years on, 1962) where elements of the gothic insinuate supernatural occurrences even as the theme is about family pride, revenge, and retribution. In this text, and in many others of a similar kind, the gothic is a framing device for the revenge theme to take its course and not for a rethinking of the received (colonial) form. My concern in this section will be primarily with the second type of the gothic, and my proof texts are the two exemplary films already noted: *Mahal* and *Madhumati*.

Mahal is dedicated to Himansu Rai, the maker of *Achhut Kanya*. More precisely the dedication should have also indicated the film's indebtedness to Himansu Rai's director, the German Franz Osten, whose camera work is followed by *Mahal*'s director of photography, Joseph Wirsching. Directed and scripted by Kamal Amrohi, the film is arguably the first significant Indian gothic. Despite subsequent imitations at regular intervals, it remains unsurpassed in the genre. Like the founding text of the English literary gothic, Horace Walpole's *The Castle of Otranto* (1764), *Mahal* also foregrounds the space of a mansion/castle in its title. And it is the space (of the mansion) that triggers in the new owner a desire to connect with a prior, repressed narrative. In the canonical literary Gothic (Walpole, Reeve, Radcliffe, etc.) the castle draws into its space the dominant figure of the ruthless father, the pliant woman, and the obedient mother. The reader also participates, vicariously, in the sexual transgressions that might take place in the mansion/castle. As a nightmare house, the mansion/castle is a space of residual unconscious material in which sexual, genealogical, and psychological struggles will take place. But despite the threats that it poses to the subject, and the reader, the space of the mansion has this enormous power of attraction, drawing people inward into its mysteries, and keeping them there. The fascination of the mansion/castle to the subject is what marks the beginnings of the subject's complicity in the unspeakable narrative that the castle contains/gives impetus to.

After the credit stills in *Mahal* a man's voice-over is heard. It begins, "Thirty years before on a wet, stormy night . . . close to the city of Allahabad, next to the banks of the Jamuna a magnificent mansion called "Sangam Bhavan" lay neglected for years. . . . It is said that when it rains heavily one

can hear the pitiful cries of a woman. . . . An old gardener lives in the house."
A young man enters a silent, cold mansion, and the simulated sounds of
winds whistling and someone's cry may be heard. An old gardener meets the
man, and takes him inside. The gardener speaks first, "Yes, my master," and
relates, as he lights the candles in the chandelier and slowly pulls the attached
chain to drag it up, the narrative of the previous owner of the mansion. A
young man had built this mansion so many years before. He had come with
a woman who would wait for his return all day. At midnight he would come
and then disappear early in the morning. One night he was drowned on his
way back. Kamini, who heard his ghostly voice imploring her to be patient
("Do not pine, my love, I will come"), was found drowned sometime later.
"You have come," adds the gardener, "to redeem that pledge, to complete an
unfinished tale." At this moment the new owner, Hari Shankar (Ashok
Kumar), remarks rather ambiguously that yes, he has come to complete the
tale. As he walks toward his bedroom a large portrait that was hanging above
the door frame falls suddenly (as indeed it did in many gothic tales). Hari
Shankar turns back, looks at the portrait, and the camera takes a close-up of
his face as he recoils from the picture. The look of horror is followed by a shot
of a portrait of a bearded man, the same age as Hari Shankar and his double.
Next to the portrait is a clock, which is about to strike 2 in the morning. The
hero speaks to the portrait: "What is this secret, why are you exactly like me?
Is it that I am your second incarnation?" The clock strikes 2 and immediately
a woman's voice is heard singing the signature refrain of the film, "āyegā āyegā
āyegā āyegā āne vālā" (He'll come, he'll come, he'll come, who is destined to
come will come). The song and the shots that follow establish the signifying
system or practice of the Indian gothic. The portrait and its uncanny resemblance to the hero, the viewer's specular participation in the uncanny (the
effect of the doppelgänger), the set-piece conventions of the figure of a veiled
woman, the furious swinging of the chandelier, the candle suddenly going
off, the girl on a swing who mysteriously disappears as the hero approaches,
the figure of a lonely girl on a boat, a glance and a look from a woman in a
boudoir, and the black cat, all become set conventions of the Indian gothic.
The hero touches his fist with his cigarette to see if he is in fact awake. The
arrival of his friend the barrister Shrinath from Kanpur breaks this sequence.
But the desire engendered cannot be solved by the logic of a lawyer. "Is it that
in my past life I built this mansion and participated in a doomed love? Have
I come to complete that love?" Shankar asks. And even though he agrees to
return home with his friend so that his fiancée will not be aggrieved, the
power of the mansion, which he sees from his train compartment, is so great

that he must return to the scene of the mansion so as to repeat, compulsively, a prior, Othered narrative.

"You have returned," says the girl, "I knew you would. Why are you so agitated, I'm no ghost, no dream? But look at me intently, do not touch me, just look." The emphasis here is on the look just as the camera, functioning as voyeur, concentrates on the woman's face. She says little, but the look, occupying the entire frame, seems to underline the woman's own request to the hero, "Just look." It is only at the very end of the film that the girl, Asha/Kamini (Madhubala) actually touches Hari Shankar's body. The audience too simply looks at her as she gazes just off camera throughout. This is a kind of "slanted" spectacle binding, which remains the controlling image of the film. If the look is complicit with desire then the sound, the chiming of the clock at 2 in the morning, is the second, aural, moment of complicity. Between the two—desire propelled by the imperative of the gaze, and memory of time signified by the clock—the film situates the enigma of the hero, who is convinced of the identity of portrait and self, of a past life and its duplication in the present. But it is the trajectory of desire that dominates the film throughout. At one point the girl in the mansion (she says she has been waiting for his return all these years) asks him, "You desire me? Do you know the consequences of desire?" "Yes," he replies, "My death." She also reconstructs his past life reminding him that while he escaped through rebirth, she was kept waiting. For her to find peace he must first die. The solution she offers—the willful killing of the gardener's veiled daughter—is accepted by Shankar but not followed through. Another dharma, the duty toward his betrothed, of which he is so forcefully reminded by his father, leads him to breakoff his infatuation with the lady in the mansion. He marries Ranjana, his betrothed, but on his wedding night the clock chimes 2 just as he is about to unveil her (he has never seen his wife's face before), the refrain "āyegā, āyegā" is heard, and he rushes out, leaving behind an agitated wife. Since the proximity of the mansion is responsible for his strange behavior, he leaves the comforts of his city life and goes traveling with his wife and a guide for two years. The landscapes they inhabit during these years are eerie, marked by leafless trees and sunless skies. Into this sojourn is inserted a dance macabre by tribal people involved in a ritual dealing with a wife's infidelity. It is a primal dance of the indigene, aboriginal Indians, who are used here as a form of the return of the repressed. Another gothic set piece is an attack by bats from which Ranjana is saved by the timely intercession of a snake. The wife's woes continue, as Shankar is agitated whenever the clock strikes 2 at night. One day she stops the clock so that it won't chime at 2. This triggers a sympathetic reaction in the clock in the mansion which also stops. The gardener tries to correct it manually but falls off the clock tower as soon as he does so. The synchronicity returns, as does Shankar's unease. The wife finally discovers Shankar's obsession with the lady of the mansion, takes poison, tells the police that she was poisoned by her husband but writes a letter to her sister-in-law explaining her decision to take her own life.

An obligatory courtroom scene now ensues in which it is revealed that the gardener's daughter herself was the mysterious lady. She explains, in a manner borrowed from any number of Ann Radcliffe's gothic tales, the mysterious happenings in the mansion. She tells a story of how as a young girl she had heard the tale of the lovers from her father and, obsessed by it, had decided to play out the role of the lady of the mansion. She too wanted to become "the object of desire." When Shankar arrived she was struck by the resemblance between the portrait and him and convinced herself that he was the former lover. So she acted out the role of the mysterious woman but knew nevertheless that as a gardener's daughter she would be unacceptable to him. But once she realized that he was desperately in love with her she persuaded him to kill the gardener's daughter in the hope that upon seeing her face he would desist and instead of killing her would embrace her. Shankar is, however, sentenced to death for the murder of his wife, Ranjana. He is subsequently released but dies soon afterward though not before seeing Kamini in bridal costume married to his lawyer friend, Shrinath. The camera shifts to give a frontal view of Kamini's face, then moves up to disclose the portrait of the first owner of the mansion (who had an uncanny resemblance to Shankar). The closing shots and the diegesis remain ambiguously open-ended as gothic desire remains unfulfilled. *Mahal* is clearly the great precursor text of the Indian gothic. It remains the final achievement precisely because it lacks closure and has ambiguous moments built into its very structure. But what has interested me most here is the way in which the Indian gothic has internalized a colonial discourse by strategically incorporating into it elements from the vast tradition of Indian thought. The use of the Hindu theory of reincarnation in fact expands the capacities of the gothic form and ultimately connects it with an underlying impulse toward the sublime that characterizes Hindu aesthetic theories generally.

In *Madhumati* (1959), the Indian gothic is gradually naturalized through a more direct relationship between rebirth, spirits, and ghosts. In *Mahal* the theory of reincarnation is firmly in the mind of Shankar. In *Madhumati* the supernatural itself makes its presence felt. Both *Madhumati* and *Mahal* clearly suggest that the particular type of reincarnation Bombay Cinema advances is one in which a violent death occurred in one's previous life: Shankar's earlier incarnation drowned; the spirit of the dead girl lures Anand, in *Madhumati*, to his death. The genealogical connection that we make between *Mahal* and *Madhumati* is hinted at in *Madhumati* itself. Apart from the fact that Bimal Roy, who did the editing for Kamal Amrohi in *Mahal*, is the director of *Madhumati*, another connection is made through the obvious echo of the name of the actress who played the part of Kamini in *Mahal*, Madhubala. *Madhumati* after all echoes Madhubala, creating through this echo a string of interrelated signifiers: *Mahal*, Madhubala, and *Madhumati*. The central song of *Mahal* ("āyegā, āyegā") is replaced in the later film by "ājā re pardesī" (O come to me stranger). Like its earlier prototype, this song too punctuates the film at crucial moments, and both are sung by Lata Mangeshkar in her radically new falsetto voice. Finally, the chiming of the clock reappears, though in *Madhumati* the crucial moment is not 2 in the morning but 8 at night.

Ritwik Ghatak, best known for his neorealist Bengali films of the 1960s, penned the story of *Madhumati* in 1955 (Banerjee 1985: 17). The screenplay, however, was by the well-known Indian novelist Rajinder Singh Bedi who probably had a greater say in the form the narrative finally took. What is of interest to us in *Madhumati*, however, is the way in which the ambiguity of Shankar's past life (in *Mahal*)—of which the portrait is the only evidence— is now replaced by a full reincarnation narrative. Where Shankar simply wonders whether he is the portrait's double in this life, Devendra (Anand reincarnate in *Madhumati*) actually recollects upon seeing the landlord's portrait (which he as Anand had painted in his previous life) in this life a complete past narrative dealing with his short stay as the manager of the landlord's timber estate. In this memorially constructed past life, which is the main narrative of the film, his beloved Madhumati plunges to her death after her pastoral innocence was violated by the Zamindar-rapist. In terms of filmic representations, however, the Indian gothic in this instance, too, follows the codes established by *Mahal*. These codes include an empty mansion into which the hero enters one stormy night, an old servant who remembers the lives of the past inhabitants of the mansion, the absence of suitable lights (candles, hurricane lamps, an old chandelier are used), sounds that only the hero can hear, a woman's scream, a hidden passage (as in *Mahal*), a spiraling staircase, and a hero who is acutely sensitive to sight and sound. The opening scenes of *Madhumati* use almost all of these (and some nondiegetic features too). Ten years after *Mahal*, however, the Indian gothic is beginning to look, outwardly at any rate, less colonial. A more thoroughly indigenized form of representation replaces the trappings of the court, the Anglo-Indian mannerisms of actors, and the look and gaze. The portrait shows marks of a distinctive Indian hand, and the heroine, the eponymic Madhumati, played by Vijayanthimala, displays characteristics we would associate with the Indian folk tradition. She is full of life, she is energetic, and she dances as well as sings. Where Madhubala remained a study in the number of shots of the face a cinematographer can take, Dilip Gupta's photography in *Madhumati* rarely dwells on the face and instead captures movement as Vijayanthimala gyrates, wriggles, and swings her way through duets and collective folk songs. This significantly postcolonial gothic is also a lot more redemptive in its ideology. The lovers are reborn in this life and complete, through marriage and the birth of a child, their partially completed earlier lives. *Mahal* ends in an illusory hope; *Madhumati* ends with the shot of a laughing child with his loving parents, Devendra and Radha (Anand and Madhumati reincarnate in this life). In doing so, *Madhumati* effectively closes off the gothic canon; after *Madhumati,* tales of recall will not deviate too much from this narrative, and certainly would not return to the open-ended narrative of *Mahal.* How *Madhumati* achieves this is discussed next.

We have already noted the importance of recall in the space of the gothic "ruined" mansion. In this space the *Madhumati* narrative also emphasizes the uncanny "I have been here before" feeling. A portrait once again triggers a past memory as white silk curtains blow into Devendra's face. Images of a horse rider, a mansion, a chandelier come before his eyes before the narrative of past life begins. A decisive feature of *Madhumati* is the use of the gothic's threat to woman, and this feature takes the form of the rape of Madhumati by the owner of the estate, Ugra Narayan (whose own name echoes the fearsome man-lion avatar of Lord Vishnu). In the recollected narrative, Anand traps Ugra Narayan into confessing the rape of Madhumati by using her double, Madhvi. But before Madhvi appears to confront the landlord, dead Madhumati herself appears to elicit the incriminating evidence from him. As she alludes to a detail about her death which no one else would have known, Anand suddenly becomes aware of the fact that this is the real Madhumati. In an echo of an episode from Matthew Gregory Lewis's *The Monk,* where the apparition replaces the real, Madhumati beckons Anand toward her. He follows and falls to his death as the ghost of Madhumati walks off the balcony. In the next reincarnation, Madhumati returns as her own double as does Anand. In this respect the Indian gothic continues, perhaps in a much more explicit form than the English gothic, the law of the imaginary return and of the double ("My form is a filthy type of yours," the Monster tells

Dilip Kumar and Pran in Bimal Roy's *Madhumati*, 1958. A look that foretells evil. Courtesy National Film Archive of India.

Frankenstein). But present in all that I have said about the ways in which the genre was established lies the song text. In *Mahal* and *Madhumati* the key songs—the haunting extradiegetic "āyegā āyegā āyegā" and "ājā re pardesī"— are used to mark the special nature of the attraction to the other (as sexual object, as uncanny) and are rendered by women.

Like its complex literary antecedent—the gothic novel—the Indian gothic draws upon the discourses of melodrama and sentimentality. To these we need to add Indian aesthetic theories of the wonderful, the horrific, and so on, and the very Indian narrative of reincarnation, or rebirth. Through the latter, gothic tales of the uncanny, where the narrative is locked into a compulsion to repeat an earlier moment or revisit an earlier scene, are underpinned by a belief that is theosophical and religious. In *Madhumati*, a theory of reincarnation redeems a narrative of sexual violation and rape through the triumphant reunion of the lovers (for so it is suggested) in another life on earth. In this sense the scandal of violation (which can rip apart the Indian social order) is addressed and yet contained within a narrative of social stability and continuity. The final shots of the latter-day Anand and Madhumati (Devendra and Radha) underline social harmony and sexual bliss. In one sense the Indian gothic is the medium through which a textual elision in the normal run of melodrama is allowed to resurface, and transgression, "the scandal of pleasure," to use the title of Wendy Steiner's fascinating book on the battles for the autonomy of art (1995), is momentarily avowed before a lid is placed on the surfacing of the repressed. The Indian gothic—and *Madhumati* especially—reminds us of the power of the repressed, and the spectator's complicity in that power since Ugra Narayan, the dark figure of the mansion, is, in one sense, the erased identity of the spectator, the id to the spectator/Anand's superego. Sex as the violation of the moral order is always the palimpsestic text of Bombay Cinema. And yet, without the possibilities of that violation (which is invariably contained at the level of the manifest text) there is no melodramatically rendered pleasurable scandal, and no Bombay Cinema.

Chapter Three

THE TEXTS OF "MOTHER INDIA"

When Camoens da Gama, Aurora's father, enters the room to which Aurora had been momentarily banished, he sees a painting covering the walls and the ceiling. This huge painting of imperial and post-imperial history, of family saga and those yet to be born, replete with the emotions of love, hate, rage, and defiance, he observes, were all set upon the figure of "Mother India herself . . . who loved and betrayed and ate and destroyed and again loved her children" (Rushdie 1995: 60–61). The woman who portrays Mother India is, however, none other than the painter's own mother, dead at 33, when Aurora was only 13. Salman Rushdie writes at this point in *The Moor's Last Sigh*, "at the heart of this first immense outpouring of Aurora's art was the single tragedy of her loss, the unassuaged pain of becoming a motherless child" (61). Motherhood, or more specifically "motherness," we are subsequently told by the narrator, Moraes Zogoiby ("the Moor"), "is a big idea, maybe our biggest: the land as mother, the mother as land" (137). A big idea certainly, but one that enters the discourse of the novel not through a goddess (Kali, Durga, Parvati, Lakshmi) or a warrior queen (the queen of Jhansi, for instance) or even a female renouncer (Sita, the medieval devotional singer Mira) but through Bollywood cinema's greatest epic melodrama, Mehboob Khan's foundational film *Mother India* (1957). Here is the narrator/Rushdie's critical reading of the film:

> The year I was born, Mehboob Productions' all-conquering movie *Mother India*—
> three years in the making, three hundred shooting days, in the top three all-time
> mega-grossing Bollywood flicks—hit the nation's screens. Nobody who saw it ever

forgot that glutinous saga of peasant heroism, that super-slushy ode to the uncrushability of village India made by the most cynical urbanites in the world. And as for its leading lady—O Nargis with your shovel over your shoulder and your strand of black hair tumbling forward over your brow!—she became, until Indira-Mata supplanted her, the living mother-goddess of us all. (137)

   In *Mother India*, a piece of Hindu myth-making directed by a Muslim social-ist, Mehboob Khan, the Indian peasant woman is idealised as bride, mother, and producer of sons; as long-suffering, stoical, loving, redemptive, and conservatively wedded to the maintenance of the social status quo. But for Bad Birju, cast out from his mother's love, she becomes, as one critic has mentioned, "that image of an aggressive, treacherous, annihilating mother who haunts the fantasy of Indian males." (138–39)

These passages are examples of vintage Rushdie prose: broad strokes of the pen that combine an accessible popular style of seeming superficiality (the postmodern "surfaces" without depth) with an ironic commentary function-ing as disingenuous social critique. But they also have metacritical value since embedded in them are ways of theorizing *Mother India*. There is the kind of reading that would see female "peasant heroism" ("O Nargis with your shovel over your shoulder") as a project aimed at strengthening the nation-state. The village community (and even the family or the tribe) in this read-ing is the larger national community but one that is itself undergoing extensive transformation (Vasudevan 2000a: 17). "Until Indira-Mata sup-planted her" refers to the way in which former Indian prime minister Indira Gandhi projected herself as India: "India is Indira." The argument (the sec-ond reading embedded in the Rushdie passages) has been brilliantly analyzed by Rajeswari Sunder Rajan (1993: 109–10) who has shown how the iconic-ity of Nargis as Mother India was appropriated (not very subtly but to good political effect) by India's first woman prime minister. Using a preexistent trope of nation = mother = soil, Indira Gandhi in a sense interpellated her own political self through a figure that had become a central symbol of the Indian popular imaginary: Nargis as Mother India. The Rushdie passages allude to something else as well (the third and fourth readings). Rushdie refers to the Muslimness of the producer/director Mehboob Khan though not Nargis's. There are a number of texts and histories at work in this con-text. The first ("a piece of Hindu myth-making directed by a Muslim social-ist") is the highly syncretic, hyphenated Hindu-Muslim nature of Bombay Cinema discourses, production practices, and indeed its very ideology. Some of these features surface remarkably in Saadat Hasan Manto's recently translated account of his days in the Bombay film industry before partition (1998). The discourse of Hindi cinema remains to this day markedly Urdu and many of its key personalities have been Muslim—Mehboob Khan and Nazir Hussain (producers/directors), Javed Akhtar and Majrooh Sultanpuri (scriptwriters and lyricists), Naushad and A. R. Rahman (music directors), Dilip Kumar, Madhubala, Aamir Khan, Shah Rukh Khan, and, of course, Nargis (actors). Add to this financiers and the largest single group of Hindi/Urdu speakers (some 120 million), and we begin to get some sense of the importance of Muslims to the industry. The cultural syncretism is so complete that even when, as at present, there is an implicit directive to work within the formal determinants of Hindu culture (in some ways a more rigid directive to conform to the metatextual traditions than before), the cinema continues to represent itself through that syncretism.

The above commentary takes us to Nargis's own Muslimness, absent from Rushdie's account but something which, in a sense, has been the thematic center of much recent writing on *Mother India*. This is an interesting trend since, as we shall see in the next chapter, Nargis the star was never constructed in terms of her Muslimness per se prior to her role as Mother in *Mother India*. Nargis the glamorous "star" before *Mother India* (T. J. S. George's sycophantic biography calls her "the first lady of Indian cinema") had the kind of personal history (and persona) upon which (male) voyeuristic desire could be readily projected: daughter of a *koṭhevālī* (the courtesan, actor, and singer Jaddanbai), unscrupulously marketed as a star by her mother from the age of 14, lover of the debonair Raj Kapoor, and so on. A key critical study in the refiguring of Nargis is to be found in Parama Roy's *Indian Traffic* (1998). In her chapter on *Mother India* she works through a number of filmic and profilmic features as well as the star's post–*Mother India* life to demonstrate the complex ways in which Nargis's Muslimness enters into a general theory of the construction of "the iconicity of the actress" (154). As Roy asks: "how does the Other [marked by an inescapable Muslimness] become an icon that represents [Indian] nationness?" Roy's argument is that the construction of Nargis's body as the modern national goddess (Sita incarnate, so to speak) is not identical with the film but has to be seen in terms of both *Mother India* the film as well as its sequel, the life of Nargis after the film. In our next chapter we shall write about the prequel to these narratives; here with Roy we need to examine the manner in which the signifier "Nargis" has acquired surplus value. To do justice to this argument one needs to unpack, however cursorily, the information given by Roy. Of course, there may be a simpler (or at least an alternative) answer to the question posed by Roy: the Mother of *Mother India* is not Indian after all; it is an artificial filmic construct that grew out of Bombay Cinema's Zoroastrian-Judaic-Christian-Islamic construction of the enabling and defiant woman (Das Gupta 1991: 119–23). In the latter argument, what Mehboob's *Mother India* finally brings together is a tendency within Hindu culture toward a "West Asian code of female honour." This tendency was directly linked to the Muslim dominant culture in India during a good part of the second millennium. Das Gupta characteristically overextends his case, but there is something in the empowering presence of the Mother, the Mother as an active agent (in realistic and not in religiomythical terms) that is quite unlike the Mother as the person who suffers. If Das Gupta's implicit argument is that Nargis's Muslimness is the outward iconic representation of the new syncretic Indian woman (who comes into being because of the symbiosis of two cultures), then only a Muslim woman could have captured this newness. With a slightly different inflection, Parama Roy reinforces this reading: "If *Mother India* is, at least partially, an allegory of the repudiation of Muslim difference and of a becoming Hindu, then only a Muslim can assume the iconic position of that maternal figure" (168). The difficulty with the Roy argument, however, is that intense discussions about Nargis's Muslimness is very much a post–*Mother India* phenomenon and more specifically, it seems, a post-Ayodhya phenomenon when both her husband, Sunil Dutt, and her son, Sanjay Dutt (the latter arrested and charged under the notorious Terrorist and Disruptive Activities Prevention Act or TADA in April 1993 for allegedly smuggling arms and ammunition), were seen by the Hindu body politic as Muslim sympathizers. If there is a decisive image that can be isolated from the film it is the image of the Mother with her two children directing villagers not to leave their homes despite the terrible famine. The directive is, of course, via the medium of the typical Bombay Cinema song ("please don't leave," sings the playback singer Lata Mangeshkar) and is sung against the backdrop of an undivided pre-partition India. Roy sees this as an image that also reinforces Nargis's renunciation of partition (and of her own Muslimness). This observation is certainly true in terms of reception but falters if we recall that the historical time of the profilmic event is itself pre-partition India.

Moor Zogoiby's mother, Aurora, never becomes close to Nargis; nor does she attempt the kinds of theorization that cultural theorists have subsequently advanced. Because she cannot distinguish film from reality, her interest in Nargis is that of the gossip who seems to have uncovered a dark secret. To Nargis, who played Sunil Dutt's mother in the film, she disarmingly declares, "And now look—you have gone and marry-o'ed him!" Rushdie is, of course, playing postmodern games by collapsing the divide between real lived history and fictionally transformed history, but what he does, thematically, is no different from the Indian spectator's own conflation of the filmic and pre- or postfilmic lives of stars. And it is here that *Mother India* has become a proof text for readings well beyond its own declared aim of representing the great dharma of India. If we follow Das Gupta's claim that there is no "Great Mother in the canon" (1991: 111), we may read Mehboob Khan's film as a text that artificially constructs this figure out of a complex and heterogeneous religious and social history; if we recall Lalitha Gopalan's astute reading of the avenging women in Indian cinema, *Mother India* becomes a prototype of that avenging woman (who is also a mother). In these arguments *Mother India* generates meanings of the kind we associate with seminal texts of the culture.

Mother India is, of course, a cultural artifact and, as we have foreshadowed, a pervasive one too. It occupies a central place in Indian cinema history, and especially in the variety of cinema—Bollywood cinema—that constitutes the target texts of this book. But because of its centrality, especially in the North Indian cultural imaginary, the film takes us directly to a key issue in cultural representation: cultures, after all, use their artistic forms to represent themselves (Said 1985: 7). For all its melodramatic design, for all its detachment from the "real," Bombay Cinema is self-consciously about representing, in the context of a multicultural and multiethnic India, the various disaggregated strands of the nation-state—political, social, cultural, and so on. In the symbology advanced here, these strands are reaggregated around an idea—that of the Mother—which, as Rushdie's narrator had enthusiastically noted, was the biggest idea in the land. *Mother India* reworks this "biggest idea" into the most powerful symbolic statement on Indianness and was instrumental in giving it such a wide currency. Even bazaar and calendar art defer to it. There are few Bombay films that do not, in some manner, cash in on this equation.

Released during Diwali week, October 1957, *Mother India* ran for a whole year at Liberty Cinema, Bombay. It received rave reviews in key film journals such as *Filmfare* and *Filmindia* and in *Bharat Jyoti* (Reuben 1999: 261–68) and went on to become the Bombay film dubbed and subtitled more than any other. Baburao Patel called the film in his *Filmindia* review "the greatest picture produced in India during the forty and odd years of film-making," to which he added in a later paragraph, "Remove Nargis and there is no *Mother India*" (Reuben 1999: 266). When shown on Britain's

Channel 4 during its tribute to Bombay Cinema in 1983, *Mother India* was presented as the film by which that cinema is measured. In India it continues to be shown regularly and is part of a small number of Bollywood films (along with *Kismet* [Fate, 1943], *Mughal-e-Azam* [1960], *Sholay* [Flames] 1975), and *Hum Aap Ke Hain Kaun* [Who am I to you? 1994]) that have been granted the apocryphal status of films that are shown somewhere in India every day of the year. Now in its forty-fourth year, it continues to be invoked as the "definitive" Indian film text. Along the way it has won many awards in India, has been widely acclaimed in the Middle East and Southeast Asia, and gained an Oscar nomination in the category of best foreign film in 1958.

Mehboob Khan (1909–74), son of a Gujarati policeman with strong agrarian roots, had been associated with Indian cinema since 1935 when he directed *Judgment of Allah*. Five years later he began to produce his own films, initially for a studio (National Studios) but from 1943 under his own banner (Mehboob Productions). Between 1940 and 1957 he produced some extremely popular films such as *Aurat* (Woman, 1940, an early version of *Mother India* indebted to Pudovkin's socialist realist cinematic adaptation of Maxim Gorky's *Mother* [1926] and MGM's *The Good Earth* [1937], based on Pearl Buck's portrayal of a Chinese peasant family), *Anmol Ghadi* (A priceless watch, 1946), *Mela* (The fair, 1948), *Andaz* (Style, 1949), *Aan* (Vow, 1952), *Amar* (Forever, 1954) as well as the controversial *Humayun* (1945) for which he was accused of being a revisionist on matters of Mughal history. The "socialist realist" antecedents that I invoke here need to be looked at in the context of the Indian nationalist movement of the 1930s and '40s. Among the many issues canvassed by the nationalists, two of the most significant dealt with the secular ethos of the nation and sectarianism. Mehboob Khan's films were in some sense located within the tensions generated by these two issues. Whether it was Western modernity in India (as in *Andaz*) or the reformation of the Muslim *madarsā* schools (as in *Elan*, [A declaration], 1947) or, more significantly, woman as the focal point of social cohesion and genealogical purity (as in *Aurat*), one detects that in Mehboob Khan's populist interpretation these themes cannot be dismembered from the larger nationalist program. And this program was always predicated upon a visionary egalitarianism dramatically at odds with the real social divisions in the country. There was, however, something else besides in Mehboob Khan that attracted Bombay film critics and the middle classes who would have also patronized Hollywood movies. This is Mehboob Khan's technical mastery, and it is also why many of his films (*Aurat, Andaz, Aan, Mother India*) have had more cinematic durability than those of many other filmmakers. *Aan,* in fact, received a letter of commendation for its technical virtuosity from none other than Cecil B. de Mille!

Mehboob Khan's last major film—and the film for which he is best known—*Mother India* is in some ways more diffuse and contradictory than his other films. As suggested by Rushdie, it is in fact not one film but a number of films; not one text but a multiplicity of texts. To come to grips with *Mother India*'s heterogeneity we need to think through the layers of meaning that have accrued to the title itself. The first text is obviously embedded in the title itself. *Mother India* goes back immediately to Katherine Mayo's antagonistic and racist book of that name published in 1927. Mayo's book was a best-seller that went into some dozen reprints in just under three years, and was used as a powerful propaganda tool by the British against the Indian Nationalists, Gandhi included. Mayo herself had excellent credentials as a social advocate, having bravely published major exposés of corruption in the Pennsylvania Police Force, as well as taking up issues such as sexual harassment, women's rights, antiquated rape laws in the United States, and so on (Emilsen 1987). She was so implacably opposed to any form of real or perceived sexual harassment and the degradation of women and minorities that in *The Isles of Fear* (1925) she opposed the granting of independence to the Philippines on the grounds that the safety of Muslim and other minorities could not be guaranteed. *Mother India,* published two years later, took her even further into her committed areas of sexual violence and sexual exploitation. It became the most widely read book on India in the first half of the twentieth century and had an enormous impact upon Western attitudes toward the Indian Nationalist Movement. Years later, in 1957, A. M. Rosenthal captured the impact of the book: "There are few people more important in the relationship between India and the United States than Katherine Mayo, few books if any, that contributed more violent coloring to the American mental image of India than 'Mother India'" (621).

In Britain, Clifford Sharp, the editor of the *New Statesman,* called *Mother India* the "most powerful defense of the British raj that has ever been written." So persuasively did Mayo make her case that Gandhi (who privately agreed with many of Mayo's sentiments and whom Mayo had interviewed between October 1925 and March 1926) condemned her to his Indian audiences and sent Sarojini Naidu and C. F. Andrews to the United States to counter the quite staggering influence of *Mother India* upon American attitudes. But the damage had been done. Despite valiant attempts by Indians to counter her charges, and the publication, some years later, of C. F. Andrews's *The True India* (1939), Mayo's version of India remained crucial and influential. Much to the delight of the critics of India, the 1928 Joshi Report on the Age of Consent commissioned by the Indian Legislature singled out child marriage (a key theme in Mayo's book) as the cause of many of India's social problems. The English title of Mehboob Khan's film may be seen as postcolonial India's response to Mayo's thoroughly colonial thesis.

The title, of course, had been used by the popular film industry before Mehboob Khan. In 1938, Ardeshir Irani (maker of the first Hindi talkie *Alam Ara* [1931]) produced a film called *Mother India*. In the context of Mehboob Khan's *Mother India* one expects something of the extended mythic symbology that the title carries. Nothing of that cultural investment is evident in Irani's film. Rather, the theme of the film, as *Filmindia* pointed out (March 1939: 35), was the rather bland "the hand that rocks the cradle rules the world," an obvious reference to one of the recurring motifs in D. W. Griffith's *Intolerance* (1916). The narrative here is pure melodrama with melodramatic solicitations from the spectators more important than attention to plot or character. It is difficult to see why the film was given such a loaded title unless of course it too was meant as an answer to Mayo's work since it showed, at the level of plot at any rate, an Indian women's struggle spread over two generations: a village woman is left alone to look after her son following her father's imprisonment and her husband's departure because he couldn't bear the poverty at home. It could be that when reworking *Aurat*, Mehboob Khan's original 1940 version of *Mother India*, he had this *Mother India* text in mind as well.

Even as the title "Mother India" has circulated as critical discourse (Mayo's) or as popular culture (Ardeshir Irani's melodramatic saga), there remains something terribly removed, detached, and alien about the term itself. In Indian culture "Mother India" is a transcendental signifier; it has hegemonic privilege and presence, but it doesn't have a single, unproblematic, originary moment. It is a term around which has accrued many referents and meanings: it carries echoes of the very loaded Hindi *bhārat mātā* ("mother India"), the softer, poetic Urdu *mādre hind*, the more autochthonous Sanskrit compound *matṛbhūmī* ("mother-earth") as well as Bankim Chandra's famous nationalist song *Bande Mātaram* ("I bow to you, Mother"). Indeed, Mehboob Khan's film opens with the nondiegetic strains of the song *dharatī mātā* ("mother earth") as the typically establishing shots of the land are given so that the spectator has a firm sense of where the action is taking place. Through yet another system of transformations one can actually connect *matṛbhūmī*, mother-earth, with the figure of Sita, the heroine of the *Rāmāyaṇa*, the *dhīram bhāryam* (the steadfast wife) who, in the North Indian popular imaginary, is one of the mythic/religious prototypes of "Mother India." "Sita" means "of the furrow" and indicates via this name her autochthonic origins. In this respect "Mother India" is a way of talking about Sita, the figure who is really a stand-in for India. Historically, however, Sita is not a given; she has never been there in that form all along; she had to be fought for as Hindu culture and Brahmanical ideology came to terms with what in the epic tradition was the uneasy narrative of Sita's abduction and restitution. In that act of struggle, a whole Sita idiom evolved, and a number of post-epic texts were written to make Sita other than herself. (In the medieval vernacular epic—the *Rāmacaritamānasa* of Tulsidasa—only her image is violated by the demon king Ravana.) The culture invested Sita with excessive meaning, overdetermined her through massive semantic and mythic overcoding, but could not quite remove her epic violation. The guilt surrounding Sita's "contamination" led to excessive circumspection and cultural bracketing for woman generally. This congruity of Sita/Mother–India/Woman thus surfaces as an artificially constructed ideological phenomenon in culture. In projecting that affinity the ruptures and discontinuities are glossed over. Instead we get an excessive insistence upon dharma, the law of culture, and an excessive valorization of genealogy so that Sita may be granted a central position in Indian consciousness. If Mother alone knows the secret of your birth her power within culture becomes inviolate and beyond falsification. "Mother India" then represents a monumental problem of Motherness, Sita-ness, and Otherness in Indian culture. Indian culture, which endorses a predominantly patriarchal point of view, has countered this problem of absolute identity of Mother with a single iconic figure by dispersing the symbols onto a number of icons. Through this iconic dispersal Mother is associated with Goddess (here Sita is Lakshmi), with Wife (here Sita is Draupadi), with Lover (here Sita is Radha), and through the slightly contradictory iconography of Kali and Durga, with the Avenger or Destroyer, where Sita embodies Shiva's female principle. In this final historical compromise woman (femininity) is seen as a total counterpart of the two crucial masculine gods, Vishnu the Preserver, and Shiva the Destroyer.

Mehboob Khan's initial version of the Mother India theme did not carry this loaded title. It declared itself simply as "Woman" (*Aurat*) and was praised, like another film of the period, V. Shantaram's *Aadmi* (Man, 1939), for its "sheer documentary value" (*Filmindia*, June 1940: 35–37). The film was singled out for its "detailed portrayal of village life," for its combination of realism with popular form, and for Sardar Akhtar's interpretation of the mother figure. Some forty years later, the fanzine *Movie* (January 1, 1984:

96–97) returned to this version of *Mother India* and quoted, approvingly it seems, from K. A. Abbas's original review of *Aurat*:

> From the heart of rural India is drawn the story which is familiar because it is ele-
> mental, eternal. In its tremendous sweep it is a saga. Pictorially *Aurat* is outstand-
> ing. Cameraman Faredoon Irani has hardly missed anything that ever happens in a
> village . . . the fields of corn waving in the breeze, the graceful village maidens, the
> village well, the mud huts, the spinning wheel, the mango groves, the spectacular
> bullock cart race. Contrasted with this are the "documentary" shots of vultures
> hovering over dead bodies, the cracked earth, famine and the parasitical money-
> lender.

Retrospective reviews of this film often involved comparisons with the 1957 remake. In these comparisons *Aurat* invariably emerges as the stronger film. *Star and Style*, another popular fanzine, called the later version "a sad commentary on the uneven development of the Hindi Cinema" (October 2, 1970: 9). What it noted, furthermore, and rightly I think, is the centrality, in *Aurat*, of the woman character. The film is about her and not about the village and its social problems. But even as it shifts the emphasis to the woman, the film continues to frame her in the melodramatic tradition of Bombay Cinema. *Star and Style* continues the comparison between the two versions by endorsing, after Ajit Merchant's original review in *Bharat Jyoti* (quoted in Reuben 1999: 262), Anil Biswas's musical score in *Aurat* over the heavy orchestration of Naushad's music in *Mother India*. The magazine *Movie* (1984) too made its preference for Anil Biswas's music clear but went even further to favor *Aurat* at every point: Sardar Akhtar over Nargis; Yakub over Sunil Dutt as Birju. The aestheticization of *Aurat* (at the expense of *Mother India*) in the '70s and '80s may have come about because of a nostalgia during the Rajesh Khanna–Amitabh Bachchan years for what seemed like the less heterogeneously produced austere realist texts of colonial India.

Two powerful words, one specifically connected to Indian womanhood, the other more generally connected to civility, dominate the text. These words are, from Sanskrit, *lāj* (shame, honor, a sense of shame) and, from Perso-Arabic, *izzat* (honor, respect, self-respect). These words are so culturally specific that the English gloss fails to capture their cultural resonances. In the context of a colonial discourse of India that registered especially Hindu Indian womanhood in terms of the iconography of the "burning" or the child bride (where both were seen as signs of a decaying culture), the use of these words as thematic strands in the film is understandable. But Mehboob Khan's film does not leave these words there. It links them to an eternal order that declares the non-negotiable primacy of the eternal dharma in Indian culture. Although such a statement is powerfully metaphysical, its use is fundamentally political as its targets are the writings of people like Katherine Mayo and the Christian evangelists. These "big" themes (themes that underpin Indian culture itself) are, however, recast in a form that is distinctly Bombay melodrama, which, as we have already noted, is a colonial form that mapped European sentimentalism upon Indian notions of karma. Crudely redefined as forms of poetic justice, karma (a highly complex theory of acts and responsibilities) then becomes expanded as a narrative of predestined ends that coexists comfortably with melodrama. As a result, in Indian hands European melodrama is considerably enriched by the concept of karmic suffering. *Aurat* then signals the primacy of *lāj* and *izzat*, of Indian womanhood, even as it manipulates and extends the generic structures of Bombay Cinema. In dialogic terms *lāj* is the first term that strikes the spectator in the film. It occurs after Faredoon Irani's long crane shots that establish Mehboob Khan's auterial style. When the new bride discovers that her mother-in-law (Sundar Chachi) mortgaged her land to pay for the wedding she says to herself: "bhagvān lāj rakhna" (O Lord save/keep my *lāj*). The word *lāj* with all its connotations of woman's virtue, but especially of sexual virtue is thus used very early on. Implicit in the term is thus the whole question of chastity in the Indian world, its defense by the Indian, and its function also as a marker of the worth of woman. Its preservation (akin in power to *tapas* or austere practices) can shame even gods who intervene to save a woman's *lāj*, as happens when Sukhilala, the village landlord, wants to take sexual advantage of the hapless mother's destitution. He is struck down by a falling tree, and the drought breaks. What *lāj* finally says is that woman is a commodity to be measured in terms of her chastity. Whatever else the narrative might point toward, this fact alone, this primacy of *lāj*, will dominate the text. Even before the narrative is given full expression, it closes in upon itself, predicting a narrative unfolding in which *lāj* will be its crucial determinant. One wonders therefore what the agenda of *Aurat* in fact is. If *lāj* is metonymic of womanhood in Indian society, what freedom does she have? Could Bombay Cinema ever write a narrative in which *lāj* itself is contested, one that would demonstrate the conditions under which a woman might sacrifice her *lāj* for the greater good, for *her* greater good, or indeed for her desire, as Tabu declares to her husband (Sachin Khandekar) in a much later film, *Astitva* (My being, 2000)?

Let us accept, for strategic reasons, the prescriptive nature of the narrative. Is it then possible to see how Mehboob Khan might destabilize the form? One feature that strikes the viewer is the juxtaposition of the outer and

Sardar Akhtar and Kanhaiyalal in Mehboob Khan's *Aurat*. A Woman's *lāj* under threat. Courtesy National Film Archive of India.

Sardar Akhtar and her two children in Mehboob Khan's *Aurat*, 1940. Courtesy National Film Archive of India.

the inner. Outwardly even in *Aurat* the Indian landscape is rendered essentially pastoral with long establishing shots of millet fields where peasants sing folk songs and celebrate Hindu festivals, notably Holi. Within, however, the pastoral harmony is broken by two things. The first, at this early stage in the film, is Radha's pregnancies, about which even the husband despairs. Cinematically the husband's words of despair are cut to a montage shot of a caged bird, forcefully suggesting that unwanted pregnancy is also a form of caging. The point being that in the seemingly unselfconscious melodramatic narrative are embedded significant social issues that were equally part of Gandhi's nationalist agenda. Under conditions of severe hardship, children tax resources and create tension in the family. The husband, helpless and considering himself a failure, leaves home and disappears. Before departing he wipes off his wife's *bindī* (the large, round forehead mark that distinguishes a married woman), touches his mother's feet, pats his bullocks, and looks back forlornly. We see him walking off toward the sunrise. Distraught, his mother dies soon afterward.

A second form of instability—and this time a contestation that is not simply within the form but is activist—occurs in what may be called the text of Birju. Played by the actor Yakub, Birju is the rebel son who gambles and lies to his mother. He is shorter than his brother and has a clean-shaven head. Ramu, the obedient elder son, is played by the singer Surendra (whose academic degrees, B.A. LL.B., often appeared on publicity stills). He is tall and handsome, and he has a healthy relationship with a village maiden, Jamuna. In a well-known shot, the mother momentarily confuses Ramu with Shamu, her lost husband. But this identification is in fact illusory: it is really Birju who is temperamentally like his father and who symbolically displaces him. The final phase of the film works through subliminal Oedipal desire and the kinds of characterological contrasts intrinsic to the form. Unlike the later version of this film (as *Mother India*) where the Birju narrative is more centrally cast in a revenge theatrical structure and is organized around the metadiscourse of justice, in *Aurat* the Birju narrative is more staggered and even disjointed. Yakub brings an erratic element to Birju's character and perhaps even a sense of psychological instability because of the absence in his life of a father figure. Birju's life is represented in terms of tableaux shots that show him gambling, stealing a gun, and hitting his mother, brother, and his soon-to-be sister-in-law. He is abusive to the villagers, to the landowner Sukhilala (whom he stabs to death), and is disrespectful of the inviolate concept of a woman's *lāj* and the culture's *izzat*; he abducts the woman he had long desired (but whom he could not marry because their horoscopes were divergent) on her wedding day. It is in the latter context that *Aurat* confronts the impossible, the radically incommensurable (in terms of the culture's valorization of sons) act of a mother killing her son. Although the genre could not have allowed Birju to live, the manner in which Birju dies—he is shot dead by his mother even as he tries to abduct Tulsi on the day of her wedding—marks a decisive shift in Bombay Cinema. The defense of *lāj* is paramount because *aurat,* woman, is indeed *lāj* incarnate. An anticolonial movement cannot succeed unless it too maintains this equation. Before she herself dies the mother tells the villagers and, in particular, Kamla, Tulsi's mother: "I had given my word to the villagers and I have kept it . . . the Lord has taken the life of a son so that the *lāj* of a woman might be saved." The final shots are of the mother's face, juxtaposed against the figure of a woman carrying a load of wood on her head.

Aurat was released a year after V. Shantaram's *Aadmi*, the latter, as we have seen, a self-consciously "social" film. But whereas Shantaram's modernity was the modernity of the city and offered a critique of sexual hypocrisy, Mehboob Khan's *Aurat* locks itself into a nationalist ethos in which the grand narrative of the village and the presumed values it has always enshrined are seen to be redemptive of the nation. For a postcolonial India to come into being it was necessary to return to the idealism of the past, to capture an organic worldview, both epistemologically and materially, so that the epistemes of *lāj* and *izzat* would also be the conditions under which the capitalist bifurcation of use value and work value would be transcended. But it is also clear that Mehboob Khan had inherited a form, not unlike the novel itself, which, being younger than photography (just as the novel is younger than print) allowed him to constantly redefine, fine-tune, and expand on its possibilities. In its dominant form it came to be seen as distinctly melodramatic, but not in any prescriptive fashion, so that epic forms and themes could be unproblematically inserted into it. Beyond the possibilities of a counter ideological critique (*lāj* is, after all, an essentialist patriarchal dogma unrelated to the real conditions of woman in a feudal Indian world order), *Aurat* may also be read cinematically (not just thematically) as the first full attempt at constructing an epic cinema in India. Faredoon Irani's camera work uses the long shot and montage, constructing images that repeat themselves. In this respect there is perhaps an ideological statement that is being made through the form of a quasi-epic realist cinema about the value of representationalism in cinema. Here the emphasis is on the semiotic system itself as signifying auteurial practice. Faredoon Irani, who won the *Filmfare* award for best photography for his work in *Mother India,* said in an interview with the magazine published November 30, 1962:

[Film producers] spend huge amounts in paying the fees of their stars but they attach little or no importance to photography and production values. After all how can anyone exploit to the fullest advantage a highly paid star unless competent photography presents the star at his best?

Irani, of course, does not go far enough in his words. In a sense the emphasis on cinematography (and Mehboob Khan's concern with the technical side of filmic production) in *Aurat* meant that in his hands cinema remained an epic spectacle that bonded the spectator to the image (of the mother).

Between the production of *Aurat* in 1940 and *Mother India* in 1957 a number of significant events intervened: the Second World War, Indian independence, and the partition of India into two countries. For Bombay Cinema, two other things stand out: crippling taxation on the film industry by the new government and the 1952 First International Film Festival, which was held in India. The first affected the amount of money that could be spent on film production as returns went straight to the government treasury. The second had a tremendous impact on a film industry that had hitherto been modeled by and large on Hollywood. The film festival rather dramatically brought to the attention of Indian film producers the neorealist films of Vittorio De Sica and Roberto Rossellini and the epic cinema of Akira Kurosawa. An immediate consequence of this exposure was the increase in outdoor shooting and naturalist settings for Indian films (George 1994: 109 –11). In 1953 Bimal Roy consciously used neorealist techniques in *Do Bigha Zamin*. A by-product of the festival was Rossellini's return to India in 1956 to work on a film entitled "India 57" which received the enthusiastic support of Nehru himself. The venture fell through because Rossellini fell in love with Sonali Dasgupta, wife of his associate, and both departed quite abruptly for Rome. Mehboob Khan's reworking of the *Aurat* theme in *Mother India* needs to be looked at in this varied context. It could be that Mehboob Khan wished to combine Kurosawa's epic realism with the kind of nationalist agenda that Nehru had in mind when he supported Rossellini's project. This is not to say that *Mother India* is primarily a nationalist ethnographic narrative where the cinematic sign has (or claims to have) a largely indexical quality: the "this is really how it is" or "would have been" argument (Nichols 1981: 241). Obviously *Mother India* (or any other Bombay film) cannot possibly pass primarily as an ethnographic narrative, that is, as a text that directly links image with referent. Nevertheless there are some indices in the film that enable spectatorial transformation of diegesis into cinema verité. The opening scenes of the film, in which Congress Parliamentarians in Nehru caps persuade the

Nirupa Roy and Balraj Sahni in Bimal Roy's *Do Bigha Zamin*, 1953. The realist aesthetic. Courtesy National Film Archive of India.

Mother to open a new dam, are meant to direct the spectators' view to the profilmic India of 1957, ten years after independence. In this respect some degree of documentary (and even ethnographic) framing of the film is part of its conscious design. In one sense this possibility—the spectatorial transformation of diegesis into cinema verité—is to be conceded for every Bombay film. But the critical spectator also knows that the representational processes have been carefully ordered and the indexicals are really iconic and even arbitrary signs. To Western readers (or to readers unfamiliar with the signifying practices of this cinema) Bombay Cinema remains, in one sense, ethnographic, an index of cultural practices, what Bazin had called "films with documentary quality" (Bazin 1971: 2.20). It was the absence of the directly ethnographic (realism as denoting an experience of the land) that led the London review *Film and Filming* to despair that *Mother India*, which it called an "extravagant orgy of Technicolor," would be more appropriately titled "Through Blood, Flood, Fire and Mud with Mother" and was "far removed from the austerities of Satyajit Ray's masterpieces" (*Movie*, September 1984).

To proceed with my reading of *Mother India* I want to return to a key icon with which we began this chapter, the figure of the Mother in Indian culture. The text is obviously held together by this figure, but at one level the

Mother is structured through what may be called the economy of the super-ego, as the censorious object that carries the burden of culture. In other words, although we are meant to identify with Mother India, the metaphorical congruity so essential for absolute identification is not possible because the film is not about Nargis the star (the point of entry in the economy of desire) but about Nargis as Mother, which is how Rushdie's narrator reads her as well. Publicity for the film made the latter point very clearly. An advertisement for the film in *Filmfare* (February 2, 1958), for instance, carried the caption: "From India The Ancient Cradle of Humanity, Two Mothers Rise, Earth and Woman . . . !" Nargis's head is superimposed on top of the northern end of India. In her hands she has a piece of clay which she is examining rather intently. Beneath her gaze India is represented as a mega village. In the film itself, we recall, it is as "the Mother of the village" that she is asked to open a new dam just constructed in postcolonial India, and appropriately in 1957, ten years after independence. Mehboob Khan's original black-and-white version, *Aurat,* did not carry this baggage, largely because the country could not be legally claimed as Indian territory.

The danger posed by collapsing the sign and the referent, the actor as Mother India and the latter as sanctified body is that the film may become associated, however improperly, with the uncompromisingly Hindu mythological genre of Bombay Cinema. *Mother India* is, quite defiantly, not a religious but a secular epic of the new, modern India where a universal moral principle transcending religious and caste difference is the dominant dharma. To maintain that secularity, what was not particularly important for purposes of interpretation with *Aurat* (a product of colonial India) had to be more clearly stated both in name and representation in *Mother India* (a product of post-colonial India). For this reason, although the names of the chief characters in both films are the same, we need to unpack their associations in *Mother India* (and not in *Aurat*) to see how Mehboob Khan bypasses a prior Mother = Goddess (or India as goddess) equation. No epic of India, not even a defiantly secular epic of the nation can totally bypass that equation—this much any reader of Indian cinema has to concede. It is nevertheless important to address the issue as a problematic. The Mother, it strikes us, is not named after Sita or even Durga, Parvati or Lakshmi, names that come to mind immediately when the Hindu thinks of "Mother." The Mother is in fact called Radha, a "goddess" marked by her strong will and illicit passion for Krishna (in one version she is already married). Radha, therefore, is open-ended, canonized as the ideal devotee (of Krishna) but sufficiently flexible so as not to generate an already sanctioned cultural response. Sita, the

Nargis and her two children in Mehboob Khan's *Mother India*, 1957. "This lump of clay calls you home." Courtesy National Film Archive of India.

Nargis and Raaj Kumar in Mehboob Khan's *Mother India*, 1957. Mother as wife and lover. Courtesy National Film Archive of India.

preferred candidate, although historically deeply ambiguous herself, remains extraordinarily predictable. As a result, Indian cinema can do very little with a figure like Sita. Her field of operation is limited; her relationship with the audience carries with it a very closed and systemic repertoire of expectations and prior readings. I think it is for this reason, among many others, that in *Mother India* the Mother, the Woman, is not called Sita, she is called Radha after Krishna's jovial consort, immortalized in Jayadeva's Sanskrit masterpiece *Gītagovinda*, the song of Krishna. So while Sita is fundamentally religio-epic, going back to the *Rāmāyaṇa*, Radha is "vernacular" or local. Against Sita who does not have referential freedom—she is closed, fixed, immutable, existing only in endless replays of sameness and foregrounds through her iconic presence the primacy or the efficacy of the religious—Radha's presence enables the typically Indian concept of life as play, as a game, as ludic, to surface. In *Mother India,* "woman" is therefore represented as wife, as lover, as Mother in both her role as a preserver and destroyer, so that in representational terms she can bypass, at crucial moments, the censorship of the superego.

It is the erotic in Radha as woman (but suppressed in Radha as Mother) that creates the unstable sexual politics of the Mother's love toward the younger son. The relationship conforms to cultural norms (and these are formal cultural norms) but at the same time endows that love with a replay of the Radha/Shamu (her husband) desire so cruelly brought to an end in the first hour of the film. From this possibility the older brother Ramu is excluded (as a young child Ramu in fact does not say a word throughout the film except perhaps to scream "māṁ" [mother]). Indeed those who give in to the Law of the Mother, like her husband and her older son, are symbolically castrated and made inarticulate (unlike in *Aurat,* in *Mother India* her husband loses both his arms). It is clear that in making the younger son Birju more like his rebellious father, the film connects sexual potency with rebellion against the Mother even while it plays, unconsciously, with the much more frightening narrative of the Oedipal triangle. Birju in fact dies holding a pair of blood-soaked *kaṅgan*s (his Mother's marriage bangles) he had recovered from the tyrannical landlord Sukhilala. As a son's symbolic restitution of his mother's honor, it is an image that brings to the fore the many transgressive undercurrents of the text.

The mythic-structural antecedents that I draw upon here are not lost on Salman Rushdie. In the section dealing with the encounter between Aurora Zogoiby and Sunil Dutt and Nargis, Vasco Miranda dismisses the mother-son relationship summarily as "sublimation" (1995: 138), and adds that sublimation of "mutual parent-child longings is deep-rooted in the national psyche." Let us follow how Rushdie reprises the argument I've advanced above:

> The use of names in the picture makes the meaning clear. This "Birju" moniker is also used by God Krishna, isn't it, and we know that milky "Radha" is the blue chap's one true love. In the picture, Sunil [Dutt], you are made up to look like the god, and you even fool with all the girls, throwing your stones to break their womby water-pots; which, admit it, is Krishna-esque behaviour. In this interpretation. . . . *Mother India* is the dark side of the Radha-Krishna story, with the subsidiary theme of forbidden love added on. But what the hell; Oedipus-schmoedipus! (138)

Rushdie's agenda is, or course, rather different as he uses *Mother India* as the intertext for Moor Zogoiby's own rebellion against his mother. And insofar as the real-life relationship of Nargis and Sunil Dutt shadows the mother-son fictive relationship in the film, this composite text of actor, wife, and mother shapes the world of Rushdie's Moor Zogoiby as well. Recounting the episode, Moor Zogoiby also establishes two further connecting threads. First, like the husband of Mother India in the film, who is made symbolically impotent when his arms are crushed by a rock, his own father may have become impotent. Second, Birju's desire for his mother in the film may be Moor Zogoiby's own: "I have been keeping my secret for too long," he says (139).

Though the foci of the commentaries I have drawn upon in the preceding pages vary enormously, one thing remains constant: "Mother India" is a complex site for the production of meaning. Against the received sanctity of the symbol and a narrative of the proper *lāj* we also have a counter or alternative narrative that is constructed through cinema's endless possibilities around "image-as-word." In one sense in film narratives, the visual dimension, the juxtaposition of stage "properties," produce a body of "suprasegmentals" that ambiguates the dialogic narrative (Penley 1988). Film (as visual medium) has a greater capacity to carry multiple meanings than its prototype, the realist novel. In what is clearly a predominantly male representational form, the visual allows for points of resistance to surface, gaps to be created (a return look that just misses the eye of the camera, for instance) that rupture any presumption of an authorial point of view. In cinema there can always be a collective identification/misidentification against the seemingly seamless nature of the film's representational apparatus. For instance, the Oedipal narrative of separation from the mother and identification with the father (*Awara, Laawaris, Shakti*) that is a cultural dominant in both Hollywood and Bollywood may be undercut by the grammar of visual coding. The Oedipal narrative is based on a triadic system of mother, father, and child. The child's initial desire for his mother is deflected onto another female object of desire because of the threat of castration that comes from the father. In *Mother India* the absence of the father leads to an identification with the mother, from whence comes a similar threat of castration. But the "mother" is a body with a lack since the womb is an absent penis. So we have a subject that duplicates a father's aggressivity but succumbs to a threat from precisely the object that it desires (in the absence of the father) but an object, as lack, which should have no power to castrate. The highly contradictory relationship that Birju has with his mother (a relationship that has spilled over into the real-life marriage of Sunil Dutt and Nargis) comes across through the visual narrative of incestuous desire. It is the mother's strength that Birju cannot accept—and which he therefore fetishizes. She cuts him down to size because Birju never completes the Oedipal narrative of separation from mother and identification with the father. The sign of "Mother India"—so effectively deployed by Indira Gandhi—absorbs patriarchal authority into itself. This is why so many power relations do not conform to the established narratives of female lack and disempowerment in Bombay Cinema.

As we have noted, it is through visual ambiguity that *Mother India* turns a lack into something more, into a nonlack, into a sign of such foreboding and relentless negativity that it disrupts the dominant (Western) narrative of the Oedipal triangle. In moving the father out, *Mother India* confronts the spectator with an Oedipal narrative without its third element, the father. In doing so *Mother India* returns cinema to the (dis)comforts of the mother-son binary, to a system of representation in which the father exists only in the periphery of the narrative: *Deewar, Amar Akbar Anthony, Khalnayak, Baazigar,* to name a few. If some visuals introduce a repressed economy of desire and shift our reading of the film to the patriarchal (and stable) domain of *lāj* and the dharmik order, other visuals reinforce *Mother India* as an allegory of indigenous postcolonial reconstruction and redemption after the ravages of the feudal/colonial order. The latter reading requires us to return to the ways in which the film structures its narrative, visually and thematically.

Except for the opening prequel and the final coda (a return to the prequel) the entire film has two identifiable parts. These parts are differentiated both formally (or filmically) and discursively (that is, at the level of narrative). In the first half of the film the epic form of visual representation is relatively unified. Here the text is much more centrally epic in its design, with the great Russian masters of the form—Eisenstein, Pudovkin, Mayalovsky—as the cre-

Sunil Dutt, Rajendra Kumar, and Nargis in Mehboob Khan's *Mother India*, 1957. Land as nation; sickle as class symbol. **Courtesy National Film Archive of India.**

ative antecedents. In this part, classic epic shots—long shots of bullock carts stretching on the horizon, a man gazing afar from the top of a scaffolding, mother and sons against the backdrop of bullocks and fields under water, or in profile holding sickle and harvest in their hands—are used to underline land as nation. The narrative is relatively clear-cut and sustained; it begins with Radha's marriage to Shamu, goes through the loss of Shamu's arms and his disappearance, and effectively ends with the growth of the two surviving sons, Ramu and Birju. Although rural India continues to function as a sign of cultural continuity (an idea endorsed by Prime Minister Jawaharlal Nehru even as he feverishly followed the Soviet developmental model of heavy industrialization), in the second half of the film the narrative is much more diffuse, both filmically and discursively. The center shifts, and the film offers rasas of love and hate, desire and sexuality, comic buffoonery and the tragic, in ways not very different from that offered by the Bombay film genre as a whole. In this second narrative, epic cinema is much less sustained as the text, in fact, acquires different centers: the Mother; the defiant younger son, Birju; the landlord, Sukhilala; and the woman schoolteacher who finally becomes the revolutionary intellectual and who points out the need for action after Birju fails to learn accountancy. But since this second text, the second narra-tive, is complex and discontinuous or fractured, its unity has to be found elsewhere, beyond the textual domain, beyond the film *Mother India* as we see it, in the base culture itself. It is here that *Mother India*, like the genre of Bombay Cinema, requires a multiplicity of self-justifying and self-explicating discourses.

An informed analysis of *Mother India*, therefore, takes us away from the surface expressions of culture to those imaginary relationships (or ideologies) in the presumed "deep" structure of Indian culture that hold Indian society together. Rather simplistically Louis Dumont once declared: "There are two kinds of men in Hindu India, those that live in the world and those that have renounced it" (1960: 33). Dumont was of course invoking a binary that had been documented in early Sanskrit texts in which dharma itself had been referred to as either *pravrttidharma* (the dharma of real social relations) and *nivrttidharma* (the dharma of transcendental absolutes exemplified in the figure of the renouncer). In terms of this proposition one either followed the dharma of the man-in-the-world or the dharma of the renouncer. In real social terms, this abstract binary cannot account for questions of agency, nor of human motivation and individuality. But if we stay with this as an organizing principle in the domain of art, and as a structure for the construction of meaning, we are struck by a number of things. The first is that the figure of the Mother in *Mother India* becomes an active agent (for the primacy of the dharma of *lāj*) when she symbolically affirms the code of the renouncer. We see this in her looks, in her black clothes, in her dark face. We see a figure who seems to be marked by austere practices, who is capable of the great act of *tapas* (immense piety and self-denial) that moved gods in Hindu cosmogyny. Here the renouncer (like the Mahatma himself) is not the Dumontian (or the Hindu canonical) ascetic whose self-denial implies rejection of the world as it is. The figure of the Mother then intervenes into a hallowed abstraction and transforms it into a social force. This much is clear enough and seems to get cultural endorsement. Where it becomes unstable is when the renouncer is mapped onto the figure of the rebel who doesn't simply "interpret" dharma but believes that the point of rebellion is to change metatexts themselves. If Mother as philosopher can only interpret the world (for which the killing of the son is necessary), the son as revolutionary must change it. It is this point that leads to narrative and representational uncertainty. So the question of justice and the ethics of revolutionary change get telescoped through other imperatives. If Sukhilala is the ultimate feudal lord, he is a father as well; if he wishes to defile other women, he has a daughter as well. Between the roles of feudal lord and father, between the lecher and the father it is the figure of the father that acquires greater significance and makes his killing an act against dharma even when it is just. Thus *Mother India*—ostensibly about struggle against tyranny/feudal colonialism—is faced with a real dilemma between an old metaphysics that had sustained a civilization (or so the Brahmanical texts had argued) and a new modernity in which the feudal past may be laid to rest. The difficulty here is that dharma cannot take sides on the basis of historical truth; it can only act in terms of its own absolute imperatives. The logic of the dominant epic would have led to the triumph of Birju through self-sacrifice in which his death (not at the hands of his Mother) would have been redemptive, with the visuals of a new dawn endorsing this. Since *Mother India* the film cannot countenance this, the dominant epic narrative has to be distorted.

There is then a shift in the narrative order. Since rebellion cannot be condoned—but in fact is condemned outright—it has to be located in a subplot that is not a direct continuation of the blighted lives of Mother and two children under a tyrannical overlord. The subplot is about the honor of a village girl (the landlord's daughter) who is abducted by Birju the renouncer/revolutionary toward the very end of the film. It is this subplot—so far completely irrelevant to the underlying revolutionary impulse of the text—that suddenly becomes the narrative in terms of which *Mother India* resolves the terrible crisis of the Indian revolutionary in a postcolonial world. Mehboob Khan's ploy here is to introduce a facet of Mother India we've already outlined. In the face of the shame brought upon the village girl, Mother India must now be reinscribed into her role as the law, as the renouncer who is also the upholder of dharma. Thus in reintroducing the notion of law as dharma, the film returns Mother India to the larger paradigmatic narrative that has generated this complex discourse as well as to the "nation-building project as inscribed in the popular cinema" (Chakravarty 1993: 126). The end of the feudal world order comes not because Birju kills Sukhilala and abducts his daughter, but because in upholding the eternal dharma, the Indian body politic effectively demonstrates its own moral uprighteousness. It is this specific conjunction of Mother as upholder of the law and Mother as the renouncer/avenger that bespeaks the radical impossibility of action in Indian society. United India after Independence needs a guerrilla warfare like a hole in the head. In allowing a son to be killed by a mother, *Mother India*, the epic of postcolonial India, bares the contradictions upon which this massive civilization is based. The resolution, when it comes through Birju's death at the hands of his mother, remains incomplete because the immemorial difference between the serf and his feudal lord remains virtually untouched. In an interview recorded on December 26, 1990, Sunil Dutt, by then producer, director, and parliamentarian, made the following remarks when asked about his filmic portrayal of Birju:

> He [Birju] was revolting against the system in his own way like a Bhagat Singh; the Mother was rebelling likewise but in a Gandhian way. Birju's way is not the way since revenge and hatred cannot bring about reform. You need understanding. And also in abducting the daughter of the village bania Sukhilala Birju was doing what Sukhilala had tried to do to Birju's own mother when he was young. If Birju hadn't done that she wouldn't have killed him. You can't have revolution over *lāj*. Birju is a totally emotional human being; his responses were therefore not based on social sense but on attachment to his mother whose suffering he had seen when young. *Mother India* is not a story about revolution; it is a story about a personal vendetta, a rebellion based on a personal tragedy. The revolution solution in India is through non-violence. Gandhi shook the might of the British Empire through non-violence.

Here we have the principle of "hermeneutic containment." Transgression, whether social, sexual, or caste, is inadmissible to the domain of interpretation because it is somehow "false"; somehow transgression needs to be excised from the spectatorial mind. In recalling *lāj*, Dutt invokes yet again another metanarrative, the time immemorial principle of the containment of shame—because *lāj* is a woman's worth defined in terms of its opposite, sexual transgression. The allusion also confirms the post–*Mother India* image of Nargis as wife and mother: the only important film she appeared in after this film was *Lajwanti* (The chaste wife, 1958). The point about *Mother India* is that it is precisely the moments of ambiguation, the moments when the film ceases to be cinematically and thematically seamless—when, for instance, the camera breaks the eyeline matching of mother and son, husband and wife, daughter-in-law and mother-in-law and indeed ruptures the suture of shot reverse-shot—that an alternative meaning is posited. At these moments spectatorial binding or suture is both broken and ideologically deflected. Broken because the spectator's pleasure is no longer contained within a predictable line of response, and deflected because the spectator is allowed freedom of transgressive identification.

As we have intimated all along, *Mother India* moves inexorably toward a decisive moment of transgressive identification. Before this there is a moment of celebratory bonding when Birju stabs Sukhilala, the feudal lord. The dialogue here revolves around the question of what constitutes true knowledge. Faced with Birju's hatred of the written word (Birju is illiterate), Sukhilala insists that his books of accountancy, his ledger books, are in fact repositories of knowledge and as knowledge they should not be defiled. To this Birju replies, "I have no time for this knowledge (*vidyā*). This is the knowledge that took my land away, this is the knowledge that took my bullocks away, this is the knowledge that led to the defilement of my mother." Birju declares that he will not forgive and concludes before stabbing Sukhilala, "You are a bandit, and I too am a bandit; the law (Urdu *kānūn* here, not Sanskrit *dharma*) will not leave you alone; it will not leave me alone." Although Birju does not raise the alternative to knowledge, the fact of challenging the sanctity of knowledge (*vidyā*) introduces the need for a rethinking of the nexus between knowledge and power. This the spectator endorses. When the transgressive moment comes, the filmic situation is tense as the nondiegetic music and foley effects presage an eerie end. Dressed in black, Birju rides a horse. He has abducted Sukhilala's daughter, Rupa, and she is now "impure," her *lāj* has been violated. He is stopped by his mother, also dressed in black. She carries a gun and gradually lifts it.

> Rupa: Radha Auntie, Radha Auntie, save me!
> Mother: Birju, leave Rupa alone or else I'll kill you.
> Birju: You can't kill me, you are my mother.
> Mother: I am also a woman.
> Birju: I am your son.
> Mother: Rupa is the daughter of the entire village, she is my honor, too. Birju, I
>   can lose a son. I cannot sacrifice my honor.
> Birju: If you dare, shoot—shoot. I too shall not break my vow.
> (Mother screams "Birju" and fires.)

The final triumph of the Mother confuses and places into disarray the revolutionary act essential for postcolonial reconstruction, but it also establishes a "dialogic" convention (going back to *Aurat*) of a dramatic encounter leading to the killing of a loved one by the socially authorized subject. In *Gunga Jamna* (1961), the younger brother (as dharmik police officer) shoots his older brother (Dilip Kumar); in the Deepak Sadashiv Nikhlaje–funded *Vaastav* (Reality, 1999), the chief protagonist is an underworld don who is shot down by his mother (Nikhlaje is the brother of Chota Rajan, who was recently wounded [in Bangkok], and a bitter enemy of underworld figure Dawood Ibrahim); in Khalid Mohamed's *Fiza* (2000), the Muslim terrorist (Hrithik Roshan) is tracked down by his sister (Karishma Kapoor) and shot (at his request, though). The sister's act here (unheard of in cinema before *Fiza*) redeems not only Indian womanhood generally but more significantly the misunderstood Muslim. The language of the mother in *Mother India* (as of the other upholders of the nationalist ethos in the films mentioned) is the humanist discourse of the mother in Aimé Césaire's tragedy *Les Armes mirac-uleuses (Et les chiens se taisaient)* quoted by Frantz Fanon in his seminal *The Wretched of the Earth* (1990: 68–69). In Césaire's tragedy the Rebel speaks of the specificities of race and class, those conditions necessary for the raising of class consciousness, while the mother reaffirms the colonial language of brotherhood, religion, and the human race. However, since the mother in *Mother India* triumphs (in the form of Mother as Durga) and upholds dharma as law—Rajeswari Sunder Rajan has called this "her transcendence of motherhood" (1993: 110)—the film refuses to accept the concept of action based upon political (rather than cultural) necessity. That political necessity finds its cause elsewhere—in spectatorial identification with Birju. Thus in allowing this kind of identification to take place, the director's complicity in subverting the law of the Mother (and of culture) and in advancing political action (which may necessitate a radical change of the social order) comes into play. In shot after shot, suture is maintained with Birju. Birju's gaze is the spectator's gaze even as he denounces Hindu ideology and contradicts the spectator's age-old cultural assumptions. In the process, the film is shot through with contradictions precisely of the kind endorsed by Krishna in the battle of Kurukshetra. An action has a legitimacy if it has moral force; in terms of selfless action (*karmaphalatyāga*) it is Birju who triumphs and not the Mother. Perhaps it is the only way in which Mehboob Khan can make his political statement about India: let the Mother affirm the law, dharma, but let the spectator confirm Birju's actions in much the same way in which the Mehboob Khan Production Marxist Logo of the hammer and the sickle is framed by a fatalistic proclamation of divine destiny in Urdu. In this way the overt textual ideology of the film (which is also a symbolic mapping out in fiction of the nationalist agenda of progress within Hindu values) meets a kind of spectatorial conspiracy with the antinationalist agenda of Birju (Césaire's Rebel). Couched in such a contradictory political agenda, *Mother India* becomes outrageously "conforming," yet so defiantly subversive.

Chapter Four

AUTEURSHIP AND THE LURE OF ROMANCE

Mehboob Khan was an auteur, a director whose major works can be defined in terms of certain expressive styles of filmmaking. These styles were both cinematographic and discursive: a preference for particular kinds of shots, the organization of the mise-en-scènes in a special way, recognizable ways in which key themes (nationalism, honor, and so on) were dramatized. We may refer to Mehboob Khan as a controlling consciousness whose films are read as authorized products of the mind. Such an expression, however, takes us to the heart of the auteur problematic since it implies the presence in the filmic text of a creator who is equivalent to the literary author. In a literary text the author writes the text and shows, where necessary, an authorial point of view or ideology. This could be done through the detached narrator (narratorial voice), ironic undercutting or commentary, and, among other techniques, through the construction of a "character voice" with whom the author is clearly sympathetic. In none of these techniques (or even in a combination of all) is the author present as transcendent meaning because texts are intentional objects (not intended objects) that presuppose a text-reader (spectator) transaction. The reader is part of the meaning of the text and mediates between text and author. In film the transaction requires, as in literature, textual codings that are then recoded by the spectator as part of the film's design. The words of a sympathetic character and the manner in which a particular image has been constructed (the mise-en-scènes around that image are important indices) parallel the techniques of the literary text. Nevertheless, the fact remains that the nature of filmic production—linked as it is to capital, technicians, the work of the camera, the general labor of production—is such that there is no single person with quite the same control over the film that we find in a literary text. Despite Stanley Kubrick's well-known pronouncement—"One man writes a novel. One man writes a symphony. It is essential for one man to make a film" (*Edmonton Journal*, March 8, 1999: C3)—the conflation of writer, composer, and director is not all that simple. So where do we locate the "controlling genius" of the filmic text? An argument that I will pursue in some detail below comes from Roland Barthes (via Kaja Silverman 1988) who distinguished the author "within the body of the text" from the author "outside the text." If we consider authorial index as something within the body of the text, as in fact the corporeal of discourse, we can begin to construct a narrative theory of film where the shift is from an "auteur" (Stanley Kubrick vigorously defines him through his literary avatar) to a cinematic structure through which the controlling mind (here the director) of the work is given expression.

When the *politique des auteurs* (or auteur theory) was first raised in the pages of the film magazine *Cahiers du Cinéma,* the idea of author as owner of intellectual property had to be superimposed on a figure in the complex apparatus of cinema who could be said to be identical with the author of a literary text. While the theory of auteurship that emerged in the pages of this magazine did not specifically define who or what a filmic auteur was, it is clear that the director was the closest analogue to the literary author. André Bazin had in fact declared as early as 1943: "A film's worth stems from its authors. . . . It is much safer to put one's faith in the director than in the leading man" (quoted in Bordwell 1991: 45). The first significant critic of auteur theory in Anglo-American film studies, Andrew Sarris, used the term "criterion of value" to speak about the director as auteur (1992). The use of the phrase itself and Sarris's elaboration of the criterion of value in terms of matters of style, structural design (technical competence), and interior meaning indicate the dependence of auteur theory on a theory of literary production. In the latter the author's signature is his or her style, which is what Sarris is concerned about (585–88). Indeed Sarris is very precise on this point: "The way a film looks and moves should have some relationship to the way a director thinks and feels" (586). And the way a director thinks or feels becomes part of the "interior meaning" of the film, which for Sarris is like an *élan vital* (after Bergson) that cannot be rendered in "noncinematic terms," just as the spirit of a literary text cannot be rendered in nonliterary terms.

Sarris's notion of inner meaning and its filmic specificity (which also implied that the director was aware of the entire filmic tradition in which he or she worked) were bound to valorize art cinema over and above the popular because the controlling eye of high modernist directors (Bergman, Fellini, De Sica, Satyajit Ray, for instance) is more readily discernible in works that have a self-conscious aesthetic intention and where, for obvious reasons, there is considerable directorial control. The kinds of visual and semantic unities achieved by art cinema made the use of auteur/director (behind whom always stood the figure of the literary author) less problematic and certainly more rewarding in the critical/evaluative arena. Directors of popular cinema such as Howard Hawks, John Ford, Steven Spielberg, or Fred Zimmerman could not be read in terms of this "high art" definition of the auteur for one simple reason: too many other factors contribute to the creation of popular cinema. So a fully articulated auteur theory would argue against any direct connection between director and text and would want to explore a host of complex signs that go into the "materiality" of cinema. In Peter Wollen's important contribution to auteur theory (1969; 1992: 589–605), it is cinema as a process—a way of bringing material together, a structure with authorial imprimatur firmly embedded in the text—that is the crux of an auteur theory. A director's corpus is thus marked by an identifiable style located in both what the film represents and what it says. In one respect, Wollen's ideas here are not unlike Barthes's concept of the author within the body of the text, although in recasting the "author" as "source" of latent desire, Wollen erases him or her completely from the manifest text. This is what he had to say in his 1972 postscript to his 1969 work on auteur theory:

> What the *auteur* theory argues is that any film, certainly a Hollywood film, is a network of different statements, crossing and contradicting each other, elaborated into a final "coherent" version. Like a dream, the film the spectator sees is, so to speak, the "film façade," the end-product of "secondary revision," which hides and masks the process which remains latent in the film "unconscious." Sometimes this "façade" is so worked over, so smoothed out, or else so clotted with disparate elements, that it is impossible to see beyond it, or rather to see anything except the characters, the dialogue, the plot, and so on. But in other cases, by a process of comparison with other films, it is possible to decipher, not a coherent message or world-view, but a structure which underlies the film and shapes it, gives it a certain pattern of energy cathexis. It is this structure which *auteur* analysis disengages from the film. (167)

If we follow closely the logic of this passage, auteur theory situates itself in the spectator whose job, like that of the analyst, is to retrace a film's manifest content to its latent meaning. Film, then, is like a dream text marked by significantly overdetermined practices (such as displacement, negation, condensation, and so on). The "meaning" of a film—and the role of the author behind the manifest text—is to be located at the level of "film work," which is analogous to "dream work." In one sense, each auteur has a distinct way of overdetermining the material, of transforming the "ur-" or "pre-" text into the cinematic text; to be able to grasp how film work shapes the manifest text, how the auteur's hand is at work, we need to examine the auteur's entire oeuvre. This does not mean, as dream analysis itself would dictate, that we trace the surface text to its source, or attempt to do so (although even here, as Freud pointed out, there is a point beyond which analysis can go no further, what he called the "unplumbable" regions of the labyrinth); rather it means that the spectator-critic traces the latent structure within the work, follows through the transformations that underlie the seamless product of cinema. Wollen calls the film auteur "an unconscious catalyst" (1992: 602) who is not the same as the literary artist. The procedures outlined by Wollen could be applied to a literary text, however, because there too, in terms of psychoanalytic theory, the author has to be located at the level of the text's latent structure. What has happened, however, is that, unlike Sarris, Wollen is not writing about the auteur as director whose *élan* gives the film a particular vitality or character. What he has done is shift auteur theory away from its dependency on theories of intention and authorial meaning (the auteur as artistic genius) to questions about the production of meaning. In the spectator's act of constructing meaning one glimpses (and again through the text) a structure (not a message) within the work. But the spectator is also faced with a radical act, one that locates interpretation at the level of a text's deconstructive capacities, at the level where the cinema disrupts the codes of cinema, where the text is in fact "unbalanced," out of gear, where meaning cannot be contained within the limits of the frame. In this respect, the act of reading a film is not about locating a (romantic) vision of the artist; it is about what Stephen Heath has referred to as the understanding of the text's "ideological formation" (quoted in Silverman 1988: 198). But insofar as an ideological formation is a façade, an illusion that offers an unproblematic, unmediated vision of the author at work, Heath's use, and before him Wollen's reference to dream work, make the same larger theoretical observation, which is that "cinematographic projection is reminiscent of dream" (Baudry 1992: 698). Pushed to its logical conclusion auteur theory locates the auteur in the spectator's field of analysis. Even more powerfully than in a book—where the reader activates authorial intent—in film the spectator is the (camera) eye that sees. If the cinematic point of view is to be located at the level of the eye of the camera, then the spectator is in effect that eye.

Two kinds of conflation follow from the above. The first is a curious conflation of spectatorial ideology with cinema ideology, which explains the spectator's compulsion to return to his or her self-projection. The second, more significant conflation, is that of a camera desire and spectator's desire that is more than just libidinal. It is in fact a desire that places the cinematic image as the image of the nation itself. The question of desire—and the spectatorial production of meaning—from within a voyeuristic subject are best addressed through the work of Christian Metz. I want to hone in specifically on Metz's 1975/1976 essay "Story/Discourse (A Note on Two Kinds of Voyeurism)" subsequently included in *Psychoanalysis and Cinema* (1982). Here too there is a mapping out of Wollen's "film façade" and Heath's "ideological formations" onto the way in which the film "obliterates all traces of the enunciation, and masquerades as story." What one has to do—along with Heath and Wollen—is examine what film masquerades, what it hides, which would mean uncovering its discourse. Presented in identificatory terms, with its apparatuses of production (its presentational processes) hidden from view, story effortlessly fulfills desire, it presents cinema as an "exhibitionist" form that "relentlessly [erases] its discursive basis" (94) because it wishes to remain unaware of the pleasure it gives its spectators. But that site, the "site of cinematic enunciation" (Silverman 1988: 201)—as discourse and not story—is precisely what is not exhibited; the site as the latent content is smoothed over because cinema "is unaware of being watched" (95). The spectatorial gaze then is the gaze through the keyhole of the primal scene. The spectator as voyeur is presented by Metz as the crucial element in our reading of cinema, but it is a reading in which cinema is always complicit: the actor, writes Metz, behaves "as though he were not seen" (96). And since the sign of enunciation is obliterated in the story, the voyeur occupies the position of the subject of enunciation. In this identification of a story without a teller with the spectator—an identification that, according to Metz, can happen only if the primary identification of the spectator is with the camera (97)—we find an economy of voyeuristic identification which is at the heart of the cinematic experience. Metz identifies this specularity more precisely with the Lacanian mirror stage in which the child reads his or her own image as an Other's image but internalizes it as an "I." The economy of the mirror stage is, however, incomplete in the specularity of cinema because one's own image does not appear: the screen is its own image, not a mirror. So in a sense there is no complete voyeurism as there is no reciprocal gaze of the striptease. Metz's points—through the mediation of the mirror phase—are two. The first is that there is a process of identification because the spectator occupies the position of enunciation (the story exhibits only its outer form, not its discourse). The second is that the act of seeing ("the brute act of seeing," as Metz terms it) is what establishes the moment of cinematic reading.

There are a number of elisions that must be commented on at this stage. Metz recognizes the ways in which the "story" of cinema hides its deep fissures, and the ways in which the gender of the spectator is occluded in the economy of the voyeur (who is always male). But for him authorship is really a matter of cinematic reading, of the spectacle of cinema located at the level of the viewer which is not to say that cinema critique never goes beyond this. Since cinema is like a dream, the auteur is rather less important than the reader of the text. There are other questions, though, about the auteur that need to be raised. The first relates to the question of who does the looking in the text. Is the camera eye located within the eye of a character in the film? Does the director create a series of images that connect back to the gaze of a particular character in the film? Is this gaze in any way marked, insofar as it picks up elements that one associates with a particular race, sex, or class? Could one then make connections between ideology as espoused by the text and that of the director/auteur? A key "transition" text here is Laura Mulvey's classic essay "Visual Pleasure and Narrative Cinema," first published in 1975 (1988a). Mulvey's aim is to isolate the links between cinematic ("visual" or "seeing") pleasure and a deeper, one could say insidious, phallocentrism predicated upon the figure of the "castrated" woman as the object of (male) desire. At the heart of this representation of woman—more accurately the structural necessity of woman in the male economy of desire—is her indispensability once the child has entered the order of the symbolic. In Freudian-Lacanian reading the child's entry into the symbolic (the order of language, of difference beyond the endless iterability of the imaginary) requires the "recognition" of the castrated mother because it is only in this recognition that the real threat from the father (that the child, too, may be castrated) finds actual expression, and creates the necessary deflection of desire from the mother (because of the real threat of castration) to an "other" woman. The Oedipal narrative is, of course, the classic narrative of a transgression that does not succumb to the Law of the Father, or to the threat of castration. So "woman," as Mulvey goes on to establish,

> stands in patriarchal culture as signifier for the male other, bound by a symbolic order in which man can live out his fantasies and obsessions through linguistic command by imposing them on the silent image of woman still tied to her place as bearer of meaning, not maker of meaning. (1988: 58)

Although it is true that alternative cinema (cinema consciously formed against the Hollywood norm of the spectator as voyeur) challenges spectatorial positionings in radical ways, the cinema that forms the archive of this book does not. I will return to this larger question later. For the moment I want to follow up Mulvey's reading, as it is an important contribution to auteur theory.

Mulvey brings together two elements of the spectator/voyeur we have already discussed with reference to Christian Metz. The first is the Peeping Tom figure for whom the object is the source of sexual stimulation. Here desire is constructed on the principle of scopophilia. The second is the narcissistic "misrecognition" of the image on the principle of the Lacanian mirror stage when the child "misrecognizes" himself as an Other in the mirror. Although the processes are dissimilar (objectification versus identification) there is, in one sense, an overlapping of the two in the filmic experience, where desire for the Other gets framed, from the male perspective, by the identification with the hero in his desire for a woman. Mulvey keeps the two separate on analogy with Freud's distinction between "sexual instincts" (the object as desired) and "ego libido" (the self as desired). The center of Mulvey's thesis—a center that is central to my reading of Raj Kapoor as auteur in this chapter—is that whereas women are displayed as erotic objects, it is men who enjoy the look. Indeed, for Mulvey, a woman's "visual presence tends to work against the development of a story line, to freeze the flow of action in moments of erotic contemplation" (62). But her "visual presence" may undergo change. Since the spectator identifies with the male protagonist (and here this figure also carries the auteur's point of view), any shift in the sexual dynamics of the woman and the protagonist leads to a kind of mediatized eroticism on the part of the spectator because the protagonist's possession is read as his own. There is also a considerable weakening of woman as icon of desire here. Since in Bombay Cinema possession cannot really happen except through marriage, the latter is always postponed until the end, and even then can only be signaled as a postfilmic event.

If we keep pace with Mulvey's decisive reading of the gaze, we get to a crucial element in the processual nature of cinema. "It is the place of the look," she writes, "that defines cinema, the possibility of varying it and exposing it" (67). It is here, too, that I would want to connect auteur theory with reception theory in the sense that an auteur theory is primarily about the look and the general question of spectatorial (mis)identifications. Of course, at the bottom is cinema as the language of the imaginary, an illusion imposed by the camera upon profilmic events from the privileged, patriarchal position of the male ego. But it does not follow, as Laura Mulvey goes on to suggest in the concluding paragraph of her essay and in a follow-up essay published in 1981 (1988b: 69–79), that there is always complete foreclosure. The "look of the camera" can be freed, especially if we are to radically postulate a female spectator and, equally strongly, if we are to return to the centrality of the female character in the genre of melodrama.

At one level—perhaps even at the primary level—auteur theory is about locating the dominant authorial voice of the text. But the voice itself—principally male, patriarchal, and dismissive of women—may not be as readily identifiable as in a literary text. In film, as Kaja Silverman has observed, "there are an enormous number of other productive elements, not the least of which is a whole textual system which often persists intransigently from one directorial corpus to another" (1988: 208–209). In examining the auteur in Bombay Cinema, the same principles are readily discernible. The Bombay auteur is part of a textual system—one that is in every way as "monolithic" as Hollywood—that brings to him (rarely "her") a prior system of cinematic practices, with their own material and discursive formations. It is in the context of this form—the form that established the genre—that we need to discuss two auteurs of Bombay Cinema: Raj Kapoor and Guru Dutt, auteurs who, according to Das Gupta, occupy an intermediate space between the reformism of preindependence cinema and the neotraditionalism of contemporary popular Bombay Cinema (1991: 31). For both a number of general observations must be made at the onset. First, Raj Kapoor and, to a lesser extent, Guru Dutt are also "stars," and their auteur-presence cannot be prized out of their status as "stars." In fact there is a larger principle at work here that needs to be spelled out. For a very long period, and with rare exceptions such as Mehboob Khan and Bimal Roy, or Prakash Mehra and Manmohan Desai, only auteurs who were stars as well circulated as auteurs in the popular imagination. In other words, up until very recently—perhaps with the arrival of Mani Rathnam, Aditya Chopra, and a few others—auteurship, from the spectator's point of view, could be conferred only upon actor-directors. Second, our auteurs tend to fuse author ideology and text ideology through what Silverman, speaking about Hitchcock, said was a "position of phallic dominance" (1988: 209). And finally, eruptions in the ideological control have to be discovered in moments of transgression, countercoding, the subversive look, the song text, diegetic audiences within the text, and so on, that occur within the productive interstices of the form. The key to an auteur lies precisely in the ways in which secondary revisions (or the grammar of transformations) can be recovered through processes of interpretation.

Not all the films I will consider here were directed by Raj Kapoor or Guru Dutt—in some they were under the direction of other filmmakers. But there is little doubt that Kapoor and Dutt had considerable control over all their respective films. Of Raj Kapoor's films I examine key films from what is defined as his classic phase, from *Aag* (1948) to *Jagte Raho* (1956). The period also coincides with Raj Kapoor's well-documented relationship with Nargis, the leading lady of all the films of his classic phase. Guru Dutt's major phase occupies the next five years, from 1957 to 1962. To isolate Raj Kapoor and Guru Dutt does not mean that they were the only auteurs of Bombay Cinema even in the restricted terms of the definition. My argument here is that historically in Bombay Cinema the auteur has surfaced only when there has been spectatorial involvement in him through the spectator's prior identification with him as actor. This may not make good sense in the domain of art cinema but in popular film it means that the bazaar commentarial tradition so crucial to the popular can be brought to bear on the actor as auteur. Nor do I wish to conflate two radically different individuals by juxtaposing Raj Kapoor and Guru Dutt. One, Raj Kapoor, is the showman (at the 1998 Filmfare Awards ceremony Amitabh Bachchan referred to Raj Kapoor as "the greatest showman this cinema has ever produced"), an extrovert who played to the gallery. He is part of a film dynasty that has survived to this day (Purohit claims that members of this dynasty were in 286, or 16 percent, of all Hindi films between 1931 and 1966). The other, Guru Dutt, is sensitive, introverted, self-denying, and, within the limits of Bombay Cinema, much more willing to transgress the demands of the genre. But they are important because between the two one gets a range of filmic articulations, in the guise of romance, of "the reformist/restorative function that the State was required to accomplish politically" (Rajadhyaksha 1999: 144). The grand omission here is of course the figure of Dev Anand, an actor/auteur who clearly controlled many aspects of films produced by his production house, Navketan. Although his key films, *Taxi Driver* (1954), *House No. 44* (1955), *Nau Do Gyarah* (The con artist, 1957), *Kala Bazar* (Black market, 1960), and *Guide* (1965) were directed either by his brothers Chetan Anand and Vijay Anand or by M. K. Burman, Dev Anand does open up the possibility of a different manner in which the auteur in Bombay Cinema may be approached. To digress to Dev Anand so perfunctorily is not to dismiss him, only to suggest that he requires analysis of a kind I don't offer here. But to invoke Dev Anand also reminds us of the "composite" formation of the auteur and the link between the auteur, the actor, and a host of other workers. In particular we need to mention and indeed to bracket with the auteurs discussed here the names of the cinematographers, especially Radhu Karmakar, Raj Kapoor's cameraman in *Awara*, *Shree 420* and *Jagte Raho*, and V. K. Murthy, Guru Dutt's cameraman in almost all his films from *Jaal* (The net, 1952) to *Sahib Bibi Aur Ghulam* (King, queen, knave, 1962).

RAJ KAPOOR: AUTEUR AS VOYEUR

Raj Kapoor (1924–88) was perhaps the first of the distinctive auteurs in the sense in which Wollen defines the term. What I have called his classic phase is marked by an output that may be examined as a series of loosely connected texts. Three of these—*Aag* (Desire, 1948), *Barsaat* (Monsoon, 1949), and *Aah* (Sighs of the Heart, 1953)—are straightforward romances. Two others— *Awara* (The vagabond, 1951) and *Shree 420* (Mr. 420, 1955)—though also romances, have a more obvious social message. *Jagte Raho* (Stay awake! 1956), his most artistically accomplished film, is the film that is closest to a realist text and may be seen as an important precursor, in the tradition of *Achhut Kanya*, *Devdas* and *Aadmi*, of what came to be called Indian Middle (or "middle-brow") cinema of the '70s and '80s. Raj Kapoor's own hand is least evident in this film—Sombhu and Amit Mitra, the directors, stay close to the film's Bengali antecedents—but the film is, nevertheless, ideologically of a piece with *Shree 420*, the tale of a tramp in an inhospitable city. Raj Kapoor made a number of films after these six and acted in at least three— *Jis Desh Men Ganga Behti Hai* (Where flows the Ganges, 1960), *Sangam* (The confluence, 1964), and *Mera Naam Joker* (The joker, 1970). They are not discussed here because they depart from the relatively homogeneous form of the six films mentioned above. There are many reasons for this. Three of the most important are that Kapoor lost his leading lady Nargis after *Jagte Raho*, the colonial underpinnings of India began to fade away ten years after independence, and the romantic hero/tramp was replaced by a more worldly urban hero as the cityscape changed quite dramatically in the 1960s. But the first ten years of Indian independence, transformed into sentiment and song, belonged to Raj Kapoor. (Indeed, Andrzej Fidyk's wonderful documentary on Indian mobile cinema (roaming cinema), *Battu's Bioscope*, begins and ends with music from Raj Kapoor's films.) I want to examine the texts of the classic phase under the broad themes of the tradition of colonial romance, Indian definitions of the filmic auteur, and the globalization of cinema aesthetics.

If we glance back at those films that established the genre (*Achhut Kanya*, *Devdas*, *Aadmi*, *Kismet*, *Aurat*) what strikes us is the manner in which nationalist aspirations, including social reform, the necessity of a pan-Indian mass culture, get transformed into what Ashish Rajadhyaksha has called "the idiom of

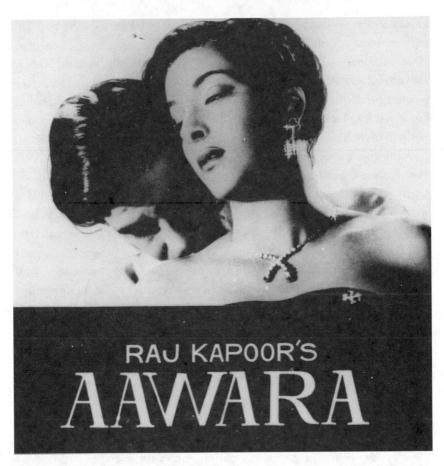

Publicity Poster for Raj Kapoor's *Awara*, 1951. Courtesy National Film Archive of India.

melodrama" (1993: 56). I have indicated that the dominant genre of Bombay Cinema may be called sentimental melodramatic romance linked to dharmik codes. Raj Kapoor worked from within this ideological system but revolutionized romance in two significant ways: first he made song and music texts in their own right so that played by themselves one could memorially reconstruct the absent narrative, and, second, he manipulated what film does best—the politics of desire and the subject/self/spectator's insertion into that desire. Here I think the concept of the body—the female body—is important. Raj Kapoor has defended the body fetish by referring to erotic art; but there is something illicit, almost pornographic, in his use of the camera as voyeur. It is the camera eye capturing the primal scene, so to speak, the scene to be censored by the mature subject, that surfaces over and over again. If the space of social realism in a film such as *Awara* is the space of the symbolic (where meaning as difference is produced), the space of the female body is the space of the imaginary (where the fetish is compulsively repeated). Not unusually, in films such as *Barsaat* and *Aah* (the original version) Raj Kapoor's narcissistic urge toward the pleasure principle leads to the death of one of the key characters. The (phallic) eye of Raj Kapoor so dominates these films that he appropriates the spectator's position (the class differences here being irrelevant) as his own, transforms that position, and then feeds it back to the spectator as something that the spectator had discovered himself. The fact that we do not gloss "himself" here is intentional. There are no women spectators in Raj Kapoor's films: men desire, women are only desired or, as Laura Mulvey pointed out, the filmic apparatus simply forecloses women's desire. That particular type of female fetishization, which had been carefully circumvented in the genre through at times carefully placed parallel narratives that define a larger pan-national consciousness (cinema here as a social document for change), now returns as a haunting signifier of Indian sexual repression. For Raj Kapoor, alongside the eternal law of dharma existed the equally eternal law of desire, the principle of *kāma*. The *Kāma Sūtra*—that demotic text on desire—is the marginalized text of the Indian that resurfaces in his cinema. Indian aesthetics had transformed desire into the declaratory *rasa* of *śṛṅgāra* (eroticism); now it is being redefined as the pleasure principle that would leave Kewal in *Aag* disfigured, Raj in *Awara* behind bars, and Raj in the original version of *Aah* dead.

Before I turn to Raj Kapoor's films in some detail, the law of desire and the economy of the gaze require a critical gloss with reference to Madhava Prasad's valuable work on the absolutist gaze and spectation (1998: 72–87). I raise his critique of the voyeuristic look (Metz's "unauthorized scopophilia") because my argument with reference to Raj Kapoor is that the spectator's implied entry into the private world (as voyeur) is central to the structure of the Kapoor film. On an important level this contradicts Prasad's argument that in the melodrama of the 1950s and 1960s voyeurism was curtailed through the subjection of the spectator to a mode of filmic production that normalized the spectator's gaze into a structure of looking that deflected identificatory relation. Performance (like Parsi theater or *Rāmlīlā*) had its own rasa and its enjoyment was an aesthetic relish that came "pre-textualized," as part of the social in itself. In Laura Mulvey's argument, as we have seen, the subject's identification is with an ego ideal whose representative in the cinema is the star. The theory presupposes a post-Enlightenment individuated subject who singly identifies with the object in an imaginary (as distinct from symbolic) order. In Prasad's argument (which he applies directly only to what he calls the Hindi feudal family romance—a romance that functions within a patriarchal order), the Indian look is defined by a premodern, pre-textual structure of spectation that is "embodied in the tradition of *darśana*" (74). The theory—a forceful one—cannot explain, however, the textual complexity of the signifying system because bodies do erupt, and "*darśanik* gaze" is no guarantee that actual subjects in fact are bonded to that gaze. To account for the persistence of the scopophilic moment, Prasad has argued that Bombay Cinema punctuates the text with standardized moments (often nondiegetic, such as the song sequence) when the voyeur is allowed into the scene of surrogate identification. There is much more at stake here—corporate identity versus individual identity; state versus the citizen; free acts of consciousness versus formal aesthetic laws, and so on—but the overall thesis is that the absolutist gaze persists because the "consensual" is at the heart of spectation. When, however, female desire required fulfillment as in *Sangam* or *Dil Ek Mandir* (The heart is a temple, 1963), the object of desire had to die through an act of heroic self-denial. For Prasad's argument the archetypal actor was Rajendra Kumar whose deaths in these films combined personal sacrifice with national virtues. The theory of reception advanced here has great merit and quite possibly some relevance to certain types of cinematic narratives, but it has difficulty accommodating a filmmaker whose camera work is consciously deployed toward the spectator as voyeur. This is as true of *Awara* as it is of *Sangam,* which is a key proof text for Prasad.

Many of the essential features of the Raj Kapoor classic corpus are foreshadowed in his first film *Aag* (literally "Fire" but better translated as "Desire," 1948): the invocation of Vedic chants by Raj Kapoor's father, Prithviraj before the credit stills, the figure of a man with a violin in one hand holding a woman as the production house's signature, the theme of the hero as a sentimental Werther figure, the juxtaposition, again in sentimental terms, of the conflict between outer looks and inner essence, and the significance of the male gaze that constructs, for the spectator, the sublime object as an impossible ideal. In this sense the spectator was always framed as male. So far as women are concerned, if Laura Mulvey is correct, they underwent symbolic transvestism as they adopted, in the words of Constance Penley, "another role in order to 'read' the image" (Penley 1988a: 7). Since laws of censorship made exposure of the body and any form of sexual contact (including kissing) impossible, the face was all that was left as the object of fetishization. In this respect Raj Kapoor reshaped the representation of the secular goddess for millions of Indian spectators. In *Aag* the auteur inserts the narrative of his own life into the text by presenting it as a melodramatic romance in which the metaphorics of fire (borrowed directly from Charlotte Brontë) loom large and where the spectator, the auteur, and the hero are united through a kind of erotic glue. The look, the symbol, and the song become crucial signifiers. Women become raw material for the gaze as a "scopophilic eroticism" binds the text. The camera performs a subjective function as we see whatever Raj Kapoor (or his heroic alter ego in the film) sees. We pause here to watch as Nargis enters the Raj Kapoor filmic syntagm for the first time in this film (the cinematographer is V. N. Reddy). A woman sits on a chair. She has a fashionable blouse on, she looks down, her long flowing hair unbraided. Kewal (Raj Kapoor) looks, and Rajan (Premnath), his theater-partner and painter, recognizes her as the model of his paintings and the women he loves. The camera closes in on her face, glamorizes it, and drags the spectator into its point of view. She has no name (as she insists), and is the only survivor of the Punjab massacres during *baṭvārā* or partition. (In 1948 viewers would have been aware of the many cases of abduction and rape surrounding *baṭvārā*, and the attempts being made by the government of India to locate women who had been abducted by both sides.) She comes without genealogy, a not uncommon feature of the genre. Even as the camera constructs Nargis as the object of desire, the wish to transcend looks and enter into her soul is strong for Kewal (Rajan's obsession, "What a voice . . . like an angel," is followed by Kewal's response, "I wish to peep into her soul"). Perhaps Kewal's (and Raj Kapoor's) verbal insistence here is a screen, a form of censorship, a diegetic ruse, a willed repression of desire, a disavowal that confirms the opposite. Secure in the clichés about the soul ("There is a great difference between Rajan and I. He loves the flesh, I worship the soul," he tells the girl), the camera can act out another narrative. Thus as Nargis sings "nā āṁkhoṁ meṁ āṁsūṁ nā hoṁṭhoṁ pe hāy" (No tear, no cry) it is the camera that does the looking that Kewal had disavowed. Nargis lies on a couch, she turns around, she looks. The camera lingers on her face as she moves her head from one side of the pillow to the other. There is a full frontal shot of her face. The camera does not move as it takes in the magnificent beauty of this woman in white, Raj Kapoor's preferred color for Nargis. As the song comes to an end she stands, looks away from the camera and walks, dragging the spectator on her way out of the frame. As Rey Chow has pointed out, non-Westerners also gaze, they also participate in illicit pleasures (1995). But with Nargis—and only with Nargis—there is also a kind of sexual violence exploding into the collision of bodies that undercut the serenity of song. At one point in the film Kewal grasps Nargis's hair with considerable force and pulls her face toward him. The symbolic sexual violence demonstrated here is a kind of proto-macho violence of male superiority that undercuts Kewal's erstwhile claims about the beauty of one's soul. But this physical gesture will be repeated again in other films as it becomes a coded way of insinuating the silenced sexuality of the Bombay film. The corporeal, the body (not the angelic soul) finally wins as Nimmi (Nargis) leaves Kewal for Rajan when she discovers Kewal was seriously disfigured in the fire that destroyed the theater. The sentimental hero once again is left alone as another Nimmi leaves him: "to is tarah yah nimmi bhī calī gayī" (In this manner this Nimmi too left me). But the lure of romance lies precisely in the illusion of continuity, as Kewal's bride, to whom the story is narrated, turns out to be none other than his childhood sweetheart, also named Nimmi. "I'll make you another theater," he tells her. "I will be Bilwamangal," says Kewal, recalling a popular stage play and early film. "And you?" he asks. She replies, "Chintamani," Bilwamangal's beloved, and they embrace, cinematically rescuing two features so common to the form: frontality and framing within the invisible proscenium arch.

Kewal, Rajan, and the last Nimmi in *Aag*—Raj Kapoor, Premnath, and Nargis—reappear a year later in *Barsaat*, another romance but with two clearly marked sets of lovers. The film effectively begins with the seduction of an innocent hill-country girl, Neela, played by a new Raj Kapoor discovery, Nimmi (named after the three Nimmis in *Aag*) by Gopal (Premnath). Against Gopal's attraction to the physical (the common narrative of the repressed desire of the city sophisticate for the rural rustic) Pran's (Raj Kapoor's) intense love for Rashma (Nargis) reflects a spiritual coming of minds. But once again, since the woman in question is Nargis, Raj Kapoor's camera-eye tells another story: through the camera work the spectator begins to get glimpses of the Raj Kapoor-Nargis passion as played out in real life. In other words, the camera compulsively foregrounds a sensuousness that the narrative diegesis tries to hide. As in *Aag* claims about the inner purity of the self, the importance of detachment and reflection made by the hero (Raj Kapoor) are undercut by a camera work that offers a different point of view. So, as Nargis sings "mujhe kisī se pyār ho gayā" (I have fallen in love with someone), the camera (of Jal Mistry) concentrates on her face, taking full frontal shots of her face, which now covers the entire screen. When the song ends Pran (Raj Kapoor) pulls her by the hair in a conscious repetition of a similar scene in *Aag*. This act of violence, meant to "teach" Rashma the meaning of true love, is different from the exhibitionist love that the camera eye had captured. It becomes clear in these early films that Raj Kapoor carefully projects Nargis as the object of voyeuristic fantasies even as the narrative diegesis tries to make her, especially through songs sung for her by Lata

Nargis and Raj Kapoor in Raj Kapoor's *Aag*, 1948. Defining desire. Courtesy National Film Archive of India.

Mangeshkar in her virginally pure voice, a symbol of the lovelorn, *viraha*-stricken, constant woman of the canonical literary texts of love. To heighten the latter the narrative must work on the theme of the melancholic lover established in Barua's *Devdas* (1935). There the hero's dedication to Paro is such that he abrogates his right to live.

Raj Kapoor's homage to *Devdas* is best seen in *Aah* (recall that in Bimal Roy's *Devdas*, the last word of the title character is "aah," which may be translated, in that context, as "oh, the pity of it all"). Though directed by Raja Nawathe, Kapoor's auteur hand is evident throughout. Once again the drama is about love and sexual attraction consciously predicated on the spectator's sense of identification with the hero, which is why the film works on sexual fantasies at considerable length. I want to pick out the final scenes from this film as they replicate Barua's and Bimal Roy's treatment of the journey of the sick hero back to the home of his beloved. It is the day of Neelu's (Nargis's) wedding. In a re-play of the classic final scenes of *Devdas* (1935/1955) Raj (Raj Kapoor) is seen traveling in a train with his trusted old servant and a doctor from the sanatorium. On the night of the marriage Raj, like Devdas, takes a horse cart to the bride's house. The actor who plays the driver of the cart is none other than the playback singer Mukesh, who sings in his own voice and, for himself, the memorable song:

Life is so short;

And youth shorter still;

Your narrative, a tale of woe.

Raj dies upon reaching Neelu's neighborhood; the wedding procession passes by the dead body. At least this is how I recall the ending of the film shown in the Empire Theatre, Fiji, in 1954. The video copy of the revised film tells a different story. In this version, Dr. Kailash, Raj's friend, and Neelu do not marry; a car carrying almost all the main characters of the film collides with Raj's carriage. It is suggested that thousands of years before, Savitri's devotion brought her husband, Satyavan, back to life. And of course the implication here is that Neelu's love can cure Raj of his terminal illness. The final scene is of Raj and Neelu, now married, watching a religious pantomime on stage in which Krishna kills an evil demon (Death). The change destroyed the thematic unity of the text and, in particular, the special pathos of the song text throughout. Bunny Reuben concurs and offers a rationale behind the changes. "The film had some of Shankar-Jaikishen's loveliest music, and a 'Devdas'-ian tragic ending which was changed to the conventional happy ending because the film didn't do well in its first release" (105).

Raj Kapoor's account of his experience in the theater during one of the early screenings of the original version is worth noting:

> I did not have to wait until the premiere of Aah, at its third screening, to know its fate. I was in the darkened auditorium, at the first show (matinee) at the Opera House in Bombay listening to what the atmosphere had to tell me. The atmosphere in an auditorium is like a living, palpitating thing. It told me, again and again: "Your picture is a flop." (Reuben, 107–108)

Beyond the competing claims of the value of the revision, two revealing features about Kapoor as auteur arise out of juxtaposing the two quotations. The first is that the Raj Kapoor auteur reads a filmic text purely in terms of popular reception. The second point is that even for Raj Kapoor, cinema was essentially a commercial venture, so that the artistic unity of the text as created by the director could be mutilated (in artistic terms) by Raj Kapoor the "real" auteur of all his films. The auteur, as seen through the Raj Kapoor corpus, is not the isolated artist pouring his passion into cinema for aesthetic pleasure alone but is a function of popular taste.

If there is one film that is equated with Raj Kapoor as auteur that film must be *Awara* (The vagabond, 1951). It remains to this day the most popular and the best known internationally of all his films. It broke into the

European and Soviet markets and did, predictably, extremely well, in the traditional Middle Eastern and South East Asian markets. It has been claimed President Putin asked for tapes of *Awara* (and *Shree 420*) music to be left in his presidential suite when he visited Delhi in September–October 2000. In the Indian diaspora it began fashions and life styles that changed an entire generation. Its phenomenal success, however, came as a total surprise to Raj Kapoor. K. A. Abbas, the screenplay writer of *Awara*, declared: "No one connected with *Awara* ever expected that it would achieve such phenomenal popularity" (*Movie*, March 1985: 99).

Awara is the classic Oedipal narrative. A son searches for his father, whose whereabouts he does not know and whose very name has been suppressed by his mother, who is appropriately named Bharati (the feminine form of *Bhārat*, the Sanskrit word for India). Once he discovers the name of his father and the history of his mother's rejection, though not its cause, he seeks to kill his father. By this time, the mother is dead, and Bombay Cinema can comfortably declare that displacing the father for the mother's affections is no longer at issue. As a narrative problematic at the level of the psychic development of the subject, the decisive third term is often missing from Bombay film narratives. Instead of the familiar tripartite ideal of father-son-mother or father-daughter-mother, one often finds either father-daughter (not unusually varied to guardian uncle-daughter) or mother-son bipolar familial structure at the beginning of many narratives. In *Awara* the third term (father/mother) is missing from the domain of both man and woman. In the case of Raj (Raj Kapoor), it is the father figure who is initially missing; in the case of Rita (Nargis) the mother figure is absent throughout. What is clear is that in the absence of the ternary item (mother and father from both equations) desire is not resolved through a proper, admissible deflection. In the event desire gets locked into the "dual," the binary in these relationships. Without the third factor (which is so crucial for resolution) what gets reproduced is an "overinvestment" in these relationships (Vasudevan 1995a). Given that the shift to the symbolic (from the imaginary) is therefore played out in the parallel space of the father's and the mother's domains, these two spaces emerge as highly charged spaces for the production of cinematic meaning. This "meaning" is often projected onto social binaries such as rich versus poor, urban versus city, modernity versus tradition, and, more radically in *Awara,* the conflict between geneticism and behaviorism. They circulate as well through song texts that often begin to have lives of their own. So we find songs about lovers separated by *mahal* (the mansion) and *kuṭi* (the shack or hovel) or wealth (*dhanmān/ nirdhan*: literally the "rich and the poor"), and so on. Additionally, in the narrative of the absent father, we need to keep in mind the parallel narrative of actors, in fact their profilmic lives. By the early 1950s, Prithviraj Kapoor, Raj Kapoor's father, was no longer the towering actor of Bombay Cinema. The son had already displaced him in popularity. The possible tensions between father and son, although replayed in fictional terms in the film itself, are not lost on the audience.

This retracing of the abbreviated Oedipal drama, and the social message of the film, however, takes place in the shadow of the foundational myth of Rama. In the *Rāmāyaṇa*, Rama rejects Sita because he could not, finally, allow rumors about his wife to threaten the ship of state itself. In a clear reference to this episode, Judge Raghunath's sister-in-law threatens him with the Hindu horror of pollution when she demands that he too should reject his wife, who had been abducted by a thug. In the Vulgate *Rāmāyaṇa,* the rejected wife, Sita, gives birth to twin sons who, toward the end of the epic, harness Rama's horse during the *aśvamedha* ceremony in direct defiance of their father. In a replay of the rules of epic genealogy Raghunath stands for geneticism and pure genealogical transmission while his son is the postcolonial social determinist in rebellion. Within the oppositional simplicity of the popular, Raj Kapoor presents the colonial and the postcolonial as a simple opposition: do children of thieves grow up to be thieves and children of well-to-do parents grow up to be decent citizens regardless of their upbringing? Can the colonial bourgeoisie never change in a postcolonial world order? In a very real sense the matter rests there because the film really endorses neither.

If *Awara* unsettles the purity of "epic genealogy" by introducing the self as socially constructed, *Shree 420* moves into the domain of truth and social responsibility on the part of the capitalist nation-state at large. By 1955, we are well into the first five-year plan that Nehru so proudly declared would make India an industrialized nation. Gradually the utopian ideal of the unity of work value and use value constructed by Gandhi around the village artisan ideal became less and less important in India's modernization process. Capitalism and the commodification of labor are here to stay, and Raj Kapoor picks these themes up. Why not examine some of the excesses of free enterprise and place them against the alternative ideal of "cooperative" capitalism? So, in one sense, the Soviet communes are replaced in *Shree 420* by capitalist self-help cooperatives. At the same time the social imperatives that would necessitate, in terms of Soviet realism, a heroic struggle are transposed onto the figure of the innocent country tramp (albeit one with a Bachelor of Arts degree) brutalized by the sophistication of the city, Bombay, where "clocking" in to work implied a mechanical rotation of labor.

Bombay Cinema is spatially located in a great postcolonial metropolis, and Indian modernity is projected primarily onto this city. In *Shree 420,* as in *Awara* before and in *Jagte Raho* later, the city looms large and is in need of humanization. Raj (Raj Kapoor), a college graduate from Allahabad (stories of unemployed people with B.A.s in India are legendary), an orphan, something of a buffoon and an Indian nationalist, comes to the great postcolonial city. He is a traveler on the road, a picaresque hero, whose life simply gets dragged into momentous events. He sings his own version of the song of the road, which Salman Rushdie in the opening pages of *The Satanic Verses* (1988: 5) translates as follows:

> O my shoes are Japanese,
> These trousers English, if you please.
> On my head, red Russian hat;
> My heart's Indian for all that.

The Indian picaro in the song declares his local inscription even as he is commodified by the global. Indeed all that remains Indian in this version is the relatively unimportant heart, because it cannot be converted into an item of value. In his first words—"Bombay 420," uttered as he reads a road sign—are captured, through the extended meaning of the phrase, the idea of the world being essentially fraudulent. Which is why the phrase "Bombay 420" strikes the Indian spectator immediately. Although in the context of the road sign it means "Bombay is 420 miles away," its other meaning through the ellipsis becomes the crucial descriptor of the city. Glossing the use of the 420 motif in Rushdie's *The Satanic Verses,* Srinivas Aravamudan (1989) noted:

> The hold of "420" on the Indian imagination does not result from the previously mentioned movie [*Shree 420*], which is its product; rather, its origin lies in the juridical apparatus installed by the British imperialists to better govern the country. . . . culminating in the Indian Penal Code, which was finally promulgated in 1860. As in many postcolonial societies, the colonial apparatus forms the basis for current law: the numeral "420" in India is still readily understood as an abbreviated reference to the section of the Code of Criminal Procedure under that number: "Whoever cheats and thereby dishonestly induces the person deceived to deliver any property to any person, or to make, alter or destroy the whole or any part of a valuable security, or anything which is signed or sealed, and which is capable of being converted into a valuable security, shall be punished with imprisonment. . . ." . . . "Section 420," frequently the abbreviated explanation for an arrest in Indian newspapers, alludes to those who attempt small-scale fraud

Nargis and Raj Kapoor in Raj Kapoor's *Shree 420*, 1955. A frame that supplants the text. Courtesy National Film Archive of India.

and confidence tricks; however, in the popular imagination, the scope of "420" extends to the more significant villainy of politicians and businessmen. (7)

To break past the fraudulent world of "420," Raj has to choose Vidya (Nargis) over Maya (Nadira). Vidya (literally "knowledge") and Maya ("illusion") create a simple opposition in which, for the moment, the latter triumphs. But the role of Vidya is once again played by the star Nargis, who is indispensable to any study of Raj Kapoor as auteur. Our attention now shifts from social politics (the Raj Kapoor corpus imbued with social democratic textures) to another kind of politics—sexual politics.

In a fascinating essay, "Sanctity and Scandal," Rosie Thomas (1989) has examined in some detail the manner in which Nargis the star was constructed through her filmic history as well as a parallel ("real-life") history made up largely of fanzine discourses (gossip, studio dissemination of (mis)information for dramatic effect) through which the spectator-voyeur has historically constructed Nargis as an elusive courtesan with a subcultural history. This history in fact has displaced the official version so comprehensively that "Nargis" has no real referential meaning. (Indeed in the *Moor's Last Sigh* [1995: 174] Salman Rushdie uses "Nargis-y" to allude to both the name of the star, Nargis [the narcissus], and to the meaning of the adjectival form ["resembling the narcissus."]) Part of this construction of "Nargis" is also a result of the very special manner in which Raj Kapoor as auteur constructed this figure. I have made some references to her cinematic construction through the economy of the voyeur. I would now like to extend my treatment of Nargis as the sublime object of the Indian spectator's desire, and Raj Kapoor's defining moment as auteur.

Nargis thus becomes a site that brings together issues relating to male Indian sexuality, the projection of women, the cinematic apparatus, the physical space of the cinema hall, and the sexual pleasure of looking. Writing about the last of these—the act of gazing—E. Ann Kaplan (1988) specifies three kinds of looks:

(a) within the film itself, men gaze at women, who become objects of the gaze;

(b) the spectator, in turn, is made to identify with this male gaze, and to objectify the women on the screen; and

(c) the camera's original "gaze" comes into play in the very act of filming.

I do not wish to critique these "gazes" here. Rather I am interested in the manner in which Raj Kapoor exploits these gazes toward the ends of Indian sexual fantasy which, in this instance, are in turn predicated upon his real-life relationship with Nargis. In very general terms the spectator gets titillated and, as if in a dream, participates in a profilmic relationship reenacted in the filmic text. In the case of Raj Kapoor the "as if" has less force since the films are consciously designed as texts of sexual fantasy. In this fantasy (where the object of desire is Nargis), the spectator is always "male." Women's desire, to follow Laura Mulvey, can take place only through the perverse logic of transvestism. In the melodramatic texts of Indian cinema, however, one senses that the hegemony of the male perspective is not necessarily totally overpowering. Melodrama tends to rework a primarily female agenda into the text as well since the genre's emotional excess destabilizes the rigid, detached, male worldview and makes way for a degree of female spectatorial engagement.

I now want to examine a sequence from *Awara* in which the male gaze is not simply a gaze that looks passively, but is complicit with the ravenous appetite of the camera (Jameson 1990: 123). The camera, in this instance, carries with it a "possessive," compensatory force armed to defend the male psyche against female empowerment. Cinema thus denies women objective existence because they can only be recipients of the gaze as captured by the camera at the "behest" of the male spectator. In psychoanalytic theory the

Nargis in Raj Kapoor's *Awara*, 1951. The camera lingers on the face. Courtesy National Film Archive of India.

"sexualization and objectification" of the gaze goes beyond mere eroticism since "it is designed to annihilate the threat that woman (as castrated and possessing a sinister genital organ) poses" (Kaplan 1988: 31). We find in Raj Kapoor "excessive use of point of view shots" (Mulvey 1988: 89) that both reinforce the fantasies of the camera as voyeur and implies what Mary Doane called in another context the "terrorist act" of directing the camera toward the female body (1988: 216).

The scene is from *Awara*. A man and a woman are in a small boat. The full moon can be seen. The man clasps the woman, who replies that the moon is watching over them and their actions must therefore be discreet. They look at the moon. The woman begins the first line of the song slowly as if in a whisper—"dam bhar jo udhar muṁh phere" (if for a moment you would take your gaze away), she sings to the moon—and the camera captures her face emerging, like the moon from below, in the same manner in which it had been done in *Aag* three years before. One side of her face remains dark, the other luminous as she sings to the moon, but also to Raj the spectator's conduit through whom he too finds sexual gratification. As Nargis sings and gyrates—bodily palpitations are endorsed by the *Kāma Sūtra*—the camera captures her youthful exuberance while Raj remains the subdued male to whom she dances and sings. When it comes to his part of the duet, Raj is somewhat sullen, unappreciative, even, it seems, of the bodily pleasures being poured all around him. The actor-auteur now inscribes his own person as the desired being for the woman while she is being constructed as the man's possession. The male spectator then constructs his fantasy of the courtesan and at the same time defines himself as the desired man of the woman. But what he is given, apart from the glorious shots of the face, are suggestive narratives veiled in images and metaphors. When the song ends their faces are captured in the water with the moon in between. As they come closer there is a sudden agitation in the pool of water, and the pending embrace can only be inferred. (Sanskrit poetics called this the rhetoric of suggestiveness, *vyangya*.) Again seduction is only hinted at, both discursively and imagistically. "I'll capsize the boat if you come any closer and then . . . ," says Rita/Nargis. "So?" asks Raj. "Then let it be capsized," she replies, changing the anticipated logic of the syntax completely. He comes close to her, but their embrace, shown from behind the foresail, remains veiled. In matters of desire the "dam bhar jo udhar mumh phere" song sequence endorses as explicitly as any other moment in the Raj Kapoor corpus (the director of photography here, as in many of his other films, is Radhu Karmakar) the fact that a woman's desire is subject to male desire and must be veiled.

ROMANCING THE AESTHETIC: THREE MOMENTS OF GURU DUTT

For students of Bombay Cinema, Guru Dutt (1925–64) stands out at one end of an entire tradition that began to take shape with Himansu Rai and P. C. Barua. His "innovation," his individuality, might be better assessed in the context of the nature of the form itself and its cultural antecedents. Nowhere is the nature of that form as a "mode of cultural production/assimilation" (as distinct from formal genre governed by aesthetic norms) (Rajadhyaksha 1993: 59) clearer than in Guru Dutt. There is, in one significant way, no further development of Bombay Cinema as a genre. As Rajadhyaksha has put it, in Guru Dutt "the several streams that have made up Indian Cinema from its inception culminate, achieve a synthesis" (Rajadhyaksha 1985a: 226).

The first significant moment of Guru Dutt on film is *Pyaasa* (The thirsty one, 1957), a film dedicated to Gyan Mukherji, the maker of *Kismet* (1943). The central theme of the film is the Romantic/bourgeois conception of the artist in isolation. This is essentially a Romantic image that made its way into Indian literary consciousness (mediated no doubt by Bengal literary modernism) the moment the colonizer established his foothold in India. Behind the idea of the tortured, isolated artist lies the figure of Shelley, whose lines from "To the Skylark" ("Our sweetest songs are those that tell/of saddest thought") are paradigmatic of the condition of the sensitive hero cum artist in Bombay Cinema. (Talat Mehmood's well-known song, "hair sab se madhur vo gīt jise ham dard ke sur mem̐ gātem̐ hai," in the film *Patita* [The fallen, 1953] is a literal Hindi translation of Shelley's lines.) Superimpose this literary inheritance upon the principle of *nivṛtti*, renunciation, and you get the figure of the Romantic artist who is riddled by philosophical doubts (and is effectively antisocial), becomes totally incompetent, and is excessively sentimental. In terms of rasa theory, the figure evokes once again the aesthetic emotion of *karuṇa*, the dominant rasa of all Indian literature.

Not surprisingly, Guru Dutt's rendition of the auteur/artist—who is lyrical as well as radical—is situated within what Shyam Benegal has called a "profoundly romantic vision of life" (Benegal 1983: 161). Bombay Cinema, of course, can handle this vision extremely well, since the Romantic as renouncer (especially after the success of P. C. Barua's *Devdas*, 1935) is a recognizable "sign" in this cinematic practice. The narrative of *Pyaasa* has this predictability about it. Vijay (Guru Dutt), the spurned poet-lover, is rejected by woman and family alike. The rejection is by people who stand for a rationalist worldview and for whom living in the world necessitates sacrificing love, sexual or motherly. Thus while Vijay's Romanticism can be transformed into verse, packaged, published, and commodified, he himself cannot achieve an authentic social existence. Without wife and family, the social order cannot, finally, allow him self-definition. The Romantic becomes the eccentric, the poet, a lunatic, and poetic emotion generates conundrum and chaos. When Vijay finally appears as the living author of poems published "posthumously," the reaction of the audience itself is one of ambiguous savagery in the wake, first, of a blackout and, second, of a denial by the "true" poet of his own identity. "The Vijay you wish to welcome . . . I am not that Vijay. I am not Vijay," the poet announces on stage. And all hell breaks loose.

In a way, Bombay Cinema had anticipated *Pyaasa*. Devdas, the hero troubled by a death wish, makes way for Vijay, the poet unable to come to grips with the redefinition of the poetic vocation under postcolonial Indian capitalism. But this is to overlook what Guru Dutt finally does with the form. In his hands the form is twisted quite radically, the narrative loosened up, and we get glimpses of the possibility of the reworking of the epic form in the new capitalist order. In this reworking, the text is less rigidly structured, its plot not quite so carefully measured, and the heroic action remains ambiguous to the end. To achieve this, Guru Dutt introduces the figure of a heroine who is neither an *achūt kanyā* (the untouchable girl of Himansu Rai's film of that name) nor a crippled *nartakī* (the dancer of *Kismet*). What we get instead is the figure of the "unromanticized" prostitute, someone like P. C. Barua's Chandramukhi (in *Devdas*) but without her reformist tendencies. For a brief moment women in Bombay Cinema come of age and begin to anticipate their radical representation in Indian Middle Cinema films such as *Ankur* (The seedling, 1974) and *Arth* (Substance, 1983). But for a moment only, as Guru Dutt continues to work within what Ashis Nandy has referred to as popular middle-class cinema. *Pyaasa* must be read, in the final analysis, not through the thematizations of the hero as poet but through the manner in which it reads the marginalized Indian woman. With all his Romantic limitations—Waheeda Rehman as Gulabo is both far too attractive and her sensibility is far too labored—Guru Dutt nevertheless makes the relationship between stars and audience much more complex. In the end the text remains fragile. Despite the elements of the popular—song and sanitized representations that characterize the genre—the text's fragility (formal and ideological) draws us to Guru Dutt as auteur.

The incorporation of the poet into the world of the prostitute, however, must be done, as the form demanded, through some form of devotional mediation. In *Achhut Kanya, Kismet, Devdas,* and even *Awara,* it is the nondiegetic background song or the singing of road minstrels that offers a commentary on the foregrounded situation. In *Pyaasa,* it is the Baul (Bengali devotional) song of love-longing—*bhakti* (devotionalism) crossed with *śṛṅgāra* (erotic love), the tradition of the oscillation between *vipralambha* (love-in-separation) and *sambhoga* (love-in-union)—that has this mediating and, in this instance, purificatory role. (One remembers *Patita* [1953] and *Sadhna* [1958], where quasi-devotional songs have a purificatory role, too.) The itinerant group sings:

> Clasp me closer to your body my beloved
> So that my life may find a meaning.
> The agony of the heart, the fires of my body,
> May they all find peace.

This is a pure Bombay Cinema device that allows for the accommodation of the aberrant or the justification of a karmic event. Unlike the heavy orchestration that we find in *Toofan Aur Diya* (The storm and the lamp, 1956) or the "jis kā koī nahīṁ uskā to khudā hotā hai" (he who has no one still has the Lord) background song of many other Bombay films Guru Dutt uses the moment of sacralization through song (drawing upon the *saguṇa bhakti* of Bengali devotionalism) to connect the woman Gulabo with the itinerant minstrels. The connection opens up the perennial filmic question, "What do women desire?" Framed in a devotional song of love-longing (where profane codes are translated into the sacred) desire is presented as an aesthetic of love-longing. Against the staged spectacle of audience adulation turning to rejection (of the poet), the framing device of the song prepares for a redemptive ending. Although the film ends with an intrusive, if not markedly obsessive, romantic sentimentalism as Vijay explains to Gulabo that he wishes to go to the place "from which I needn't go any further," and asks "sāth calogī" (Will you go with me?), this is no walking-toward-the-sunset scene. The world is renounced, in the Bombay film fashion, but the road to that renunciation has been sufficiently destabilized for the film itself to become a critique of its own limitations. The democratization of the world (that the poet had yearned for) becomes no more than a wish fulfillment, an impossible desire for the nation (Rajadhyaksha 1999: 145). That very impossibility, however, enters the "spectator's reason." Brecht had noted how in epic theater "instead of sharing an experience the spectator . . . [comes] to grips with things" without totally denying "emotion to this kind of theater" (Brecht 1974: 23). The Guru Dutt text locates itself at the cusp of feeling and reason, and invites the spectator to make the choice: romancing the aesthetic does not deprive it of ideology.

When he moved from the representation of one kind of artist, the literary artist, to another, the filmmaker, the broad outlines of the synthesis achieved in *Pyaasa* were taken a step further. In *Kaagaz Ke Phool* (Paper flowers, 1959), Guru Dutt recasts a version of the history of Indian entertainment cinema in a quasi autobiography. Two intertexts that loom large in the film are P. C. Barua's *Devdas* (1935) and, without directly commenting on it, Bimal Roy's remake (*Devdas*, 1955), the latter dedicated to both P. C. Barua and K. L. Saigal. The effect of this is the inscription of a filmic textual tradition from the mid-1930s to the late '40s into the text. Quite early on, for instance, we see the filmmaker Suresh Sinha (Guru Dutt) leaning from the balcony of a theater where Pahari Sanyal and Prithviraj Kapoor's big hit of 1937, *Vidyapati*, is being screened to a full house. The self-conscious reference to another film is nothing new as V. Shantaram had done a mild fillip on *Achhut Kanya's* pretensions by highlighting the contradictions between its lyricism and its ideology in *Aadmi* (1939). In *Kaagaz Ke Phool*, however, the filmic tradition and the *Devdas* intertext signify the first struggle over the nature of this form. In demonstrating how systemic this cinema is, Guru Dutt must deconstruct it first.

At one level, the narrative of *Kaagaz Ke Phool* is a kind of an allegory of the filmmaker, a less complex version of, say, Fellini's *8½*. In terms of historical representation, *Kaagaz Ke Phool* is further removed from its moment

Guru Dutt in Guru Dutt's *Pyaasa*, 1957. The artist estranged. Courtesy National Film Archive of India.

Guru Dutt and Waheeda Rehman in Guru Dutt's *Kaagaz Ke Phool*, 1959. The sentimentalist's self-pity. Courtesy National Film Archive of India.

of creation than *Pyaasa*, in which history was really postcolonial history, the years immediately following Indian independence. At one point, in *Pyaasa*, Vijay makes the historical context explicit by informing the publisher, Mr. Ghosh (his erstwhile lover Meena's husband), that he went to college during 1948–50. It could well be that the events recounted in the fictional world of *Pyaasa* are contemporary with their moment of creation. *Kaagaz Ke Phool* covers an earlier period, more or less from 1935 (the moment of *Devdas*) to the late 1940s. Although there are no dates (no specific year is given), the Anglo-Indian world is readily evident in Sir V. B. Varma's unshaken faith in the efficacy of colonial institutions: "british insāf par mujhe pūrā bharosā hai" (I have full faith in British justice). There is little of the colonial world in the filmic text itself unless we pay careful attention to English breakfast, British idioms, Westernized dress, the English public school system, the linguistic absurdity of colonial Hindi ("kyā māṁgtā hai tum ko," says a receptionist), the affected accent of the Anglo-Indians, and so on. Like *Pyaasa*, however, the generic center of the text is romance. What holds history together is a narrative around a romance structure: hero meets orphaned girl Shanti (Waheeda Rehman) with whom he cannot establish an enduring relationship because he is not totally free. Even after a divorce the family man is not free to act as he wishes. The tension that ensues cannot be resolved by action since the sentimental hero cannot reject his past totally. Drunken Suresh Sinha, the idealist filmmaker, looks back at drunken Devdas, the fictional character, for understanding. To aestheticize romance, the Bombay film must produce its *becārā* complex: the romantic hero renounces love, and history, to celebrate sentimentalism. In the process what triumphs is not narrative structure but rasa theory. History gets displaced by the aesthetic imperative; the king becomes a lover in distress; Rama cries, "priyā hīn ḍarpat man morā" (Without Sita my mind is in agony). But Guru Dutt doesn't do what Barua and the sentimentalists after him did to the form. Tragic love does not explode into a triumphant, cathartic moment. In *Devdas*, Paro rushes out when she hears of Devdas's death, but the gates of the house are closed. In the original version of *Aah* the wedding procession goes past the lifeless body of Raj. In Guru Dutt the sentimentalist either walks away with a mundane question "Will you come with me?" or is seen dead on his chair. The spectator cannot quite get the implied dominant mood of *karuṇa* rasa here since the underlying emotion doesn't have a corresponding *bhāva*, a structure of feeling, in the real world. There is then a degree of "disidentification" between spectator and hero here, a slight mismatch, a slant in the principle of equivalence.

This is not a criticism of Guru Dutt; rather it is a reading of Guru Dutt as a moment at the end of a tradition to which he brings a level of individuality. Central to this individuality are two important features. The first, once again, is the role of women; the second, that of the inscribed intertext. We have already examined the first, and we can simply underline its importance here. Shanti (Waheeda Rehman) is once again a version of Gulabo, without genealogy and operating from the margins of traditional Indian society. She is the woman capable of love and individual happiness. "I've only had a moment of happiness in my life—this single joy—and you wish to deny me even that," she tells Pammy, Suresh's daughter. Against this, the traditional wife is all duty (though Veena is pure antiduty) but not impassioned love. The entry of the "wife" (a category that is effectively indistinguishable from "mother") cancels out love. But the marginalized woman Shanti (who becomes a superstar) is also Waheeda Rehman, whose own relationship with Guru Dutt in the real world (in real, lived history) is couched in such ambiguity. When Guru Dutt committed suicide on October 10, 1964, it seemed as if *Kaagaz Ke Phool* was a poor prelude to a real drama about which no film could be made. "I've seen the loves of this world, one by one everything passes by," the background singer tells us in the movie. There is no confirmation here, only a loss, an absence, a nostalgia. This nostalgia takes us to the second crucial feature of *Kaagaz Ke Phool*—its intertextual resonance, especially in the context of P. C. Barua's seminal film based on Saratchandra Chatterjee's novel *Devdas*.

Cinematically, *Kaagaz Ke Phool* is presented as one seamless flashback: the aging director, Suresh, returns to his former studio and recalls his life. Memory initially centers on the filming of *Devdas* and the director's unease with the star actress who is asked to play the pivotal role of Paro. What the event generates is a history as well as a theory of the construction of the Romantic hero. As history, the intertext clearly alludes to P. C. Barua and also, from the audience's point of view, to the later remake of Barua's classic by Bimal Roy in 1955. The citation of the Barua text establishes a point of reference as well as an autobiographical motif. Is Suresh reenacting the life of P. C. Barua? Hardly. Why, then, does Guru Dutt use it? In one way Barua's text offers a more realistic alternative to Himansu Rai. It is to (Barua's) Calcutta New Theatres rather than to (Himansu Rai's) Bombay Talkies tradition that Guru Dutt largely defers. Yet the expected unity of design one associates with the New Theatre tradition is now broken. For instance, though Saigal/Dilip Kumar's dystopic vision is only occasionally punctuated by the ironic humor of Devdas's companion in the brothel (Pahari Sanyal/Motilal), Dutt presents, as in *Pyaasa*, the infectious humor of Johnny Walker and his parody of Anglo-Indian values which belong to the Bombay Talkies' tradition. Guru Dutt's deference to *Devdas* in *Kaagaz Ke Phool* is thus situated in two not necessarily complementary studio traditions. When the hidden *Devdas* text finally surfaces, it is through palimpsestic cinema. Instead of the completed Waheeda Rehman/Paro text of the inscribed *Devdas* within *Kaagaz Ke Phool*, we are given a fragment of P. C. Barua/Saigal's 1935 version. The intrusion of this text occurs at a particularly significant moment in the film.

In a mechanic's shop, white-haired Suresh writes on a makeshift desk. His daughter is outside in a car; she wants to tell her father she is getting married. Suresh doesn't wish to see her, even though Pammy recognizes the mechanic, an old hand at her father's studio. She goes to Shanti in the hope that she might know her father's address. Distraught, Shanti can't be of any help as she replies disjointedly, "[Suresh] doesn't even know his own life, yesterday, today, tomorrow. . . ." After this, the scene shifts back to a drunken Suresh, who is with a group of equally drunk people. Saigal's song can be heard: "apnī khuśī nā āī nā . . ." (Happiness never came to me . . .). Someone introduces Suresh: "he is the director of *Devdas* . . . there is no certainty in the film world: today the sky's the limit, tomorrow in the gutter." A factual statement such as this is couched in the discourse of the fictive world of film. Saigal's fragment designates that fiction. And *Kaagaz Ke Phool* absorbs that citation only to find itself confined by its limitations. The triumph of the sentimental melodramatic romance is also the triumph of the Bombay film. At best Guru Dutt can aestheticize it, but he cannot explode its conventions totally for fear that the effort would be parodistic. So Guru Dutt consciously constructs a text that locates itself tenuously in the tradition of uncompromising art and the grand syntagm of Bombay Cinema. The point is that faced with the realized, fully articulated realist principle, Bombay Cinema can function, artistically, only as a text like *Kaagaz Ke Phool*. This is what Guru Dutt understood so remarkably well. When he read the form again, he produced, in a singularly tight historical context, a film where once again romance is aestheticized from within the generic principles of Bombay Cinema.

In Wordsworth the subject remembers "spots of time" in a "sense of place." The two establish a profound spatiotemporal nexus for the play of memory which takes the poet to "Tintern Abbey," to the stagnant pools of the Leech Gatherer, and to the many anecdotal narratives that make up *The Prelude*. Bombay Cinema finds a similar fascination with place, which is often a decaying *havelī* or mansion to which the hero returns. Mansions have a solidity, a history that is absent from the *saṃsārik* rendition of life and history found in Indian culture. Guru Dutt's *Sahib Bibi Aur Ghulam* (King, queen, knave, 1962) is all about a mansion and its inhabitants and it is structured like *Kaagaz Ke Phool* (the present—flashback—the present). As in Wordsworth, place in Bombay Cinema becomes a haunting and haunted site, what Geoffrey Hartman, after Mircea Eliade, has called an "omphalos" (Hartman 1971: xii). So we recall *Mahal* (The mansion, 1949), *Nadiya Ke Paar* (Beyond the river, 1948), *Madhumati* (1958), and *Bees Saal Baad* (Twenty years on, 1962), films that use the mansion motif as the occasion for recollections. In *Madhumati,* entry into a mansion triggers Devendra/Anand/ Dilip Kumar's memory ("I remember clearly, probably in my past life . . . "). Similarly, Guru Dutt's film (although Abrar Alvi was the director, Dutt's style is evident throughout this film) begins with the final destruction of a decaying mansion by a construction firm of which the hero is the overseer. In *Madhumati* Dilip Kumar hears the sound of someone sweeping; here Guru Dutt hears a haunting melody ("Come to me, slowly, my beloved") and reconstructs, in his mind, the mansion to which he had come from his village so many years before. Given the self-conscious invocation of the earlier Indian gothics, the film's form too echoes many of the representational characteristics of the gothic: ruined mansion, retrospective narrative, discovery of an object in the ruins that triggers memory, and so on.

The more immediate setting of *Sahib Bibi Aur Ghulam* is the declining fortunes of the feudal classes in Bengal as they struggle to come to terms with the new industrial-capitalist order. The text recalls Satyajit Ray's magnificent *Jalsaghar* (The music room, 1958), on which it is partly modeled. But where Ray, the realist, had opted for unity of design by juxtaposing, finally, precapitalist Indian sensitivity (represented by the feudal landowner) and crass materialism (represented by the emergent industrialist), Guru Dutt, the consummate Bombay auteur, introduces the parallel text of romance. The chronicler of the decaying feudal world is Bhootnath/Atulya Chakravarty (Guru Dutt), the village rustic and *ghulām* (servant). Romance is introduced as an allegory of this condition, as a form of expressiveness through which a critique can be mounted. Bhootnath becomes the pivotal figure in two moments of romance: his own, which is conventional, and that of his feudal master(s), which is disruptive and open-ended. Bhootnath's own romance with Jabba (Waheeda Rehman), daughter of the Brahmo Samaji Subinay Babu, is an occasion for demonstrating the progressive social ideology of the Samajis (the Sanskrit line "brahmakriyā hī kevalam" [nothing but proper action] is displayed on the wall of Subinay Babu's home) who espouse social change over the radicalism of the schoolmaster, for whom violence is essential for anticolonial struggle. Unfortunately *Sahib Bibi Aur Ghulam* doesn't make much use of the politics of the Brahmo Samajis, their lofty intellectual theism, and their historical connections with their founder, Ram Mohan Roy.

In the feudal mansion, romance is of a different order, since in a traditional Hindu marriage, as the saying goes, there is an inverse relationship between a woman's duty and a husband's sexuality. Husbands therefore find fulfillment of desire elsewhere, especially in the house of courtesans, in the space of the *kothā* where men seek "refined companionship and erotic dalliance" even as the wife, unaccustomed to "Lucknow-derived tawaif culture," continues to be "incarcerated inside the home" (Das Gupta 1991: 141–42). The world of the courtesan (*tavāyaf*) allows Guru Dutt to use formulaic features of Bombay Cinema—the mandatory song-and-dance sequences, and the incorporation into the text of the classic *mujrā* dance of the courtesan. The second parallel text is enacted in the space of the mansion. In her desire to keep her husband at home in the evenings, Choti Bahu, the wife played by Meena Kumari, seeks the help of Bhootnath, who provides her with cosmetics and liquor. The collapse of the feudal order is metaphorically generated through the wife's desperate act to possess her own husband but not without insinuating an illicit desire for Bhoothnath. Choti Bahu's nameless addiction, her ambiguous rendition of desire, and her murder by the older Chaudhari brother parallel the final collapse of the economic wealth of the owners of the mansion, whose decadent lifestyles had not prepared them for the new bourgeois world order. The decline of the feudal world and the introduction of new capital (against the backdrop of anticolonial revolution) is designated by Guru Dutt (the auteur) through the modernist (after Bergman) figure of the Timekeeper, the Ghari Babu, who screams, "Run back, run away from these mansions; time is the destroyer of illusions; mansions won't last; only time will, tick, tick, tick, run away, run away." Time, *kāla* (which in Sanskrit also means death), the logic of history, is a madman's scream, leading to suicidal rather than redemptive action. Dramatically staged, the intrusion of the Timekeeper's discourse is crucial to Guru Dutt's rendition of the occluded history behind the space of the mansion, the history that informs us that the man who sells the worthless coal mines to the feudal lords is British. But such is the power of this dramatic staging that, through the universalism of time, we are drawn back into the general aesthetic impulse that controls Guru Dutt's art. Guru Dutt was neither radically altering the form nor offering pure realism. What he achieved in a very significant manner was a reconceptualization of both (Bombay) form and technique.

Auteurs, as I suggested in the theoretical section of this chapter, work from within the entire tradition of cinema. They demonstrate a consciousness of the form, and work in its shadow, even as they present a coherent, "individual" vision. The difficulty, of course, is that although auteur theory began as the search for cinema's equivalent of the author of the literary text (who may have total control of his/her product) it soon became obvious that filmic auteurs are premised on a rather different structure of the production of meaning. Here both the literary author and the literary reader undergo considerable changes. The auteur, whom Andrew Sarris had located at the level of "interior meaning," cannot exist independently of editor, cinematographer, musician, and so on and in this respect is radically different from the literary author. Nor is the reader the same as the spectator since the site of cinematic enunciation is linked to the fulfillment of desire. There is, however, an identifiable style or a coherent vision of the manifest material that stands out, and the aim of cinematic interpretation is to get to the heart of this coherent statement.

As spectator/analyst I have tried to retrace the manifest contents of Bombay auteurs Raj Kapoor and Guru Dutt to their latent meanings. As the qualified subheadings show I have suggested that the identifiable style of Raj Kapoor has to be seen in a quite explicit manipulation of the spectator as voyeur (and desiring subject) and of Guru Dutt in a self-conscious aetheticizing of the Bombay romance. Their film work shapes similar material or interpretive indices—the significance of the song text, a consciousness of the cinematic eye, the mapping over of the personal onto the artistic, a social agenda—but to rather different ends. Because in the Bombay definition the auteur, until relatively recently, has to be star too, film work has to take into account the manner in which the auteur arrives as an already constructed star. In many ways Metz's account of voyeurism finds a remarkable proof text in Raj Kapoor, whose films are self-consciously created to fulfill desire. They are, in other words, relentlessly exhibitionist. Even as the voyeur watches from the keyhole, the Raj Kapoor cinema is "unaware of being watched." Where Raj Kapoor read the eye as the scopophilic eye, Guru Dutt saw the eye as a heavily coded system that spelled out hidden meanings. From within the conventions of romance (and sincerity to the genre is a formal prerequisite of the Bombay auteur), Guru Dutt dragged the spectator into questions about ideological formation so that the significant moments in his text were those that destabilized the seamless narrative: the Timekeeper with his maddening prophecies, the skeleton and the bangle discovered in the excavated site, the song of the minstrel, the invocation of the intertext, and camera work that gave bodies a "random quality" (Mani Kaul). The camera as a structure of desire (Raj Kapoor) and the camera as a means of organizing the ideology of the aesthetic within discourses of romance (Guru Dutt) are crucial markers of the two auteurs discussed in this chapter. These auteurs also carry the dynamism of Bombay Cinema of the 1950s and early 1960s and insinuate idioms that arose in the first full burst of the postcolonial Indian sense of artistic self-assurance.

Chapter Five

THE ACTOR AS PARALLEL TEXT: AMITABH BACHCHAN

To speak about an Indian "actor text" presupposes some cultural understanding of the concepts of "acting" and performance especially in the
domain of drama. The dramatic tradition in India is vast and heterogeneous,
the commentaries on it equally large and complex. An important North
Indian dramatic presentation with a wide currency in North India at least is
Rāmlīlā, a folk theater based on the *Rāmāyaṇa*. In her study of an important
Rāmlīlā in performance—the *Rāmlīlā* at Ramnagar—Anuradha Kapur
(1988) sets up three key modes of representation with which one can begin
to theorize the idea of actor as parallel text. The first may be called the redun-
dant gesture where an actor would repeat "insistently, illogically, passionately,
a single gesture" (7). The aim here is to draw attention (diegetically) and
spectatorially to an important emblem through which he/she has been
marked. It could be the long hair of Sita, a widow's insistence on applying
sindūr or vermilion to the hair-parting (although for the rest of the world her
husband is dead) or simply a wisp of gray hair. The second is the way in
which "spectators collaborate with the actors" in creating intersubjective
meanings since the "*līlā* [play] in performance says something to us about
ourselves" (5). Finally, character in a *līlā* is only a *pātra* (vessel). In this definition a character is like a vessel that contains "qualities of a character" being
portrayed; the actor, in the words of Geeta Kapur, conveys "the attributes and
emotion of a 'character' to the viewer while himself remaining intact" (1987:
89). Although cinema is not a *līlā*, the spectator comes to cinema with a critical vocabulary that grew out of a pre-cinematic experience. The father of
Indian cinema, Phalke, was certainly conscious of that tradition of audience

participation in a performance. From the second half of the nineteenth century especially, Parsi theater fused folk dramas like the *Rāmlīlā* with Western dramatic forms and created a relatively fixed form that was more centrally controlled by the colonial space of the proscenium arch theaters (Anuradha Kapur 1993). We have already seen the ways in which many aspects of Bombay Cinema—frontality, thematic and semiotic eclecticism, the fusion of the realistic with the fabulist, the persistence of the song and music texts, acting as display, and so on—have had a significant impact on the thematics and materiality of this cinema. In isolating the role of the actor as parallel text, one needs to keep these varied indices of theatrical production in mind.

That said, there is no unproblematic antecedent of the Bombay cinematic hero as such. What Bombay Cinema inherits is the form or discourse of various folk theaters, plus their dramaturgical and epic antecedents. As complex signs embodying historical, cultural, and economic meanings, Bombay stars are cultural "compromises" of a bewildering complexity. At the same time as locating and emphasizing the culturally specific antecedents of the Bombay star, it would be foolish to ignore a second crucial problematic—the role of Hollywood stars in this genealogy. For the fact is that Hollywood films dominated Indian middle-class viewing habits until at least the late 1940s. Many of the early Hollywood "stars" had considerable following among Indian audiences: Eddi Polo, Charlie Chaplin, and above all Douglas Fairbanks Sr., whose *The Thief of Baghdad* was immensely popular and spawned many imitations, including *Hind Kesari* (1935), *Husn Ka Chor* (1953), *Baghdad Ka Chor* (1934/46/55). Bombay stars modeled themselves, in part, on them, as readily seen in Raj Kapoor's imitation of Charlie Chaplin, Ranjan and Mahipal's imitation of Douglas Fairbanks and Errol Flynn, and later, Shammi Kapoor's imitation of Elvis Presley (the singer and the star). In Bombay Cinema, stars began to come into their own the moment they were used by independent producers to undermine a burgeoning studio system, which, by the mid-1950s had either closed down or taken over by merchantile investors for hire to independent producers. From around the early 1950s onward, they were wooed away from the studios, where they had been salaried employees, through the offer of vast payments to appear in films made by independent producers. Thereafter, the "star" became the single most important aspect in the production, circulation, and exhibition of films. Popular cinema in India, perhaps even more so than in Hollywood, became the cinema of the star rather than the cinema of the director or the studio. Writing almost exclusively about the construction of the Hollywood star, Dyer (1979) and Ellis (1982) advanced a model for an analysis of stars that has considerable heuristic value. Their key points may be summarized as follows:

(i)   the star's roles should be examined in regard to a culture's precursor text(s);

(ii) through these manifold roles or narrative placements on screen a star gradually accumulates his or her own symbolic "biography";

(iii) the screen biography and the star's actual life intersect, often generating industry deals and occasional political placements;

(iv) the star is a material phenomenon, a physical body with idiosyncratic or stereotypical voice, physiognomy, gestural repertoire, physical agility, and costume;

(v)   the star is iconic whose public reception is manifested in shrines, calendar art, comics, T-shirts, and so on.

To account for the Indian star, this model needs to be expanded. In particular, I will argue that song and dialogic situations constitute two overarching systems that lead to the memorial construction of the star in Bombay Cinema.

To illustrate how stars are constituted in cinemas other than Hollywood I want to examine in some detail the star persona of Amitabh Bachchan. In the ninety-year history of Bombay Cinema no actor has achieved the status of Amitabh Bachchan, and none certainly has found a place in Madame Tussaud's London waxwork museum. He was also, arguably, the last of the pan-Indian film heroes. As sociologist Shiv Vishvanathan has observed (*Sunday Times, Times of India,* September 24, 2000: 1), the current crop of Bollywood heroes have varying constituencies even among Hindi/Urdu speakers: Bobby Deol and Ajay Devgan are popular in Northern India, Sanjay Dutt in Maharashtra and Shah Rukh Khan in the diaspora. From 1973 (the moment of *Zanjeer*) to 1990, Amitabh Bachchan was the dominant figure in Bombay Cinema. He continues to have a major influence through his massive investment in film production and cable TV, through his work as the host of India's most popular quiz show *Kaun Banega Crorepati* (Who wants to be a millionaire?) as well as through his continued, albeit intermittent, appearances in films such as *Hum* (The collective, 1991), *Major Saab* (The major, 1998), *Mohabbatein* (Varieties of love, 2000), and many others. He has starred in literally dozens of films, not all of them successful; he has dominated the fanzines that are such important props of the Indian popular cinema and has consistently been an item of interest in news magazines; and at key moments he has acquired social and political prominence. There are a number of reasons (which I will elaborate in greater detail below) for his phenomenal success. First, Bachchan is the first post-partition major star who came from the Hindi-speaking heartland of Uttar Pradesh and who was thoroughly conversant with standard Hindi as well its dialects, notably Avadhi. Second, his film persona challenged the figure of the noble, transcendent Rama as the dharmik model of the hero. His roles deployed features that belonged to the antihero Karna in the *Mahābhārata* while the generic frames of his films destabilized the dominant cinematic form much as the baroque *Trauerspiel* destablized German tragedy (Mazumdar 2000: 239–40). Finally he projected this antiheroism onto the very modern notion of the angry young man in rebellion (an Indianized John Osborne character) and grafted this onto the figure of a subaltern hero "as an agent of national reconciliation" (Prasad 1998: 141). The rebelliousness thus synthesized reflected the disenchantment, the oppression, the hopelessness of the slum dweller who saw in Bachchan's acts of "antiheroism" a symbol of his or her own aspirations. The rags-to-riches theme that always paralleled the narrative of personal revenge in Bachchan's films was the imaginary fulfillment of the slum dweller's own fantasies. To get the social context right we need to recall that the slum dweller provides cities like Bombay and Calcutta with its everyday labor force, a labor force that would include professional tailors as well as stevedores and extras in films. It is the class that is gradually supplanting the middle class as the primary spectators of cinema. It is also the class that has been the prime victim of an economic liberalism that has heightened the differences between rich and poor. As Fareeduddin Kazmi has pointed out, "It is the articulation of this marginalized sector that largely explains the phenomenon of Amitabh Bachchan" (Kazmi 1998: 140). What is not mentioned by Kazmi is Bachchan's own (contrary) reformulation of the source of this anger in markedly bourgeois (and genetic) terms. *Movie* (September 1983: 41) quotes Bachchan: "There seems to be a strong sense of revolt within me. Probably it is in my genes. I have seen rebellion in my father's writing, in his early life. . . . When I tried to show anger on screen, it seemed to come through beautifully." It is ironic that someone with impeccable middle-class roots (poet father, socialite mother, connections with the Nehru/Gandhi dynasty) begins to espouse the dreams of Bombay shanty dwellers and speaks for them. Since the latter constituency does not have access to fanzines (which circulate only in middle-class literate India) the star persona (as received by the slum dweller) has to be constructed through an essentially oral transmission of the star as a cinematic presence. This is where we need

Amitabh Bachchan in Yash Chopra's *Deewar*, 1975. Rebellious dialogue with God. Publicity Still Kamat Foto Flash.

to take up the construction of the star with reference to the song text and the "dialogic situations." Thus even as we examine our fanzine archives in some detail we need to keep in mind the ways in which "emotion" or "sentiment" actually circulates with reference to a star. Speaking about the failure of Amitabh Bachchan's *Shaan* (1980) the producer Ramesh Sippy stressed that what Indian audiences want most of all are sentiments, "even in the midst of action" (*Movie,* October 1982: 83). We need to keep a critique of emotional judgment firmly in mind as we proceed.

AMITABH BACHCHAN AND FANZINE CULTURE

The fanzine archive I shall use for a reading of the construction of the star in Bombay Cinema ranges from *Filmfare* (latterly a glossy fare with a website and ads that include Cindy Crawford's *Revlon* products and *Durex* condoms), *g, Stardust* (the "most foul of the bitch fanzines"), *Movie, Cine-Blitz* to *Showtime, Screen,* and Hindi magazines such as *Jī-Stār* and *Māyāpurī.* A number of these fanzines are registered in overseas cities such as London (*Stardust*) and Colombo, Sri Lanka (*Screen*). The Indian diaspora, of course, has its own fanzines—many rather ephemeral—such as *Indian Movie News* in Malaysia, *Mehfil, Aaj, Bollywood West,* and *Bollywood Times* in Canada.

Despite the growing internationalism of the movie fanzine market, we need to keep in mind the limited readership in India of fanzines written in English. As the advertisements show so clearly, the target readers of the English-language fanzines are largely middle-class urban dwellers with disposable incomes for whom fanzines are also catalogues of consumer items and fashion. Although there is some overlap, Hindi fanzines have a different, though not necessarily larger, target audience, and need to be considered in any examination of fanzine culture because the ways in which lower-class workers, itinerant city dwellers, migrant labor force, peasants, indeed the general subaltern class, respond to cinema are captured more accurately in the Hindi fanzines. Compared to English fanzines, Hindi fanzines have fewer salacious details, they present the material in a more subdued, suggestive manner, and they don't carry glossy advertisements of expensive luxury items. One need only look at the very subdued *salwar-kameez*–clad August 1993 centerfold of Karishma Kapoor in *Jī-Stār* and the interviews given by Rishi Kapoor in *Māyāpurī* (August 19, 1993) and Aamir Khan in *Jī-Stār* (August 31, 1993) to see a second-order representation and discourse through which Bombay film is disseminated. The contrast between Hindi and English fanzines (a contrast we need to keep in mind always) illustrates the differing levels of reception of Bombay Cinema captured in Hindi and English fanzines. Although it is unwise to construct from the Hindi fanzine a complete subaltern aesthetics of cinema, it is nevertheless an important reminder that there is more than one narrative of reception available to a student of this form.

Clearly Hindi and English fanzines commodify stars rather differently, and it could be argued, and persuasively too, that the use of English fanzines may even lead to a very different reading of the star phenomenon. This qualification should be kept in mind as I return to both Indian and diasporic fanzines for a narrative of Amitabh Bachchan as parallel text. To begin with, English fanzines are a classic vehicle for the crossover of industry publicity and policy and the filmic text, which is the ultimate posit of the star. Industry publicity, control, and policy represent the social institution that produces and determines, in major part, the social consumption and circulation of film as commodity. In the case of Bachchan, industry publicity provides fanzines with a continuous barrage of information: his relations to other stars (male and female), his relations to "starlets" (the ultimate commodity), his achievements in stunts that are used to confirm his masculinity, his ambitions and desires, and speculation about his personal life. When *Time* magazine (April 8, 1991) carried a short piece on the Bombay film called *Hum* (1991), which marked the return of the 48-year-old Amitabh Bachchan and demonstrated

Amitabh Bachchan in Mukul S. Anand's *Hum*, 1991. "Jumma give us a kiss," Bachchan's triumphant return. Publicity Still Kamat Photo Flash.

his staying power, it observed, "During the '70s Bachchan [was] . . . No. 1 through No. 10. There was no one in between." To stay number one through ten, Bachchan consciously cultivated a screen biography of the aggressive underdog, and a personal, real life biography of a disquieting, dark, brooding spirit drawn toward beautiful women as some kind of an aesthetic act.

In constructing a Bachchan "star biography" through the fanzine literature I want to begin by examining a small booklet that appeared with the January 1991 issue of the very upscale (30 rupees or £3 for Indians overseas) fanzine called *g* (a play on "G-string," "gentleman," and the Hindi honorific "jī" meaning "sir"), a glossy magazine in the old *Life* magazine format. The booklet, entitled *Junior g*, carries an account of Amitabh Bachchan's life as told to *g*'s editor Bhawna Somaya. In this account, Amitabh Bachchan frames his recollections in the genre of narrative fiction, recalling, initially, memories of the old gramophone in the house or a particular *dhun* on the sitar. Memories merge into discussions of his father, a Cambridge-educated Hindi poet and English literature academic, his mother, a strong-willed Sikh-Punjabi woman from Lahore, and his younger brother, more intelligent than he but less rebellious. Bachchan attended the University of Delhi and ended up reading for a degree for which he was ill suited—in science. He regrets this, recalling his immense interest in

Shakespeare and Shaw. He moved to Calcutta and did a few years of clerical work, but all the while, he had a burning desire to join the film industry. A pause in the narrative occurs here. Jaya Bachchan (Bhaduri), his wife, speaks now, and her narrative is about how she, also a well-established actor, in fact a Satyajit Ray find, was courted by Bachchan when he was an aspiring actor. (In *Movie*, April 1985: 32, Amitabh Bachchan says that in marrying Jaya he "deprived the Indian screen of a fantastic actress" . . . "I feel Jaya was my best co-star," he added.) Marriage is followed by the meteoric rise of a star who is linked romantically with a number of leading cinema ladies—Zeenat Aman, Rekha, and Parveen Babi—though Jaya herself does not specify any names. She simply adds as an afterthought, "women have always been a problem with Amit. It was so, even when he was not a star." But passions are constructed in a Byronic manner: there is in Bachchan that dark, brooding melancholy, an inwardness at odds with his film persona. And there is poetry too, as is clear from a chapter in the booklet entitled "The Poet's Son." The father, Harivanshrai Bachchan, was the author of a well-known series of poems distantly modeled on Omar Khayyam's *Rubaiyat*, called *Madhuśālā*, which had gone into its twenty-fourth edition by 1979. Composed in 1935, its subsequent English translation by Marjorie Boulton (*The House of Wine*) carried a foreword by Jawaharlal Nehru, India's first prime minister. The offhand transcription of his father's poem in the *devanāgarī* script in *Junior g* underlines the homage that the popular makes to high art.

The "stargraph" offered by *g* magazine came after Amitabh Bachchan had reached his peak. Despite the success of *Hum* later that year, by 1991 Bachchan's own star appeal was on the wane. So what we must do now is look back at the preceding twenty years and trace that career forward to the present. I will do this by reconstructing a Bachchan narrative once again through a selective citation from the surfeit of material available on him in the fanzines.

Let me begin with an early account of the actor given in *Star and Style* (May 1, 1970: 33):

A science graduate of Delhi University and son of the famous Hindi poet Bachchan, Amitabh possesses a sensitive face and his peculiar manner of parting his hair gives him a gentle look, a point which might have gone in his favour when K. A. Abbas interviewed him and at once selected him to play a role in his "Saat Hindustani."

Amitabh portrays a meaty role in the film—that of a meek poet among the seven Indian revolutionaries who cross into Goa to fight against the Portuguese. . . . The young actor is very grateful to Mr Abbas who has given him such a well-etched role to play in his first experience with grease-paint. Amitabh is also playing key roles in Sunil Dutt's "Reshma aur Shera" [where he plays the role of a mute brother] and Mehmood Productions' "Bombay to Goa" based on a Tamil hit.

Neither *Saat Hindustani* (Seven Indians, 1969) nor the other films mentioned in the passage above were in any way significant. His performances in these films were no great shakes, and Bachchan was happy to accept, even as these films were in production, a lesser role opposite the reigning superstar Rajesh Khanna in *Anand* (1970). Yet *Anand*, a thoroughly professional work by director Hrishikesh Mukherji, brings out many of the later characteristics of Amitabh Bachchan. There is the same anger, the same unease with the definition of the heroic role. These get expressed by a slightly different gaze at the camera and one that counterpoints significantly the free-flowing movement of Rajesh Khanna. One also sees in Amitabh Bachchan's portrayal of the doctor hints of the rebelliousness for which he was to become famous. "When I signed on *Anand*," says Amitabh, "I was more excited about working with THE Rajesh Khanna." He adds, "Then came *Zanjeer*" (*Movie*, April 1985: 26–32, 26).

Then, indeed, came *Zanjeer* (The chain, 1973). The phrase is reprised, with variation, in the fanzines many times. So we read in *Movie* (September 1984: 41):

[Before *Zanjeer* Amitabh was] written off as a disaster. Then the "impossible" happened: *Zanjeer*. Made by a nearly bankrupt Prakash Mehra, the film went on to become a sensational hit (sold for 12 lakhs, it raked in 60 lakhs per territory) and launched the new, angry, young, violent Amitabh Bachchan.

Zanjeer is so important for the construction of the Amitabh Bachchan parallel text that we must pause to examine it in somewhat greater detail. The main role was offered to established actors first—Dev Anand, Dharmendra, Raaj Kumar, even Dilip Kumar—and came to Amitabh Bachchan on the rebound. The theme of this film is revenge placed in the context of cure for a personal trauma and public responsibility since the hero is now a police inspector. In challenging a notorious criminal, the police inspector brings about the end of a thoroughly unscrupulous and despicable bootlegging mogul but he also cures the cause of a recurring nightmare about a dark rider on a white horse. Revenge here is clearly a cure for a repressed memory going back to the Diwali night when his parents were shot by Teja, the crime boss. But revenge is also shown as a pleasurable but transgressive moment, which is why the dharmik order closes in upon itself soon after the lid on repressed pleasure has been lifted. The film also marks the return, in a radically different form, of an earlier Bombay genre of revenge. The role of the villain Teja is played by Ajit (Hamid Ali Khan, a Muslim, who changed his name in the early 1950s), the swashbuckling hero of earlier films on the theme of revenge, notably *Samrat* (1954) and *Baradari* (1955), as well as the lapsed believer in *Nastik* (The atheist, 1956). In these films vengeance is not linked to a social cause and is purely generic. In *Zanjeer* vengeance carries a quasi-revolutionary fervor (public revenge) that is also directly linked to a private trauma. This is why the dream text in *Zanjeer* is significant. It is true that the dream sequence fills no more than a few frames of the film, but it is a highly concentrated dream text. The use of the horse taps into the importance of the *aśvamedha* (horse sacrifice) and the *aśvins* (the twin horse-headed gods) generally in Indian consciousness. Wendy Doniger O'Flaherty (1980) has written sensitively on the subject, and I can do no more than gesture toward her conclusions. It is clear that the *aśva* (horse) enters Indic consciousness at a crucial phase, displacing the bull and effectively effacing the mare. After this phase the stallion and the cow reign supreme in Indian mythology. In *Zanjeer* the horse and the rider frame the villain as father substitute and castration threat in the general symbology of the phallic horse in Indian culture. The first representation of the *aśva* nightmare in the film is presented as a twice repeated shot of the horseman crossing the frame left to right. This is a slightly unusual form of Bombay representation because the Bombay film normally codifies such sequences through repeat zooms as in the flash visions of Rishi Kapoor in *Karz* (1980) or as a single shot as in *Babul* (Childhood home, 1950). For us the significance of the shot lies in the manner in which it metonymically connects with the miniature horse that was on the villain's bracelet the night he slaughtered the hero's parents. As a child, the hero sees this from the closet where he is hiding. What *Zanjeer* does is connect the power of horse symbolism (always threatening, always ambiguous) with the figure of Amitabh Bachchan. The conjunction of actor and the symbolic horse creates Amitabh Bachchan as a "complex text" sanctioned by mythology and able to respond to the need for rebelliousness in the restless Indian lower-middle and slum-dwelling classes (the target population of the Indian film industry as a whole) and a resurgent patriotism after the 1971 Indo-Pakistan war. Although the immediate response to the film by the fanzines was not particularly positive—*Star and Style* (June 8, 1973: 35), for instance, declared that it was a poor imitation of *Dirty Harry*, already plagiarized in the same year by F. C. Mehra in *Khoon Khoon* (Murder! murder! 1973), and

**Publicity poster for Prakash Mehra's *Zanjeer*, 1975. Bachchan's career-making film.
Courtesy National Film Archive of India.**

Filmfare (June 1, 1973: 35) gave it a score of 1 out of 4—the film is the foundational Amitabh Bachchan text and one that will have a special place in any survey of Bombay Cinema.

After *Zanjeer*, *Deewar* (The wall, 1975), *Sholay* (Flames, 1975) (for which he was paid only 1 lakh rupees, though the taxation department has never believed him on this), and *Amar Akbar Anthony* (1977) followed in quick succession, and his preeminence was sealed. By the end of the decade he had no equal. "After 1980," writes *Movie* (September 1984), "Amitabh went from strength to strength, soon getting to be regarded as a 'one man industry.'" More enthusiastically we are told "he was undoubtedly the greatest *star* in the history of the Indian film industry." From 1980 to 1984, *Movie* informs us, he starred in nearly every major hit: *Dostana* (Bonding, 1980), *Naseeb* (Good fortune, 1981), *Laawaris* (The orphan, 1981), *Namak Halaal* (The ungrateful, 1982), *Khuddar* (Shreds, 1982), *Andhaa Kaanoon* (Blind justice, 1983), *Coolie* (1983), and *Sharaabi* (The drunkard, 1984). Even his minor films grossed more at the box office than the films of almost all the other film stars. In fact, of the fifty-seven releases up to 1984, only five of Amitabh's films were in the red: *Zameer* (1975), *Faraar* (1975), *Alaap* (1977), *The Great Gambler* (1979), and *Do Aur Do Paanch* (1980). As we have already indicated, *Zanjeer*, his thirteenth film, was a superhit. Between that

time and the success of *Hum* (1991), however, seven others had reached the
great distinction of what Indian fanzines call a "super-super hit": *Deewar*
(director Yash Chopra), *Sholay* (Ramesh Sippy), *Amar Akbar Anthony*
(Manmohan Desai), *Muqaddar Ka Sikander* (1978; Prakash Mehra), *Naseeb*
(Manmohan Desai), *Laawaris* (Prakash Mehra), and *Coolie* (Manmohan
Desai). Fanzines invariably make comparisons between Amitabh Bachchan's
success and Rajesh Khanna's meteoric rise between 1969 and 1972 (from
Aradhana to *Apna Desh*) when he too rewrote the annals of Bombay Cinema
by single-handedly wiping out other major film stars and rewriting the record
book of popular film hits. But soon afterward Khanna fell, probably a victim
of his own cockiness and—such is the morality of Bombay Cinema and the
fickleness of the filmgoers—his overhasty marriage to Dimple Kapadia, a sensational actor of 16 who was largely responsible for Raj Kapoor's hit *Bobby*
(1973). The fanzines dwell fondly on Bachchan's punctuality, his profession-
alism (*Cine Blitz* [April 1982] and *Movie* [April 1985]), his dedication, his
willingness, his careful improvisations on the script, and his extraordinary
sense of commitment to artistry in an industry that really functions on the
basis of shift work. There are also carefully constructed commentaries on the
voice behind the corporeal body. In *Laawaris* we hear his voice first, and then
we see his face. In *Chupke Chupke* (Silently, silently, 1975) he speaks to
Dharmendra for a full three minutes before he is shown, and in *Hum* the
powerful narrative voice-over is Amitabh Bachchan's. (Satyajit Ray used his
voice in *The Chess Players,* too.) There is also a dialogue in *Hum* on the differences between biological and social bacteria—all done more or less in
monologue—in which "Tiger"/Bachchan speaks to Jumma's brother
Gonzales for a good five minutes. The allegorical nature of this narrative—
biological bacteria can be killed by insecticide, moral bacteria infects society
and destroys it—means that standard metaphors of the slum are deployed to
make abstract statements about the ethical order. The fanzines point out on
many occasions that without Bachchan's voice all these scenes would have
collapsed. But there is also a carefully publicized selective biography in which
a comfortable middle-class life is reclassified as the picaro who comes to
Bombay with only his driving license, not unlike the Raj Kapoor character in
Shree 420 and *Jagte Raho,* who also came to the city-without-compassion and
is rejected by it.

Just as *g* celebrated its second anniversary with a special feature on
Amitabh Bachchan, so did *Movie* (September 1983) when it opened an office
in London to cater to the large British South Asian diaspora. In basing its first
"international" cover story on Amitabh Bachchan—"One Is a Lonely

Number," the heading triumphantly declared—*Movie* affirmed Bachchan's huge appeal both in India and in the diaspora. Apart from the predictable news that is the staple of fanzines (an actor's many affairs with glamorous leading ladies, his love-hate relationship with gossip columnists, and so on), the article isolates two key elements of Bachchan's personality: a brooding melancholy plus explosive anger. The former is clearly a contrived poetic effect through association with his father, the second a feature of his own filmic personality. What gets stressed again and again is a hero in rebellion, a hero who is egalitarian but introverted and incapable of romance. In short, even as Bachchan is celebrated, the flip side of him marginalizes the female actor and excludes her from the center of the cinema. In this respect, Bachchan altered a major component of the practice of Bombay Cinema, thereby foreclosing, in a sense, the heritage of the female star. Except for Rekha, few female actors of any real power emerged until Madhuri Dixit in the late 1980s. As Rajadhyaksha and Willemen have observed, in Bachchan's films women can be no more than melodramatic mothers or liberated girl-friends (1999: 49–50).

The change brought about by Bachchan in the traditional concept of the hero ("the latest poet of mass culture," as Shekhar Hattangadi called him in *Filmfare,* November 16–20, 1978: 20–25) had an enormous impact on Bombay Cinema. The antihero now manipulates the revenge theme (where he can best function) to rewrite the hitherto ridiculed figures of the failed husband (*Do Anjane* [Two strangers], 1976), the innocent turned avenger (*Ganga Ki Saugandh* [I swear on the Ganges], 1978), the hireling (*Sholay,* 1975), and the zealous cop (*Zanjeer,* 1973). As late as *Hum* (1991) the two sides—hero and antihero—function side by side. In this film, "Tiger" (Amitabh Bachchan) runs away from violence only to find that he must return to it years later because the moral order had turned cankerous once again: "When there is adharma on the ascendant, then do I reincarnate myself," Krishna had told Arjuna in the field of battle. There is something deep-seated here, as if the entire politics of nonviolence did not, finally, lead to the kind of moral uplift Gandhi had in mind when he raised nonviolence to the highest principle of action. Amitabh Bachchan's anger is possible only in an India no longer comfortable with the Gandhian ideology of nonvio-lence. Indeed, contemporary India is a very violent nation in which almost unparalleled killings—by the state and by the insurgents—have been con-doned. The growth in "private gangsterism and parallel government," the passing of the Terrorist and Disruptive Activities Prevention Act and the introduction of a number of repressive laws (Kazmi 1998: 153) constitute the backdrop to the Bachchan hero in rebellion. Can one say that Bombay Cinema has quietly (and inadvertently) colluded with the rise of separatist and communal violence in India by justifying, in art, the efficacy and imperative of individual revenge outside of the law? Does sanitized violence in cinema spawn the frighteningly real violence outside? There is, of course, epic antecedent at work here in the figure of none other than Karna, the *Mahābhārata*'s antihero in rebellion, the eldest finally throwing his weight with the enemy. But just as Kunti has no place in Karna's world—the mother's pleas fall on deaf years when Kunti confesses the dark secret of Karna's parentage to him—so women remain totally in the margins of the Bachchan text. Masculine domination is such that Amitabh Bachchan's films are really one-actor genres whose closest counterparts are the Hollywood westerns. The fanzines do not overlook the antiwoman, antifeminist, and sometimes even antimother stance of the Bachchan persona in films. In *Filmfare* (February 1–15, 1980: 17–21), Sheela Naheem points to hints of "misogyny" in Bachchan's films and notes that rarely does the hero enter into "warm heterosexual relations." Bachchan thus redefines the Romantic hero—the tradition from K. L. Saigal to Rajesh Khanna—and banishes the centrality of romance. Vengeance precludes love; the Jacobean revenger cannot love, as dying Vindice in *The Revenger's Tragedy* (1607) declares at the end, "when we ourselves are foes." The Amitabh Bachchan hero propels the antihero into that position but does not give him Vindice's voice. In the end, as fanzine critics like Shekhar Hattangadi had noted (*Filmfare* 1978), the genre of revenge itself became exhausted, as did Bachchan. In Amitabh Bachchan's films anger and revenge become rituals which, finally, destroy the idea of "character." Motivation is replaced by generic predictability; the twist at the end that kept many of the earlier romances in business—will the woman in question return to the hero?—is no longer part of the design of the narrative. For Bombay Cinema to survive, the romantic twist had to return. And so as Bachchan's star waned, romance returned. From *Maine Pyar Kiya* (Yes I've fallen in love, 1989) to Mani Rathnam's *Dil Se* (With love, 1998) and the recent films of the comic-hero Govinda (*Maharaja, Dulhe Raja, Naseeb* [Destiny], 1997) romance underpinned the social as well as the political and once again became the centerpiece of Bombay Cinema.

As we reconstruct the star personality through the fanzines we also come across carefully placed self-reflections. At the end of the interview with Pammi Bakshi in *Movie* (September 1983), Bachchan frames his own future (and demise) as a kind of a Guru Dutt figure. In a conscious echo of *Kaagaz Ke Phool* and to K. A. Abbas's own account of how he, Abbas, first inter-

Amitabh Bachchan in Tony's _Insaniyat_, 1994. An older Bachchan safeguarding the nation with a semi-automatic. Publicity Still Kamat Foto Flash.

viewed him and offered Bachchan a role in _Saat Hindustani_ (Abbas 1977), he projects a future for himself in which the "star" is constructed as an ephemeral being whose name is followed by a director's dismissive comment—"please do not waste my time" (48):

> Then one day while shooting with a crowd of about fifty junior artistes, the director will ask his assistant, "Woh crowd mein lamba kaun hai? Familiar lagta hai."
>
> The assistant will give a second look and say, "Sir yeh woh actor tha na?"
>
> "Kaun?"

"Sir, woh Amitabh Bachchan!"

"Achcha, achcha, mera time mat waste karo! Ready everyone?"

"Sound—Camera—Action."

There are three subtexts (the third is primarily nonfanzine based) around the figure of Amitabh Bachchan that I should now wish to examine. The first two are central to his star persona, the third draws us to the links between star and power in Indian culture. The first subtext is Bachchan's relationship with heroines (an important element in the construction of the star); the second subtext is the narrative of his near fatal accident on the sets of *Coolie*. The third subtext—the Bofors affair—was taken up by highbrow journalism in light of his close friendship with Rajiv Gandhi and his very brief foray into Indian politics.

AND THEY CALLED HER REKHA

In the interview already referred to above, Pammi Bakshi asks Amitabh Bachchan, "Where does Rekha stand with you today?" The question is linked to earlier questions about two other leading stars: Zeenat Aman, a onetime Miss India, and Parveen Babi, whose face appeared on the cover of *Time* magazine on July 19, 1976. Both had been romantically linked with Bachchan. In the case of the Rekha question the answer is an abrupt, "What do you mean where does she stand with me *today*? Rekha was my leading lady. *Just that*." The overemphasis in the case of Rekha suggests something deeper in the relationship and requires a second look. Rekha emerged as the consummate Bollywood female actor in the late 1970s and early 1980s. In *Movie* (January 1984) Supriya Pathak said that she had everything: "charm, grace, warmth," and Anita Ray placed her in the tradition of Madhubala, that extraordinarily beautiful face of the 1950s whose haunting looks were put to such effective use by Kamal Amrohi in *Mahal*. Daughter of the Tamil/Hindi actor Ganeshan, Rekha came with classical good looks, a tall frame, and real acting abilities. Although the genre does not require or nurture real acting talent— the scripts do not allow for character development, and the piecemeal nature of the filming procedure (up to five shifts a day on five different films in some instances) makes concentration difficult—Rekha became one of those rare actors who brought a real sense of character to the films. The Bachchan-Rekha affair was extensively documented in the fanzines, and like another more open affair—that of Hema Malini and Dharmendra—it probably added to the growth of what sounds like a quietly sanctioned counternarrative by Bachchan himself. When Amitabh Bachchan began to be hounded by pop journalists, he finally banned them from his presence, which added to his mystique and to an even more extensive treatment of the relationship in the fanzines. But no such act of censorship took place with *Silsila* (Continuity, 1981), where film avowed through fiction what the star disavowed in the real world: the triangular relationship of Jaya Bhaduri, Amitabh, and Rekha. In Rekha's case the disavowal was considerably less. When the authoritites raided her flat for tax evasion, she told *Filmfare* (November 16–30, 1984: 12): "Every woman expects the man she loves should come and support her. But that didn't happen." She reflects, "He wasn't my husband, what duty did he owe me?" Then she constructs an image of herself as the other woman, the seductress who is hated by her lover's family. Without making the point explicit, she more or less implies that had she been Jaya Bhaduri, she would have left him: "Without respect love is nothing." Unlike other stars involved in relationships, such as Nargis and Raj Kapoor, Rekha makes no attempt to rewrite the past, either in real life or filmically. There is, in other words, no film like Nargis's *Lajwanti* (The chaste wife, 1958) in which she symbolically rewrites her past and gives the spectator an alternative narrative of herself.

In isolating this relationship I want to underline the nexus between the construction of a star personality and a star's relationship with his leading ladies. Although Bachchan denied having had an affair with Rekha, we note that he is aware of the importance of the relationship and its use in the fanzines as a crucial component of his own image as star. The star is thus not simply a screen image; he or she is also a product of a fanzine culture that successfully conflates filmic and real lives. Before I move on, there is a coda to this narrative of Rekha that needs to be noted. In February 1990 she married, rather abruptly it appears, a businessman named Mukesh Agarwal. (It must be said that this is not uncommon among Bombay stars. In October 1999, the reigning queen of Bombay stardom, Madhuri Dixit married, equally suddenly it seems, a Los Angeles–based nonresident Indian doctor.) By July, Rekha's marriage had reached a dead end, and within days Agarwal committed suicide (the popular press declared that he hanged himself with Rekha's *dupaṭṭa* or shawl) while Rekha was in New York. The marriage was strange to say the least. She had met him only once before. Marriage and a too brief London honeymoon only showed her all the reasons why they should not have gotten married. He wanted glamor and easy entry into the glittering world of Indian cinema, as well as political introductions. Asked by a reporter why she had rushed into this marriage (*Filmfare,* December 1990: 29) she replied: "But there is no logical answer. All I can say is that it was destined to happen. It was God's will." At the time of the interview, she was also making *Phool Bane Angaray* (Flowers became embers, 1991), a film that uncannily echoed her own recent past.

DEATH OF THE HERO OF OUR TIME

> On August 2 [1982] I was declared clinically dead. Jaya had gone to the Siddhi Vinayak temple and she rushed back. Panic-stricken she stood outside the ICU [intensive care unit], watching the doctors' attempts to revive me . . . apparently in vain. Suddenly she screamed from outside. Don't give up, I just saw his toe move. Please keep trying. The doctors started massaging my feet upwards. And I came back to life.

In the interview (*Movie*, September 1983) Bachchan continues, "The doctors had told me to report for work sometime in August 1983. I reported on January 7, 1983. And started from where I had left off—the same sequence of *Coolie* that I had left incomplete." Indians have shown their epic capacity to mourn. Singers who die young like K. L. Saigal were mourned by the entire nation. Thousands also lined the funeral procession when two other great singers died: Mukesh and Mohammed Rafi. But nothing in Indian film history—not even the death of Raj Kapoor in 1988—had the same impact on the Indian nation as the weeks in which Amitabh Bachchan lay in a hospital fighting for his life in 1982. As I've done throughout this chapter, I will reconstruct the narrative of what I've called "Death of the Hero of Our Time" from accounts of it in the fanzines, and again as a means of filling out the construction of Amitabh Bachchan as parallel text.

It is a typical Saturday afternoon in July 1982. There is nothing significant in Hindu astrological terms about the date, which is the 24th. And Bangalore, the garden city of southern India, is certainly less humid and sticky than the rest of India, where monsoon rains have held their sway for almost three months. Manmohan Desai (the co-director) is working here on parts of his film *Coolie*, a typically ordinary narrative in the style of the post–*Zanjeer* films of Amitabh Bachchan. The scene being shot is an indoor scene—which could have been filmed in any number of studios in Bombay—in which the hero is punched in the abdomen by the villain. The villain, Puneet Issar, a Kung Fu sixth-degree black belt and karate expert, goes through the rounds of simulating a punch at Bachchan's stomach, then at his face, after which he is to be thrown upon a desk. As a general rule the simple simulated punch would feature Amitabh Bachchan and Puneet, but the more difficult sequence (the falling on the desk) would require the services of a double. It is an ordinary steel-rimmed office table with drawers made of soft wood or chipboard so that if need be it will easily break upon impact. Amitabh Bachchan, however, thinks the shot will be more realistic if he does both sequences, taking the simulated punch to the abdomen and the face, a sudden fall on the desk, then executing a half-somersault that will land him on the other side of the desk. The director agrees and Bachchan gets his way. The sequences with Puneet Issar and Amitabh Bachchan go very well, and the camera crew does not ask for a retake. However, as Bachchan gradually collects himself, his face tense and discolored, he says he is in some pain. The others check his stomach and see no signs of bruise or cut. Bachchan walks about and goes through the routine exercises of moving himself sideways and bending down to touch his toes. But the pain lingers, and with it a faint, nauseating taste in his mouth. The next day, Sunday, he stays in his hotel all day, his condition worsening, and by nightfall he is in considerable pain, with bouts of loss of consciousness. On Monday he gets himself admitted into St. Philomena Hospital in Bangalore. The doctors take X rays of his chest and abdomen, find no signs of abrasion or broken bones, and shrug off the case. On Tuesday, however, Bachchan is in extreme pain. He is incoherent in his speech, fails to recognize people easily, and confuses names. At this point, as in a Bombay film, enters the figure of Dr. H. S. Bhatt from the prestigious hospital in Vellore. He is shown Bachchan's X rays and immediately spots a dark shade around the intestine area and becomes worried. Seventy-two hours after the accident, the undigested food could have turned poisonous, and the body's immune system would be hard-pressed at this late stage to neutralize the poison in the blood system. The only solution is immediate operation.

Dailies in Bangalore were rife with rumors. Puneet Issar was targeted by all as the villain who had a grudge against stars and had purposefully made his punch lethal. Others changed the fifteen-second sequence into a complicated fight sequence in which fists as well as legs were used. The hero's fall was magnified into a twenty-foot fall. Amitabh Bachchan's screen presence as the indestructible hero made people think that only an extraordinary event could have led to his injury. Yet the accident itself was minor, and as *Filmfare* points out, Amitabh Bachchan was a victim of the "VIP syndrome." "An ordinary man would have been quickly operated upon and survived" (September 1–15, 1982: 12). It was because septicemia had set in that matters became complicated—so complicated, in fact, that for a week he needed a tracheotomy tube to breathe.

On August 2, 1982, Bachchan was declared clinically dead at the Breach Candy Hospital in Bombay. It was then that Jaya screamed from outside the

ICU that she saw signs of life and doctors revived him. His condition deteriorated on August 5, and there was panic in the hospital (*Filmfare*, September 1–15, 1982). Throughout India dramatic scenes were being performed. A child offered to give his life to save his hero. For once there was no shortage of blood donors in India. Both in Bangalore and subsequently at the Breach Candy Hospital in Bombay, pilgrims from all over India came and went. Fans thronged the hospital every day, temples, mosques, churches, and *gurudvāras* were full. The hospital visitors list included Shashi Kapoor, Prakash Mehra, Amjad Khan, Manoj Kumar, and Zeenat Aman. Rajiv Gandhi cut short his American trip to visit his friend in hospital on August 5. Prime Minister Indira Gandhi, too, made a "purely personal and private" visit (*Filmfare*, September 1–15, 1982: 11) on August 8. But Rekha did not come, and gossip columnists picked this up, remarking, as if faking Rekha's point of view, "the hero is a straw dog after all" (*Filmfare*, September 1–15, 1982: 11). A 6 P.M. bulletin was issued daily by the hospital to keep journalists and inquisitive visitors informed. The statements were characteristically vague but comprehensive enough to give journalists something to work from.

The hero survived. And on January 7, 1983, Amitabh Bachchan was back on the sets of *Coolie* to complete the sequence broken off because of his accident. Billboards proclaiming "God is Great! Amitabh is Back" could be seen in cities from Bombay to Patna. When the film—*Coolie*—was released later that year, the producers capitalized on Bachchan's close encounter with death by freezing the moment of the decisive punch and holding a caption to the frame that explained to the audience the significance of that incident in the life of the nation: the hero of our time becomes pure simulacrum.

THE BOFORS AFFAIR

In 1985 Amitabh Bachchan entered the Indian Parliament from the Allahabad constituency as a gesture of support for his politically inexperienced friend Rajiv Gandhi, who had become prime minister on a sympathy vote following his mother's assassination the previous October. Two years later, in 1987, Bachchan quit politics. In one sense this was a very natural thing to do—unlike Bombay Cinema, Indian politics cannot be cleaned overnight through the intercession of the angst-ridden modern epic hero. But soon there was talk of underhand deals between Rajiv Gandhi and a Swedish supplier of military hardware. There were persistent rumors that the Swedish firm Bofors had bribed key Indian politicians, including the prime minister, to ensure that the Indian government would buy Bofors's tanks. In the two years that Bachchan was a parliamentarian he held no cabinet position and clearly had no direct dealings with decisions made by the cabinet. But he was a close friend of Rajiv Gandhi, he probably had connections with banks, and more important, he had easier access to hard foreign currency than did Rajiv Gandhi himself. In 1987 Bachchan and his brother, Ajitabh (then a Swiss resident) were connected to a forged letter (a letter rogatory) relating to the Bofors purchase. Although both Rajiv Gandhi and the Bachchan brothers denied wrong dealing, allegations of bribery persisted and were a contributing factor in Gandhi's defeat in the 1989 elections. Immediately upon gaining office the new National Front coalition government led by Prime Minister V. P. Singh began a thorough investigation into Rajiv Gandhi's involvement in the scandal. In the course of investigations the Swedish paper *Dagens Nyheter* claimed (on January 31, 1990) that one of the six accounts under investigation in the Bofors affair belonged to the Bachchan brothers. Amitabh Bachchan immediately sued *Dagens Nyheter* for libel "for naming him as the man behind a Swiss account containing money from payoffs in the Bofors deal" (*India Today*, August 15, 1990: 39), but the case was not defended. Instead the newspaper editor, Christina Jutterstrom, offered an apology in the English high court on July 19, 1990, in which she said that she had been misled by Indian government investigators. This was followed, in December 1990, with the judge of the Swiss cantonal court clearing the Bachchan brothers of any involvement in the payoff by Bofors. Public scrutiny of the brothers didn't end there, however. The Singh government opened up investigations (through the Commerce Ministry) into possible tax evasion and violation of foreign exchange laws by the Bachchan brothers. As so often happens in India, another change in government meant that even these investigations were discontinued. The Bofors affair was recounted at various levels in both fanzines (peripherally) and serious journalism (extensively). Some people, it was suggested, did run away with the Bofors booty (by way of payoffs): the Gandhi family, some claimed openly (a charge sheet belatedly filed in a Delhi court on October 22, 1999, named Rajiv Gandhi as one of the accused), the Bachchans quite possibly. In a curious way the years of the scandal (1987–90), following hard on the heels of a disastrous two-year political foray, marked the decline of Amitabh Bachchan as star. Between 1988 and 1990 almost all of Bachchan's films flopped at the box office. These included *Gangaa Jamuna Saraswathi* (1988), *Main Azaad Hoon* (Freedom, 1989), *Toofan* (The storm, 1989), *Jaadugar* (The magician, 1989), and *Agneepath* (The path of fire, 1990). It wasn't until August 1990 that something of the old Bachchan reappeared in *Aaj Ka Arjun* (The modern Arjun, 1990) and a year later in *Hum*. The latter led to a lead article in the

Illustrated Weekly of India, February 9–10, 1991, under the title "A Quiet Comeback" in which the success of *Hum* is placed alongside interviews with Bachchan about the Bofors affair.

The correlation between scandal and failure is far too neat, and at any rate no causal connection between the two should be made. The decline of Bachchan as hero, as a parallel text that is, has to do with the 1990s return to romance and song (the key film here is *Hum Aap Ke Hain Kaun*), precisely the kind of things that Bachchan had turned his back on so as to carve out a new space for the Bombay hero. This is not to say that in terms of publicity 1990 was not one of his best years. In May 1990 he performed at the Giants Stadium in New Jersey to a packed audience of forty-five thousand, and four months later, in September, he made a spectacular entry on a white horse for a performance ("Jumma Chumma in London") at Wembley Stadium. The 1990s, however, saw the arrival of actors in their early twenties with a different modern agenda, as reflected so consummately in Shah Rukh Khan. If the 1970s and '80s are marked by *Zanjeer, Sholay, Amar Akbar Anthony, Deewar,* and *Coolie,* the decisive films of the '90s are *Maine Pyar Kiya* (Yes I've fallen in love, 1989), *Khalnayak* (The antihero, 1993), *Hum Aap Ke Hain Kaun* (Who am I to you? 1994), *Dilwale Dulhania Le Jayenge* (Lovers win brides, 1996), *Dil To Pagal Hai* (The heart is a wild thing, 1997), *Dil Se* (With love, 1998), *Kuch Kuch Hota Hai* (Sometimes things do happen, 1998), and the films of the talented comic hero Govinda (*Dulhe Raja,* etc). The turn of the millennium has created films—*Fiza, Mission Kashmir*—that invoke the unity of the Indian nation-state and the new, vulnerable but heroic film sensibility of actor Hrithik Roshan.

I have argued that Bachchan's preeminence in Indian popular films, his status as a star, his social significance, and potential political eminence attest to the power of cinematic discourse. While fanzines can be quickly dismissed as ephemera, and a legitimate claim made that the construction of the star primarily through an English fanzine archive elides the value of fanzines in the vernacular, the position they accord Bachchan is underscored by the more serious Indian press, as shown in *India Today*'s treatment of him. Referring to Bachchan's injury while filming *Coolie,* it wrote:

> Bachchan, the near indestructible superstar who had battled seemingly insur-
> mountable odds in thousands of celluloid frames, was fighting the most epic and
> riveting battle of all—for his life. . . . Childhood friend Rajiv Gandhi broke off his
> trip to the United States . . . among Prime Minister Indira Gandhi's first appoint-
> ments after her return was a flying visit to see the stricken star. (August 1982: 32)

The uses we have made of the fanzine material provide the kind of commentary that is crucial to the construction of the Dyer and Ellis model. There are, however, some unanswered questions that remain if we return to the heuristic model referred to earlier in the chapter. First, how does Bachchan, or the parallel text, get inscribed into Indian consciousness? What is the nature of the initial moment of text and audience response that leads audiences to flock back to the cinemas? What makes *Deedar*, *Awara*, or *Mother India* films that remain popular because of their respective stars: Dilip Kumar, Raj Kapoor, and Nargis? The Dyer morphology establishes an effective model through which the nature and manner of the dissemination of the star may be grasped. I am not totally convinced, however, that the political economy of the marketing and distribution of star capital can fully explain my conception of the parallel text. There is something symbiotic and emotional, a form of an aesthetic relish in the materiality of the star, something resonating deep in Indian psychology that explains the initial moment of conjunction of star and spectator. It is this that explains why few stars in Bombay Cinema have generated parallel texts. To find that parallel text—one that vies for place with the film itself (as character to plot)—we need to examine the reception of texts beyond the construction of both text and star by the fanzines. We need to examine how two legacies of the tradition of drama and *Tamasha*, of folk performance as well as temple ritual are received by the spectator as these are reworked in the film act. To do this it is necessary that we examine the use of song and the dialogic situation in the construction of the actor as parallel text.

SONG AND DIALOGIC SITUATION

Fanzines are important sources for any reading of popular culture. But the point I have made is that fanzines in India are not read by the film's slum constituency although it is clear that fanzine constructions of stars grow out of slum responses to them. If we are to construct a narrative of how films circulate in this constituency, we need to go back to the oral underpinnings of filmic reception. I want to advance the hypothesis that the parallel text is also constructed and carried by the song and dialogic situation. In other words, the "star" is the product of a "labor" of memory, the essentially "oral" traditions of the Indian, as much as of industry publicity. To isolate this we need to expand the levels that made up our heuristic model. In this argument, our study of the parallel text hitherto arrived at through Dyer and Ellis will be subsumed under the superparadigms of the song and dialogic situation, which may be considered as sites for the identification of actor with spectator. In other words, the symbolic identity of spectator with text/actor has to be located in a theory of narrative transaction that is not identical, in any absolute sense, with the way in which that transaction functions in mainstream Hollywood cinema. In the end the difference reflects both the manner in which the Indian cinematic commodity has come into being (its historical antecedent, its links with a parallel folk culture, its indebtedness to orality, and so on) and a complex theory of Indian textual reception. And, of course, it goes without saying that these two indices are not value free: they are fissured by categories of gender, power (patriarchy), and social class.

In *Cinema Cinema* (1983), a videocassette introduction to Bombay Cinema, the role of the song or the lyric was analyzed in some detail by the two film producers interviewed. Both Kamal Amrohi, himself an Urdu poet and director of *Mahal* (1949) and *Pakeezah* (1971), and Raj Kapoor, actor as well as auteur, found the interweaving of "song" in the filmic narrative a defining characteristic of Bombay Cinema. They argued on the grounds of cultural antecedents and emotional representations (*jazbāt*), indicating through such correlation the inextricable unity of song and character in Bombay Cinema. Amrohi's defense is indeed couched in the language of cultural "difference": songs are a defining feature of Indianness. Birth, growth, marriage, death are all informed by or translated into song. Songs are significant emotional correlatives, they extend dialogue or filmic image. A heroine in distress is either presented through the montage of a severed kite, a storm, or through a song. Like much else in contemporary Indian culture, the latter device—the song as filler—also has an honorable antecedent in the dramaturgical texts. One remembers the well-known episode in Kalidasa's *Śakuntalā* where the director asks his wife to sing a song while the performers are getting ready. Spectators must be entertained or else they will leave, is the argument here. "What do you want me to do?" asks the wife/actor. "What else but to charm our audience with a song," replies the director/dramatist. The actress needs no further coaxing. She knows that at moments like these the song sung should be about nature and seasons. So she sings a song about summer, the season in which the play is being performed (Kalidasa 1981: 42):

> Acacia flowers whose filaments
> With trembling lips
> The bee has known,
> Plucked now with careful fingertips,
> For ornaments

> To women's ears are gone.

The contemporary Indian reader/spectator quickly makes a mental shift at this moment and recalls any number of songs about seasons. A classic song in this style is in the movie *Rattan* (Invaluable jewel, 1944):

> O clouds of monsoon months go tell my beloved,
> It had to be so, my lover do not cry.
> O clouds of monsoon months.

For the stars in question here—Karan Dewan (who is also the male singer) and Swaranlata—the song became their "signature" in the sense that their "star capital" was constructed by the song. There is a moment of synchronicity between playback singer and the actor: the actor text enters popular Indian consciousness through a song syntagm. Before Amitabh Bachchan, no actor without the support of the song had ever become a parallel text in Bombay Cinema, and that includes great stars like Dilip Kumar and Raj Kapoor. For the Bachchan star personality, it is not song but the dialogic situation, where a dramatic encounter is verbally developed, that is crucial. Thus the ideal dialogic situation is one in which a lengthy debate takes place between two people: mother and son, brother and brother, father and son, hero and villain, mother and daughter, or most important perhaps, man and woman. Film work here, of course, draws attention to the many screenplay writers and lyricists who construct such dialogic situations around the heroes, and this should not be forgotten. In the case of Amitabh Bachchan the dialogues written by the Salim-Javed team were carefully scripted with Bachchan's persona in mind.

SONG AND DIALOGUE IN AMITABH BACHCHAN

Let me expand on Bachchan's dialogic situation by examining a dialogue from *Deewar* (The wall, 1975), which produced two popular critical terms for the dialogic situation: "kyā scene hai" (what a scene!) and "kyā dialogue mārtā hai" (what a way with dialogues!). We enter with the camera as it focuses on the face of Ravi (Shashi Kapoor). Ravi's top half occupies the left side of the frame, and he is foregrounded. In the background, at an angle, in the right-hand side of the frame, stands Amitabh Bachchan. The dialogue develops in the following fashion:

> *Kapoor:* No, our principles and our ideals will not let me do this.
> *Bachchan:* Oh! your principles, your ideals. Can they provide you with a square
>   meal? You risk your life for these ideals. What have they given you? A police

job, a pittance of a salary, rented rooms, two changes of uniform. Look at you and look at me. We grew up on the same footpath. But look where you are today and where I've got to. Today I have property, buildings, homes, cars, a bank balance. What have you got?

[*Long pause follows, shot reverse-shot*]

Kapoor: I have a mother.

Bachchan as the elder brother is here abrogating those dharmik laws that go into the making of the elder brother in Indian society. But as a dialogic situation it is indicative of one of the many moments in the construction of Bachchan as parallel text; it is a kind of a *smṛti* discourse, a "memory-text," that audiences would recall and participate in. It is the younger brother who uses words like *wasūl* ("principles" for Urdu speakers) and *ādarś* ("ideals" for Hindi speakers) to establish the higher law. The older brother, normally Rama, the upholder of dharma, is in fact Karna here, the *Mahābhārata's* hero in rebellion. This essential generic shift from the relatively predictable registers of the pre-Bachchan film also requires a firmer grasp of the ways in which screenplay writers work in Bombay Cinema. My point in recalling this dialogue as an instance of the "dialogic situation" so crucial for the construction of the parallel text is to demonstrate how "memorial reconstructions" of texts work hand in hand with industry publicity to create the "star" in Bombay Cinema. Although the mother (and woman generally) is removed from the emotional discourse of Bachchan, her power remains even as that of woman-as-lover diminishes. In the end Bachchan returns to the arms of his mother. "I feel so tired," he tells her. Motherhood remains something rather special in Bombay Cinema, and even Bachchan's wry cynicism cannot remove her from her central position in Indian culture.

In another well-known instance, Bachchan deconstructs one of the great enabling discourses of Bombay Cinema. I take a segment from *Naseeb* (Good fortune, 1981) in which a very thin line divides a Bombay film's sincerity to its generic conventions and a parody of precisely those conventions. As we enter this dialogic scene a singer-dancer Miss Asha Singh (Hema Malini) is about to be molested by a gang of five thugs led by the son of the evil hotel owner with a complex rags-to-riches history of his own. As she tries to escape from them, doors close around her and she is trapped under a net thrown at her by a female accomplice. She writhes helplessly, shakes and quivers, when suddenly five silver bangles are seen rolling down one of the ramparts of the parking lot toward the thugs. Enter Amitabh Bachchan as John Jani Janardan. After wisecracking about male bullies who should first wear bangles before they molest a girl he beats the daylights out of them. Though crudely choreographed by the stan-

Amitabh Bachchan, Nirupa Roy and Shashi Kapoor in Yash Chopra's *Deewar*, 1975.
Mother and sons. Publicity Still, Kamat Foto Flash.

Nirupa Roy and Amitabh Bachchan in Yash Chopra's *Deewar*, 1975. Mother and dying
son. Publicity Still Kamat Foto Flash.

dards of *Zanjeer* and *Shakti*, the hero is at any rate triumphant. What follows
is the following dialogue between Hema Malini and Bachchan.

> Malini: Many thanks to you.
>
> Bachchan: I knew this.
>
> Malini: What did you know?
>
> Bachchan: Where the story will begin. You will first thank me, and then you will
> ask me my name, and I will reply that my name is John Jani Janardan. Then
> you will ask how can one man have three names? To which I will reply a
> Christian mother gave me birth, a Hindu fed me milk, and a Muslim brought
> me up. Then you will ask me where I live. And I will reply in a hotel. Then
> you will ask what work I do. I feed people. . . .
>
> Malini: But why do you want to tell me all. . . ?
>
> Bachchan: Wait, please do let me continue. See in every Indian picture this is exactly
> what happens. The villain molests the heroine with his four thug friends. At the
> right moment enter the hero. The audience claps. Then the hero mercilessly
> pummels the daylight out of the villain and the thugs exactly as you have just
> seen. After that love develops between the hero and the heroine. Then marriage.
> Happy ending. The audience gets its money's worth. The end.
>
> Malini: Nothing of that sort is going to happen here. There is no picture ("picture-
> wicture") being made here. I am not used to listening to someone's idle prat-
> tle. Could it not be that you hired these thugs so that having overcome them
> (as you assumed I would have thought) you really wished to impress me?
> [This is a clear reference to an earlier episode in England, in which Bachchan's
> childhood friend Vicky (Shatrughan Sinha) helped her out when she was
> being abducted by a couple of English thugs. Later, one of the thugs told her
> that Vicky had hired them to stage the abduction so that he could establish
> his own chivalrous credentials in her eyes.]
>
> Bachchan: What is your name? If this were a film shooting then this is certainly
> what would have happened. But it so happens that this is not a film shooting,
> this is reality (*haqīqat*), and if I hadn't arrived on time it would have been the
> end of you.

The film as *haqīqat* (reality) is not unlike fiction's claim that it is more real
than reality. But the parody works because it is done by Amitabh Bachchan,
whose star status is such that he can deconstruct the text in which he is star.
Earlier in the film there is a scene in which the golden jubilee of a Hindi film,
Dharamveer (a Manmohan Desai film made in 1977), is being celebrated.
Real stars (Dharmendra, Raj Kapoor, Randhir Kapoor, Rajesh Khanna,
Waheeda Rehman, etc.) come to this jubilee. Amitabh Bachchan entertains

them with a song ("I have seen all local and English films, and after seeing each one I thought of being an actor"). At the end he asks Raj Kapoor to play the accordion à la *Sangam* (1964), which Kapoor does. At this point in the film Raj Kapoor ceases to be himself as he now simulates the playing of the accordion to playback music. Raj Kapoor enters the *Dharamveer* jubilee as the grand actor of old but leaves it as the character in *Sangam* playing the accordion. Amitabh Bachchan moves in and out of the film as a star whose presence transcends the text. The actor as parallel text, in the case of Amitabh Bachchan, subsumes the text itself.

If the dialogic situation effectively displaces the old song syntagm in Bachchan (the videocassette *Follow that Star: Amitabh Bachchan* has no songs), the song nevertheless is adopted by Bachchan as a different kind of tool for the construction of the parallel text. What we find in Bachchan is the appropriation of Indian folk songs rather than the carefully modulated lyric. Thus in *Laawaris* (1981) Bachchan adapts a well-known North Indian folk song "mere āṅgane meṁ tumhāra kyā kām hai," (Why are you here in my backyard?) commonly associated with Indian *hijṛās* (eunuchs). Bachchan dresses up as a woman to sing this song, which is based on the formula of transforming personal deficiencies into virtues. Thus the song would suggest that husbands with large wives should not despair because, of course, they would not need pillows in bed. This is clearly one type of folk song built around a series of innuendos easily recognized by the audience. A more careful modulation may be detected in *Silsila* (1981), in which perhaps the best known of all folk songs, the *holī* song, is sung by Bachchan. The moment of the song, a ritual that momentarily allows men and women to break the laws governing physical contact, is used to designate Bachchan's desire, in this instance, for a married woman. In his study of carnival, Bakhtin (1968) had drawn our attention to precisely this subversive feature of the moment of the carnival: the lifting of censorship within cultural constraints. As we have already remarked, the film plays on the real-life triangular relationship between Bachchan, his wife (Jaya Bhaduri), and his lover (Rekha). The song "raṅg barase bhīge cunarīyā re raṅg barase" (Colors rain upon me, they drench the edges of my shawl), is a clear variation on "holī āī re kanāhī raṅg bhar de sunā re zarā bāṁsurī" (*Holī* has come, fill me with colors, Krishna, to the tune of your flute), which we remember from *Mother India*. But while the *Mother India holī* song was meant to reinforce a collective village ethos, Bachchan's song is centered upon him totally and has strong adulterous undertones. The choreography stresses Bachchan's central place in the song text. The point is that in both the *Laawaris* and *Silsila* songs, as well as in the dialogic situations, Bachchan self-consciously reinscribes himself into the basic laws that govern the construction of the parallel text in Bombay Cinema. There is a clear inscription of the actor into the received tradition of "actor construction," as well as carefully positioned departures from that tradition.

A HERO RECONSTITUTED

I wrote off the hero of our time prematurely. Suddenly in 2000, Bachchan is everywhere, thanks to cable and satellite television. The sources I have used to construct the Bachchan parallel text have been popular print material. In the second half of the 1990s, especially, electronic material became more important. In cyberspace Bachchan has been suddenly reconstituted through his own website, through Internet fan clubs (the Cyberbollywood Amitabh Bachchan site, for instance), and through discussion portals. Additionally Star TV's immensely popular *Kaun Banega Crorepati* (Who wants to be a millionaire?), for which he is the host, has created a new Bachchan who has redefined the role of the quiz master. "Who Wants to be a Millionaire?" has many audiences in many languages around the world but nowhere has it received the kind of frenzied following that it has in India, where theaters are rescheduling their evening shows on Mondays to Thursdays so as to not coincide with the program's evening time slot. Launched in July 2000 by Star TV (controlled by Rupert Murdoch's The News Corporation) on the Hindi Star Plus channel, the program seems to have started fierce competition with rivals Zee TV and Sony Entertainment TV since becoming the peak viewing Hindi language program in India, especially in the cities. This is how one of the many Bollywood film portals (www.idlebrain.com) introduces the "new" Amitabh Bachchan:

> Amitabh Bachchan is on a winning streak of gigantic proportions. . . . He becomes an early televisionary, exhibits how a quiz show should be hosted . . . after it seemed as though his on screen glory belonged to the past, he returns triumphantly to the present tense as an actor-star with *Mohabbatein*. The man seems to have worked out some deal with destiny. He had all but hit rock bottom. As a star, after a disastrous comeback, he was dangling dangerously from the edge of the A-list. As a businessman, he was swamped by debts. But within the last few months, what a dramatic reversal of fortunes!

This is a not atypical electronic discourse on Bollywood. For our purpose what it indicates, however, is the enormous resilience of the Bachchan star persona and its reconstitution via pay TV. As the website commentator explains later in the article, Bachchan's success as the disciplinarian rector of a prestigious college (in the film *Mohabbatein*) is directly linked to his Star Plus role as quiz master. Some of the key phrases used in the quiz—"fifty fifty," "lock kiyā jāye"—have become not uncommon spectatorial responses every time Bachchan appears on the screen. The success of Aditya Chopra's *Mohabbatein* (Varieties of love, 2000) (which premiered simultaneously in the Indian diaspora and in Bombay) is thus related to the manner in which the star persona circulates through the medium of TV and on the Internet. With the increasing overlap between cinema and TV (especially cable and satellite) in India and in the diaspora, star persona will be created through the ways in which the image-dominated electronic media project and redefine his or her personality. The many film-oriented TV programs (reviews of films, talk-back shows with actors, and so on) now create the star in a manner that is gradually shifting interest away from fanzines (important as they continue to be) to TV and Internet websites.

Except for my remarks on Internet fan clubs, I have not followed up Bachchan fan clubs in India during the period when he dominated the film industry. It is sufficient to allude to the work of S. V. Srinivas on Chiranjeevi fan clubs (Chiranjeevi is a very popular Telegu film star) and suggest that his observations on these fan clubs could be similarly applied to the Bachchan fan clubs, both print and electronic (1996: 66–83). Srinivas makes two crucial points. The first is the importance of fans in bringing audiences back to theaters, especially since the slab system of taxation (taxation based on the grade of the theater and not on actual ticket sales) means that repeat audiences are crucial for profit. Although fans are not to be seen as working in tandem with theater owners or distributors or even film producers, it is clear that "fans ensure[d] sustained interest in stars." However, and this is Srinivas's second point, fans do contest, and indeed struggle against, the hegemonic constructions of stars by the film industry and are not, contrary to what the dharma police often say, themselves surrogate heroes/anti-heroes in their own social lives (1999). In this way Bachchan fan clubs imbibe critical discourses even as they deploy "the vocabulary of excess, hyperbole, adulation/devotion/admiration" (1996: 68).

In devoting this chapter to the actor as parallel text what I have attempted is to both demonstrate the highly complex way in which the star in Bombay Cinema is constructed and capture the dynamics of spectatorial desire and cinematic construction in the 1970s and 1980s. In the case of Amitabh Bachchan we have argued that his success has been a result of a very careful manipulation of tradition and individual talent: he has imbricated himself in the received tradition of Bombay Cinema even as he has parted company from it and destabilized it. Thus, in studying the parallel text "Amitabh Bachchan" we discover a carefully modulated and subtly self-conscious presence that manipulates the song and dialogic situations (the super-

Publicity poster of Aditya Chopra's *Mohabattein*, 2000. Bachchan in the afterglow of *Kaun Banega Crorepati*.

paradigms through which this cinematic practice creates its actor texts) to seemingly endless effects. Behind this manipulation (which is intersubjective since the audience "specularly" connives with the parallel text anyway) I think lie carefully positioned departures from earlier formulations of the heroic personality. Responding to modern needs and cultural shifts, especially the shift in the target audience from the middle class to slum dwellers, and yet conscious of his precursor texts in ways the early actors never were, Amitabh Bachchan transcended the status of stardom to become a text in his own right. It is in this context that Bachchan is both ubiquitous (one can speak of pre- and post-Bachchan Bollywood cinema) and a parallel text constructed through a process that goes beyond the construction of "stardom" as outlined by Dyer and Ellis. To deconstruct this text would require skills of a bewildering complexity as well as a consciousness about popular reception through both popular print and electronic media. In India mainstream cinema can be the site for both high and low cultural forms and their aesthetic critiques. To this end, "Amitabh Bachchan" has been an indispensable text around whom almost a quarter century of Bombay Cinema has congealed.

Chapter Six

SEGMENTING/ANALYZING TWO FOUNDATIONAL TEXTS

The title of this chapter is borrowed, in part, from Raymond Bellour's seg-mentation of *Gigi* (1976: 331–53). My aim here is to extend Bellour's dis-cussion of a Hollywood musical to two key texts of Bombay Cinema. The first is *Baiju Bawra* (1952), which I use to further exemplify the significance of the "song text" in Bombay Cinema; the second, *Amar Akbar Anthony* (1977), I use to explore the principle of symmetrical narratives that have something of the rhythm of classic Hollywood cinema. Bellour's segmenta-tion of *Gigi* is based on Christian Metz's *grande syntagmatique*, a term he used to refer to the grammar, the deep structure, or the *langue* of cinema. According to Metz, the *grande syntagmatique* is the series of autonomous "syntagms" (Bellour's "segments") that make up the picture track. To grasp this, one suspects Metz had to read cinema as a language of shot sequences which, in Bellour's words, is "a sort of theoretical operator [that] actualizes the concrete possibility of a semiotics of cinema" (332). The procedure came under strong criticism, notably from the Italian semiotician Emilio Garroni, on the grounds that any procedure based on a "division of the filmic text into autonomous segments" would deny filmic message its "pluricodicity" (Henderson 1980: 151). Metz, of course, never offered seg-mentation as a "*total* analysis of the filmic message," seeing it rather as a "subcode" of cinema (Metz 1974: 189) that was not meant to elide the semiotic complexities of the filmic image. Further defense for segmentation has to be mounted here because Bellour himself has declaimed the proce-dure on the grounds that segmentation (of the kind I attempt) relies on the analyst's use of segments as discrete citations of the film. Since written texts alone can be cited in print, the citation of filmic segments can be no more than a literary paraphrase.

> But this seductive body [the filmic text] is an elusive body; it cannot really be quoted nor grasped. It is polysemous as well, in an excessive way, and its matter, moulded by iconicity and analogy, pushes language into check. This irreducibility of the filmic substance, which fascinates and stimulates (as do all such elusive objects), serves to limit analysis: the readings of films have been unable to produce the equivalence brought out in readings of "Les Chats" or in *S/Z*. This does not simply result from the analysts' lack of genius, but primarily from the exceptional resistance put up by the analytic material. (Bellour 1985: 54)

Behind these comments stands Bellour's essay "The Unattainable Text" (1975) in which, curiously, he claimed that filmic texts were unattainable (because they were uncitable) even as in his own practice (in his analysis of *Gigi* for instance) segmentation and citations of filmic images continued to be made. The added difficulty with citations, Bellour noted, is that neither the description of the segment nor the citation of the filmic "framed" image can "restore . . . that which only the projection apparatus can render: a movement, the illusion of which guarantees its reality" (Bellour 1975: 25). However, as Larry Crawford has argued in a brilliant piece on Bellour's essay, "The status of the projector, for film theory and for the methodology of film analysis (including the filmic citation) must not be left as a brute fact or paralyzing given, with general semiotic importance attributed to it" (1985: 66). There are three additional points I want to make before I leave this section and proceed with my analysis. First, the ontological primacy of the written text (as the only form of "writing" that can be adequately cited) is an overdetermined epistemological relation that need not invalidate other modes of citation (including the prose paraphrase of the filmic segment) (Crawford 1985: 70). Second, the materiality of the text (its means of production as well as its mechanics) in themselves do not constitute the citational text (the projector, the computer, and so on). To collapse the two would mean, for example, that a novel read on the computer would be less valid for purposes of citation (given the different materiality of computer production vis-à-vis the book). Finally, as Bellour's own analyses have shown, segmentation is both a legitimate form of citation of narrative units in a film and a useful methodology with which to detect patterns of repetition and emphasis.

I return to Bellour despite his autocritique for the simple reason that segmentation allows me to work through those rhythms that are a mark of Bombay Cinema. In the great realist texts/films of the West specific rhythms or repetitions would be built into the structure to emphasize those features of the narrative that would lead to the construction of the artistic object as an harmonious whole. The aesthetic ideology at work here is clearly drawn from a latent distinction that is being made between meaning and significance. The meaning of the text resides in its paraphrase, which is how an uncritical spectator reads the text. But embedded in the diachronic structure are moments that connect the text with other segments through principles of repetition, allusion, montage, and so on. This procedure underpins a text's significance. A scene may be repeated, or the actions of characters may duplicate something that has already happened. In a continuous and thoroughly systemic cultural practice like Bombay Cinema all films become part of a grand intertextual system. Here Metz's *grande syntagmatique* has to be read as a syntagm that defines Bombay Cinema as a totality, as each film is in one sense a "segment" of a much larger semiotic continuum. It is this qualification, which also leads to the recognition that each segment is "pluricodical," that persuades me that *grande syntagmatique* (and segmentation generally) can be located in terms of a differential system of filmic codes. The principle of segmentation is thus the first step on which a "codic analysis" (Henderson 1980: 158) of the kind I attempt in this chapter will operate.

Baiju Bawra finds its rhythm in the relationship between two forms of diegesis: dialogue and song. In the larger discourse of the film (as image and as word) the film gets its cultural capital (as a classic song text) from the fact that it locates itself in the midst of the high point of Hindu-Muslim cultural synthesis and symbiosis even as it, finally, demonstrates through a surreptitious narrative built around the primacy of song the triumph of the Hindu indigenous form over the Muslim courtly Baroque. Working from Bellour's division of the *grande syntagmatique*, what is of great value to me is the way in which the song text (which, in some sense, is a generative structure) may be inserted into the filmic language. If we go to the accompanying chart at the end of this chapter, we see that *Baiju Bawra* may be divided into sixteen sections, twenty-three suprasegments, thirty-one segments, and some one thousand shots. One cannot be precise about the exact number of shots because the film has not survived in its complete form. Moreover, the transfer of film onto video (my working text for purposes of segmentation) may lead to the loss of a good many shots. Even with this proviso, though, each of the segments, here defined as a major narrative unit, has a tendency to lose its sense of discreteness and spill over into the adjoining segment. Thus it is hard to tell whether suprasegment II, for instance, is made up of two or three segments. On the face of it, there is a sequential continuity here as there is no dissolve or other markers of dramatic shift in the scene. The camera simply moves away from the gaze of Ghasit Khan, the affable singer of the masses—the subaltern agent—to take in a group of Hindu minstrels who walk onto the stage (here the city street). I have read this as one segment on the grounds that there is no technical marker to distinguish the two scenes. This tendency is not an uncommon feature of *Baiju Bawra*, especially toward the end of the film, where a number of scenes—preparations for Gauri's marriage, Baiju's arrival, the crossing of the river, Gauri's frantic run toward the river, and the death of both Baiju and Gauri by drowning—effectively make up one segment with nine subsegments. It could, again, be argued that these subsegments should have the status of segments in their own right.

The relationship between shots and segment may be examined with reference to the two initial suprasegments of the film. Again it is quite legitimate to ask whether the first autonomous shot of the film's logo is a suprasegment in its own right (as the opening shot, it can't have an independent segmental status since segments must function within a suprasegmental network). The logo shows a woman raising herself up from a bowed position on top of a dome that signifies the earth. At the base of the dome is written "Lead Kindly Light" and "Prakash" (light). At one level this is no different from the logo of Paramount Pictures or Metro-Goldwyn-Mayer, but the citation of a line from a Christian hymn and the emphasis on light (given in romanized Hindi) shift this pure icon to the level of a statement. The words are written in English so that already large sections of the audience are being excluded. Those who can read English—the colonial middle classes left behind by the British—quickly connect this with Gandhi who was particularly fond of this first line from the hymn "Lead Kindly Light," possibly because it came so close to the Vedic gāyatrī mantra itself: "tamaso mā jyotir gamaya" (lead me from darkness to light). Thus an autonomous shot, and a logo, too, moves from one discourse to another, from pure image to a plea to postcolonial India: do not forget your recently departed Mahatma. The opening shot then becomes something like the Law of the Father whose thematics would be keyed into the text proper. Nehru picked up precisely this theme when on the occasion of Gandhi's *samādhi* he said, "the light is gone." Indian Republic Day celebrations continue to repeat this motif through the lone trumpeter who plays "Lead kindly light" at the end of the ceremonies. The implicit Law of Gandhi (the Father of the Nation) gradually invades the text, as the controlling force of the narrative momentum—vengeance—is tempered by love. The idea of vengeance is established quite early in the film as young Baiju loses his father in a skirmish. The origin of this skirmish is in fact the great court singer Tansen's directive that no music or sound should interfere with his compositions of new ragas. The cause of the father's death is thus directly linked to the whole question of the freedom of song upon which, paradoxically enough, the great court singer Tansen himself has now placed a caveat. Baiju's vow to revenge his father is then linked to the imperial narrative of *Hamlet* where Hamlet's desire to "sweep" to his revenge is obstructed by both philosophy (a brooding mind) and love ("we will have no more marriages"). Baiju too must get past these impediments and take up his revenge through the nonviolent weapon of song and not sword. This triumph—which also comes with the Hamlet-like confession about "a special providence even in the fall of a sparrow"—is closely linked to Baiju's acquisition of the entire repertoire of Indian ragas. Thus what makes *Baiju Bawra* such an exemplary text for purposes of our analysis is the productive nature of space occupied by the song syntagms in the text. What I would like to demonstrate is the function of song as segment/syntagm in this film. Is it possible to claim that the song text had its own thematic continuity in the classic Bombay Cinema?

The first song occurs in section A, suprasegment I, segment 2. This segment is made up of one shot framed by the performance of a lone singer in the evening. The singer sits on the right of the frame with his tamboura. The credits move from the bottom up on the left side of the frame. At the end of the formal credits an introductory statement is given in English, Hindi, and Urdu. The statement reads, "Among the popular figure gathers many a legend that obscures History. If any . . . and what is history but legend agreed upon?" The film thus makes a double claim: the work is possibly fictional but it may be true if we begin to believe in it. The construction of history as a tradition agreed upon without, necessarily, any evidence (paleographical or archaeological) implies the Hindu primacy of the *śruti* text, the oral text that a community of speakers accepts as designating truth. The flier about history—as agreed upon legends—thus gives the text an historical force that accepted academic practice would reject outright. The legend of Baiju, which this film creates (the legend is not anterior to the film) then becomes an "historical" fact through the film's collapsing of legend and history. The segment under discussion, is however, marked more significantly by the voice of the singer Tansen as he sings a *rāga mārvā*, a primarily devotional evening raga sung in a serious tone. This raga is a classical raga largely uncontaminated by other influences and may be seen as a kind of a Baroque city raga. At the onset, then, this segment establishes one of the great themes of the film: the city is marked by a courtly opulence symbolized also in the form of the ragas that Tansen sings. These ragas lack full semantic content as they simply rework, with variations, a set of key words such as (in the case of the raga sung by Tansen) *torī jay jay kartār*. Pure raga over semantic content (the *khayāl* style) is characteristic of the court and of Tansen. Raga here becomes music made by voice as an extension of a musical instrument. In terms of segmental classification this segment merges into segment 3, shots 3 to 14 as the singing of Tansen comes to an end and is followed by the applause of the crowd. The silhouetted shot of Tansen, which frames the credit stills, is now sequentially linked to shots of the city and of Tansen singing in his music room. The break between this sequence and the next is marked by an autonomous shot (shot 15) of the skyline of the city at night.

The second raga establishes the first of the conflicts in the film and cinematically offers the first instance of the kinds of alternation we associate with classic cinema. Against Tansen's Baroque, a people's singer breaks into *rāga bhairavī*, an extremely flexible raga that paves the way for the minstrels' song in the next connected sequence. Segment 4, subsegment (a) begins with an interdiction from Tansen that he should not be disturbed. As he tunes his tamboura, he hears the vigorous *bhairavī* sung outdoors by the people's singer, Ghasit Khan. Since Tansen should not be disturbed, the guards jostle the singer only to be distracted by the minstrels' song, "sāṁco tero rām nām" (Sing the name of Rama). Against the essentially *khayāl* style of the court singers, this devotional *bhairavī* has adapted many of the folk styles of the Sannyasins and may be referred to as the *ṭhumrī* style of the Hindu world of Baiju and the villagers. The *bhairavī* also reflects the song text which has come to be associated with Bombay Cinema. In this film the key musical motif is really another *bhairavī* which is sung by the adult Baiju ("tū gaṅgā kī mauj meṁ"). The tune of this song and its opening invocatory line—"ho jī ho"—mark out the domain of the lovers Baiju and Gauri, and has what Das Gupta has referred to as the "climactic, orgasmic function" of song in the cinema (1991: 67). In the minstrels' song, while raga remains the controlling force, the singing lacks the improvisations of the classical musician. In this respect the devotional song is marked by a semantic excess which, combined with its religious intent, challenges the aesthetic superiority of the pure raga. It is clear that Baiju, the protagonist of the film, will be located on the side of devotional excess against the Baroque order of Mughal India. The alternation between the two and the redundancy of the song syntagms are all features of the classic cinema. But the song also has a cardinal narrative function, as Roland Barthes defines it (Barthes 1977) because the minstrels' song leads to the death of Baiju's father. The adolescent boy of 12 now takes a vow to revenge his father's death (B.III.4b:46). But since the origin of the law that leads to his natural father's death comes from Tansen in the first instance, the dead father himself is now transformed into the living father in the form of Tansen. Baiju's narrative of revenge as desire now replays one of the classic narratives of the Oedipus triangle.

The signature song of this film—"tū gaṅgā kī mauj meṁ"—is intricately connected to an entire suprasegment (VII) so that segment 10 and the suprasegment are identical. Although the song doesn't get under way until eight shots later, it cannot be read, like the swing song (D.V.6a: 81–85), as an autonomous unit made up of a segment. Since this song has been anticipated, it links themes that are essential for the classic continuity of the narrative. Thus the frame of the song is the river and a boat. References are made to the earlier episode (segment 5) in which Baiju is saved from drowning by Gauri. This has an anticipatory value in the sense that the river and Baiju's incapacity to swim will lead in the end to the death of both Baiju and Gauri. Thus the river that touches Tansen's city is the site of a different kind of life here. Where Tansen's city walls exclude the river, in the village the river marks the ebb and flow of life and has a history all its own. Baiju's song is linked on the one hand to the aberrant singing of Ghasit Khan, whose *bhairavī* was good enough only for the city subaltern, and on the other hand to Baiju's father's singing. There is, then, a connection through ragas between three songs: Ghasit Khan's pure raga, Baiju's father's devotional song, and Baiju's own love song. The song is sung to Gauri as she rows away. As the song comes to an end the entire village participates in the song, symbolically accepting the union of the lovers:

> In the tempestuous flow of the Ganges,
> You are the Jumna stream;
> Likewise our union will remain, mine and yours,
> Our union will remain.

Love, union, the river, and *rāga bhairavī* impose a classical unity on the text. The kinds of repetition we detect here are thus as much a poetic repetition as purely narrative repetition. Just as this song occupies an entire segment/suprasegment, the next song (segment 13) is also a unified segment, though I have divided it into subsegments (a)–(d). The song proper takes up only twenty-two of the fifty-one shots, but the preceding and following scenes are closely linked to the song itself. The song is the companions' song as they tease Gauri: "dūr koī gāye dhun yah sunāye tere bin sajnā re." Again the companion motif is borrowed from medieval texts where the dancing, singing Radha would be seen in the company of the other cowherd women (*gopīs*). The chief characteristic of this raga (*rāga pāharī*) is that it is very much a folk song of the hills, with lilting tunes and a semantic content drawn from nature. One of the underlying features of this folk form is that the idea of the echo is built into the structure of the raga. Segments 6, 10, and 13 are therefore relatively independent segments that may be read as rhetorical tropes meant to establish musical connections with other singers (a genealogy is implied here) and to intensify a particular situation. The situation so far (in these three songs) has been passionate love.

The song at segment 18 marks a shift in narrative. The highly unified form of the narrative (about the nature of singing and love) is broken by the intrusion of a form that has often been used as a *deux ex machina* in Bombay Cinema. This is the dacoit interlude. A subgenre in its own right, this particular form is utilized to advance the narrative through some form of abduction or capture. Under normal circumstances (as in *Awara*), it is the woman who is abducted by the male dacoit. In *Baiju Bawra* the dacoit leader Queen Roopmati demands Baiju as payment from the villagers. Before she does this Baiju stops the carnage of the villagers by singing a *rāga torī*. The song "insān bano" (Be human) is a devotional raga connected with lament and renunciation. (Tansen composed a special variety of this raga which is called *miyām̐ kī torī*). However, in this instance Baiju is drawing upon the established form of the *torī*. It is the only one of the five songs discussed thus far that does not have a complete segment to itself. The song takes up only twenty-five of the eighty shots that make up this segment. The other shots are simply a formal device leading to the estrangement of the lovers and, in this instance more specifically, to the return of the revenge theme.

I want to pause at suprasegment XII, segment 19 at this point. This is a segment of eighteen shots that is devoted entirely to one song sung by Gauri. It is based on a sad, simple raga, *rāga sarpada bilāvala*, a highly melodious but very touching morning raga ideally sung during the first quarter of the day. The mise-en-scène of the song is a shot in which Gauri runs along the ridge of a hill while, in the foreground, the dacoit Queen Roopmati and her followers march out with Baiju. The close-up shots, however, show a very different image. Gauri is in a desolate garden, singing this dolorous song. Staged performance bonded to the laws of the proscenium arch theater and realist principles exist side by side in one of the more obvious instances of a practice not uncommon in this cinema. The illusion is maintained through the continuity of the song and not through any continuity in representation. The argument here is that the force of the raga as a totally overpowering semantic unit is such that the spectator will be completely taken in by the song.

This is certainly the case with this song, a highly sentimental rendition of childhood love and loss ("bacpan kī muhabbat ko"):

Don't forget our childhood love . . .
When memories return
Pray that we may meet again.

Why does the spectator get so totally taken in by the song? What is the nature of the "voice" that is being lip-synced by Gauri? Indian spectators in 1952 would recognize that the voice is a relatively recent one, perhaps no more than three or four years old. And yet, this voice—of the playback singer Lata Mangeshkar (b. 1929)—will not only become the glorious, the definitive voice of the Bombay filmic heroine, but it will also remain the dominant voice in the second half of the century. Such will be its preeminence and power (given the significance of song in the genre) that the singer Lata Mangeshkar alone would command royalties (most other singers are paid a set fee by the producer). Moreover, during her long reign she would be able to marginalize significant music directors like O. P. Nayyar and new Lata-like singers such as Suman Kalyanpur. Even her own sister Asha Bhosle was not immune from Lata's wish to control the agenda of the female voice in Bombay Cinema. Her voice was so well established as the representative voice of Bombay Cinema that Lata clones like Alka Yagnik, Anuradha Paudwal, Kavita Krishnamoorty, and Sunidhi Chauhan continue to replicate it. In segmenting *Baiju Bawra* I have restricted my commentary on the film as a "song text," and chosen it as the exemplary text of its kind in the genre. It circulates as a syntagm of songs, often disembodied from the film as such. In this circulation, in the "traveling history" of the film through song, we need to pause for a moment and address the key female singer in *Baiju Bawra* and her role in the development of this cinema.

THE HEGEMONY OF LATA MANGESHKAR

As Peter Manuel has pointed out, until well into the 1970s (when cassettes revolutionized the dissemination of music in India), "commercial popular music was virtually synonymous with film music" (1993: 41). Even so, the vast bulk of cassette music continues to be Indian film music, and the female voice that dominates Indian, especially North Indian, popular culture is that of Lata Mangeshkar, who is included in *The Guinness Book of Records* as the singer of the largest number of recorded songs in the world. The kind of varied vocal styles one detects in much non-Western music is largely absent from the Indian popular, whether filmic or nonfilmic. Writing specifically of the homogenizing voices of film music—Mohammad Rafi, Kishore Kumar, and Lata Mangeshkar are the giants here—Manuel notes that the varied vocal styles of the rich and complex tradition of Indian regional musics ("from the intense shouting of Haryanvi men's songs, to the nasal timbre of Garhwali singing and the classicized coloratura of Rajasthani Manganhar and Langa music" [52]) are missing from their voices. I want to take up Lata Mangeshkar's voice since *Baiju Bawra* not because this is when it reached its distinctive falsetto form but simply because 1952 could be seen as the year that brought to an end the richly textured and individually timbred voices of an earlier tradition of film music that included Wahidan Bai, Husnbanu, Mehtab, Amir Bai, Noor Jehan, Suraiya, and Shamshad Begum. Even the extraordinarily gifted Geeta Roy, who carried the tradition of the Bengali Kanan Bala, survived only marginally, and that through the continued patronage of her husband, filmmaker Guru Dutt. In displacing these varied voices—Shamshad Begum, who brought a range of styles to the songs of the film *Shabnam* (Dew 1949), for instance, ceased to be an important voice of leading female stars and is remembered primarily as the voice of loss and departure (*bidāī*) as in *Mother India*'s "pī ke ghar āj pyārī dulhaniyā calī"—Lata prized out the female film voice from its great, heterogeneous tradition. In Bombay Cinema her voice projected the pure, uncontaminated, virginal qualities of the heroine who in a film might be even a prostitute or a courtesan. One remembers the courtesan song in *Sadhna* (1958)—"bolojī tum kyā kyā kharīdo ge" (Pray tell what else would you buy from me?)—which, in Lata's voice, emerges less like the raw, seductive singing of Wahidan Bai or even Suraiya and more like a girlish flirtation. The unique "shrill falsetto" of Lata, as Manuel remarks, probably doesn't exist in North Indian folk music. Manuel quotes from an important commentary by the Indian music critic Raghava Menon:

> The ultimate measure of sweetness in a woman's voice [was to be found in Lata's voice]. Its chief characteristic was the skillful use of a particular kind of falsetto which did not exist in quite the same way before her coming. . . . Lata brought this curiously stupefying voice into our light music. And the technique narcotised all forms of light music. Even the folk genre seems to have tried out this technique. (53)

The success of the marketing of this virtually nonexistent Indian singing voice is deeply indicative of the power of Bombay Cinema in affecting the music tastes of a vast and heterogeneous population. Resistant forms could not compete because alternative forms were never marketed by the monopolistic Indian gramophone industry (HMV), which basically churned out primarily film songs. By the time cassette culture made it possible for independent singers to enter the market, the Lata-filmic hegemony had been so strong that even they were Lata clones. It is only in the past few years that Lata's "sacred" status has been touched. In *Saaz* ("A Gift of Song," 1996) Sai Paranjpye took the unusual step of modeling his narrative on the rivalry of the Mangeshkar sisters (Lata and Asha Bhosle). And in the 1990s generally other voices began to emerge primarily in response to the burgeoning independent music industry in India and in the diaspora. In Govind Nihalani's *Thakshak* (The serpent, 1999) Lata disappears completely as Nihalani brings together voices that carry the heterogeneous tradition of Indian singing: Asha Bhosle, Alisha Chinnai, Hema Sardesai, and Sujata Trivedi.

But why would a film industry cultivate such a singular voice and hold onto it for a full half century? And why would the nation-state, too, read Lata as the representative voice of Indian nationalism and appoint her, in 1999, to the Indian Rajya Sabha, the Upper House? In a fascinating article Sanjay Srivastava (forthcoming) tries to answer these questions, and I want to develop his arguments further. Srivastava argues that Lata's voice has to be seen as the "marker of 'modern' Indian female identity" produced by the "modernization of patriarchal norms" in Indian culture. In this reading, Indian patriarchy commodified and packaged Lata's voice, and sold it as the authentic, uncontaminated, postcolonial voice of the Indian woman. There are a number of subtexts here that we need to keep in mind, subtexts that, in a sense, threatened the patriarchal order. The first is the representation of the nation as Mother. Here the problem arose because Mother as protective goddess could also be Mother as defiant avenger, condemning the avaricious and rewarding the just. So if woman had to be worshiped, she had to be controlled too. If that was one kind of woman—woman as Mother and goddess—who needed to be controlled, the other was woman as she had hitherto been constructed by the profilmic biography of the star. Here postcolonial Indian cinema had inherited a tradition of the courtesan-star often with her own own rich and idiosyncratic singing voice, but with an uneasy personal history as well. "Enter Lata," writes Sanjay Srivastava, and adds:

> What Lata's voice does is present a viable solution: at the same time that women's bodies became visible in public spaces via films, their presence was 'thinned' through the expressive timbre granted them. The heroines for whom Lata provided the singing voice may well have been prancing around hill-sides and streets while performing a song-sequence, but this gesture which otherwise threatened male dominance of these spaces, was domesticated through the timbre and tonality which marked that presence.

In *Baiju Bawra*, the singing voice of Gauri is always Lata Mangeshkar's, which also means that Meena Kumari (who plays the role of Gauri) gets recoded, through Lata's voice, as virginal and pure and removed from her personal history as Mahzabin, the daughter of a courtesan. (A similar process was under way with Nargis as well when she "adopted" Lata's voice in *Barsaat*.) Embedded in the *Baiju Bawra* song text are thus two narratives: the narrative of the song text as a signifying practice in Bombay Cinema and the narrative of a voice—Lata's—that takes its distinctive form in this film. Space does not permit us to extend the obvious—the manner in which filmic song texts are in fact generated by specific singers and the impact films as song texts have on our readings of the Bombay Cinema. When we return to where we left off—Gauri's lament on love –we find that from there on there is only one complete song by Lata: "mohe bhūl gaye sāṁvariyā" (a base *rāga bhairav* normally associated with serious morning devotion crossed with a complementary erotic-devotional grammar) in which Gauri wonders whether Baiju has in fact forgotten her (segment 26). After that the songs are sung either by Baiju or by the court singer Tansen. Except for a quick return to Lata's voice in the signature song of the film at the end (segment 31), Lata's voice disappears altogether from the film, but not before it established itself as the voice of the Bombay film heroine.

CLASSIC ALTERNATION: *RĀGA DARBĀRĪ*

In the realist text there is always a scene that is far richer in meaning than any other scene. Very often the scene in question is not particularly long or complex, nor does it necessarily have an extended narrative. What often happens is that a poetic principle of symbolic organization establishes resonances between this scene and earlier or later ones. In *Baiju Bawra* such a scene occurs at segment 21 when Baiju, sword in hand, climbs into Tansen's music room with the aim of killing him. As he approaches, he is struck by the raga *rāga darbārī* that Tansen has just composed. As Baiju listens to the raga in *svar* only (which is made up of the musical notes *ga, re, sa, ma, pa, dha, ni, sa*), he loses his resolve. On the walls he sees paintings of music personified into its male and female principles, as Raga and Ragini. These figures coalesce with those of Krishna and Radha, giving music a decidedly religious twist. When he gets a grip on himself, and, as Tansen's raga moves toward its grand finale (it ends in a crescendo of rising *svar*), he swings his sword and smashes Tansen's tamboura. The surrogate father's magnificent music makes it impossible for Baiju to take the decisive action for which he had prepared himself all his life. To kill music one has to find a superior music; to override a father's voice, an equally compelling voice must be found. For a segment that lasts for no more than six minutes, there are eighty-one shots here. This is partly because the confrontation between man, music, and painting leads to quick cuts and repeat zooms to all three as the music continues to be played. What Tansen tells him is that he can be destroyed only by an equally sad raga: "jāo dard bharā gīt lāo" (Go and find a sad song). The relationship between sad songs and the power of cinema was so strong that right up to the moment of Amitabh Bachchan there were very few successful films that did not have a sad song or two.

The center of the film now shifts almost exclusively to the song syntagms as Baiju masters in quick succession the key ragas: *rāga lalit* (a morning raga), *rāga gauṛa malhār* (the raga of the rainy season), *rāga bhāgeśvarī* (an evening raga about *saṃyoga śṛngāra*, love in union), and so on with the help of Tansen's own guru Swami Haridas. The result of this training is seen in the first complete song that he sings after "insān bano" (segment 18), located at segment 27, subsegment (b):

> My mind yearns to meet Hari,
>
> Without you my entire world is chaotic.
>
> Listen to my devotion and save me.

Set to *rāga mālkauṁsa*, the song ("mana tarpat hari darśan ko āj") moves away from the primarily folk-based light ragas of the pastoral period. As a purely devotional raga, *rāga mālkauṁsa* (whose base *ṭhāṭh* is in fact *bhairavī*) is universally known for its very precise form and its overall seriousness. It is a late night raga, normally sung during the third quarter of the night. In a very significant manner this raga marks the transition from the world of the country to Tansen's world. Baiju's father had sung another devotional song but in the lighter, less tight morning *rāga bhairavī*. The son's devotionalism is now one with Tansen's as he shows mastery over the intricate grammar of Baroque (city) ragas.

Patterns of alternation, repetition, and duplication, the rhythms based on symmetries, are to be found at every point in the text. One that is of immense consequence to the resolution of the narrative "enigma" is the duplication of Tansen's own *rāga darbārī* in a manner not unlike the return of a fetish (Tansen creates this raga) to its original owner, but tainted because of this re-routing. We have seen that Baiju is struck by the intense nature of this raga, and especially the power of the new kind of crescendo with which the raga ends. He had heard it in *svar* (note) form alone. At segment 27, subsegment (g), Baiju now fleshes out Tansen's *svar* by singing a song in Tansen's own *rāga darbārī*.

> O keeper of this world listen to my heart-broken notes,
>
> Listen to my heart-broken notes.

Cinematically this song marks the final preparation of Baiju. Beginning with a devotional refrain the song moves into the lyric of love and absence, representing these through the paradoxical, "inverted" language of *sandhyā bhāṣā* (twilight language) through which the devotional poets of old captured the massive contradictions of life. But the sense of loss and failure, of desire, moves to another domain as the scene gradually shifts from the ruined Shiva temple, with which it opens, to the streets of Tansen's city (L.XIX.27.g). There Baiju discovers nothing but lonely streets because, paradoxically, music had been banned in the name of music itself so that Tansen could work in peace. His raga now moves into a higher pitch as he lifts the refrain to even loftier levels of music, something that Tansen had demonstrated only in *svar* form to him early on.

Segment 27 ends in *rāga darbārī*, Tansen's raga given expressive form by the young Baiju. Through the song text a new assertiveness comes to Baiju and he challenges Tansen to a musical competition. Of the 105 shots that make up segment 30, 95 are devoted to one song. The segment marks the final encounter between Tansen and Baiju in the presence of Emperor Akbar. Baiju comes prepared, having overcome desire for revenge and replaced it with the majesty of song. To defeat him, as Tansen had suggested, Baiju had to first find a sad song. In "o duniyā ke rakhvāle" (O keeper of this world), he had demonstrated precisely that, filling out Tansen's own *rāga darbārī* with the kind of devotional content that was his father's signature. So they sing the final raga, *rāgu desī*, a complex, difficult, city raga, so precise in its grammar that it rejects deviations: āj gāvat man mero jhūm ke terī tān bhagvān. A pure form, this is the raga of the second quarter of the day and best sung at midday. In this duel it is Baiju who is triumphant. The pattern with which segment 2 began— Tansen's singing and the subsequent interdiction against singing—now repeats itself. The unity of the song text at this level is complete.

But there remains a coda that is linked to the love narrative, the story of young lovers who meet and separate. Like much else in Bombay Cinema, the central mode here is melodrama. The space in which the lovers have functioned has been the river and the village. In this space Gauri, the girl, is at home in both village and river; Baiju only in the village as he cannot swim. When we see her again, Gauri is betrothed to another and the village Panchayat insists that the marriage should go ahead since Baiju has disappeared. At this point, another textual tradition—the tradition of doomed lovers enshrined in the Persian-inspired *mathnavīs*, *Lailā Majnūn*, *Shirīn Farhād, Sohinī Mahivāl*—now brings that genre into play. This is the genre of tragic love, which is also one of the founding genres of Bombay Cinema. The river which Baiju had transformed into his beloved Gauri ("tū gangā kī mauj meṁ jamnā kā dhārā") now shows its real *mauj*, its tempestuous self. Baiju's boat capsizes as he approaches the village; Gauri rushes out of her house, attired for marriage, to save her beloved, but the currents, the *jamnā kā dhārā*, are far too strong and they both drown. The city text ends with the classical raga, the pastoral text ends in death. The song syntagm in Bombay Cinema creates its own narrative since it leaves behind another memory, the memory of the song through which classical Bombay films get constructed. Through the song text a single unity is eschewed in favor of parallel texts that can be located in both the diegetic and non-diegetic space of the narrative. And here we need to also acknowledge the utilization of a wide variety of rasas—*śṛngāra* most certainly but also *karuṇa*, *hāsya* (certainly in the figures of Narpat, Ganju, and Ghasit Khan) and even *adbhuta* (the drowning scene)—that links the filmic text to a spectator-response theory going back to ancient dramaturgical treatises. More significantly the response is a *darśana* in all its complex meanings: seeing, observing, having an audience with, visiting, having a philosophical point of view, and so on.

To get another sense of the classical pattern we must now look at a film in which the relationship between song and text is slightly different. The narrative domain becomes more specious, and the song texts are used not as set scenes with largely poetic connections between character, emotion, and meaning but as variations on the narrative itself. In our next exemplary text we cannot use the song text as a "poetics," as a code that shows (as in the case of *rāga darbārī*) a form of symbolic empowerment over a dominant city culture. In this respect our second film works on a version of epic melodrama that was to become a dominant feature of many of the highly successful films of the late '70s and '80s. The variations on this epic melodramatic narrative and their uses in the cinema of specularity can be seen in *Amar Akbar Anthony* (1977).

TEXTUAL SYMMETRY/ASYMMETRY

Amar Akbar Anthony, another of Amitabh Bachchan's "superhits," may be divided into thirteen sections, thirteen suprasegments, twenty-five segments (with subsegments), and some 1,632 shots. The formal design is quite explicitly based on the principle of complementarity, congruence, repetition, and alternation. In this respect every segment has a tendency to compress the larger macronarrative metonymically and reinforce the intense synchronicity of the form—to know one segment, one fragment, is to know the synchronous moment, which is the grammar of the entire film.

We can examine the idea of repetition by looking at a number of subsegments, which we can initially summarize as follows:

   (a) A/I/1b and K/XII/23c

   (b) A/II/2a and E/VI/7a (1–2) (Cleans shoes)

   (c) A/II/2g and E/VI/7b (Gold)

   (d) G/VIII/18 a–g (Song sequence AAA)

   (e) A/II/2 b; F/VII/11c; J/XI/21c; L/XII/24d—24e (Santoshi Maa)

   (f) E/VI/7x^1; J/XI/21e; K/XII/23c; L/XII/24b; L/XII/24e (August 15, 22 years ago)

   (g) J/XI/21e; K/XII/23c; K/XII/24e (3 recognition scenes)

The first three—(a) to (c)—are instances of visual and/or oral/visual repetition. The fourth—(d)—is a series of duplications constructed around one song sung by the three brothers and their girlfriends in three separate localities. The fifth—(e)—inserts a goddess recently resurrected from oblivion by Bombay Cinema in another film. The fifth—(f)—is a reference to August 15, twenty-two years before, when the three children of Kishenlal were separated from him. The last—(g)—is a recognition scene. It need hardly be stressed that the film ends where it began with the re-establishment of the patriarchal order. Speaking to Robert, Kishenlal says, "yah kahānī maiṁ tumhāre sāth śurū kī thī aur āj tumhāre hī sāth ise khatm kar dūṁgā" (I began this tale with you and it is only fitting that I end it with you).

The first of these duplications—(a)—deals with the question of responsibility by the syndicate for which a criminal works. In the first subsegment (A/I/1b), Kishenlal, a former criminal, is released from prison, and returns home to find his children destitute and his wife suffering from tuberculosis. He asks his wife, Bharati, if his boss Robert had looked after her when he was in prison. The wife replies in the negative. In the symmetrical repetition at K/XII/23c we see Kishenlal twenty-two years later, now enormously wealthy, entering the house of a woman in his former neighborhood and apologizing to her because one of his lieutenants had not kept the underworld code of honor which required that wives of workers should be cared for. Like Kishenlal before, her husband too is in prison, this time because of the nature of Kishenlal's own criminal business.

In the second case of duplication (b) a scene is repeated with the reversal of roles. Here a copper coin is returned to its rightful owner but within a dramatically altered economy of power. In the first subsegment (A/II/2a), Kishenlal goes to Robert for money and an explanation of why he did not keep his side of the bargain. Instead of responding to Kishenlal's queries, Robert asks him to wipe his shoes and then throws him a copper coin. "What did you expect for shoe shining, ten thousand rupees?" he asks Kishenlal.

Years later the tables are now turned (E/VI/7a^1–a^2). Robert has been destroyed by Kishenlal, and he works for Kishenlal as a laborer. Robert asks, "Where's my daughter?" and is told to clean his shoes. When he completes this action, Kishenlal throws him a copper coin. "This is the same copper coin you threw at me so many years before," he tells Robert.

After confronting Robert, Kishenlal manages to escape in a black car. He rushes to his home to find that his wife had disappeared, leaving behind a suicide note. He takes his children with him, dropping them off in a park under a statue of Gandhi (A/II/2c). Robert's thugs are in full pursuit, and Kishenlal's car crashes. Before he escapes he notices that the car has a crate full of gold bullion (A/II/2g). He gets hold of this crate as he disappears. Immediately after Kishenlal's encounter with Robert (noted under (b)), there is a police raid. Robert rushes out but not before he sees a crate of gold bullion that belonged to Kishenlal. He grabs hold of this crate, wounds a police inspector, and he too disappears (E/VI/7b). The fantasy of gold is now repeated and the process of stealing one's boss's gold is neatly reversed. Gold made Kishenlal a Robert; it again makes Robert rich.

The segment isolated under (d) is centered around a song "ham ko tum se ho gayā hai pyār kyā kare bolo to jīye bolo to mar jāye ham" (I have fallen in love with you, what can I do; tell me to live or tell me to die). The segment moves through sixty-eight shots in which the loves of the three brothers Amar, Akbar, and Anthony are combined. Beginning with Anthony's relationship with Jenny, where the mise-en-scènes are a speedboat and a horse-cart, the camera cuts to Amar and Lakshmi and to the somewhat unromantic surroundings of their house and garden (they live together). After this scene, the camera cuts to the third pair of lovers, Akbar and Salma, as they sing and dance on a joy-train. The sequence of three scenes is repeated in exactly the same order. Anthony and Jenny ride on a horse cart, Amar and Lakshmi sing in the rain in their garden, Akbar and Salma sing from the top of a train. The song ends with a return to Anthony and Jenny (with whom it had begun in the first instance) as they embrace in the sunset. The distribution of shots and the amount of space given to the pairs are interesting: Amar and Lakshmi get twelve shots, Akbar and Salma twenty-five, Anthony and Jenny thirty-one. The bias is clear. The younger brothers have greater scope for romantic interludes than the eldest. This is not surprising because the role of the eldest and his spouse, in Hindu society, often repeats the role of the patriarch and the matriarch. This is also part of an epic given in the culture.

At (e) we move into more complex symbolic repetitions. The repetitions here do not occupy anything like the space given to those we have already examined. Instead the emphasis is on the symbolic resonances of the icon. The icon in question is a picture of Santoshi Maa, a goddess largely created by Bombay Cinema in 1975 through the release of the film *Jai Santoshi Maa*. *Amar Akbar Anthony* exploits the popularity of this film by giving the picture of Santoshi Maa the status of a talisman. Kishenlal touches a locket with Santoshi Maa's picture as he reads his wife's suicide note. In the note she exhorts him to stay true to this goddess. The pendant is seen by Anthony when he is introduced to Kishenlal in his palatial house. The pendant surfaces again in the operating theater of the hospital where Robert and his thugs are masquerading as doctors. Robert snatches the pendant from the unconscious Kishenlal and exclaims, "So this has been the source of his strength." The dying Catholic priest clutches onto this pendant which Anthony immediately recognizes as belonging to Kishenlal. Finally, the pendant is returned to its rightful owner, and in the process a letter, too, is returned and a recognition scene takes place. Picture, letter, and recognition all form part of a narrative of returns.

Under (f) I have summarized the film's repetitive use of the number 22 and the date August 15. It is twenty-two years since Kishenlal was separated from his wife and children. The precise day was August 15, Indian Independence Day, but the year is not given. The film does not specify its present moment, not that it needs to because in Bombay Cinema the pro-filmic historical moment and the filmic moment are often presented as being the same. Whatever the year of the initial moment of separation—1947 or 1955—the narrative of "partition," of division and displacement, of break from the collective family, is a theme that gets played out often enough in the genre. In this sense the narrative of *Amar Akbar Anthony* gestures toward the grand epic narrative of the painful founding of the nation-state. Appropriately the figure of Gandhi looms large. The first reference to the events of twenty-two years before occurs at segment 7, subsegment (x^1) through a flashback in which the abduction of Robert's daughter by Kishenlal is recounted. It is repeated when Bharati (Kishenlal's wife) is recognized by Akbar's adoptive father, who recalls how on that dark night of August 15, twenty-two years before, he had saved her (J/XI/21e). In another scene Kishenlal reminds Amar of the incident twenty-two years before when he lost his children. Amar's discovery of a toy pistol he hid that day (in shot 8 of the first segment Amar is seen running out of the house with a toy gun) connects his father's statement with his own vague recollections of the event. At L/XII/24b the Catholic priest tells his congregation how he found Anthony twenty-two years before. Jenny, who is in the congregation, rushes out to phone Kishenlal to tell him the good news because she realizes that Anthony is Kishenlal's long-lost son. At this point, however, a slip occurs that the director does not correct during editing. Jenny tells Kishenlal, "uncle āp ne kahā thā kī āj se paccīs sāl pahle azādī vāle din āp ke tīn bete kho gaye the in mem se ek kā patā mil gayā" (Uncle, you once said that twenty-five years ago, on Independence Day, you lost three sons. Out of the three we have found one). Whether Jenny's memory is weak (after all, the uncle seems to have said this only once) or whether Parveen Babi (the actor), who was never renowned for her skills in speaking in Hindi, confused *paccīs* (25) with *bāīs* (22) one can't be too sure. But it seems to me that the error is left uncorrected because it is an essential component of the slippage that takes place in the general problematic of the place of the historical in the structure of Indian cinema and in Indian culture generally. Again like the minstrels of the oral tradition it is the frequency of the occurrence of the number rather than an occasional deviation from it that is significant. My own feeling is that the Indian audience completely ignores this, or it doesn't register it because Parveen Babi's function in the film is very different from that of the other two women. We shall return to this later. The final reference to twenty-two occurs when Kishenlal reads his wife's suicide note composed twenty-two years before.

The three scenes specified as "recognition scenes" (all within the same suprasegment) coincide with those moments when references are also made to the events of twenty-two years before (subsegments 21e, 23c, and 24e). In the first recognition scene the youngest, Akbar, is united with his mother, who had been blind for twenty-two years. Their relationship is more intensely drawn than the mother-son relationship of the others. The bond between the mother and Akbar is further demonstrated by the offer of *sindūr* (sign of the fact that her husband is still alive) by Akbar at K/XII/22b. What is striking is that Oedipal longings remain less sublimated in Akbar than in the other brothers. The second recognition is between the eldest, Amar, and Kishenlal (K/XII/23c). Here a fragmentary narrative of the toy gun collapses with the discovery of one's origins. The law of the police inspector now finds further authority in the Law of the Father. The final recognition scene, this time between the father and his second son, Anthony, is also the moment when a letter, and a pendant (Santoshi Maa) are rediscovered (K/XII/24e).

AFFIRMING THE SECULAR NATION-STATE

The oblique symmetries that we find in all cases of repetition, however, encode another more important narrative, which is the narrative of the nascent Indian state itself. The double coding—the cinema of the imaginary locked into pre-

Oedipal fantasies of harmony working in tandem with a nationalist ideology—confirms the resilience of the secular nation-state. The key to *Amar Akbar Anthony* is this confirmation of the secular nation-state and its great resilience. It is achieved at a number of levels. The first is through the grammar of the eternal dharma, the ultimate Law of the Father, the social unconscious of Hindu India without which filmic narratives would cease to have a central core. The eldest son—as the policeman—occupies the discourse of dharma and remains largely above the "effects" of genre mixing (the hero occasionally as the comic-buffoon, the *vidūṣaka*) associated with Akbar and Anthony.

This confirmation is achieved, second, through the figure of the mother, who confirms the primacy of blood—"yah sac hai koi kahānī nahiṁ khūn khūn hotā hai pānī nahīṁ" (This is the truth, it is no fantasy, blood is blood, it is not water). Blood is thicker than water, a cliché that clearly marks the text's ideology. And this is reinforced by the simple fact that as the song is heard and the credit stills flashed, the three brothers are giving blood to Bharati, their real mother. In one way the film's success is based on the presence of the mother who confirms, for the Indian spectator, the simple fact that the genealogical "disturbance" in the text will not go uncorrected. The spectator can then participate in this imaginary world (as a *darśanik* communion) knowing full well that the disturbance is only momentary. In the context of partition—to which I turn in the next chapter—the trauma of the violence done to the unity/sanctity of Mother India is repeated in a narrative of atonement and confirmation of a presumed earlier sanctity. In the end Mother India remains inviolate.

The third level at which confirmation of the nation-state is achieved is through the iconography of Gandhi. As we have seen in our segmentation of the film, two themes are linked at the level of narrative progression: Indian independence and Indian secularism. The figure who combines the two is Gandhi. He is also a kind of a Yuddhishthira figure whose statue bears the line "ahiṃsā paramo dharma" (Nonviolence is the highest dharma). The locus of independence also allows the film to now represent India, symbolically, through three brothers who grow up in different religions but can come together as one in a secular India. Religious differences do not get in the way of the secular ideal, and in fact religious practices, especially Hindu and Muslim ones, are confined to the margins of the text. The crucial scene of the return of the Mother's eyesight takes place in the Shirdi Sai Baba *dargāh* or shrine (the Sai Baba here is not the current Afro-haired guru). The supernatural event again unites Indian secularism with religious fervor, but since this fervor is now acted out in the context of a nonsectarian and peripheral saint,

Sai Baba, it mediates between the two dominant religious groups in India. In a characteristic fashion, Bombay Cinema confirms all religious and cultural dominants of India through a sleight-of-hand deflection where an aberrant tradition becomes a stand-in for the major (Hindu) one. The secular can be celebrated provided that (Hindu) dharma remains intact, and intermarriage is acceptable provided that the participants finally return to their true genealogy. The telling insinuation here is that Mother India is also the Muslim Mother.

I return to the question of classical Hollywood films, and more specifically to the writer whose work has provided me with the critical apparatus for this chapter. Speaking about "the principle of classical film" Raymond Bellour had observed that "the end must reply to the beginning; between one and the other something must be set in order; the last scene frequently recalls the first and constitutes its resolution" (quoted in Lyon 1988: 249).

At M/XIII/25/l, which is a coda made up of five shots constituting a song scene, it is the second-last subsegment (at 25/k) that replies to the beginning. Here we see Kishenlal in prison with Robert. He tells Robert that the story began and ended with the two of them. The opening shot of the film (A/I/1a) was of a man outside the "Central Jail"; the penultimate subsegment is of the same man and his erstwhile boss inside.

In examining the *grande syntagmatique* (which is also to be read as a structural theory of the heterogeneous practice of Bombay Cinema) through segmentation we need to acknowledge, as both Metz and Bellour have done, that although the procedure does not exhaust the text, segmental citation (despite Bellour's later rejection of it) has analytical value. The *grande syntagmatique* is itself structured around principles of desire and reception, of frame and image, of the construction of the actor-as-parallel-text and has its own dynamic relations with the spectator. I want to conclude by gesturing toward aspects of the Bombay Cinema (as a self-inclusive total structure) that must be constantly factored in. I want to return, in my concluding remarks, to Laura Mulvey's essay (1988) in which she made a case for the male gaze as a controlling patriarchal mode of viewing that dominates, represses, and denies real definitions of womanhood. Woman becomes the object of desire, glimpsed through a keyhole, an object of voyeurism and fetishized to the extent that her real conditions of existence within patriarchy are never rendered truthfully. In the process the male gaze makes woman a commodity without legitimate meaning, an appendage to the greater male history being played out. In Laura Mulvey's thesis this is the condition of the classic filmic narrative in the sense that without this gaze the form itself would be very different. Interestingly enough, the female spectator, too, is no more than a male-substitute viewer, a "transvestite" who is ideologically conned into viewing her own condition through male eyes oblivious of the fact that it is she herself who is the object of that look or gaze. In our reading of Raj Kapoor we claimed that his construction of Nargis was an exemplary instance of precisely the thesis advanced by Mulvey. It is also true that Raj Kapoor is probably the only auteur who consistently employed this mode although even he restricted his gaze to Nargis for reasons that required us to enter into matters of biography as well as film theory. Raj Kapoor's enormous success arose out of the manner in which he substituted the spectator's gaze for his own (or vice versa), reinforcing in the process the repressed sexual desires of the Indian male generally. The camera eye here is that of a Peeping Tom whose fantasies are even greater because the keyhole limits his vistas. Later filmmakers realized the value of the gaze and manipulated it for the same ends but not with the same success. Raj Kapoor's films were a lot more about desire than about social justice or anything else. *Amar Akbar Anthony* is about unity in diversity with a dharmik chocolate coating. But the film also plays on another kind of knowledge. This is the knowledge of stars through the fanzines, a point that we made at length in our chapter on the actor-as-parallel-text. The actor who was the subject of that chapter, Amitabh Bachchan, is the towering star of *Amar Akbar Anthony* as well. But his heroine in this film is Parveen Babi, a glamorous actor whom the fanzines had romantically linked with Bachchan. Thus whereas Lakshmi [Shabana Azmi] (Amar's lover) and Salma [Neetu Singh] (Akbar's lover) are represented through relatively neutral shots that eschew any close bodily contact, Jenny [Parveen Babi] is represented through full frontal shots and close body contacts with Bachchan. There is a sinister ideology at work here that more or less says that a Christian Indian is a legitimate object of desire. The desire is derisively strengthened through shots of Jenny scantily dressed so that in an entire sequence (I/X/20b, shots 989–1070), her long legs and black panties are exposed. Since the fanzines had made much of Bachchan's real or illusory relationship with Parveen Babi, and her sexuality, the construction of Babi in this manner superimposes spectatorial desire onto that of Bachchan's profilmic desire for Babi. What is significant for the theory is that the spectator perceives desire as such. My point is that segmentation and the importance of the *grande syntagmatique* in film analysis need to be tempered by the ideology of the point of view, especially with reference to the female object of desire. In referring to the male gaze and the use of Parveen Babi's body in *Amar Akbar Anthony* I simply want to foreground this proviso and place my segmentation exercise in the larger problematic of reception and representation.

BAIJU BAWRA

Section	Supra-Segment	Segment	Place	Sub-Segment	Characters	Shots	Syntagma	Music	Action
A	I	1	[Producer/Title]	a	Woman	1	Autonomous shot	Music	Woman bows over dome:"Lead Kindly Light."
		2	[Titles over singer and background synopsis]	b	Tansen	2		Song/music: "tori jay jay kartār"	Man sings: titles and background synopsis in English, Hindi, and Urdu
B	II	3	Inside palace		Tansen	3–14	Scene	Song continues	Tansen sings. End of song. Crowds disperse as he takes applause.
						15	Autonomous Shot		Guards disperse crowd. Night.
	III	4	City at night outside palace	a	Tansen & Ghasit Khan	16–30	Sequence	Song: raga	Tansen tells guard there should be no noise as he is composing a new raga. Ghasit Khan, the people's singer, sings and is stopped by guards.
			City	b	Singers; Young Baiju & father	31–52	Sequence	Song: "sāmco tero rām nām"	Group of singing minstrels approaches. Guards try to disperse them. Baiju's father is killed in the skirmish. Dying father asks Baiju never to forget this incident and seek revenge on Tansen. Baiju vows to take revenge.
C	IV	5	Countryside	a	Young Baiju soldiers Priest	53–59	Scene		Young Baiju tries to steal a sword, is caught by a guard but gets a reprieve as a passing priest offers to take care of him.

Section	Supra-Segment	Segment	Place	Sub-Segment	Characters	Shots	Syntagma	Music	Action
			Riverbank	b	Priest, Baiju	60–66	Scene	Music	Priest takes Baiju to his village across the Jamuna river. Baiju narrates his story.
			Riverbank, river	c	Priest, Baiju Girl	67–75	Scene	Theme song played in background: "tu gaṅgā ki mauj meṁ" (music only)	Meets girl on boat. His name is Baijnath, the girl's Gauri.
			Riverbank, river	d	Gauri, father (Mohan), Baiju, Priest	76–80	Scene	Music	Baiju meets Gauri's father (Mohan). Baiju gets agitated whenever he hears Tansen's name.
D	V	6	Riverbank, swing	a	Baiju, Gauri	81–85	Scenes plus autonomous shot	Song: "jhūle meṁ pavan ki āī bahār"	Baiju and Gauri sing.
			Swing, garden, river	b	Adult Baiju & Gauri	86–106	Sequence	Song continues	Both grow into adulthood.
VI		7	Garden		Baiju, Gauri, rival suitor, comic, and villagers	107–120	Scene		Baiju and Gauri's relationship disturbed by entry of rival suitor and comments by villagers about Baiju's obscure genealogy. The suitor claims that he'll marry Gauri in the next season.
		8	Gauri's house		Mohan Gauri	121–134	Scene		Father (Mohan) comes looking for Gauri as she milks cow because villagers tell him that Gauri has been flirting with Baiju.

	9	Baiju's house		Baiju's father [Priest]	135–140 Scene		Baiju overhears villagers' complaint. Father comes in, and Baiju is despondent, saddened both by love and harsh words. Father assures Baiju he'll be a great singer.
VII	10	Riverbank	a	Gauri and Baiju	141–147 Scene	Background music	Baiju and Gauri talk as she gets off the boat. Conversation about swimming and drowning as Baiju can't swim.
		Riverbank	b	Father	148 Autonomous shot		Father sees Gauri and Baiju.
		Riverbank, river	c	Gauri, Baiju & villagers	149–192 Sequence	Song: "tū gaṅgā kī r̤auj meṁ"	Baiju sings the signature song of the film as Gauri pulls the boat away. Villagers gather as Baiju's father, too, watches.
		Bank	d	Gauri and female friends	193 Autonomous shot 194 " 195 " 196 " 197 " 198 "		Friends tease Gauri in these individual shots.
VIII	11	House		Mohan and Baiju's father	199 Autonomous shot		Mohan tells Father that Baiju and Gauri are in love.
	12	House		Rival suitor comic	200–202 Scene		Suitor wishes to learn how to sing. Comic recalls a singer in Agra, Ghasit Khan.
	13	House, garden	a	Gauri, friends	203–207		Friends ask Gauri to join them. She is lonely.

Section	Supra-Segment	Segment	Place	Sub-Segment	Characters	Shots	Syntagma	Music	Action
			Garden	b	Baiju	208–219	Scene	First line of signature song	Baiju calls one of the female friends.
			Garden	c	Gauri, friends, Baiju	220–242	Scene plus autonomous shot of Baiju	Song: "dūr koī gāye dhun yah sunāye"	The friends sing as Baiju intermittently sings chorus of signature song: ho jī ho.
			Garden	d	Baiju, Gauri friends	243–253	Scene		Friends joke with Baiju about Gauri, who runs into the house.
E	IX	14	City		Clown (Ganju), Ghasit Khan, etc.	254–259	Scene		Clown (Ganju) meets Ghasit Khan and invites him home to act as tutor to his master.
	X	15	Outside home	a	Suitor and friends	260	Autonomous shot		Suitor waits for Ghasit Khan and proclaims he'll get married the next season.
			Gauri's courtyard	b	Suitor and Mohan	261–284	Scene		Suitor tells Mohan that Gauri is seeing Baiju. Mohan calls Gauri.
			Father's house	c	Father, Mohan, and Gauri	285–303	Scene		Mohan comes to Baiju's father's house. Father tells Mohan Gauri is already "married" to Baiju in a union of pure love. Mohan agrees to raise it at the Village Council, and, if need be, agrees to pay for breach of promise.
		16	Garden	a	Baiju	304	Autonomous shot		Baiju walks alone.

Section	No.	Location	Sub	Characters	Shots	Type	Song	Description
		Garden	b	Gauri, Suitor	305–308	Scene		Gauri runs to Baiju. Bumps into suitor.
		Outside	c	Clown, Ghasit Khan	309–314	Scene		Clown and Ghasit arrive.
		Garden	d	Gauri, Suitor (Narpat), Ghasit Khan	315–317		Suitor (Narpat) tries to sing	Cut to subsegment *a* as Gauri and Suitor seen together. Ghasit hears Suitor's atrocious singing and reproaches him. Suitor runs to meet Ghasit Khan.
	17	Garden	a	Gauri, Baiju	318–330	Autonomous shots	Baiju plays tamboura	Gauri runs toward Baiju saying that her father, Mohan, has agreed to their marriage.
F	XI							
	18	Outside (streets, etc)	a	Crowd	331–343	Scene		Shots fired, horses. Gauri falls down on the road and is hurt. Some villagers rounded up by dacoits.
		"	b	Looters, Mohan	344–356	Scene		Woman leader of gang asks for 2,000 gold sovereigns. Dacoits grab women's jewelry.
		"	c	Father, crowd, Baiju, crowd, Looters	357–381	Scene	Baiju sings: "insān bano"	Affected by Baiju's song, dacoits put their swords/guns down.
		"	d	"	382–409	Scene		Dacoit Queen desires Baiju. Agrees to leave the village/town if Baiju goes with her. Gauri tries to stop him but the Dacoit Queen is adamant. Reluctantly Baiju takes leave.
XII	19	Countryside men on horses desolate garden		Baiju, Dacoit Queen, Riders, Gauri	410–427	Scene	Gauri sings: "bacpan ki muhabbat ko"	Gauri sings as Baiju rides away. Mismatch of Gauri's long shot and close-up of her singing in a desolate garden.

Section	Supra-Segment	Segment	Place	Sub-Segment	Characters	Shots	Syntagma	Music	Action
G	XIII	20	Inside Dacoit den	a	Baiju, Dacoit Queen	428–436	Scene		Dacoit Queen confesses that she is the daughter of the village chief killed by the notorious Man Singh. She had vowed to take back what was hers by right. Baiju rejects her love.
			"	b		437	Autonomous shot (flashback)		Baiju recalls his own father's call for vengeance.
						438–439	Scene		Baiju confesses Gauri's love had made him forget his vow and now she, the Dacoit Queen, has reminded him of his duty. He grabs a sword and rushes out to fulfill his vow.
			"	c	Dacoit Queen and guard	440–442	Scene		Dacoit Queen prevents guard from stopping Baiju.
H	XIV	21	Palace wall and inside palace	a	Baiju and Tansen	443–496	Sequence	Tansen sings classical rāga Darbāri	Baiju climbs wall and closes in on Tansen as he sings. Quick shots of Tansen, Baiju, and paintings of Raga and Ragini (personifications). Entranced by the music, Baiju wavers, then strikes the musical instrument with his sword.
			Inside palace	b	"	497–509	Scene		Tansen informs Baiju that he can be destroyed only by a sadder song.
			"	c	Baiju, Tansen, and soldiers	510–523	Scene		Soldiers come rushing in. Baiju is taken away with echoes of "bring a sadder song."

				Location	Character	Shots	Type	Song/Rāga	Description
I	XV	22		Outside	Baiju	524–539	Autonomous shots		Series of shots superimposed upon each other. In search of the perfect voice he goes to Vrindavan to find Tansen's own guru, Haridas Swami.
J	XVI	23		Vrindavan	Baiju, Haridas Swami	540–547	Autonomous shot		Haridas Swami tells Baiju that he can master music only through love.
	XVII	24	a	Forest	Baiju	548–560	Scene		Baiju wanders into a ruined Shiva temple.
			b	Ruined temple	Baiju	561–575	Scene		Speaks to statue. Repeats "om."
			c	Desolate garden	Gauri	576–577	Autonomous shots	Signature song: "tū gaṅgā kī mauj meṁ"	Cut to Gauri who hears first line of signature song.
			d	Ruined temple	Baiju	573–582	"	Rāga: "piu piu re kahat hai papīhā"	Baiju sings the following ragas guided by the vision of his guru: rāga bhairavi.
			e	Outside (in the rain)	Baiju	583–586	"	Rāga: "rim jhim badariyā barase"	Rāga malhār.
			f	Outside	Baiju	587	"	Rāga: "ajab to"	Rāga puriyā.
			g	Outside	Baiju	588–590	"	Rāga: "hari maiṁ kaise ghar āūṁ"	Rāga bhāgeśvarī.
K	XVIII	25		Village	Father, Mohan, Gauri	591–596	Scene		Baiju can't be found. Mohan has failed to convince the Village Council that Gauri's engagement to Narpat can be broken.
		26	a	Garden	Gauri	557–605	Scene	Song: "mujhe bhūl gaye sāṁvariyā"	Gauri sings as flashback shots are interwoven into the present text.

Section	Supra-Segment	Segment	Place	Sub-Segment	Characters	Shots	Syntagma	Music	Action
				b	Gauri Dacoit Queen	606–611			Gauri wishes to take poison but is stopped by the Dacoit Queen who takes Gauri away with the promise of finding Baiju.
L	XIX	27	Hermitage	a	Haridas, friends, Baiju	612–620	Sequence	"Hari Om" sung	Haridas Swami is ill. He can't walk when Baiju comes to see him.
			Outside	b	Baiju, Haridas and friends	621–683	Sequence	song: "mana tarpat hari darśan ko āj"	As Baiju sings Haridas is healed. Lots of autonomous shots interwoven into the sequence.
			Outside	c	Baiju and Haridas	684–690	Scene		Haridas again emphasizes the importance of self-denial.
			Temple	d	Baiju and Gauri, Dacoit Queen	691–722	Sequence	Signature song and "Hari Om" heard	Gauri finds Baiju with the help of the Dacoit Queen. Baiju spurns Gauri, who emphasizes love against Baiju's revenge. Baiju tells Gauri he wants to beat Tansen at singing before marrying her. Baiju leaves Gauri with the words that love in an impediment to revenge.
			Outside temple	e	Baiju, Haridas Friends and Gauri	723–749	Scene		Baiju tells his Swami that he must be a loner. Gauri overhears this. Gauri lets a serpent bite her.
			Outside	f	Baiju, Gauri, Dacoit Queen, guards	750–763			Baiju becomes crazy when he sees Gauri dead. Baiju enters the temple as the Dacoit Queen takes Gauri's body away.

M	28	Jail	g	Baiju, Ghasit, Tansen, crowd	764–817		Song: "o duniyā ke rakhvāle"	Begins singing in the temple. The statue weeps. Walks around from place to place. Reaches Agra. Tansen looks out as guards take Baiju and Ghasit Khan to jail for disturbing Tansen's peace.
			a	Ghasit, Baiju	818	Autonomous shot		Ghasit and Baiju in jail.
			b	Baiju / Gauri	819–820 " / 821–822 [inset shot]			Shots of Baiju. Shots of Gauri.
			c	Ghasit, Baiju, Dacoit Queen Guards	823–837			Dacoit Queen (Queen Rupmati) comes to rescue them and tells Baiju that Gauri is alive. He refuses to believe her. They are taken away by guards.
N	29	Mohan's house		Mohan, Gauri	833–846	Autonomous shot		Mohan insists that Gauri should now marry Narpat or face her own father's death.
O	30	Jail	a	Ghasit, Baiju	847	Autonomous shot		Ghasit Khan tells Baiju that if he wishes to see Gauri he must beat Tansen at singing. He agrees.
		Durbar	b	Baiju, Tansen crowd	848–853		Various ragas	Preliminary to the singing competition Tansen and Baiju show their singing skills.
		Durbar	c	Baiju, Tansen, Ghasit, Akbar crowd	854–950	Scene	Song: "aj gāvat man mero jhūm ke"	Final competition in front of Emperor Akbar. The challenge is to break marble through raga. Baiju succeeds. Asks for the release of his friends and that music be freed from all restrictions. Tansen's life to be spared as well.

Temple, forest city, etc.

Section	Supra-Segment	Segment	Place	Sub-Segment	Characters	Shots	Syntagma	Music	Action
				d	"	951	Scene	Signature tune: "ho ji ho"	Baiju hears music and rushes out.
P	XXIII	31	Mohan's house	a	Gauri, Narpat Mohan, crowd	952–956	Scene	Signature tune: "ho ji ho"	Gauri is getting married. She cries, hears Baiju's song.
			Riverbank	b	Baiju, boatman	957–958	Scene		The boatman can't take Baiju across as the river is flooded.
			Village	c	Father, Gauri	959	Autonomous shot		Gauri tells father Baiju has come.
			Mohan's house	d	Narpat, crowd	960–961	Scene		Call for Gauri to come to the marriage ceremony.
			River	e	Baiju, boatman	962–964	Scene		Baiju pushes the boat into the water.
			Mohan's house	f	Narpat, crowd	965	Autonomous shot		Narpat asks for Gauri.
			River	g	Gauri	966	"		Gauri rushes toward the river.
			River	h	Baiju	967	"		Baiju in the water.
			River	i	Baiju, Gauri	968–1006	"	Signature song: "tū gaṅgā kī mauj meṅ"	Both Baiju and Gauri drown.
			River	j	-	1007	"		"The End" on the water.

AMAR AKBAR ANTHONY

				Location	Characters	Shots	Type	Music	Description
A	I	1	a	Outside Central Jail	Man	1–2	Sequence	Orchestral music	Man out of jail, looks at some rupees in hand.
			b	Outside home	Man, wife, kids	3–10	Scene		A woman tells man his wife has tuberculosis. Man meets wife (Bharati), sees his three kids fighting over food. Showers them with gifts. Gives eldest son a toy gun with which he rushes out. Man asks wife if Robert sent her any money while he was in jail. Wife says he didn't.
	II	2	a	Robert's mansion, on the road	Robert, man Robert's gang	11–60	Sequence	Orchestral music	Man cleans Robert's shoes. Robert throws a coin at him. Skirmish follows as man shoots Robert who has a bullet-proof vest on. Man gets into one of Robert's cars, which, Robert says, is laden with gold. Car chase follows.
			b	Home	Man and children	61–68	Sequence		Man reaches own house. Reads wife's suicide note. Puts picture of Santoshi Maa and chain in his hand.
			c	Road, garden	Villains, man, children Police	69–110	Sequence		Policeman sees man (Kishenlal) with children. Villains continue chase. Man places children under Gandhi's statue in the garden. Child runs; wife (Bharati) runs and falls under a tree; car chase continues. Another child runs for food. Car chase. Car crashes. Police tell villains not to go to the crash site.
			d	Garden, road	Muslim man 3rd child	111–120	Scene		Muslim man picks up child sitting against statue of Gandhi. Takes him away in his car.

Section	Supra-Segment	Segment Place	Sub-Segment	Characters	Shots	Syntagma	Music	Action
		Road, garden	e	2nd child	121–123	Scene		2nd child returns with roti in hand for youngest.
		Road outside	f	Muslim man, Bharati, 3rd child	124–129	Scene		Muslim man stops car to give Bharati (suddenly gone blind) a lift. She hears her own 3rd child crying but cannot see him.
		Outside	g	Kishenlal	130–133	Scene		Kishenlal escapes from burning car. Sees crate of gold bullion. Picks up crate and leaves.
		In car	h	Muslim man, Bharati, 3rd child	134	Autonomous shot		Bharati in car with Muslim man. She touches the child.
		Outside	i	2nd child	135–136	Scene		2nd child runs toward a church. Eats roti.
		Home	j	Muslim man, 3rd child, Bharati, Policeman, Woman	137–140	Scene		Bharati is brought home. She is blind. Policeman tells Bharati that her husband and children were killed in an accident.
		Outside church	k	Priest, 2nd child	141–146	Scene		Priest finds 2nd child and discovers Bharati's suicide note.
		Road	l	1st child, Policeman	147–148	Scene		A policeman picks up the 1st child.
		Road	m	Kishenlal	149–157	Scene		Kishenlal carries gold and runs. Reaches Gandhi's

statue, but cannot see any of the children. Calls "Amar," the name of his first child.

					Characters		Type	
B	III	3	Church	a	2nd child / Priest	158	Autonomous shot	2nd child confesses to Father/priest.
			Church	b	Anthony / Priest	159–164	Scene	2nd child, grows up into Anthony, and confesses to Father about his liquor business. A man rushes in to say there's been an accident.
			Church Outside	c	Priest / Anthony	165–170	Scene	An accident outside the church. A taxi is called.
			Police station	d	Amar	171–174	Autonomous shot	Amar (the 1st child) is the policeman who answers a phone call about the accident.
			Hospital	e	Akbar / Woman / Nurse, etc.	175–185	Scene	Akbar (the 3rd child) romancing the doctor. Is asked to donate blood to the accident victim because blood from the two volunteers is not sufficient. A doctor asks names of the three donees; they reply, "Amar," "Akbar," "Anthony."
		4	Credits		Song: "yah sac hai koi kahānī nahīṁ…khūn khūn hota hai pānī nahīṁ."	186–192	Scene	Credits superimposed upon a shot of Amar, Akbar, Anthony giving blood to Bharati, who is, unknown to them, their mother.
C	IV	5	Liquor store	a	Anthony & two men	193–231	Scene	Anthony and men fight in liquor store. Anthony disposes of the men.

Section	Supra-Segment	Segment	Place	Sub-Segment	Characters	Shots	Syntagma	Music	Action
			Outside	b	Anthony, Akbar	232–234	Scene		Akbar gives Anthony a ticket to his musical performance that night.
			Outside theater	c	Akbar, Mother Anthony crowd	235–253	Sequence		Blind mother (Bharati) gives flower to Akbar. Anthony takes her into the theater.
			Theater	d	Akbar, Anthony, mother, Akbar's beloved's family, audience	254–369	Scene	Song: "pardā hai pardā hai"	Akbar sings a *qawali* on stage. Throws flower at woman doctor (veiled) who walks on stage and touches Akbar.
D	V	6	Police station	a	Amar Policeman	370–371	Scene	Orchestral music	Policeman tells Amar about a girl who steals from men.
			Outside	b	Amar, girl crooks	372–419	Sequence		Amar gives a girl a ride in his car. The girl screams "rape" and threatens to call the police if she is not given money. Girl's brother and other crooks fight with Amar. Amar gives them a beating. Girl confesses that she had been used by her stepmother and stepbrother.
			House	c	Girl, stepmother, old woman Amar	420–435	Scene		Girl tells stepmother her brother has been taken by police. Amar steps in to arrest stepmother and to take the girl and her grandmother home.
E	VI	7	Outside near the sea	a¹	Kishenlal Robert	436–446	Scene	Orchestral music	Smuggler Kishenlal (now phenomenally rich, speaks with an English accent) is stopped by Robert, now one of his workers who speaks with an Indian

No.	Location	Segment	Characters	Shots	Type	Music	Description
	Home	x¹ (flash-back)	Kishenlal, Robert, young girl	447–449	Scene	Orchestral music	accent. Kishenlal tells Robert to clean his shoes. Robert wants to know his daughter's whereabouts. Kishenlal kidnaps Robert's daughter, leaving a note behind.
	Outside near the sea	a²	Kishenlal Robert	450–463	Scene		Kishenlal throws a coin at Robert pointing out that it is the same coin he had thrown back at him many years before. He had made a pauper of Robert through his own gold.
	" "	b	Police, Kishenlal Robert	464–480	Sequence		Police arrive. Robert runs off with a crate of Kishenlal's gold bullion and wounds a police inspector, Amar's "father."
	Street	c	Anthony, Robert	481–489	Scene		Robert bumps into Anthony, who notices the gold bullion and helps Robert escape from the police.
8	Hospital		Amar, inspector, doctor	485–489	Scene		Amar visits his inspector "father" in hospital. Declares his determination to catch the culprits.
9	Jail		Amar, crooks, inspector	490–497	Scene		Amar beats up crooks. Inspector Desai tells Amar that Robert was seen with a man named Anthony.
10	Outside		Amar, Anthony, crowd	498–561	Sequence		Amar and Anthony fight.

Section	Supra-Segment	Segment	Place	Sub-Segment	Characters	Shots	Syntagma	Music	Action
F	VII	11	Jail	a	Anthony, Amar, policeman, mother	562–590	Scene		Anthony behind bars is visited by mother (Bharati). Calls both Amar and Anthony her sons.
			Inside police van, street	b	Anthony, police	591–601	Sequence		Inside police van. Someone throws smoke bombs, and Anthony disappears.
			Inside house	c	Kishenlal Anthony, crooks	602–631	Sequence		Anthony is seen with Kishenlal sitting around an expensive table. Kishenlal asks for Robert's whereabouts. He gives Kishenlal the mother's flowers and sees the picture of Santoshi Maa around Kishenlal's neck. After a scuffle Anthony escapes.
		12	Police station	a	Amar, Anthony police	632–640	Scene		Anthony makes his way back to jail. Agrees to take Amar to Robert upon hearing that Robert is a criminal.
			Anthony's den	b	Amar, Anthony, man, priest	641–649	Scene		Robert has escaped from Anthony's custody. Amar gives Anthony a month in which to find Robert. Priest/Father tells Anthony to get married.
G	VIII	13	Airport	a	Robert Kishenla, Jenny, girl, crooks	650–663	Sequence		A girl arrives. She is abducted by Robert and his cronies because Robert thinks she is his lost daughter.
			In car	b	Kishenlal, Jenny	664	Scene		Girl (Jenny) with Kishenlal who tells her that Robert was responsible for the loss of his three children.
			Home	c	Robert, girl, crooks	665–670	Scene		Girl abducted by mistake holds a gun but is overpowered.

	Location		Characters	Shots	Type	Song/Music	Description
	Home	d	Kishenlal, Jenny, bodyguard	671	Scene		Kishenlal introduces Jenny to her new bodyguard.
14	Church		Anthony, Jenny, bodyguard	672–715	Sequence	Church music; Film music	Anthony sees Jenny in church. He is infatuated by her. He drags Father to meet her, but she disappears.
15	Dance hall		Anthony, Jenny, bodyguard, crowd	716–787	Sequence	Song: "My name is Anthony Gonzales... maiṁ duniyā meṁ akelā hūṁ"	Anthony sings song and delights Jenny. Gets drunk and is beaten up by Jenny's jealous bodyguard.
16	House		Anthony	788–789	Scene		Drunken Anthony speaks to his image in the mirror. A comic scene.
17	Church		Jenny, Anthony	790–800	Scene		Jenny confesses to Father about love, but the Father turns out to be Anthony.
18	Outboard, beach	a	Anthony, Jenny	801–829	Scene	Song: ham ko tum se ho gayā hai pyār kyā kare . . .	Anthony and Jenny sing on a boat, from a horse cart.
	House, garden	b	Amar, Lakshmi	830–840	Scene	Song: "	Same song continued by Amar and Lakshmi in their house.
	Joy-train	c	Akbar, Salma	841–864	Scene	Song: "	Akbar and Salma sing same song on a train.
	Beach	d	Anthony, Jenny	865	Scene	Song: "	Anthony and Jenny on horse cart as the sun sets.
	Home	e	Amar, Laksmi	866	Scene	Song: "	Amar and Lakshmi in the garden in the rain.
	Train	f	Akbar, Salma	867	Scene	Song: "	Akbar and Salma on the roof of train.
	Beach	g	Anthony, Jenny	868	Scene	Song: "	Anthony and Jenny at sunset.

Section	Supra-Segment	Segment	Place	Sub-Segment	Characters	Shots	Syntagma	Music	Action
H	IX	19	Salma's house	a	Akbar, Salma	869–876	Scene		Akbar coaxes Salma to come down from her balcony. Akbar has brought a camera.
			House	b	Taiyyab Ali and woman	877–887	Scene		Akbar takes a photograph of Taiyyab Ali (Salma's father) haggling with one of his former mistresses.
			Outside	c	Akbar, Taiyyab Ali, Salma, Hijrās, crowd	888–952	Scene	Song: taiyyab ali pyār kā duśman hāy hāy merī jān kā duśman hāy hāy	Akbar sings with a group of Hijrās accusing Salma's father for being the enemy of love. Taiyyab Ali sends some hooligans to beat Akbar up.
			Office, hospital	d	Anthony, Taiyyab Ali, Kazi, Salma Akbar	953–974	Sequence		Anthony comes rushing in. Lifts Taiyyab Ali from his desk and takes him to the hospital with a Kazi to marry Salma and Akbar. Akbar refuses to marry Salma without her father's permission. Akbar espouses nonviolence.
I	X	20	House	a	Jenny, D'Bisco	975–988	Sequence		Jenny's bodyguard (D'Bisco) suddenly turns around and tells Jenny he wants to marry her. When Jenny refuses, he phones Robert to tell him of Jenny's whereabouts but insists that he should be allowed to marry Jenny. Kishenlal arrives and choloroforms D'Bisco, releasing Jenny, who had been tied to the floor.
			Outside	b	Jenny, Kishenlal, D'Bisco, Robert, and gang	989– 1070	Sequence	Orchestral music	Kishenlal and Jenny chased by Robert and gang. The chase is witnessed on the road by Anthony and Akbar. Jenny and Kishenlal separate to confuse their pursuers. Jenny is saved by Anthony and Kishenlal

								by Akbar. Robert's car crashes into a pool. Robert and his gang survive.
J	XI	21	Hospital	a	1071–1074	Scene	Akbar, Kishenlal		Akbar takes Kishenlal to hospital.
			Robert's house	b	1075–1080	Sequence	Robert, D'Bisco, Robert's twin		D'Bisco persuades Robert that he should marry Jenny by introducing Robert to his long-lost twin brother.
			Hospital	c	1081–1102	Sequence	Mother, Kishenlal, Akbar, Robert, Salma, crooks		Mother comes to see Akbar (who had been hospitalized there after being attacked by Taiyyab Ali's hooligans) but is told that Akbar (in fact Kishenlal) has been taken into the operating theater. Inside the theater, Robert and his gang, disguised as doctors and nurses, persuade Salma, the doctor, and Akbar's lover, to bring Kishenlal back to consciousness. Robert pulls Kishenlal's Jai Santoshi Maa pendant and exclaims, "This is the source of his power." Mother knocks on the door, is brought inside, and is recognized by Robert as Kishenlal's wife.
			Outside	d	1103–1180	Sequence	Robert, gang, mother, Akbar, crowd	Sai Baba song	Robert takes mother away. Car crashes into a rock. Mother rolls down a slope. She hears a song coming from a Sai Baba Temple. Robert and his accomplice are stopped from entering the temple by a snake. Inside Akbar is the lead singer. Mother crawls inside the temple and miraculously regains her sight. Akbar recognizes her as the flower lady to whom he once gave blood.

Section	Supra-Segment	Segment	Place	Sub-Segment	Characters	Shots	Syntagma	Music	Action
			Home	e	Akbar's father, Akbar, mother	1181–1207	Scene		Recognition scene as Akbar's adoptive father recognizes Bharati and Bharati, the mother, recognizes Akbar ("Raju"). "Father" refers to the events of that dark night 22 years before.
K	XII	22	Home	a	Akbar, Salma, Taiyyab Ali	1208–1243	Sequence		Fire in Taiyyab Ali's timber factory. Salma is dramatically saved by Akbar. Taiyyab Ali, Salma's father, agrees to let Akbar marry his daughter. Salma tells Akbar that the hospitalized Kishenlal is the flower woman Bharati's husband.
			Home	b	Akbar, mother	1244–1258	Scene		Akbar symbolically places *sindūr* (vermillion) on his mother's forehead signifying that her husband is alive.
		23	Hospital	a	Akbar, mother, nurse	1259–1260	Scene		Nurse informs Akbar and mother that Kishenlal's doctor has taken him out of the hospital.
			Police station	b	Akbar, Amar	1261–1267	Scene		Akbar tells Amar about Kishenlal's original house. Amar vaguely remembers the house.
			Home	c	Kishenlal, man, woman	1268–1314	Sequence	Orchestral music	Kishenlal raps one of his workers for not paying the wife of one of his workers currently in jail. "I am not Robert," he says. Amar arrives and asks for the house. Kishenlal enters his old house. "God give me back my children," he says. Sees Amar digging up an old toy gun. Recognition scene takes place. Kishenlal relates the events of that fateful night of August 15, 22 years before.

L	XIII	24						
			Shop	a	1315–1317	Anthony, Jenny, Akbar	Sequence	Anthony and Jenny in Akbar's father's tailoring shop to order a wedding dress. D'Bisco sees Anthony and Jenny together.
			Church	b	1318–1355	Anthony, Jenny, priest, congregation	Sequence	Catholic Father gives sermon in church and narrates the story of a three-year-old child he found 22 years ago. This child is now going to get married. Jenny phones Kishenlal to tell him that she believes one of his three lost sons (lost 25? years ago) has been found and that she's marrying him. Before she can name him, the telephone is disconnected. Robert abducts Jenny. The priest intervenes but he is killed. Statue of Christ bleeds.
			Road	c	1356–1365	Jenny, Robert, Lakshmi, stepbrother	Sequence	Lakshmi sees Jenny in a van and places herself in it. Her stepbrother (now working for Robert) discovers Lakshmi and takes her away as well.
			Church	d	1366–1392	Anthony	Scene	Anthony speaks to priest who he thinks is praying at the altar. Tells him he has left alcohol business. He discovers the priest is dead and sees the Santoshi Maa locket (which he associates with Kishenlal) and an old letter.
			Home	e	1393–14:3	Anthony, Kishenlal	Scene	Anthony takes Santoshi Maa pendant to Kishenlal and accuses him of murder. Kishenlal narrates Jenny's phone call. 3rd recognition scene as Kishenlal reads Bharati's suicide note and recalls the events that happened 22 years ago.

Section	Supra-Segment	Segment	Place	Sub-Segment	Characters	Shots	Syntagma	Music	Action
M	XIV	25	Outside shop	a	Akbar, D'Bisco	1414–1419			D'Bisco comes to get Jenny's wedding dress. Akbar is suspicious and tells him that a tailor should accompany D'Bisco to ensure that it fits well.
			Robert's house	b	Robert, Akbar, D'Bisco, Jenny, Lakshmi, crooks	1420–1445	Scene		Akbar, now dressed as a tailor, arrives with D'Bisco. Sees Jenny and, pretending to need more material for the wedding dress, sends a note to his father, in Urdu, explaining the situation.
			Shop	c	Akbar's father, Salma, crooks	1446–1449	Scene		Akbar's father reads letter and sends Salma with a sewing machine. Sends message to Amar and Anthony.
			Robert's house	d	Robert, etc.	1450–1453	Scene		Salma and Akbar speak to Robert.
			Garden	e	Amar, Anthony, musicians	1454	Scene		Amar and Anthony take musicians and priest (on their way to Jenny's marriage) away.
			Robert's house	f	Robert, Lakshmi, Jenny, Salma, D'Bisco, Amar, Akbar, Anthony etc.	1455–1504	Sequence	Song: "anhonī ko honī karnā honī ko anhonī"	Amar and Anthony arrive disguised as musicians. They sing together with Akbar.
			Mechanic shop	g	Pedro, two cronies	1505	Autonomous shot		Cut to Pedro's mechanic shop.

Location		Type	Segment	Characters	Notes	Description
Robert's house	h	Scene	1506–1521	Robert, etc.		Song continues.
Car	i	Scene	1522–1523	Hooligans		Pedro's hooligans on their way to Robert's house.
Robert's house	j	Sequence	1524–1619	Robert, etc.		Priest (Anthony) calls for the bride, Jenny, who comes with Lakshmi and Salma. Jenny faints, and Salma, who is a doctor, declares she is pregnant. Anthony goes upstairs with the women to find the name of the father as Robert accuses D'Bisco of violating his daughter's honor. Pedro's hooligans arrive to expose the fraudulent musicians. Fight ensues in which Amar, Akbar, and Anthony soundly beat Robert and his cronies.
Prison and outside	k	Scene	1620–1627	Robert, Kishenlal, Amar, Akbar, Anthony, etc.		Kishenlal is also seen in prison with Robert and his gang. He tells Robert that this story has begun and ended with the two of them. Kishenlal speaks to his wife (Bharati) and embraces his three sons.
Road, in a car	l	Scene	1628–1632	Amar, Akbar Anthony, Lakshmi, Salma, Jenny	Song: "anhoni ko honi karna"	Amar, Akbar, Anthony with their respective spouses sing "anhoni ko honi karna." The film ends.

Chapter Seven

AFTER AYODHYA: THE SUBLIME OBJECT OF FUNDAMENTALISM

Amar Akbar Anthony celebrated the nation-state under the sign of an enlightened dharma. As politics, it affirmed the liberal ethos of India; as allegory, it demonstrated the underlying origins of all Indians—one mother but different beliefs, a variation on Savarkar's original version of Hindutva. That was in 1977. Any reader of Bombay Cinema senses that things changed rather dramatically after that. The hegemony of the Congress Party as the natural rulers of India came to an end; the nation (though not as a consequence of the end of this hegemony) teetered toward regional divisions, terrorism, and general exhaustion after the euphoria of the first few decades of independence. Outside, the Iranian revolution of 1978–79 rekindled, uncomfortably for India, the specter of Islam. Ten years after this revolution, the Iranian fatwa against Salman Rushdie (invariably referred to in the media as an Indian Muslim) confirmed old Hindu phobias about Islam's essential inflexibility. Two factors define the post–*Amar Akbar Anthony* world: the rise of Hindu fundamentalism and cultural globalization. I take up the first of these in this chapter. As for cultural globalization I take it up in the next chapter with reference to cinema and the diaspora. Between these two—fundamentalism and cultural globalization—may be located the essential "drama" of Bombay Cinema in the post–*Amar Akbar Anthony* (1977–), post–Amitabh Bachchan (1986–) period.

I want to argue that Hindu fundamentalism is symptomatic of an undertheorized silence or repression located at the very heart of national culture. What I have called the sublime object of fundamentalism in the half title of this chapter is another way of expressing a whole set of political, social, and religious conditions about which the secular state has historically remained silent. In their attempts to recast India's own highly divisive history as an unproblematic grand (national) narrative of linear assimilation, nationalist post–Enlightenment historians have placed a lid on the nation's fractious and multiple narratives. *Amar Akbar Anthony* (which endorsed a grand assimilative history) grew out of that ideological repression. The decisive marker of fundamentalist practices came in the events that culminated in Ayodhya on December 6, 1992 ("A Nation's Shame" is how *India Today* referred to that day in its December 31, 1992 edition) when the 400-year old Babri Masjid (mosque) was destroyed. Those events were possible only because an "ethics of forgetting" placed a lid on any systematic analysis and archaeology of what we were asked to forget. I believe that there are two issues here. The first would require us to examine how the discourse of fundamentalism congealed around the heroic figure of the Hindu God Rama; the second would take us to the difficult question of what it is that Indians have repressed. I will argue that "Rama" has been invoked historically during moments of crisis, and that the real repressed of the Indian is the partition (of colonial India) itself. After theorizing these two propositions, I will examine the manner in which both the narrative of Rama and the idea of partition have been used in Bombay Cinema.

RAMA/AYODHYA IN THE POLITICAL IMAGINARY OF INDIA

With the exception of some sections of southern India where Rama is seen as an Aryan invader, the vast bulk of Indians read "Rama" as the symbol of a golden age that was once lost but may be regained. What this golden age in fact was is both less precise and more diffuse than the evidence presented in the originary proof text of the myth, Valmiki's grand Sanskrit epic the *Rāmāyaṇa* suggests. In whatever form this myth has been subsequently recounted—as Tulsidasa's Avadhi version during the high point of Akbar's reign, as Ramanand Sagar's version televised in the late 1980s, or as L. K. Advani's provocative *rath yātrā* ("chariot sojourn") from Somnath in Gujarat to Ayodhya (here the narrative is metonymically encapsulated in the *yātrā* itself)—its point of departure has never been the real, feudal world of Rama but a reconstructed and non-negotiable version of an exemplary world that locked itself into meaning because in that mythic world (*rām rājya*) one knew the bliss of never wanting anything. What interests us here is not so much the issue of truth conditions themselves but the conditions under which the myth gets repeated.

A key text for our understanding of the social ontologies of the many versions of the Rama myth and their place in the political imaginary is Sheldon

Pollock's remarkable essay (1993). In what follows my indebtedness to Pollock's work should be obvious. As with the reception of Homeric epics and Greek tragic drama generally, it is impossible to recover a post-Sanskrit historical period when the heroic deeds of the warrior king Rama were not known. The tediousness of twice-told tales notwithstanding, what is clear is that at a given historical moment the Rama myth is grasped by an Indian collective and deployed, at the behest of a particular class, toward quite specific political ends. Geeta Kapur has persuasively argued that since "the primary function of myth is to define and sustain the specific identity of a community, its investigation occurs at points of historical crisis when this identity is embattled" (1987: 79). She gives the "breaking point of colonialism" as an example. I would argue that the imaginary breaking point of the nation-state (as an uncanny reprise of an earlier moment of breakup or *baṭvārā*) has triggered another return to the past as "mythic material." Should this be the case, is there something in the narrative of Rama itself that makes it so accessible, so malleable, to particular ideologies? Unlike the complex narratives of the Pandu brothers in the much grander sister epic, the *Mahābhārata*, which presents the Indian with the horrors of civic strife and presages the nuclear sublime, the Rama narrative in the *Rāmāyaṇa* offers a simple opposition between divinity and demonization. On the side of truth stands Rama, noble, sacrificial, dharmik, and democratic; on the side of evil stands Ravana, dark, brooding, "tamasic," and dictatorial. Not surprisingly the Rama narrative has been more readily appropriated or revaluated, its narrative recast during times of real or perceived crisis. But this appropriation of an empowering Indian symbology is a relatively recent phenomenon. Not until the twelfth century C.E. did kings frame their own biographies in the narratives and iconography of the mythic King Rama. Where for the first fifteen hundred years of its history, the *Rāmāyaṇa* was no more than a stimulating literary artifice, the next thousand years of its history show a high level of interconnection between politics and the Rama myth. There is nothing particularly new in what Sheldon Pollock has called the imperative of "historical imitation" (1993: 264). The entire project of British imperialism, for instance, was often recast in terms of the narrative and symbols of the Roman Empire. The desire for historical imitation (revolution as a "revivification of a cultural past") is neither culture specific nor a sign of political aberration. To us what is important is not why there was the desire for a return to a mythic past but what were the actual historical conditions that made the need for its recovery mandatory.

According to Sheldon Pollock the myth of Rama began to acquire much greater force once a somewhat problematic divination of Rama was transformed into a temple cult. This is an important moment in the development of the myth because the incorporation of Rama as a fully fledged avatar of Vishnu and the construction of quite specific temples around this deity invested the original myth with religious valences of extraordinary power. Not only is there now a personal God (an *iṣṭadevatā*) but also a God around whom exists a narrative of both territorialization or conquest and moral authority. Pollock places this shift (from the imaginative to the cultic) in the twelfth century and argues that although "*Rāmāyaṇa* representations" through the depiction of scenes from the epic in temple frescoes and sculptures had existed for a long time, these did not indicate "dedication to or cultic significance of Rama" (1993: 260). Nor were these earlier inscriptional citations any more than embellishments to existing Shaivite or Vaishnavite temples. "By the mid-twelfth century, however," Pollock writes, "the situation began to change, with a sudden onset of activity of building temples to Rama, which intensified over the next two hundred years."

About this time the Gahadvala dynasty began to build extensive generic Vaishnava temples in Ayodhya, and the Yadava dynasty built the Rama complex at Ramtekri (Ramatekdi, "Rama's Hill," some forty-five kilometers from Nagpur and the simulacral site of some of the events in *Hum Aap Ke Hain Kaun* [Who am I to you? 1994]). An inscription at Ramtekri refers to the Yadava king of Devagiri, one Ramacandra, who ascended the throne in 1271 C.E. Pollock quotes an interesting reference to this king elsewhere: "How is this Rama to be described . . . who freed Vārāṇasi from the *mleccha* horde, and built there a golden temple of Śārṅgadhara" (267). The law code (*dharmanibandha*) of Hemadri Pandit, the king's minister, provides "liturgical instructions for worshipping Rama as an incarnation" as well as a reference to the "most important festival associated with Rama, the *rāmanavamī* (the birthday of Rama)." The date of the text (the *Agastyasaṃhitā*) in which this festival is sanctioned indicates that the festival itself was relatively recent in origin. These scattered references are not much to go by, but in the total context of the conquest of eastern India by Mohammed Ghori toward the end of the twelfth century and the quite extensive destruction of temples that followed (Lane-Poole 1903: 51ff.), it is likely that the term *mleccha* is a clear reference to the Muslim invaders. This information in itself may not be particularly important. What is significant is the self-conscious writing of the duty of a king in terms of a prior narrative of Rāma. Apart from the name of the Yadava king (Ramacandra) this may well be the first instance of historical repetition, a redefinition of the role of a king through a mythic prototype. The tale of the warrior king gains currency at precisely the time when the *mleccha* armies have pillaged and looted many of the cities of North India. The identification of an historical ruler "with the divine king Rāma" and the "rakshasization" (demonization) of the Other (the Muslim *mlecchas*) fits neatly into the central theme of the *Rāmāyaṇa* itself (273). Once the identification is under way it is easy enough to see how the reign of the ruler in question is symbolically recast as a *rām rājya,* the golden age of Ayodhya itself. Unless there is a constant historical deconstruction of the procedures by which this identification has come into being, myth will always gain ascendancy since it extends the already known tale even further. As the genre of Bombay Cinema shows so clearly, India does not find the twice-told tale at all tedious.

It is not necessary to provide extensive evidence here to show the points at which the *Rāmāyaṇa* ceases to be simply a rhetorical embellishment (a discursive effect) and becomes a principle of structuration as histories of kings are recast in terms of the life and times of the warrior prince of Ayodhya. The birth of Rama—*rāmanavamī*—is celebrated, and theatrical or folk reenactments of the narrative begin to surface. Known as the Rāmlīlā, it acquired its modern theatrical form soon after the death of Tulsidasa, author of the best-known vernacular *Rāmāyaṇa,* in 1624 (Hansen 1992: 60–61). It is, however, important to confront one of the consequences of the figurative reenactment of actual history through myth. In this highly polarized dramatic representation of good and evil the sultanates and politics of the Arab world and Central Asia—the Ghaznawids, Ghors, Khaljis, Taghlaks, Sayyids, Lodis, Afghans, and finally the Moghuls—were easily represented as the demonic Other against whom righteous Rama (as the Hindu self) fought a morally correct battle. Their collective demonization produced a contrary collective divinization of Hindu kings, a process that probably marks the entry of the Rama monomyth into the political imaginary of the Indian. The correlation offered here is disquieting and probably far too neat. But the historical evidence brought together by Sheldon Pollock certainly points toward a conscious return to an earlier myth so as to convince a shocked Hindu world about the possibilities of regaining the lost pastoral. Of course, any research of the kind done by Pollock may have unforeseen consequences. The ontological connections he draws between a perceived threat to a Hindu world order and the shaping of the Indian imagination through the myth of Rama could be, and is, used by fundamentalists to justify their own attempts at a similar homology. Since the rewriting of history is always the work of a particular privileged class (such as the Historians' Forum in India) any return to the narrative of Rama is fraught with unforeseen consequences unless the manner in which this narrative is used is constantly examined and thoroughly demystified. In this respect it is a concern that both the ruling Bharatiya Janata Party (BJP) and its internationalist ideologue, the Vishwa Hindu Parishad (VHP), recast the *Rāmāyaṇa* as an epic about territorial expansion and the expulsion of *mlecchas*, not as a dharmik text in which a compassionate Rama remains ill at ease in his role as a warrior king.

Between the twelfth and fourteenth centuries, India became a site for what Marx called the "awakening of the dead," a term he used to refer to the legitimation of the present through the principle of historical imitation. But why India chose the heroic Rama, not Krishna, who probably had a more powerful pan-Indian presence or, for that matter, the great warrior figures Arjuna, Bhima, and Yuddhishthira, or the "yet-to-come" tenth incarnation, Kalki, who could have been given an altogether original history, has never been answered satisfactorily. Under the circumstances, Sheldon Pollock's answer to this question is as good as any. He argues that unlike the "tragic aporia" that marks the *Mahābhārata* and its heroes, including Krishna, the divination of Rama in the *Rāmāyaṇa* combines the powers of a God with those of the earthly king. For the worldly king, the text of Rama sanctions his own divine right because in deferring to Rama as his model, a mortal king actually becomes a divine king. Forever conscious of how literary antecedents merge with the real, the priestly caste must have connived at this conflation to begin with. And it may also be that the assertiveness of a Muslim identity on the part of recently converted Turks led, for the first time in the history of India, to a corresponding assertiveness on the part of Hindus. In terms of this argument, it is not surprising that the great compilations of the "Hindu way of life" (the *dharmanibandha*) began in the twelfth century just when the modern Rama myth began to take shape. Such a process of totalizing Hindu society became possible, as Sheldon Pollock has demonstrated, "when the total form of the society was for the first time believed, by the professional theorists of society, to be threatened" (286). By any definition they were troubled times for Hindu India and historical repetition is a time-honored means by which the difficulties of the present may be surmounted. A millennium later, we ask why is there the need for another historical repetition? Is it the belated revenge of a theocratic ideal in response to the failures of the democratic, secular principles of the nation-state? We have seen, however, that any revival of the myth requires the construction of a divine/demonic antithesis. Since Rama occupies the first slot, it becomes necessary to "*rakshasize*" the Other. Since this Other has, from the twelfth century onward, been the Muslim invaders of India, the Rama narrative comes with an already coded demonic Other. In this regard, no matter how we look at it, the political imaginary of the Hindu must create the Muslim demon the moment it hoists its ideals onto the Rama narrative. This is not simply a matter of fundamentalist rhetoric; it has structure and historical depth.

Let us quickly move to the present. We can use historical techniques to establish that even though no elaborate temple stood on the site of the Babri Masjid, the history of Muslim treatment of Hindu places of worship has, one could argue, rarely been particularly edifying. It would make sense to claim that many mosques were indeed built on the sites of temples both as an "evangelical" move and as a show of political domination. It would follow that many recent converts to Islam would want to convert the symbol of their old religion into the new one to legitimate their conversions in the first instance. Any historical research along these lines—research of the kind undertaken by staunch BJP historians such as Sita Ram Goel (1993)—certainly confirms the nexus between territorial domination and the destruction of sacred sites. From the point of view of the subjugated race, the history of a conquering race is always a history of barbarism. In many ways Indian nationalist history has been aware of the negative social payoff of this kind of historiography, and has, as a consequence, itself engaged in an "ethics of forgetting" on the grounds that a nation may indeed be redeemed through a conscious act of forgetting: those who forget history will not suffer from it (Pollock, 292; Majumdar 1970: 48–51). Both of these "negotiations with history" are, of course, profoundly unsatisfactory. A third alternative is to examine how meaning is constructed, and under what conditions an earlier moment in history is rejuvenated to explain a contemporary crisis. If we can see how the narrative of Rama has been (ab)used to explain a perennial melancholia, a loss of paradise by Hindus, and how unreal this reconstruction in fact is, we may be able to prevent the conflation of the imaginary with the real or at least speak more openly about the wounds inflicted upon the nation.

THE DEMON OF PARTITION

We have seen that the Rama narrative begins to inform the Indian political imaginary when the narrative's inherently fundamental opposition between the divine and the demonic can be superimposed upon real, lived history. In the process, however, it is history that gets fictionalized because the mythology of Rama is more powerful than history itself. In medieval times the "*rakshasization*" (demonization) of the Muslim Other was crucial to the recovery of this myth. In the latter half of the twentieth century the demonic is glued to the sign "partition" or *baṭvārā*. It is an idea that does not seem to have affected South India as is clear from the total absence of the same levels of emotional associations for the Tamil word for partition. Neither *pirivinay* (dividing, separating) nor *tuntippu* (forceful severence) in Tamil has the same political resonance. *Batvārā*, on the other hand, is universally used in North India to speak about territorial as well as emotional loss for which the Muslims as a collective group are blamed. Millions were uprooted, their narratives end-lessly retold as the unspeakable "horror and brutality of the time," their sub-sequent lives no longer equipped to deal "with the trauma that must have accompanied this uprooting" (Butalia 2000: 178–79). In the words of Urdu novelist and sometime Bombay screenplay writer Saadat Hasan Manto "the world around us had gone so completely insane that it was futile even to try to make sense of it" (1998: 75). Ritu Menon and Kamla Bhasin, who have written about the incarceration of women during partition, similarly speak of the period "as an event of shattering consequence [that] retains its pre-emi-nence even today" (2000: 208). I would argue that "partition" is the modern demonic with which North Indians generally overcode the Muslim Other. But the latter cannot be unproblematically symbolized unless, as Mushirul Hasan has brilliantly observed, one transforms it into "an exclusive category, with a shared world-view, a common outlook, and a structure of consciousness in accord with the fundamental tenets of Islam" (2000: 4). To be sure, the two-nation theory of the Muslim League itself used this absolutist ethnic defini-tion of the Muslim, but there were many others, the Jam'iyyat-i 'Ulama-i Hind collective of Indian Muslims, for instance, who vigorously opposed both partition and the two-nation theory. Like the unplumbable center of a dream, the Muslim as demonic Other (centered on the trauma of partition) can func-tion only if it can be linked to symbols of recovery. In Menon and Bhasin's argument, the recovery of Hindu women (women abducted during partition) from Pakistan (sometimes against their wishes) parallels "the current frenzy to recover sacred Hindu sites from the 'usurping' Muslims" (233). "Babri Masjid" is thus another displaced metaphor of partition that functions like a projection of the repressed in the manner in which Rey Chow recently spoke of fascist rhetoric as the "lack onto which we project all the unpleasant reali-ties from which we want to distance ourselves" (1998: 17). In this reading, projection is not the surfacing of something pathological that had been repressed, an act of negation, but the celebration, as an aesthetic, of the redeeming potential of a fascist worldview. *Batvārā* may well be seen as an alle-gory of the "Muslim demonic," and like it in the Indian imaginary the "par-tition" is also unplumbable: it structures the dream, but of itself it has no real representation; it is an absent center that quickly gets displaced. For the unpalatable fact is that in India the birth of a nation after a rather long and protracted independence struggle created not so much the wonderful *rām rājya* (the vision of the *satyagrāhī* for whom much of the struggle had been discursively recast in terms of the Hindu renouncer) but its very negation, the demonic specter of "partition," a point so powerfully made in Deepa Mehta's film *Earth* (1999). As a consequence the word itself (and its Hindi equivalent) is pushed upward a step or two in the ladder of discourse to become something of an archeseme that subsumes a number of meanings. By some estimates more than 2 million people were killed during the riots that followed partition. Some of the worst instances of violence done to women this century occurred as a result of partition. Women were abandoned, raped, dragged into prostitution, captured, and abducted. Urvashi Butalia estimates that some eighty thousand to one hundred thousand Hindu, Sikh, and Muslim women were the victims of such acts (2000: 183). There is, then, another "zone of silence around the event of partition" (Veena Das, 1996: 84) that needs to be articulated. It too is part of what Gyan Pandey has referred to as an "erasure of memory" and Don Miller as a "crypt" within the Hindu body politic itself. For my argument, "the agonies of partition" (Pandey 1992: 27–55) are in fact that moment of fissure and fracture, that point in the history of India that is probably of greater consequence to the Indian imaginary than both the struggle for independence and its celebration. In other words, there is a real history of India, its soft underbelly, its barbaric underside, that nationalist and revisionist Indian historians have consistently silenced. This occluded history of India is the unspeakable canker that is silenced through what Don Miller has referred to as the economy of melancholia. If mourning became Electra because she knew what an "uncompleted" mourning was like, then, it is melancholia that becomes the Indian because we tend to carry our loss, unresolved, as a painful splinter in our side. It is there for all to see, but we have never confronted it: what we don't wish to know we defer to the nth degree. Partition then becomes a symbol that is so enormous, so vast and obscene, that we cannot contain it; it is the Indian real that forever eludes representation. In short it becomes the sublime object that defies representation in history. Clearly there are other, simpler, ways in which the phenomenon can be explained. Gyan Pandey's use of phrases like "suppression," "tragic loss," and "collective amnesia" are alternative ways of explaining why the Indian nation-state refuses to theorize the partition itself.

In the late 1980s and the '90s the agony of partition and its "encrypting" took a slightly different and politically dangerous form through the redefinition of the concept of Hindutva. It is not a recent idea, nor is its political manipulation a recent fact. From V. D. Savarkar to the BJP, VHP, the RSS (Rashtra Svayamsevak Sabha), and the Shiv Sena, the term has been used to define an Indian identity in seemingly nonsecular terms. But whereas for pre-partition Savarkar the territorial and cultural definitions implicit in Hindutva included Muslims as well (they could, after all, trace their ancestries back to a pre-Muslim era: "A Hindu is he who . . . inherits the blood of the great race whose first and discernible source could be traced from the Himalayan attitudes of the Vedic Saptasindhus" [100]), for post-partition BJP/VHP/RSS/Shiv Sena, Hindutva has significance as an emotionally charged term only insofar as it enters into an oppositional set with the Muslims in India. The political incorporation of Muslims within the BJP notwithstanding (and there are Muslims who belong to the BJP), modern Hindutva is an exclusively Hindu idea. But the concept runs into trouble the moment it becomes more than just a rallying point for Hindus who feel that the majority religion has somehow been betrayed by secularism. To replace the apparatuses that go into the construction of the Indian secular state with another that is inspired by Hindutva itself would mean that the political as well as juridical and social machinery of the Indian nation-state will have to be recast. Since this is clearly impossible (or at any rate undesirable), a Hindu state is a massive contradiction, unless what one means by a Hindu state is no more than a theoretical premise about Hinduism and modernity. To return to the sign of "Ayodhya," what becomes clearer is that it is like W. B. Yeats's "terrible beauty" but this time born out of a rebellion in the history of ideas symbolized by the word "Hindutva." Underpinned as it has been by the enabling rhetoric of the Rama myth, Hindutva is not the projection of a lack, an absence or a negation that is in the subject, but "a search for an idealized self-image through a heartfelt surrender to something higher and more beautiful" (Chow 1998: 16), which is why, one suspects, a V. S. Naipaul (1990) sees "Ayodhya" as marking the Hindu's entry into history. What he doesn't examine further is that the "motley worn" (Yeats) by the *kar sevaks* and their (un)holy gurus signified not so much Hegel's "absolute freedom" but "absolute terror."

The events leading up to the demolition of the mosque have produced a number of research papers and books from scholars of all political persuasions. I will use a passage from just one of these publications in which archaeological evidence is used to implicitly support the destruction of the mosque. The publication is a slim volume entitled *Ramajanma Bhumi: Ayodhya, New Archaeological Discoveries* written by eight eminent scholars of ancient Indian history or archaeology.

In continuation of its earlier efforts, the Historians' Forum feels happy to place in
the hands of the public and the government this new incontrovertible archaeological evidence which proves that there did exist at this very site a magnificent temple
from at least the 11th century, which was destroyed to build a mosque-like structure over the debris of the temple in the 16th century. There is every possibility
that there existed at this site one or more temples of still greater antiquity, some of
which were built with burnt-bricks in which images of gods and goddesses made of
terracotta were installed. (Sharma, Srivastava, Gupta et al. 1992: 16)

Regardless of the value one would want to place on these claims (and the
strong counterclaim that earlier temples may well have been replaced by
Hindus themselves), the fact remains that it is in the nature of invaders to
destroy places of worship/power and replace them with their own. No other
outward sign of change can be more powerful than the substitution of one
religious symbol for another. The archaeological evidence is thus not the
point at issue; what is at issue is the new political imperative of Hindutva
for which historical/ archaeological evidence is more important than *smṛti*
or canonical knowledge. If self-evident archaeological knowledge endorses
the presence of temples as a trace beneath mosques (as, one would argue,
every Indian Muslim is in fact a Hindu), then Ayodhya is more than just a
narrative about a mosque; it is about decontamination, it is about recover-
ing a hallowed past, it is about discovering an unalloyed center, and it is
about seizing the repressed itself. It is indeed ironic that the word "Ayodhya"
itself is formed from the root *yudh* (war) and means "not to be warred
against, irresistible." If we worry over the meaning of the word it strikes us
that Ayodhya cannot be fought over, and yet it has enormous (irresistible)
power. The latter, its magnetic power, is what galvanizes people, not the
decrepit and decaying city itself. Ayodhya then becomes what it is not; the
real, contaminated city is replaced (in Hindutva terms) by the myth of
Rama; debates about it become a longing for a lost unity somehow
destroyed by invaders. "Ayodhya" is one way of articulating an unspeakable
past. But it is also a powerful means of legitimating the present as well. What
needs to be kept in focus is that in spite of the "time immemorial" claims
being made in defense of Rama's birthplace, there is a strong body of (largely
literary) evidence that shows that Rama Ayodhyapati ("Rama the Lord of
Ayodhya") has been strategically deployed by rulers and priests alike during
times of crisis. In the political imaginary of India, Rama has never really
been a neutral symbol.

INDIAN CINEMA AFTER AYODHYA

Scholars of the persuasion of the Historians' Forum take the Hindutva path, but there is a much more pervasive, far more powerful narrative that has also articulated "Ayodhya." This is the narrative of popular Indian cinema, especially of the Bombay variety. What I would want to do now is examine how Hindutva/Ayodhya has been expressed through arguably the most powerful cultural form of India after the pan-Indian Sanskrit epics. Let me, however, state quite clearly that by "Ayodhya" I do not mean only the events of December 1992. "Ayodhya" is used here as a term that signifies a number of political as well as cultural processes. In my reading of Bombay Cinema, "Ayodhya" will be read both as a temporal marker (i.e., December 1992) and as a process that has been part of the Indian unconscious for more than two millennia.

To frame my argument I will begin with *Chhalia* (The trickster, 1960), an important film about the recovery of women abducted during partition. I want to draw, again, on the immensely illuminating research of Urvashi Butalia and of Ritu Menon and Kamla Bhasin as my entry point into a film that I see as popular cinema's attempt to "cure" the trauma and mourning surrounding partition.

"A resounding silence surrounds the question of women and partition," writes Butalia (2000: 182). In any event, and specifically an event with strong communal overtones, where the phallus alone is the triumphant symbol of patriarchal power, the rape and abduction of women are barbaric "norms." Of course, the scenario is not all that simple because communalism also throws up contradictions in the role of women themselves in this barbarism. Have women too been agents of communal violence or at least silent co-conspirators because they believed in their role as guardians of the larger dharma, of the nation-state itself? These issues complicate research in the recovery of women after partition. They also show that many women refused to return to their homes because they were happy in their new lives. The Inter Dominion Treaty (later enacted as an act of Parliament) agreed upon in 1947 was the legal basis of this return, and it remained in force until 1957. But the treaty said something about the uneasy definition of India as a secular state because India's role was to recover only Hindu and Sikh women, and Pakistan's Muslim women. Although few women were in fact recovered by either side— 20,778 recovered from India and 9,032 from Pakistan, two Muslims for one Hindu/Sikh (Menon and Bhasin, 2000: 222)—"recovery" seems to have remained a matter of honor well into the 1950s. In real terms, however, the rehabilitation of women, especially on the Indian side, was not an easy matter. Hindu practices had, historically, been emphatic on the question of purity, and any woman who had had sexual relations with an alien man was by definition impure. So although the state extolled the necessity of acceptance—both Gandhi and Nehru had emphasized the morality of accepting these women—the community was less willing to do so. To change these attitudes, Butalia says, the government issued a pamphlet, apparently distributed by the Ministry of Relief and Rehabilitation, that cited the laws of Manu, and Sita's purity even when she had been violated by Ravana (for so the claim went). It seems, however, that the recovery of women remained a subject about which no one really wanted to talk, although the silence surrounding it reinforced the trauma of partition and the hold that the demonic Muslim had on the Hindu Indian imaginary. There are, however, especially in the context of Sikh women who committed suicide or were killed by their husbands or parents before they could be abducted, remembrance rituals (Butalia 2000: 204) that extol martyrdom and transform women's deaths into epic sacrifice for the nascent state. Recovery then may be seen as one of the first symbolic tussles between the two nations. In this tussle, women simply became pawns in the struggle of both nations to establish not so much moral superiority but epic chivalry. The acts of restitution were a way of overcoming transgression and effecting a return of purity to either nation. In this act, the subtext that emerged was a distinction between a Muslim Pakistan and a Hindu India. It is this eruption of the religious in a declared secular state that the Indian nation-state has never been able to control, which is why "recovery" was seen as a more generalized mode of overcoming the trauma of partition.

Chhalia is located in the ideology of recovery outlined above, although by 1960 (when the film was released) the Abducted Persons (Recovery and Restoration) Act itself had ceased to exist (it lapsed in 1957). The film begins with a couple's wedding night in Lahore even as civil strife erupts in the city. In the upheaval the couple get separated. Five years later the wife, Shanti (Nutan), reaches India with her son, Anwar. In India she is rejected by her family as a woman who must have been raped and violated. Leaving her son at school (where her husband, Kewal, is now a schoolteacher), she rushes off to kill herself. Saved by Chhalia (Raj Kapoor), she lives with him unaware, until some time later, that he's madly in love with her. At this point Shanti's Pakistani guardian, Khan Abdul Gafar Khan (Pran), appears on the scene looking for his own lost sister, Salma (a name that echoes Saadat Hasan Manto's young Muslim woman Sakina in his powerful short story *Khol Do* [Open up]). Seeking revenge, he decides to abduct Shanti, whose face he had never seen, only to be recognized in turn by Shanti and told who she really is. Dejected, he walks inadvertently toward Anwar's school and is recognized by Anwar as his own "father." Chhalia catches up with him and informs him that his permit to stay in India was due to expire that day. On the train back to Pakistan, however, his sister is delivered into his hands by an elderly Sikh man. In the narrative thus far, rape and violation are overtaken by human decency and love. The Hindu Shanti and the Muslim Salma were not abused but were taken care of by people on both sides of the border. What is significant, for our purposes, is the final restitution of the seemingly defiled Shanti back to her husband Kewal (Rehman) and the latter's acceptance of Anwar as his son. This happens in the final scene of the film, which is framed by the last day of the *Rāmlīlā* when the effigy of Ravana, the demon king of the *Rāmāyaṇa*, is burned. It is the folk celebration of the triumph of Rama over Ravana, of good over evil, and marks the beginnings of a new age. Apart from the huge crowd, the central characters in this scene are Shanti; her son, Anwar; her husband, Kewal; and her Indian benefactor, Chhalia. Despite Chhalia's efforts, Kewal refuses to take Shanti back. So Chhalia sings a song: not any song, but a song in which Shanti is recast as Sita. "Galī galī sītā roye āj naye bhes meṁ" (The modern Sita cries near and far), sings Chhalia against the backdrop of the final act of the *Rāmlīlā*. Kewal listens and is moved. The climax comes as the burning effigy of Ravana is about to collapse on none other than Shanti and Anwar. Kewal notices the falling effigy and in the nick of time saves his wife and son. Chhalia, the *becārā* figure, walks away. Although the casting of Shanti as Sita (and the thrust of the song itself) situates Kewal as Rama, the dynamics of the narrative is not about the death of Ravana at the hands of a heroic Rama. In fact the burning effigy marks the end of darkness, of absence of knowledge, of prejudice and fear. In its place there is a kind of nirvanic moment of self-awareness and humanist knowledge which the Nehruvian secular nation-state of India upholds. The Chinese border war and two wars with Pakistan have yet to happen. Militarism and "spheres of influence" are some distance away. It is not the militaristic Rama that underpins *Chhalia* but the moral Rama and the perennial message of the great epic.

I have said that the Rama myth begins to inform the political imaginary of India when the nation finds itself threatened or when its self-projecting apparatus requires the construction of the demonic Other. During its initial moment of historical repetition (in the twelfth century) the Other was quite readily defined. Since then, however, the original Other—as Muslim *mleccha*—has been totally Indianized; it is no longer an invading class but a large underprivileged class that shares many of the grievances of that class of people generally. Yet this "underclass"—even as an identifiable subaltern group—has never been given (except in occasional, and largely historical, films such as K. Asif's *Mughal-e-Azam* [1960] or Mehboob Khan's *Humayun* [1945]) the space that it deserves. Historically this may have something to do with a Hindu reading of the Muslim establishment in India even before independence, because this is certainly not simply a post-1947 phenomenon. Ravi Vasudevan (1995b) refers to the inflammatory rhetoric of the All India League of Censorship (a self-proclaimed Hindu culture police force set up in 1937, not unlike the Southern Baptists in America) which aimed at cleansing the film industry of all its non-Hindu elements. Their aim was not limited to matters of representation (of the Hindu body or of Hindu thought) but extended to the question of who should control the means of representation. In this case they drew attention to what they claimed was the contamination of the Indian film industry (in Bombay at least) by Muslims and Parsis—both groups, the "crusaders" said, had decidedly anti-Hindu agendas. The aim of the All India League was obviously to flesh out non-Hindu functionaries, and they did this by making artificial connections between textual (or on-screen) ideology with the presumed general ideology (as read by the Hindus) of the Muslims. One consequence of this was a long period from the late 1940s to the mid-1960s when many Muslim actors changed their names: Dilip Kumar, Meena Kumari, Madhubala, Ajit, Prem Adeep, and Jayant come immediately to mind.

The limited space occupied by Muslim culture and history in the popular film (even though the language is Urdu and many of the current crop of important stars as well as production team are Muslims) leads to a number of uneasy consequences. First, their marginalization may imply that they are not legitimate objects in the domain of the popular, or, more dangerously, as the women's chapter of RSS (the Rashtra Sevika Samiti) reads them, they are defined totally by a prior Hindu discourse of the atavism of "Muslim lust" (John 1996: 139). Second, their stereotypification means that their emotional range is limited. In *Balmaa* (Beloved, 1993), only fifty-two seconds of cinema time are given to a Muslim; in *Maine Pyar Kiya* (Yes, I've fallen in love, 1989), the Muslim is conventionally coded as the trustworthy friend in need. Muslims are excluded from situations in which they may come into complex emotional or physical conflict with the Hindu. In this respect their treatment is not unlike Hollywood's treatment of the African American, though in the case of Hollywood cinema African Americans now may occupy central positions as characters in film. With rare exceptions, in Bombay Cinema the Muslim as a character is simply written out of considerable chunks of cinematic history. And finally, because their social relationships are not enacted in film, their way of life remains a mystery to the Hindu. Only rarely, as in M. S. Sathyu's remarkable *Garam Hawa* (Torrid winds, 1973), a Bombay "middle cinema," do we get portraits of fully realized Muslim families. In Khalid Mohamed's *Fiza* (2000), the rebelliousness of the Muslim youth is directly linked to a growing Muslim sense of exclusion in recent years from the central issues of the nation-state. Although Aziz Mirza's *Phir Bhi Dil Hai Hindustani* (After all, the heart is Indian, 2000) does not deal with Indian Muslims, its subtext explores those antinational forces (corrupt politicians, sensationalist independent TV stations) that work through terrorist networks for a "foreign" (a code word for Pakistan) nation. Nevertheless, the silence, the absence, of the Muslim is disturbing and may be linked—and is, I would argue—to the general psychic repression of the unspeakable moment in recent Indian history: India's partition.

While failing to confront the complexities of the lives of Muslims (who make up something like a quarter of all Hindi speakers in India), Bombay Cinema has not overvalued the mystique of Rama in any vulgar way. One of the most successful films of the '90s and one that started a whole new trend about narratives built around the idyllic extended family order—*Hum Aap Ke Hain Kaun* (Who am I to you? 1994)—interweaves the Tulsidasa *Rāmāyaṇa* (the *Rāmacaritamānasa*) into the fabric of the text. The sanctified space of Ramtekri (the place hallowed by earlier dynasts) is used as the meeting ground of the two families whose lives the film brings together through marriage. The chants from the holy text and the use of temple architecture to connect, iconically, word and image, intertwine with the structural connections between the film's tradition of brother/husband, wife/sister-in-law, brother/brother-in-law (*bhaiyā-bhābhī-devar*) and the epic's grand triad of Rama-Sita-Lakshman (Mukherjee 1995). The resemblances, however, are not meant to underline the triumph of a new fundamentalist order in India under the sign of *rām rājya*. What the film in fact does is present the *Rāmāyaṇa* as central to the ethos of tolerance and liberalism, albeit within a dominant patriarchal Hindu order where a woman's sexuality/sensuality is circumscribed by respectable social norms and where the model is that of Sita as the devotee of her husband-lord. In this respect, the success of the film, in the context of severe tensions between religious groups in India, reflected its portrayal of a "pre-Ayodhya" or "pre-Amritsar" world order in which family harmony, as endorsed by the grand religious text of North India, was the microcosm of the larger nation. The fact that Rama begins to become the shaping force in so many films from around 1987 onward in a manner rather different from the way in which the myth had been used thus far takes me to the impact of

Ramanand Sagar's serialization of the *Rāmāyana* on the politics of "Ayodhya" and it's representation in popular Hindi cinema.

RAMANAND SAGAR'S *RĀMĀYANA*

Ramanand Sagar's television series *Rāmāyana* was shown over seventy-eight weeks on Doordarshan (the Indian National TV network), from January 25, 1987, to July 31, 1988. It was subsequently shown on national TV in Mauritius (1989), on BBC2 in Britain (1990–92), in Trinidad (1991–92), and in many other parts of the world with large numbers of Indians. The forty-five-minute episode was stretched over the full hour (9:30 to 10:30 on Sunday mornings) with the number of advertisements rising dramatically, from fifteen to forty, within eight months. The total time span of the serial (which had an hourlong grand finale) was sixty hours of television, making it one of the longer "performed" versions of the text. Not the longest, though, as the *Rāmlīlā* in performance has often lasted longer. Philip Lutgendorf cites the *Rāmlīlā* of Ramnagar, which is spread over thirty-one nights and covers some ninety-three hours (1995: 226–27). The serialization reached a weekly audience of some 80 million, and for many Indians it established itself as the definitive version of the Vulgate text and was treated as "a feast of *darshan* (ritualistic engagement)" (Lutgendorf 230). Any hints about Rama as a tragically flawed hero (his ambivalence toward Bali, his treatment of Sita, and so on) were omitted while at the same time the lost ideal of *rām rājya* was foregrounded. There is nothing particularly wrong about this version of the epic—most Hollywood versions of classical texts follow similar principles. What is interesting is the specific historical moment of this version, the moment of its reinvention, and the manner in which it was consumed by Indians. The second half of the 1980s, in particular, marked a singularly dangerous period in the life of the Indian nation-state. A prime minister had recently been assassinated, both Punjab and Kashmir were developing into precarious locales of religious strife, and around the disputed Babri Masjid, a dangerous discourse of Hindu fundamentalism was emerging. It is the manner in which Ramanand Sagar's *Rāmāyana* may be seen as a text with specific effects (effects not unlike those of Hemadri Pandit's twelfth-century *nibandh*s) and the extent to which it influenced subsequent filmic narratives that require closer scrutiny. In any account of the reinvention of Rama toward political and social ends this moment—the moment of reinvention— in the cultural history of India has to be spelled out.

A selection of some not uncommon remarks in the *Illustrated Weekly of India* (November 8–14, 1987) demonstrates the conflicting "reinvention" taking place around this serialization: it "has nothing to do with fundamentalism" (P. K. Iyengar, a scientist); it is "like any other Hindi movie," a cheap production that should have been given to a more skillful filmmaker (Sunil Gangadhyay, a poet); it is an incompetent production but a harmless one and can't possibly "incite Hindu fundamentalism" (Govind Talwalkar, an editor); it shows "our biggest historical personality," Rama, and is "not inciting fundamentalism" (Kalpnath Rai, a politician); it is a "most welcome" event (R. P. Goenka, an industrialist); "it has nothing to do with secularism" (Balamurali Krishna, a musician); "it is a document of values, relationships, on how purposes and goals were set, and about love and peace" (Vimla Patil, an editor); it is "an embodiment of the totality of Indian culture" (Datta Samant, a trade unionist). The comments of L. K. Advani, home minister in the current Vajpayee government, require a fuller quotation:

> But the exceptional popularity of this serial owes nothing to the script, to the direction or to the cast—the reason lies elsewhere, in the readiness and enthusiasm with which the people of India identify themselves with the characters of this great epic, and long to follow them through their trials. (20)

The operative phrase here, I think, is "lies elsewhere." It links the popularity of the *Rāmāyaṇa* with an ethos that is time immemorial, like *sanātan dharma*, the eternal *dharma* of the Hindus, whose authority lies in some unauthored, *śruti* text. Even though some of those whose opinions were canvassed by the *Illustrated Weekly* were forthright in their criticisms of the serialization (Kamleshwar, a journalist, spoke of how the "serial takes you to the backyard of nostalgia . . . and is definitely inciting Hindu fundamentalism," and the South Indian politician M. Karunanidhi read it as "nothing but a vehicle for the imposition of Hindi"!), the fact remains that people who espouse establishment Indian values endorsed this version of the epic. The *Rāmāyaṇa*, it was generally argued, made one feel good, made one self-assured about one's destiny, and made one symbolically part of the triumphant destiny of Rama. But whose destiny do we have here? And over whom or what is triumph necessary? This unconscious phantom—as the Muslim and its spatial equivalent in partition or *baṭvārā*—is never articulated, not even by Advani.

At the political level, the key actors in this serialization were exploited by political parties. Arun Govil accepted requests to campaign for the Congress Party (dressed as Rama) in the by-election for the seat of Allahabad following the resignation of the film star Amitabh Bachchan in 1987. When, despite Arun Govil's help, the Congress candidate Sunil Shastri, son of former prime minister Lal Bahadur Shastri, lost the election to the Opposition, L. K. Advani responded, anecdotally, to the use of Arun Govil by the Congress Party:

> The fact that the star happened to be playing the role of Rama only underscores the desire of the Congress to exploit religion. But it heartens me that the response of the people speaks volumes for their political maturity. I'm told that in Udhampur the audience was somewhat cold to Arun at first, but there was no hostility as such. He went on to say that people respect him because they think he is Rama. "But I am not Rama. The real Rama is different," he said. The people shouted, "Who? Who is the real Rama?" And when he said, "The real Rama is Rajiv Gandhi," there was booing and hooting. When he tried to stretch the allegory and anoint the Prime Minister with that kind of image, the reaction was very strong and adverse. It was improper for the Congress to have done what it did. (*Illustrated Weekly of India*, July 17–23, 1988: 17)

Even as Advani denounces allegory, we know of his own complicity in the politics of symbolism through India's most powerful and sustained myth of paradise. In June 1991, Deepika Chikhalia, the actor who played Sita in the serial, was elected to Parliament from a non-Hindi speaking Baroda (Gujerat) electorate on the BJP ticket. The complicity between politics and the power of myth as critically examined by the *Illustrated Weekly of India*'s reading of the television series is worth quoting in full:

> By telecasting the *Ramayan* at this ugly moment in the nascent nation's history, the government has virtually accelerated the Hindu revivalist movement which began in the early eighties.
>
> Viewing the *Ramayan* on Sunday mornings was not just one of those mindless television experiences of thousands of Indians. By its reinforced spiel, it swiftly evolved into a ritual that drove people into mass frenzy. Suffering cardiac arrests when Rama was struck down by an arrow; burning down power stations when the programme could not be telecast because of load-shedding, that sort of thing. (*Illustrated Weekly of India,* July 17–23, 1988: 13)

The conventional explanation of a nation's "collective hysteria" was given in terms of a Hindu reaction against a secular order that effectively silenced its history and its past. In other words, middle-class India turned fundamentalist not because of the serialization of a myth but because there was something uncomfortable in its own body politic that it had never fully internalized. Whatever the source of that loss—as Islamic invasions or as partition—nationalist history had placed a firm lid on it. The *Rāmāyaṇa*, in all its forms, signified the return of the repressed notion of *baṭvārā* or partition for the

Hindu, not as a Freudian negation but as a projection of a dangerously fascist idealism. Paradoxically enough, the more the nation and the middle class denied the cause of its repression, the more it was avowed (albeit in a highly mediated manner) in its cultural forms (such as Bombay Cinema). As a consequence the repressed became even more corrosive and even more malignant. In the symbolic domain of cinema the form the *Rāmāyaṇa* has progressively taken is an important index of the pulse of the nation.

SOME EXEMPLARY FILMIC TEXTS

I would like to pursue the relationship between fundamentalism and the popular through a reading of a number of recent Hindi films. My exemplary films are *Ram Lakhan* (Ram and Lakshman, 1989), *Khalnayak* (The antihero, 1993), *Insaniyat* (Humanity, 1994), *1942 A Love Story* (1994), and *Krantiveer* (The heroic revolutionary, 1994). It must be said at the outset that there is no complete homology, and there is no case of an explicit endorsement of fundamentalism by the genre. What is more certain is the pervasiveness of the discourse and the rise of key symbols—temple or the icon—as causal items in the narrative. The five-year period of the production and release of these films coincides with both the aftermath of Ramanand Sagar's *Rāmāyaṇa* and with some of the most horrifying communal riots seen in India since its independence. These films, I argue, are neither ignorant of the Rama myth nor oblivious of the precarious state of secularism in India. Although the Bombay film industry has steadfastly endorsed a general state ideology, its cinematic practice has at times parted company with that ideology. In this respect the shift in the spatial reorganization of the cinematic mise-en-scène, for instance, has enormous political and social significance. In *Awara* the spatial organization was primarily house/street/courtroom/beach. In *Mother India* it was home/land. The spatial category that didn't exist (in any extended form) in these films is the temple, which has now become an indispensable space in many films. A crucial text here was *Deewar* (The wall, 1975) where Amitabh Bachchan has a lengthy "dialogue" with Lord Shiva in a temple. This is not to suggest that in the films discussed here the temple is the primary space or even the only space for dramatic resolution. Rather what I'm saying is that the real or implied space of the temple is now part of the spatial design of many films. A typical film would now locate itself in the following generic spaces: house/hotel/temple/street/car/garden/picture-postcard overseas location. The dance sequences (and especially those quickly marketed as video clips) would be located in the space of a hotel or mansion (often the villain's) or a foreign pastoral locale. With the incorporation of these new spaces (or often with a different mixing of the old spaces) has also emerged the use of a variety of different filmic shots. Against the medium and medium long shots (shots that attempt to duplicate the spectator's view of the staged performance) and the use of carefully positioned montage, we get rapid staccato shots, zoom shots, and jump cuts. While montage made for tolerable realist cinema of the Bombay variety (Mehboob Khan, Bimal Roy, V. Shantaram used this form to great effect), the stacatto shots (and the jump cut) are much more episodic in structure as they connect a large number of filmic segments together. These new camera shots and their ensuing form came into their own in many of Manmohan Desai and Prakash Mehra's films. Indeed in *Naseeb* (Good fortune, 1981) any segmentation of shots would indicate a quite unusual ratio between the number of shots and different cinematic moments. Within the space of some twenty shots about a dozen personalities are introduced in *Naseeb*. As a consequence, at least twice the number of shots than is customary are used in this form of cinema. Apart from speeding up the film itself, the technique does not give the spectator enough time to think about questions of ideology since he or she is captivated by the sheer spectacle of cinema. The space of the temple, too, gets constructed through these technologies and presented as sheer spectacle without much room for the kinds of autocritique of ideology (or even involvement in the religious discourse) that was possible with the slower camera movements. To rephrase Ashish Rajadhyaksha's recent observation, the spectator remains glued to a "baseline address" system and doesn't become an inscribed viewer (2000: 280–81).

In my first text, *Ram Lakhan*, a key productive space is the temple. The traumatized mother (Raakhee) whose husband has been murdered by his unscrupulous cousins is draped in a *black* sari (Hindu widows normally wear white) and pours milk over an icon of Shiva. The temple is the silent but hallowed space where the narrative of her past life is recollected. But it is also the space of the dramatic monologue (notably after *Deewar*) through which the widow reaffirms, by speaking directly at the statue of Shiva, her desire for revenge/justice (*nyāya*). If the temple becomes the focus of the widow's life so far, her sons, Ram and Lakhan, will be the instruments by which the old order is reestablished. To underline the connections between the names of her sons and the brothers in the epic, the film places direct intertextual references to the *Rāmāyaṇa*. Lakhan (Anil Kapoor), the modern-day Lakshman, the younger brother of Ram (Jackie Shroff), wants shorter routes to success, wants to become a millionaire, wants to adopt a form of vengeance that is outside the law—all very *Deewar*-like themes. Against this version stands

Ram, the older brother, the police inspector who is the dharmik ideal, a modern-day Yuddhisthira. At one point Lakhan refers to the necessity of parting company from myth: "These days *Rāmāyaṇa* is only a drama, an old tale, a TV serial. It looks good, but its principles are difficult to follow." To which Ram replies, "Thousands of years of the *Rāmāyaṇa* tale cannot be destroyed by mortals who live to 70." But at the end of the film, when the two brothers unite to destroy their father's killers and also the evil drug baron Sir John, Lakhan recalls his earlier words about the *Rāmāyaṇa* and tells Ram, "Brother, you spoke the truth: no one has been able to change the *Rāmāyaṇa*, which has stood the test of time for thousands of years, nor will we ever be able to change it." The suggestion here is that even Ramanand Sagar's televisual *Rāmāyaṇa* is just one among limitless texts of the great pan-Indian epic. As these are the last words of the film, one senses that the film is a homage not so much to the secular state and its righteous police force under the firm hands of inspector Ram, but to the ways in which goodness triumphs only after the dharmik ideal of the *Rāmāyaṇa* has been internalized. The film touches something primal, almost atavistic, in the Hindu Indian. There is no ambiguous politics here: Muslims do not figure in it, and historical specificity is made irrelevant because it is not brought into the presented world of this cinema—generational changes do not reflect material changes in society. But the invocation of the *Rāmāyaṇa*, the use of the central symbols of the myth as the foundation of India, at this point in the history of the nation cannot be read in isolation from the rhetoric of fundamentalism. Even as it disavows any connection with fundamentalism, it gets trapped in the detritus of that discourse. Instead of using the *Mahābhārata*, the epic that examines the chaos of the Hindu world itself, and a text that is more in tune with internal strife over family property (the central theme of the film), Subhash Ghai's *Ram Lakhan* drags the sister epic of the *Rāmāyaṇa* into a narrative of family disorder because in the current climate of India it is this epic that sustains India's search for a lost world.

Khalnayak, also by Subhash Ghai, uses much of the same symbolism of *Ram Lakhan.* There is the same projection of a nationalist-religious fervor (the Indian flag, the Rig Vedic quotation) and a similar use of the double. Although the narrative of Rama does not exist here as the generative model for the film as a whole, it does inform the text through its discursive presence. The opening scene shows a widow dressed in white (once again played by Raakhee, the most recent, and defiant, avatar of the Sita-like Nirupa Roy of *Deewar* and *Amar Akbar Anthony*) reading the *Rāmāyaṇa*. She has a photograph of her antihero son in the book. A friend approaches her and asks,

"What is the point of keeping a photo of Ravana in the *Rāmāyaṇa?*" Both the speaker of this utterance and the statement itself are of use to us. The person who speaks is Shaukat, a Muslim, but he knows his Rama narrative well. The utterance itself, however, establishes the underlying connection between the film's antihero and Ravana, the demonic figure of the *Rāmāyaṇa*. In his filmic avatar he is the ambassador of Indian warlords who, in conjunction with foreign forces, are bent on destroying the country.

India, as the Rama figure in the film points out, opens itself to such treachery because it is always divided from within. The Rama figure is once again a police inspector who is none other than the actor Jackie Shroff, the Ram character in *Ram Lakhan*. In this film too his name is Inspector Ram (short for Ram Kumar Sinha). The film's use of figures from the *Rāmāyaṇa* does not stop with the representation of the antihero and the police inspector. The police inspector also has a betrothed, a policewoman named Ganga (Madhuri Dixit), who styles herself as "gaṅgā rām kī sītā (Ganga, who is Ram's Sita) and who is in the habit of speaking about her Ram through the language of the *Rāmāyaṇa*: "Ram can never be destroyed," she says at one point. In fact toward the end of the film after Ganga has been imprisoned because she helped Ballu, the anti-hero, to escape, the moral dilemma that faces Ram is whether he can now take a woman back whose call to duty took her to Ballu (Sanjay Dutt). This is a repeat of the well-known scene in the Vulgate *Rāmāyaṇa* in which a washerman refuses to accept his unfaithful wife, reminding her that he was "no Rama who would take his wife back after she had spent so many years with Ravana." In another form the line had occurred in *Awara* too. It is the reformed Ballu who tells the court that Ganga is as pure as Sita and Ram is the real Rama, a true son of India. He adds, "Even today this land has its Ganga (Sita) and its Rama." This is the overdetermined ideological statement that confirms an absolutist ethic. Yet in the Ganga-Ballu relationship bodies do collide, songs are sung (such as the enormously popular "colī ke piche kyā hai," What is underneath my blouse?), and spectatorial desire is firmly superimposed upon the relationship. Indeed in these sections of the film, Ganga is not seen in terms of "Rama's property." What is interesting for good readers of the complete textual tradition is that in the original Sanskrit epic of Valmiki, Lakshman's desire for Sita surfaces in the latter's accusing remark that the reason why he, Lakshman, hesitated to respond to Rama's cry for help during the hunt of the golden deer (Maricha) is that he really desired her and wanted Rama dead. The eruptions that surface are, obviously, neutralized or contained in set pieces like Ballu's courtroom disavowal of any physical contact with Ganga. In this double coding, filmic connections with dominant prefilmic narratives are destabilized (and sometimes even disestablished). So in a sense there are at least two levels of spectatorial complicity. On the surface level (as *histoire*) the dharmik codes are affirmed, and the Rama narrative is triumphant. However, on the level of "processual" spectatorial involvement (the text as *discours*) responses become varied, and indeed extremely disruptive.

Why foreground the Rama myth so laboriously when the upholding of dharma needs no justification? What does the film do with the figure of the antihero? Who is he? What shape does his evil take? What is his relationship to Ram the police inspector? Who is to be blamed for what Ram refers to as India's internal dissension? And how does the ending of the film reflect the fact that it (the ending) was filmed after Sanjay Dutt had been released on bail? Is it necessary for a film about an antihero to be loaded with the discourse of the *Rāmāyaṇa* in an era when films such as *Baazigar* (The conjurer, 1993) and *Anjam* (The consequence, 1994) were enormously successful with a schizophrenic antihero (played by Shah Rukh Khan) quite beyond redemption?

The making of the film coincided with the events surrounding the crisis over the Babri Masjid in Ayodhya. After the mosque was demolished by fundamentalist activists in December 1992, some of the worst communal riots erupted since independence. Bombay—hitherto the most liberal of all cities—got dragged into this for reasons that remain rather complex. It has been suggested that the developers in fact used Shiv Sena militants to destroy *basti*s (makeshift settlements of homeless people) that had become prime real estate. Whatever the causes (and they were complex) the Bombay riots were followed in February 1993 by a series of bombings that were immediately blamed on Muslims and Pakistan. The film *Khalnayak* was implicated in the communal riots and their aftermath through its main actor, Sanjay Dutt, who was accused of supplying arms to the Dawood Ibrahim brothers, underworld figures held responsible for the bombings. Sanjay Dutt is of course Nargis and Sunil Dutt's son; he comes to the screen, as Parama Roy has observed, as a son "who becomes Muslim" in the current crisis (1998: 156) and in whom the "Hindu right saw . . . the lineaments of his Muslim mother (and his 'Muslim-loving' father)" (170). Sanjay Dutt was arrested but later released on bail. Subhash Ghai completed the film in the context of communal tensions made worse, for him, by accusations made against Sanjay Dutt about his own connections with the Bombay underworld (which, incidentally, had historically underwritten many Bombay films). His body then reinforced what Roy has remarked as the sign of the "Muslim as the *familiar* enemy; thus the Muslim is not one of us, and the Muslim is, terrifyingly, one of us" (171). If we return to the final episode of the film with this knowledge, it becomes clear that Ballu's confession and his elaborate speech about the purity of Ganga/Sita as well as his endorsement of the capacity of Indians to actually become Rama are meant to demonstrate not only Sanjay Dutt's but also the filmmaker's acceptance of the new order of Rama that the fundamentalists have established in India. The final image of the Indian flag (an image with which the film began, and a mandatory final shot in many subsequent films) metaphorically reinforces the equation of Rama with India. In this way a film that is really about the spectator's attraction to the figure of the antihero becomes in fact a statement about the demon within. In the end we are left with a number of unanswered questions: why is a heavy and often unmitigated discourse of Rama essential for a film about drug overlords, Bombay criminals, creative song-and-dance sequences and the sacrificial mother? Why is it that when another religious icon is needed *Khalnayak* uses the image of the sacrificial Christ and not that of the many martyrs of Islam? If the connections between evil and Ravana are inevitable, is it important for filmmakers to actually foreground these connections? What is the nature of a political imaginary that forces the Indian to make the analogies in the first instance? What is really being repressed? What is it about the nation's history that cannot be articulated, represented? Is this an ethics of forgetting or a principle of misguided overcoding of the text?

I want to turn now to a film that sets out to heal communal wounds in a more explicit fashion. In *Insaniyat,* the hero's role is to act as a mediator between warring factions. The hero combines the heroic qualities of Rama with Yuddhishthira's dharma and Krishna's emphasis on karmic purity. In terms of cinematic form (the ubiquitous staccato shots persist) and generic structure it comes as no surprise that the film is contiguous with both *Ram Lakhan* and *Khalnayak*. But where *Ram Lakhan* represents a period when Bombay Cinema could not accept that "Ayodhya" was really possible (such was its faith in secularism) and *Khalnayak* gets dragged into communal politics through Sanjay Dutt, *Insaniyat* confronts an India that has done the impossible. To whom do we apportion blame? Is it the moral responsibility of the popular to educate as well as to entertain? Can spectacle ever be sacrificed? Can the cinema of the majority afford to alienate its patrons? Can it finally speak the unspeakable either by lifting repression or by condemning the *kar sevak*s (the people's army) of the BJP and Shiv Sena? Can it finally create a film that may be banned by Bal Thackeray and the Shiv Sena and hence impossible to screen in Bombay and probably in other parts of India, too? In different forms these questions have always been at the forefront of popular cinema whenever it has attempted to cross the line that divides entertainment from social comment. However, the film does attempt to confront, in simplified form, the ultimate issue of partition even if its most effective articulation takes the form of a nondiegetic polemical introduction to the film presented through a voice-over. In a brief history lesson with the aid of a map of India we are told that India alone is that saddest of nations because it has been placed on trial throughout the ages. The voice-over continues:

> People have plundered this unfortunate (*badkismat*) nation, and when they remained unsatisfied, in the name of religion (*mazhab*) they lit such a fire that even after independence I am still burning. For the past forty years I have been sold by foreigners with the acquiescence of those Indians who, in the name of Hindus and Muslims, have encouraged feuds between brothers.

No names are mentioned. The Aryans, the Ghaznawids, the Ghors, the Lodis, the Afghans, the British: who precisely were the invaders? But the blame for the partition certainly falls on religionists whose presence in the drama is marked by the Persian word *mazhab* and not the Sanskrit *dharma*. This slippage in the text is important because the use of the word *mazhab* immediately signifies a primarily Muslim religious discourse. Indirectly, then, the film does apportion blame, but otherwise the invaders, like every other evil in the film, remain nameless.

Insaniyat frames itself in India's postcolonial history by suggesting that the process of selling the country to foreign powers (the CIA is often the nameless destroyer of everything that is Indian) had been under way for forty years. This theme is relatively straightforward and can be handled within a Manichean binary of good and evil as in *Mr. India* (1987), for instance. The question of Hindu-Muslim tension (its other theme) is a much more difficult one to handle. Whereas the story of the smuggler king and a man's personal vendetta has an epic singularity, the touchy issue of communal violence doesn't sit comfortably with the aesthetics of this popular art form. The reason for this is that the communal cannot be so easily transformed into a simplistic opposition between good and evil because the communal expresses itself in highly complex ways. So *Insaniyat* transfers communal violence onto two warring gangs—one Muslim, the other Hindu—who are then read as instrumentalities working at the behest of unnamed foreign powers to destroy the country. The resolution of the conflict, in which the cultural specificities of either are downplayed, occurs through the intervention of the Rama figure of Amar (Amitabh Bachchan) who speaks of the two warring gang leaders as his "two hands," and transforms them into *deshbhakts* (soldiers

Amitabh Bachchan with Chunkey Pandey and Sunny Deol in Tony's *Insaniyat*, 1994. Hindu and Muslim as the new epic heroes. Publicity Still Kamat Foto Flash.

of the land) as they join forces with Amar (who escapes from the gallows) to destroy an underworld smug in its belief that "Ravana can never be killed!" The "rakshasha" is then none other than destructive forces within the country that create communal dissension (often at the behest of a foreign power) to destabilize the country for their own financial gain. For the demonic Other to be excised from the national corporeality, Rama has to be killed so that the Muslim Karim and the Hindu Hariharan can now become the new Ram Lakhan of modern India.

The discourse of Ayodhya in the sense in which I have used it in this chapter has led to a degree of rethinking about the Muslim and about the energizing power of Rama symbology. In the late 1980s and early 1990s in particular we see how Bombay Cinema has been reproducing Ayodhya even as it critiqued it. This double bind needs to be spelled out in no uncertain terms because the ambiguity is at the very heart of this cinema. One strategy has been to locate the demonic in the national body-politic itself, so that in films such as *Agneepath* (The path of fire, 1990) or *Mr. India* (1987) evil is concentrated in the figure of the villain. For righteousness to succeed in these films one needs the example of the heroic individual whose actions finally reestablish the moral order. Whether there is something intrinsically wrong with the structure itself, whether there is something inherently catastrophic about the appropriation of the symbol of Rama precisely when that symbol has been used to advance the project of fundamentalism, is never questioned. Consequently what succeeds as popular cinema—because it reproduces the compulsion to repeat—fails at the level of ideology since the triumph is always of Hindu dharma. The eternal law, finally, is never contested. I return to the point I have made all along: Bombay Cinema disavows fundamentalism even as it reproduces images that work on the logic of a fundamentalist binary.

More recently, however, in an act of self-purification, Bombay Cinema has moved into an hitherto area of silence by articulating the role of the Muslim in Indian society. Perhaps the easiest way in which this can be done is through another look at the Muslim in India's nationalist struggle. In a sense this is what happens in *1942 A Love Story,* though, as the title suggests, the film wishes to keep the register of romance firmly in place even as it creates a specific date. Is *1942* romantic? Is it a love story? Did romance really hit a high in 1942 or does the film refer to its own history, implying that in 1942 Hindi films were really romantic? These ironies are lost on the director Vidhu Vinod Chopra, who is clearly cashing in on recent successes of romantic films in Hindi such as *Aashiqui* (Courtship, 1990), *Dil* (Love, 1990), and *Maine Pyar Kiya* (Yes, I've fallen in love, 1989). But 1942, a year in which the nationalists were getting thoroughly exasperated and the Muslim League was gaining ground (it had declared for Pakistan in 1940), provides Chopra with the excuse to enter into the debates about nationhood and religion in India. In this love story, partly modeled on *Romeo and Juliet* (a Hindi version of which is being rehearsed in the film itself), lovers become revolutionaries, but their helpers are both Hindus and Muslims. The real villains are not Muslims, who are represented as loyalists, but the British (in the figure of General Douglas) and the hero's own father, Dewan Hari Singh, the landowner. The sanctity of father-son relationship (there can be no violence between them) is now disputed through the whole question of patriotism and nationalism. Under the sign of "Jai Hind" ("Hail India" or "Victory to India") a mother willingly sacrifices a son, a sister her brother, and a son his father. The insistence on national unity and the incorporation of the Muslim in this unity is clearly a political act of self-identity as well as of self-reassurance. In the wake of Ayodhya, fundamentalism had once again exposed the fragility of India. In its counterattack, Bombay Cinema effectively says that the villains are all outsiders, and the real problem was a legacy of colonization, which is why the Jallianwallah Bagh incident in the Punjab in 1919, in which General Dyer gave the order to shoot during a prohibited meeting to protest against the Rowlatt Acts, simply gets replayed over and over again in the film. An earlier moment, mystified well beyond the limits of reality, acquires the status of an allegory through which a post-Ayodhya cinema wishes to affirm its own investments in the Indian nation-state. In the end as the Indian flag is hoisted to the tune of the national anthem, the subtitle at the bottom of the raised flag then exhorts the audience to "Please stand and show your respects to the national anthem." The fiction of romance—and the fictiveness of film itself—is now replaced by a reality principle (however perverse it may seem to us) as the audience symbolically participates in the struggle for independence. All history, as is true of the genre of Bombay Cinema itself, becomes the eternal present.

Where *1942 A Love Story* plays on gratuitous political emotions but fails to address contemporary issues about religious and ethnic tensions in India, another film made at the same time, *Krantiveer*, at least tries to examine a well-researched thesis about the relationship between capital and the riots in Bombay in 1992. A huge metropolitan *basti* where Hindus and Muslims have lived together for a generation comes under threat. Through the hero of the film (the village boy who becomes the smart city man), the film explores two interlinked ideas: the power of capital and the nature of action. Inaction leads to oppression, and oppression leads to manipulation. Hindu karma needs to be radically redefined so that one can fight against injustice. Says Pratap, the hero, played by Nana Patekar: "*Gītā, Rāmāyaṇa, Qurān* makes no difference to people, so what of newspapers? This is the *basti* of the dead." The journalist to whom this is addressed (and who is herself a victim of a vicious rape) would want to transform Pratap's anger toward social ends. The occasion for this transformation happens when politicians, a building tycoon, the police, and a gangster (referred to as AIK 1: "All India King Number One") join forces to foment religious riots. Thugs are sent to bulldoze part of the *basti*, the police feign that they are busy elsewhere, and riots occur because the thugs are seen as Hindu agents bent on destroying Muslim homes. Ayodhya is never invoked; nor is Rama. In fact, the serious political malaise of India in the 1990s never surfaces; all that one gets are images of Hindus and Muslims (indistinguishable from the camera's purposefully distant eyes) fighting one another, staged melodramatic moments, and the discourse of the new *krāntivīr* (the revolutionary leader) who declares before he is about to be hanged (he is given a reprieve later):

> You've lived in darkness, in servitude. . . . you're now even worse, you're insects,
> not man. . . . so much so that even God is sad. This is the land of the living dead,

> there is no compassion for the nation, for anyone. I'm Hindu, I'm Muslim, I'm Sikh, I'm so and so, that's what you say. . . . Why am I speaking to this stone?

In a sense the difficulty with reading Bombay Cinema as critical cinema arises directly from the extraordinary resilience of the genre. Yet there are important eruptions, significant disturbances within the dominant ideology that the genre endorses which are worth noting. At one point in *Krantiveer* one of the politicians who has a vested interest in the tycoon's project of acquiring land in the *basti* tells the underworld leader that the *basti* is his vote bank and should not be touched until after the election. The manipulation of electorates as vote banks is a growing feature of Indian democracy. Widely used by all parties, it creates demographic enclaves that vote only in terms of their own vested interests. Since vote banks are easy prey to fundamentalist rhetoric, and since fundamentalist demagoguery is so easy to master, this discourse often works in tandem with vote banks. Furthermore—and in however unsubtle fashion—the film also draws our attention to the other side of the riot equation in Bombay. There is some evidence to support the view that in Bombay, at least, the crisis of Ayodhya was skillfully manipulated by a few key industrialists and developers (aided and abetted by influential politicians) for their own advantage. In fomenting strife, these people aimed to make shanty dwellers leave *bastis* that had become prime real estate. It didn't really matter to them whether Hindus or Muslims were in flight in a given *basti*. What was important was that a large group of people vacated their *basti*s so that they could be sold under the vacancy clauses of tenancy law. I end my examples of texts on the issue of fundamentalism with *Krantiveer* because at least it draws our attention to an alternative scenario, and attempts in however flawed fashion to turn the sublime object of fundamentalism away from the Muslim repressed (and the projection of a fascist Hindu ideal) to the more urgent questions about real, material conditions of life as seen, in Ashis Nandy's words, from "the slum's point of view" (1998: 2). In however truncated form, mythic history is replaced by a lived history.

Read in this fashion, fundamentalism and its object (that which may be demonized) is an unspeakable, unpresentable idea like the sublime. Bombay Cinema has quietly colluded with fundamentalism by "disarticulating" its source and by confirming what Ravi Vasudevan in his essay on Mani Rathnam's *Bombay* (1995) has referred to as the necessity of assuming the "masculine position" so that the link between the nation and the Hindu patriarchal hero is always maintained (1996a: 56). But these symbolic restitutions of the fiction of the Hindu hero (which in a sense normalizes readings of the nation as Hindu) do not get around the psychology of mourning that is at the heart of the heritage of *baṭvārā*. Recognition of the impossible mourning (which leads to melancholia) necessitates a critical vigilance about the archaeology of "Ayodhya" and a forthright articulation that while Rama may be *sanātan*, eternal, his mobilization is always a political act and always a reinvention, an historical repetition. In short, we must confront the sublime object itself and cure ourselves of the melancholia of fracture, of division, of *baṭvārā*. (*Chhalia, Fiza,* and Mani Rathnam's *Bombay* are films that carry these concerns as their subtexts.) Only then will we be able to get rid of the structures of thought that have led to the demonization, the "rakshasization," of the Muslim-Other. It is important, via Lyotard, to invoke a degree of critical activism here: "Let us wage a war on totality; let us be witnesses to the unpresentable; let us activate the differences and save the honour of the name" (Lyotard 1987: 82). Retheorized later as the differend, what we have to pay attention to are all those cases of conflict, of litigation, where the ground rules do not exist because of a radical incommensurability that exists between the two positions (Lyotard 1988). In India's most popular art form, there is some evidence that cinema is being deconstructed—although not as seriously as one would wish—to question those essentialisms in the Hindu worldview that lend themselves to a fascist politics of idealized projection, which is why I believe there is no direct, unmediated, connection between the popular and Hindutva politics as suggested by Rachel Dwyer (Dwyer, 2000). It is in the nature of secular art to move from absolute homology of myth to the allegory of fiction, to mediate and transform its antecedent archive so that whatever it repeats has to be read off against existing social conditions. It is here that recent Bombay Cinema has to be located in the context of a "post-Ayodhya" social history of India. I'm not suggesting that cinema has been complicit in espousing fundamentalist practices, but rather that cinema has confirmed the kinds of spectatorial identifications with the need for a redemptive history (against the history of invasion, against *baṭvārā*, against the demonic Muslim, however fictitious these may have been) reinforced by Ramanand Sagar's *Rāmāyaṇa* on television. If Sheldon Pollock's archaeology of the Rama myth is at all correct, then its periodic avowal has to be located deep in the Indian repressed. The danger that this poses, especially when it is re-shaped by India's dominant cultural form, is one of the greatest threats to precisely the nationalist secular ideal that Indian cinema has fostered.

Chapter Eight

BOMBAY CINEMA AND DIASPORIC DESIRE

Any study of Bombay Cinema must finally address the role of this cultural form in the lives of the peoples of the Indian diaspora. Although much younger than the other two major diasporas of color (the African and the Chinese), the Indian diaspora is one of the fastest growing diasporic communities in the world. It is conservatively estimated at 11 million—Europe 1.5 million (1.3 million in Great Britain), Africa 2 million (1 million in South Africa, six hundred thousand in Mauritius), Asia (excluding Sri Lankan Tamils) 2 million (1.2 milllion in Malaysia), Middle East 1.4 million (largely semipermanent guest workers), Latin America and the Caribbean 1 million (mainly in Trinidad, Guyana, and Surinam), North America 2 million (including VS H1 permit holders largely in the American computer sector), the Pacific five hundred thousand (three hundred and fifty thousand in Fiji) (Anderson 1994, modified)—and it is a very complex diaspora with deep roots in many nation-states. A corrective to the generalist theories of the Indian diaspora must be immediately made at this point: the Indian diaspora has grown out of two quite distinct moments in the history of capital. The first moment (of classic capitalism) produced the movement of indentured labor to the colonies (South Africa, Fiji, Trinidad, Guyana, etc.) for the production of sugar, rubber, and tin for the growing British and European markets. I have called this the old Indian diaspora of plantation labor (Mishra 1996b). The second moment (of late modern capital) is largely a post-1960s phenomenon distinguished by the movement of economic migrants (but also refugees) into the metropolitan centers of the former empire as well as the New World and Australia. As Patricia Uberoi (1998:

307–308) has observed, the shift in the kind of migrants that constitute the recent diaspora—generally referred to as NRIs (nonresident Indians) and largely seen as upwardly mobile—has radically reconfigured Indian readings of the diaspora and redefined as well cultural forms that see this diaspora as one of their important recipients. This Indian diaspora—the diaspora of late capital—is very different from the traditional nineteenth- and early-twentieth-century diaspora of classic capital, which was primarily working class and connected to plantation culture. The diaspora of late capital has now become an important market of popular cinema as well as a site for its production. The old diaspora broke off contact with India which, subsequently, existed for it as a pure imaginary space of epic plenitude (the exemplary text here is V. S. Naipaul's seminal novel, *A House for Mr. Biswas*). The new is the complex and often internally fissured communities of Indians primarily in the United States, Canada, Britain, and Australia who have had unbroken contact with the homeland. For many the space occupied by the new diaspora—the space of the West—is also the desired space of wealth and luxury that gets endorsed, in a displaced form, by Indian cinema itself. In reality, however, the dreams of wealth are often tempered in the new diasporas by the rise of a neo-racism even as the nation-state redefines itself through an idealized project of multiculturalism (Balibar and Wallerstein 1991). While in the old diaspora of racialized communities (the terms of reference in them are always "multiracial" and not "multicultural"), race was a pre-given category of ethnic classification to be politically sorted out (the demand for racialized constituencies against a common roll in Fiji for instance), in the new diaspora race and ethnicity are linked to questions of justice, self-empowerment, representation, equal opportunity, and definitions of citizenry. The differences between V. S. Naipaul's West Indian novels (where the diasporas are relatively exclusive social formations) and the novels and films of Hanif Kureishi, Gurinder Chadha, and Srinivas Krishna (where the diaspora is keyed into the social imaginary of the larger nation) may be explained with reference to the politics and history of the old and new Indian diasporas.

Against the idealist theory of diasporas (practiced by the Boyarin brothers, Radhakrishnan, Bhabha, Safran, Clifford), which reads diasporas as the exemplary condition of late modernity and as an incipient critique of homogeneous definitions of the nation-state, a realist turn would take us back to the complex and at times strained life-worlds of the people of the diaspora. If the consumption of Indian culture is anything to go by, first-generation NRIs desperately try to hang on to values that mark their difference from the rest of the nation-state. These differences are generally about tradition, continuity, family, and, often, the importance given to arranged marriages. A diasporic imaginary thus grows out of a sense of being marginalized, of being rejected outright by nation-states (Mishra 1996b). As a consequence, diasporic peoples find it difficult, perhaps even impossible, to present their "new" nation-states to consciousness. In the nation-state's "unpresentability" (rarely do we hear diasporas declaring "I am British" or "I am Australian"), we hear echoes of the Lacanian Real (in Slavoj Žižek's understanding of it) as that which cannot be, "which is produced as a residue, a remnant, a leftover of every signifying operation . . . an object which simultaneously attracts and repels us" (Žižek 1989: 180). Yet it must be stressed—and in this chapter it is necessary to make the connection immediately—that the failure to connect with the idea of the new state has its obverse side in the sublime otherness of the homeland which also eludes substantialization, but which nevertheless needs to be grasped under a "translatable" sign. In the diasporic production and reproduction of "India" one of the key translatable signs or a "synchronic warehouse of cultural scenarios" (Appadurai 1996: 30) is Bombay (Bollywood) Cinema which (as shown in cinema halls and viewed at home on videos and on cable TV such as ATN in Canada or Sahara TV in the United Arab Emirates) has been crucial in bringing the "homeland" into the diaspora as well as creating a culture of imaginary solidarity across the heterogeneous linguistic and national groups that make up the South Asian (Indian) diaspora. In Bharati Mukherjee's dogmatically diasporic novel *Jasmine* (1989), Nirmala, the young wife of Professorji "fresh from a village in Patiala district" (143), takes to Hindi videos with a passion in her Flushing, New York, apartment.

> Every night, Nirmala brought home a new Hindi film for the VCR. Showings began promptly at nine-o'clock, just after an enormous dinner, and lasted till midnight. They were Bombay's "B" efforts at best, commercial failures and quite a few flops. . . . [When] Nirmala had exhausted the available stock of Hindi films on tape [she] was now renting Urdu films from a Pakistani store. . . . Visitors from India left tapes of popular Indian television series, and friends from Flushing were known to drive as far as New Jersey to check out the film holdings in the vast Indian emporia. (144–45)

Film then may be seen as a crucial determinant in globalizing and deterritorializing the link between the imagination and social life in both negative and positive senses. One imagines not simply what one lives through, but identifies with images that are reconstructed across the international divide. Nevertheless, the global in this case is not to be read as a critical internationalism that transcends difference and creates a decidedly "hybrid" diasporic self overnight; rather it informs a narrow ethnicity that finds its imaginative realism through a particular kind of cinema. This cinema—Bollywood or Bombay Cinema—brings the global into the local, presenting people in Main Street, Vancouver, as well as Southall, London, with shared "structures of feeling" that in turn produce a transnational sense of communal solidarity. There is a remarkable parallel here between the way in which a shared sense of reading newspapers defines belonging to a nation and the way in which the consumption of Bombay Cinema constructs an Indian diaspora of shared cultural idioms. The various Indian diasporas are, in this sense, imagined communities that read Bollywood Cinema as a very culture-specific, self-contained phenomenon without any critical reference to other Third World cinemas such as Chinese or Iranian cinema (which is why a multicultural critical internationalism is not part of the diaspora's engagement with cinema). Electronic boards on the Internet such as contributions to "A Manifesto of an Indo-American Youth" that appeared early in 1997 on the IndiaStar website http://www.indiastar.com/anony.html reinforce the language of narrow ethnicity and difference. Of course, the repackaging of film as video-cassette has dramatically enhanced this process as well:

> It is an increasing possibility that the domestic VCR . . . has not only greatly influenced the collapse of cultural identity under globalization but has also contributed to the formation of cultural identities fuelled by the desire for a sense of community (or belonging). (Kolar-Panov 1997: 209)

The diasporic social selves that I have in mind here are not some ideal, perfect community or communities but are in fact marked by strong ambiguity and self-contradiction, by a double subjectivity, a double consciousness (Radhakrishnan 1996). Bombay Cinema, however, disarticulates this heterogeneity through a form of cultural intervention that must always keep both the non-negotiable primacy of the homeland and a unified response to it intact.

Two crucial advances in technology, the VCR and cable and satellite TV, have played an important role in diasporic appropriation of homeland culture. Coincidentally, too, these advances occurred in tandem with the NRI-dominated new Indian diaspora. I want to pause here and examine the impact of the VCR and cable/satellite TV. According to Kolar-Panov the VCR is the most "popular means of communication in diaspora, second perhaps only to the telephone" (1997: 13). In the Indian diaspora video is one of the key markers of leisure activity, and is often referred to, after its use by peanut-vendors at Indian railway stations, as "time pass." It is also a not uncommon method of transmitting cultural events (weddings, anniversaries, even deaths of significant people such as Raj Kapoor) from the homeland to the diaspora or from diaspora to diaspora. This aspect of video culture is readily understood and requires no further elaboration. The market side of video and film production and distribution in the diaspora is a lot more complex as the information is often not readily available, especially since both video distribution and film distribution in the diaspora are run by loosely linked independent family businesses. Nevertheless, the question about the kind of monetary return distributors of videos and films get from the diaspora needs to be explored, however partially.

Although returns on films and videos in the diaspora are now at their peak, export earnings of Indian films generally have been slow to gain momentum. Figures cited for 1977 and 1987 by Pendukar and Subramanyam show a decline in export earnings of some 40 percent, from 1,167 lakh rupees ($3 million) to 718.42 lakh rupees ($1.8 million). By 1970 the old Indian diasporas of Fiji, Trinidad, Mauritius, Singapore, Malaysia, and Sri Lanka made up the largest market for predominantly Hindi and Tamil movies. It must be added that the growth of the video market since the mid-1970s explains the drop in the earnings from films between 1977 and 1987. In 1991–92 the overseas video market generated more than 100 million rupees ($2.5 million) (Pendakur and Subramanyam 1996: 77 modified). Since then, however, the video market has been on the decline, and the film market has been on the ascendant. Cable and satellite TV have been the most important technologies that have affected video sales. Video outlets, not particularly profitable to begin with, can no longer compete with cable and satellite. In a city such as Perth, where access to cable channels is still limited, the total value of the video market to the film producers was never large to begin with—no more than $10,000 per year. This is based on the sale of 100 videos at $30–$40 apiece (depending on quality) to three video outlets in any given year. Film, on the other hand, will be the great export earner provided that film producers keep diasporic tastes in mind, a point noted recently by Aruna Vasudev in *The Times of India* (April 16, 1999). Cable and satellite earnings, too, will level off once most households in the new diaspora at any rate have been linked up.

Despite the drop in income for films during the 1977–87 interregnum as a direct consequence of the dramatic increase in video rentals, the general historical trend has been one of a growing and expanding diaspora market for film. The original export markets (Afghanistan, Iran, the Middle East,

Sri Lanka, Malaysia, Fiji, Mauritius, Trinidad, etc.) of the period between 1940 and 1970 have been gradually superseded by markets in the new Indian diasporas of the United Kingdom, Europe, the United States, Canada, Australia, and New Zealand. Pendakur and Subramanyam point out (1996: 79) that the United Kingdom, with one of the largest South Asian diasporic communities in the world (and with one of the highest disposable incomes) has become the dominant market for both Indian cable channels and films. In Britain the large screen (theater) market grosses more than $200,000 every week, while video outlets bring in about $30,000 each week. Indeed Bombay films now regularly feature among the top ten releases in the United Kingdom. The expansion of the market does not translate into massive increase in export earnings as the return to the Indian distributor has never been more than 10 percent of gross intake. True, there have been some recent successes in the diaspora. *Hum Aap Ke Hain Kaun* (1994) ran in a theater in Fiji for three months and for nine weeks in the New York–New Jersey area. *Dilwale Dulhania Le Jayenge* (1995), and *Kuch Kuch Hota Hai* (1998) have been similarly successful. Gradually, however, it is likely that export earning will come primarily from cable channels plus feature films shown in theaters and not from the video market. Cable TV gets to homes directly, is available round the clock, combines films with news, sports, and other entertainment from India, and is cheaper than renting half a dozen videos each week. TV Asia and ATN, the former a channel in which Amitabh Bachchan has a strong financial interest, are now available in North America through the satellite channel Direct TV. In Canada ATN cable television broadcasts eight hours of news and entertainment from Doordarshan India as well. The programs on Sky Entertainment in Fiji are an interesting example of how pay TV addresses the artistic needs of Fiji's Indian diaspora. Because Fiji TV (the national TV) makes no attempt to broadcast programs in Hindi, and is unlikely to do so in the near future given the coup of May 2000, Sky Entertainment now broadcasts more than eight hours of programs in Hindi to the Fiji Indians each day. A number of Hindi/Urdu serials (*Inteqam, Wakt Ki Raftar, Chandni,* etc.), popular programs such as *Antakshari,* and about half a dozen Hindi films are shown every week. The following extract from the Sunday, April 18, 1999, schedule of programs makes the above points clear:

01.30 p.m. Hindi Movie: *Hum.* Starring: Amitabh Bachchan, Rajnikant, Govinda.
04.15 p.m. *Khana Khazana* (Ep. 240)

04.40 p.m. *Inteqam* (Ep. 27)

05.15 p.m. *Chandni* (Ep. 29)

05.30 p.m. *Balcony* (Ep. 3)

06.05 p.m. *Bollywood Plus* (Ep. 53)

06.30 p.m. *Waqt Ki Rafter* (Ep. 14)

07.00 p.m. Hindi Movie: *Saat Rang Ke Sapne.* Starring: Juhi Chawla, Arvind Swamy, Anupam Kher.

The Sky Entertainment schedule for Fiji says a number of things about the way in which the old Indian diaspora relates to the motherland. The first point that strikes us is that, in contrast to ATN cable programs in Canada for instance, there is no attempt made here to bring news from India to houses in Fiji. What happens in India on a daily basis is of little interest to Fiji Indians. The second is that there are no cricket programs or other sports-related programs. Third, all the programs are in Hindi-Urdu, which again says something about the kinds of linguistic connections this diaspora makes with India. The very different ways in which the diaspora of classic capitalism consumes Indian culture (and responds to it) are matters that a critical diaspora theory generally needs to keep in mind. In the context of cinema and the Indian diaspora the implied dialectic, as we shall see later, assumes an NRI-dominated Indian diaspora. As such, while the old diaspora will continue to be an important market, it will not affect the form of the cinema itself. In the Indian imaginary, especially on matters such as the concept of Indian citizenry, the new diaspora will play a decisive role (Shiv Vishwanathan, *The Times of India*, September 24, 2000).

DIASPORIC USES OF BOMBAY CINEMA

In a forthright interview in *Filmfare* (September 2000), Shabana Azmi, who had just returned to India after performing in a play with the National Theatre Company, London, remarked, "The term 'British' needn't mean white Anglo-Saxon. . . . Asians [too] are now so much part of the British fabric." The extent to which they (the word "Asians" refers to South Asians) are part of the nation-state's fabric and how they define their subjectivities (which would then give us an alternative subject to that constructed by Bollywood) require us to examine the question of diasporic self-representations first. There have been some important films that take up the question of diaspora or diasporic reading of homeland. Among them are: *My Beautiful Laundrette, Sammy and Rosie Get Laid, Bhaji on the Beach, Bombay Boys, Mississippi Masala, My Son the Fanatic,* and *Masala.* Of this list I want to think through the Canadian Srinivas Krishna's *Masala* (1991) because it tackles a wide range of diasporic issues: the nature of the grand narrative of the nation, the reproductions of the homeland as an "auratic" artifact, the use of fundamentalist discourses within diasporas, and so on. One of the key things we learn from Walter Benjamin's classic essay on mechanical reproduction is that authenticity is outside of "technical reproducibility." The reproduced artifact, in a literal reading of the Benjamin argument, is one that has no auratic status. In diasporas, however, the reproduced artifact has its own authenticity, its own aura—not in terms of monetized value, but in terms of authentic emotional capital. In an insightful essay on *Masala,* Nicole Schiele (1999) makes the case that in the film, "originals are reduced to their (authentic) artefacts through several levels of reproduction." The list of "artifacts" is long: the film as an artifact of one of the worst air crashes in history, gods and beliefs as material artifacts in the grandmother's shrine at home, and memory itself as the fast-forward or rewind button on the videocassette recorder. In this sense the artifact—as commodity—enters social value. Yet the commodity fetish works in a curiously fragmented fashion since the artifacts are themselves not grounded in any unproblematic foundational narrative of the diaspora. The artifacts are presented as kitsch, the impure replica of the impossible-to-attain original. Srinivas Krishna makes the same case as follows: "*Masala* is a mixture . . . about purity and impurity, authenticity and inauthenticity, truth of self, loss of self; particularly revolving around the idea of kitsch. Because things that are impure are often kitsch" (quoted in Grundmann 1994: 23). Kitsch as a cinematic principle of the fake, the pastiche, drawing attention to its artificiality and impurity, to its own "constructedness," circumvents precisely the kinds of identificatory subjectivity at work in realistic cinema. Indeed it is the "kitschiness" of the objects in the film as well as the film itself that precludes all possibilities of spectatorial suture. E. Ann Kaplan's query is salutary here: "What happens when modernist subject-object looking structures are replaced by new, postmodernist ones, generated by a different set of technologies and by new global flows of bodies, money, ideas, and media?" (1997: 120). The structures are meant to defamiliarize spectation because in the film Canadian multiculturalism has bred its own stereotypes: the idolatry of nonbelievers, the aggressiveness of Sikhs, the benevolent patronage of the multicultural nation, and so on. In this respect, identification is not what diasporic cinema works toward since identification means embracing, in some sense, the stereotype. Instead the film is framed by a critical diaspora theory of subjective ambivalences within a definition of emotion as artifact. It precludes identification because it functions as a critique and, in some ways, as a consciously crafted consciousness-raising critique. Which is why *Masala*'s "kitschiness" is so central to its form. Schiele observes: "*Masala* seizes the risks of surveillance and spectacle precisely because of its conspicuous 'visuality,' its use of kitschy artefacts and aesthetics, its panoptical [marked by the frequent use of long takes] camera positions." Thus in an ironic double take on the authentic and the homeland as constructed by the media, the trauma of the Air India crash is itself presented as pure technology. There may be, as Kolar-Panov says, "no rewind button on the Betamax of life" (1997: 225), but there is certainly one on the remote control of a VCR. The quest for the original is thus presented for what it really is—epic memories without texts. The spoof on hallowed diasporic beliefs (religion, struggle for homelands, and, for many, integration into a benign multicultural nation), the use of parodic registers (both verbal and visual) are all meant to replace the authentic, the original, by the equally "authentic" artifacts of mechanical reproduction. To put it crudely, the Krishna on the VCR *is* the diasporic Krishna. It is not some inauthentic image of a lost original. In this respect *Masala* returns the media's complicity in perpetrating diaspora stereotypes back to the media. It situates "technologies of reproduction and circulation" (Schiele 1999) in the diegetic space of this film itself. One of the key apparatuses here is the grandmother's VCR in Lallu Bhai's living room. The Lord Krishna videotape (which together with the monitor is a shrine and a spectacle) releases "the whole TV Kitsch" (Grundmann 1994: 25) as the postmodern calendar art of Indian life, "auratic" but commodified. Lord Krishna functions both as a spectacle for the grandmother (and the *darśanik* spectator-devotee) and as the narrator and surveyor of the text itself. In a postmodern take on the *Mahābhārata* (in which Krishna sanctions and censors history), Lord Krishna becomes the "diegetic panoptician" in *Masala*. In this respect—as panoptic gaze—Krishna looks back at the grandmother and at the spectator since, in realist terms, the sublime object of Krishna is defined precisely by an always present narrative of the shot reverse shot. In this respect, to gaze at Krishna is to be gazed celestially or auspiciously by him (the key focus of Raja Ravi Varma's paintings). The grandmother's video viewing habit may be extended at this point to incorporate all viewing of Indian cinema, the point being that even as we gaze, the cinema gazes back at us because it functions as the "auratic" artifact of the lost original. Appadurai had spoken about commodities having social lives, and I think in the case of *Masala* both the film (as commodity) and the intradiegetic viewing within it of another video makes the societal nature of the (video) commodity so obvious. In the intradiegetic text the mirroring of the self is maintained since the renting of videos is itself an exercise in capturing the lost epic (without a text). In *Masala*, however, such mirroring, I want to suggest, is conspicuously foreclosed through the use of kitsch. This is how Srinivas Krishna himself explained the kitschy Lord Krishna video: "the point of this gag, lost on most critics, is to satirize nostalgic attempts by Indian emigrés to recapture something of the motherland through repeated viewings of Indian cinema—in particular, the vastly popular multi-part video extravaganzas based on the *Rāmāyaṇa* and the *Mahābhārata*" (Cameron 1992: 45).

As a critical text of diaspora theory *Masala*'s stand on spectator identification is highly ambivalent since its invitations to viewer participation are simultaneously undercut by its "conspicuous un-suturedness" (Schiele 1999). At the same time it is deeply indebted to Bombay Cinema as fetish, as an artifact that constructs desires for the homeland. Referring to *The Joy Luck Club*, Rey Chow comments generally on the need to prize films out of their "ethnic" confines:

> When we see the film not in terms of the realistic register of "ethnicity" in which it is inevitably cast by the forces of multiculturalism, but instead as a kind of idealism production through cinema, then it would be possible to locate it within a libidinal economy that will always imagine its "origins" in another time and place. (1998: 111)

To extend Rey Chow's criticism, the point I wish to make is that it is important to look at *Masala* not simply as an interventionist text of Canadian multiculturalism. In making this statement I do not wish to deny the value of a resistance theory which sees Harry Tikkoo's possession of the three-penny Beaver stamp as the challenging (and threatening) usurpation of a fragment of the nation's grand narrative by the minority outsider. What is of value to me are the ways in which *Masala* dislocates memory, makes the return to primal origins an impossible dream, disallows spectatorial identification but emphasizes the "auratic" quality of the reproduced artifact. Within its intradiegetic interstices we note the fetishization of the video commodity and the seductive power of the filmic gaze. In constructing Lord Krishna "kitschily" through Bombay mythologicals and Indian calendar art, in locating romantic fantasies as Bombay video clips, *Masala* points to Bombay Cinema not as anti-auratic replicants but as the stand-in for the original. The difference between *Masala* and the films of Bombay Cinema is that whereas *Masala* does not suture its spectators, Bombay Cinema, like Lord Krishna in *Masala*, stretches its hands out to lead the diaspora out of its morass.

DIASPORIC VOYEURS

Voyeuristic pleasure is both primal or ontological and constructed through an absence in the body of diaspora. The absence I speak of is a result of two factors: a sense of exclusion from the racialized politics of the nation-state and a need for corporeal identification and self-representation. The point (after Rey Chow), however, is that non-Westerners also gaze. They too are voyeurs and spectators and take pleasure in viewing the female body (Chow 1995: 13). However, the question of a non-Western diasporic gaze has implicit in it a prior, hegemonic, imperial gaze, or some version of it. There are two sides of the imperial gaze that we need to keep in mind. In E. Ann Kaplan's formulation there is the gaze at the spectator that "refuses to acknowledge its own power and privilege" (1997: 79) and, I sense (Kaplan does not make it explicit), presents the gaze as an ideology without bias. In this respect it stands aloof as the Enlightenment, rational ideal, and is to be taken for what it is— an ideal. But insofar as the gaze (and this is the second side of it) then breaks the principle of the viewer's right to gaze in return (or to "re-gaze" the object in the film being gazed upon), no mutual understanding is possible. A number of consequences follow from this imperial gaze: it "infantalizes," "animalizes," "sexualizes," and "immoralizes" the minority spectator. The diaspora comes with a narrative of this imperial gaze as a frame of filmic reception. But what it does—and I draw on the evidence found in the many Indian film related websites—is blast asunder the calculus of the imperial gaze through an act of radical refashioning. In other words, if the gaze in, say, David Lean's *A Passage to India* excludes Indians, the gaze in Bombay Cinema, however imperially constructed, is seen as one to which the spectator can reciprocate. So whereas the imperial gaze trivializes the object— thuggees are demonized in Spielberg's *Indiana Jones and the Temple of Doom*—the Bombay film incorporates and celebrates it.

The question of reciprocity and incorporation, though not presented in quite these theoretical terms, was raised in Marie Gillepsie's survey of the viewing habits of South Asians in Southall, England, during 1989–1990. Gillepsie takes up the question of the productive nature of diasporic space— space here is read as Henri Lefèbvre's social formation that "subsumes things produced, and encompasses their interrelationships in their coexistence and simultaneity" (Lefèbvre 1991: 73). The target texts that formed part of her investigation are Bombay films and the Doordarshan serialization of the *Mahābhārata*. She makes three important observations. First she locates Indian diaspora culture in the framework of what Robert Young (1995) was to call "intentional hybridity" against the "organic hybridity" of the African

Juhi Chawla and Shah Rukh Khan in Aziz Mirza's *Phir Bhi Dil Hai Hindustani*, 2000. Celebrating the image: the modern couple in the rain, remembering *Shree 420*. Courtesy Dreamz Unlimited.

British. In this respect, Gillespie argued, diaspora Indians consume rather than reproduce or redefine dominant cultural forms. Second, diaspora Indians are largely free from the communal or fundamentalist politics of "home." Third, the diaspora Indian's social space is marked by TV and video. These observations require some modification—there are more productive and less self-conscious acts of synthesis in the work of the Chicago-based sitarist Anand Bhatt, in Apache Indian's collaboration with Boy George, in the sarangi player Ustad Sultan Khan's work with Madonna, and in the incisively critical British-pop work of Nitin Sawhney (such as his album *Beyond Skin*). On the question of fundamentalist politics, it must be said that it has strong support among the Sikhs of Vancouver. Still, Gillespie's conclusion that the intensive viewing of Indian films is "also a response to the social and cultural marginalization of minorities from the mainstream of British society, which provides few cultural or leisure facilities for them" (79) remains valid. In this respect "racist" Britain degrades the Indian diaspora to such an extent that it retreats into the secure spectacle of Bombay Cinema even if, as Indian youths in Southall maintain, it perpetrates the schism between the "community" and the larger British society. What is interesting in Gillespie's study is that it shows the highly ambivalent ways in which different generations consume the video artifact. For the older-generation women (mothers and grandmothers), the VCR button brings the homeland into the family room. The viewing of Bombay films mediates the cleavages between an estranged diasporic culture and an "integrative" home culture. For youths it functions as a mode of legitimizing one's own existence in a culturally hostile nation-state. Even as youths recognize their parents' doomed attempts at artificially manufacturing a culture through film, they realize that these cultural "translations" are vital for the diaspora's emotional and psychological well-being (Gillespie 1995: 87). Do we in fact find here, in line with our general argument about the commodity as the lost auratic original, a replay of the compulsion to repeat a moment that is no longer available in the general space of the nation-state but which can be captured in the diasporic space of the living room? When Gillespie spent some time with the Dhani family in Southall viewing the Doordashan serialization of the *Mahābhārata* on BBC2 and Peter Brook's version on Channel 4, she discovered that the family rejected the latter, a much more creative and avant-garde version, as "targeted at middle-class theatre-going elites" (92). Here was a middle-class Southall family that connected with the lumpen proletariat in embracing the Indian *Mahābhārata* over Peter Brook's. Mass culture is curiously inverted as original and pure, whereas high culture (and its version of the canonical text) is rejected outright. The Dhani family's response takes us to something which is at the very heart of the diasporic imaginary—that is, the diaspora's fictive identification with mass culture in contrast with middle-class rejection of it back in the homeland. When Bombay Cinema began to create its own version of the Indian diaspora, one senses that it took into account the value systems of families like the Dhani family.

BOMBAY CINEMA GAZES BACK

It is one thing for the homeland to be constructed through the dream machine of Bombay Cinema. It is quite another for Bombay Cinema to create its version of the diaspora itself and, through it, tell the diaspora what it desires. Or, in an ironic echo of Marx, to display the diaspora better than it displays itself. The theme is not altogether new as relatively early on the filmmaker Manoj Kumar used the East/West binary to establish the primacy of tradition over modernity in *Purab Aur Pachhim* (East and west, 1970). More ambitiously, but unsatisfactorily, Rajbans Khanna's *Jeevan Sangram* (A struggle for freedom, 1974) used a decisive moment of trauma in the history of Canadian Sikhs—the *Komagata Maru* incident of May 1914 in which 376

Juhi Chawla and Shah Rukh Khan in Aziz Mirza's *Phir Bhi Dil Hai Hindustani,* 2000. Song and dance routine circulating as video clip. Courtesy Dreamz Unlimited.

Shah Rukh Khan in Yash Johar's *Kuch Kuch Hota Hai,* 1998. Representing modernity to the diaspora; inviting reciprocal gazing. Courtesy Yash Johar Productions/Kamat Foto Flash.

primarily Sikh would-be immigrants were kept offshore before they were sent home—to look into India's nascent independence movement. A deeply ambiguous and disturbing film such as *Lamhe* (The uncanny moment, 1991) could play on transgressive desire for the daughter of the woman Pallavi (Sridevi) loved by Viren (Anil Kapoor) by locating Viren in London and effectively keeping him there during those eighteen years when the young girl Pooja (also played by Sridevi) is growing up. Although *Lamhe* is not directly about diaspora it nevertheless insinuates that diasporic subjects are not caged within Indian social norms as such. It is in diasporic space that the declaration of love by Pooja (for Viren) takes place. Nevertheless transgressions of what may be called the "deep structures" of kinship, as Rosie Thomas reminds us (1985: 128), are less likely to be accepted by the Indian viewer, which is why, interesting as *Lamhe* is to a theory of Bollywood cinematic desire, it was not a great financial success. Between the simplistic tradition-modernity binary of *Purab Aur Pachhim* (1970) and the complex emotional politics of *Lamhe* (1991) a massive process of diasporic deterritorialization had occurred. During this period—which coincided with the biggest movement of Indians out of the country since nineteenth-century indenture—a new form of travel culture between homeland and diaspora developed. This new mobility, supported in every way by an ever-changing digital technology, created new markets for "film companies, impresarios, and travel agencies, which thrive on the need of the relocated population for contact with the homeland" (Appadurai 1996: 49). Films are therefore part of a larger culture of travel which brings star concerts, and film production units to the United Kingdom, Canada, and the United States. The star-studded (Aamir Khan, Shah Rukh Khan, Sonali Bendre) *Rangeela Dilwale* concert performed in Vancouver on May 5, 1996, before a crowd of some ten thousand is a case in point. It was underwritten by diasporic entrepreneurs and extensively advertised in a number of diasporic newspapers, such as the twice-weekly *Link*, the weekly *Asia Sun*, the weekly *Indo-Canadian Voice*, the fortnightly *Indo-Caribbean World*, and the monthlies *Hum, Voice,* and *Mehfil*. These cinematically packaged concerts (staged presentations of set video clips, for instance) mediate between diasporic culture and Indian culture *and* between diasporic culture and Western popular culture generally. In viewing the concert what one sensed over and over again was the manner in which the performers were re-presenting Western popular culture to the Canadian (East) Indians in response to the diaspora's own presumed unease about claiming Western culture as its own.

Sonali Bendre in Praveen Nischol's *English Babu Desi Mem*, 1995. Collapsing cultural codes of representation. Courtesy Daasa Movies.

Bombay Cinema's first fully blown reading of the narratives of migrancy and displacement, and an indispensable archival material for a sociology of diasporic formations, is Yash Chopra's *Dilwale Dulhania Le Jayenge* (Lovers win brides, 1995, hereafter *DDLJ*). This seminal text about diasporic representation and consumption of Indian popular culture has been extensively debated and critiqued (on one website two Dutch students even titled their travel in India "The *Dilwale Dulhania* Experience"). The success of *DDLJ* in the Indian diaspora is directly linked to the ways in which it re-projects the diasporic subject by first internalizing him or her. Yet cinema ideology here—the re-projection of a diaspora that Bollywood manufactures in terms of its own laws—is curiously at odds with the struggle for self-legitimacy and justice that underpins diasporic lives generally. The ideology in question then is not one that examines social ruptures (as in Srinivas Krishna's *Masala*) but one that reworks a number of diasporic fantasies. When these fantasies are reconfigured by the homeland as the "real" of diasporic lives, they have the curious role of actually becoming "truths" to which the diaspora aspires. I want to select two diasporic fantasies: the fantasy of the video clip (which gets reproduced by visiting impresarios in concerts like *Rangeela Dilwale*) and the fantasy of the ideal marriage (a love marriage, yes, but with parental approval nevertheless—what Patricia Uberoi has called the "arranged love marriage"). The classic text of the latter fantasy is *Hum Aap Ke Hain Kaun* (Who am I to you? 1994). To maintain these fantasies *DDLJ* must work through impossible narratives of ethnic absolutism and diasporic return so that, as the patriarch in the film says, one is not like a laundryman's dog, good for neither home nor the river.

The opening sequence of *DDLJ* shows us a Punjabi migrant feeding pigeons in Trafalgar Square. The voice-over expresses the man's diasporic anxieties immediately:

> This is London, the world's largest city [this is how colonial texts in the fifties described London]. I have lived here these twenty-two years, walked this street every day and each day the same street asks me my name, asks me: you, Chaube Baldev Singh, where have you come from, why have you come here? Half a life has gone by, and yet this land is so strange to me and I to it. Like me, these pigeons too have no home, but when will I be able to fly (like them)? But someday, surely, I too will return. To my India, to my Punjab.

A line snatched from a song to be played out in full later—"come home, stranger, your country calls you back"—and itself alluding back to Raj Kapoor's *Jis Desh Men Ganga Behti Hai* (Where flows the Ganges, 1960), marks the end of this scene as the credits are superimposed. The text proper that follows may be neatly divided into two broad sections of an hour and a half each. Let me call the first "the sanctified space of the home and the shop," within which I would also include the subset of "the fantasy of the grand European tour"; I will call the second, "home and the green, green field of the Punjab."

The shop is the center of the diasporic work ethic; it is also the stereotypical space for the Asian from the point of view of the British. "Why can't Asians play football?" "They'll put up a shop every time they get a corner." So goes the standard joke about Asians and soccer in Britain. In the shop Baldev Singh does his *pooja* (Hindu religious ritual) while his wife phones him every morning to see that he reached work safely. The space at home is occupied by their two daughters, ages 12 and 21. Since Baldev Singh has declared that he has been in England for twenty-two years, we can assume that both are British born. Yet they speak Hindi without an accent and, more important, have a body language that is totally Indian. Simran, the older daughter, even writes her diary in Hindi as she fantasizes about her lover, who will be portrayed by none other than Shah Rukh Khan (he of the Vancouver *Rangeela Dilwale* concert). There is nothing here, as cinema, that disrupts Bombay Cinema's

Publicity poster for Yash Chopra's *Dilwale Dulhania Le Jayenge*, 1995.

melodramatic signifying practices or departs from the screenplay writer Aditya Chopra's observation that "we may be in the 1990s, but there are certain things about the Indian family structure that haven't changed at all" (Uberoi 1998: 312). Yet there are some hints of a Western modernity. The sisters quickly change their tape/CD from rock 'n' roll to K. L. Saigal's "gam diye mustaqil" (O permanent sorrows) the moment the father returns to the space of home. To him difference has to be maintained or else like the disrespectful Indian boy in the shop (who managed to get a case of beer from him after closing time on false pretenses) one would have no identity of one's own. So what do we get here? Forms of ethnic absolutism? No engagement with the nation-state? No gestures toward hybridity? And home? Where is it? What one has left behind rather than where one is at? But are they also indications of a new sense of diasporic self-assuredness after years of excessive pandering to the West on matters of the popular? Or, finally, is this a re-projection of Aditya Chopra's own reading of Indian culture onto the diaspora to emphasize the culture's eternal verities to the home audience?

Whereas for the father it is the diaspora that is in fact threatening, for the daughter Simran it is the homeland that threatens. Apart from the synecdochic value of this reversal as signifying a diasporic generational gap in one's reading of the "here" and "there," the difference also works on the undertheorized question of gendered response to the homeland. For women (especially daughters) in the diaspora, the homeland may well pose a threat to their emotional freedom. So Baldev Singh's offer of an arranged marriage for Simran to a man in the Punjab is marked by the father's failure to detect any disturbance in the daughter. The father speaks in absolutist terms—"this is our culture," "I've kept India alive even in the heart of London." His triumph is expressed through the untranslatable *śarmātī hai* ("she's shy"), in itself a cliché but cognate with *śaram*. Salman Rushdie would have glossed "shame" at this juncture: "Sharam, that's the word. For which this paltry 'shame' is a wholly inadequate translation" (1983: 33).

The subset in the first half of the film (my "first section") is the "fantasy of the grand European tour." The European tour has taken two forms in Bombay Cinema. The first form, which is more common, is the unmarked use of a European backdrop for the standard romantic song. It is "unmarked" because the shift in locale (from India to Europe) is not marked by any narrative transition; rather it is part of the cinematic mise-en-scène of Bombay Cinema, the staging of the song sequence in a locale that is not internal to the text but is nevertheless presented as such. The second form, which is historically rare but is gradually becoming a standard feature of Bombay films generally, is the actual movement of people to Europe as part of the film's diegesis. The latter use took a definitive turn in Raj Kapoor's *Sangam* (The confluence, 1964), in which Europe is the site that redefines Indian sexuality and raises the question of the ethics of friendship as the *becārā* Rajendra Kumar must shoot himself in the end. Thus it is in the European grand tour (bequeathed upon the colonized Indian as an eighteenth-century literary artifact) that the lovers (Simran/Kajol and Raj Malhotra/Shah Rukh Khan) meet and play out, for both the diaspora and the Indian spectator, precisely those fantasies of the body censored from their real social lives. Europe as the untouched, pure pastoral, is the site of romance (against, one suspects, the racist reality of the Indian diaspora in Britain), but one that can also, given its pastoral semantics, keep the libido in check. Thus when Simran awakens in Raj's bed (after she had gulped a little cognac), he tells her, "You think I am an utter larrikin, but I am a Hindustani, and I know what a Hindustani girl's *izzat* (honor) is like. Last night nothing happened, believe me." "Hindustani," that coded word scripted as a defiant self-assertion of the absolute dharma of the Indian (to say that "I am a Hindustani" is a declaration of transcendental Indianness), confirms that Simran remains pure to the end.

Kajol, Farida Jalal, and Amrish Puri in Yash Chopra's *Dilwale Dulhania Le Jayenge*, 1995. The father's controlling hand. Courtesy Yash Raj Films.

Against the diasporic lovers' European pastoral, the father's pastoral is "the green, green field of the Punjab," which I have used as a shorthand for the second half of the film. The dynamics of this pastoral are rather different, indeed radically different, from the first because it is not simply a backdrop: space here has historical and emotional depth. There are few picture-postcard shots in this section, so when they do occur the critical spectator goes through a momentary sense of *ostrananie* (of defamiliarization) as the locale looks curiously European (in an otherwise Punjabi context). This is the site of an actual realization (since the parents do not return to England) of the classic diaspora narrative of dispersal and final return to the homeland. In this respect this is home with a difference; its space is neither England nor Europe, both of which are finally alien and alienating. As the train takes the family through the green fields of Punjab (a counterpoint to "England's mountains green, pleasant pastures, green and pleasant land"), the women in the fields sing the refrain "ghar ājā pardesī" (Come home, stranger, your country calls you back). Inside the family home itself, rituals contextualize a diasporic Rama's return from banishment: Baldev Singh's mother is in the dignified white sari of the widow as she performs the ancient Hindu *ārtī* and says in a grave voice, "For twenty years I have kept these tears inside. Today they swell up and flow." The threat to the idyllic space of the homeland, how-

Shah Rukh Khan and Kajol in Yash Chopra's *Dilwale Dulhania Le Jayenge*, 1995. The Grand European Tour. Courtesy Yash Raj Films.

Kajol and Shah Rukh Khan in Yash Chopra's *Dilwale Dulhania Le Jayenge*, 1995. A reprise of the *Aag* shot but less seductive. Courtesy Yash Raj Films.

ever, comes not from the aberrant diaspora, the diaspora of Raj and Simran, but from the husband-to-be, Kuljeet, who is a grasping, scheming, unethical materialist—Baldev Singh's version of the diasporic dog without a home. Against the Indian Kuljeet's unashamedly ulterior motive to use Simran as a one-way ticket to the "glamorous" British Indian diaspora, the diasporic Raj is presented as the proper, chivalric, and ultimately dharmik Indian lover.

It is Raj who refuses to run away with Simran even though she is clearly being married off against her will. "We do need the blessings of the parents before any marriage can be called proper," he says—echoing, as Patricia Uberoi reminds us, his real-life struggle to marry his Hindu wife, Gauri (321). The force of Raj's honesty is such that finally the father relents, and in a replay of their first encounter when Raj gives Simran his hand and pulls her into the train on their way to Europe, the girl is united with the hero. As the father lets go of her hand he says: "Go Simran go, no one can love you more than this boy. Go Simran, go with your Rama, go live out your life, go daughter go." One assumes that Simran returns to the diaspora to continue her life, but as an Indian untouched by the diasporic experience; the father remains behind. Rajeshwari Singh, the younger daughter, will probably have an arranged marriage in the Punjab. For her the diaspora would have been an interregnum, a home away from home, best forgotten.

These are the film's diasporic messages. Why then is there a remarkable congruity between the success of this movie in India and in the diaspora? Is this one of the great triumphs of this form, that it has in fact transcended diasporic difference and established an imaginary that belongs to both homeland as well as diasporic Indians? This point certainly surfaces when we see how the film feeds the diaspora with fixed Indian practices, and especially Indian practices that are predicated upon women as sacrificial victims. One such ritual is the Karva Chauth, when married women observe a fast and worship an earthen pot in the lunar calendar month of Karttik (October–November). Along with the ritual of marriage, the fast of the Karva Chauth is one of a handful of productive spaces that is reprised in current Bombay Cinema. In *DDLJ* the Karva Chauth is inserted into the wedding celebrations to bring a "pure" Indian ritual of the homeland to the diasporic spectator. It is a predominantly Punjabi fast and not necessarily pan-Indian, which says something about the target audience of the (new) diaspora. During the Karva Chauth, Simran fasts (her first Karva Chauth fast, as she proudly declares) and continues to do so well into the evening until Raj turns up. As a gesture to the diaspora's presumed sophistication on feminist critical theory we are told that Raj too has fasted all day. Even as *DDLJ* advances a rather reactionary ideology vis-à-vis the diaspora, there are moments of controlled transgressions (moments of disruption as we have noted on a number of occasions) that introduce a disharmony, an ambiguity, into the social.

TAKE ONE: MOTHER-DAUGHTER

The scene takes place in the "pure" space of the ancestral home. It is the space where the perfect arranged marriage can take place. But a strange disequilibrium has crept in: the pastoral has come under threat through desire—and a desire contrary to a social practice that locates desire in an arranged marriage. In the scene two women—mother and daughter—sit at opposite ends of a modified bay window. Lajo, the mother, speaks, and Simran listens:

> Throughout my life I have worked at the behest of others. When I was young I was denied proper education because my brothers were more important. I was simply married off. I had my joy only when you came. On your birth I promised that my daughter will have the joys, the freedom I never got. She won't be another sacrificial victim to the patriarchal order. But I was wrong. It is not for us to make promises or keep them. This is the cruel truth of being a woman. Therefore, I have come to ask you your happiness. Forget him daughter, forget him.

Let us follow the tantalizing dramatic structure of this seemingly dialogic moment. The voice is self-assured, and it comes across, in the beginning, as the voice of the (M)other, the voice of protest. But it succumbs under its own weight. It succumbs even as it enunciates a different order, or at least the possibility thereof. What resurfaces in the non sequitur is that woman must sacrifice and daughters are constituted (as subjects) by the patriarchal order (to which the mother's discourse finally pays deference). But is this cinematic moment to be closed off as such? Is there, as Monika Mehta has suggested, a directive to Kajol, the actor portraying Simran, by Farida Jalal, portraying the mother, that to survive in Indian cinema young female actors must play sacrificial roles? (1999). Read against the grain, the mother's discourse certainly makes this reading a real possibility. But the filmic presentation of the diegesis and the spectator's own response need to be considered, too. The mother's monologue is presented in fifteen shots. The camera moves from mid-range shots to close-ups, but never to a close-up of any specific part of the face such as the eyes. What is striking, however, is that when there is a reverse shot it is not over the head of the other speaker but at an angle, so that in these shot reverse shots (four instances in all) gazes do not suture, there is no superimposition of one gaze upon the other. The camera work, therefore, introduces a small ideological disruption indicating that the daughter's point of view cannot be glued onto the mother's. In this respect, the camera silently avows an alternative narrative of rejection, not one of sacrificial complicity. It is here too that we need to bring in the spectator: both the home spectator and the diasporic spectator. These two have, quite possibly, contradictory readings of the same scene. I would want to suggest that in this scene it is the homeland spectator, that is, the Indian spectator, who finds the mother's solution disturbing while the diasporic spectator reads it as a confirmation of the ungraspable perennial values that are not available in the diaspora. If I am correct in my conjecture here, then, to invoke a theoretical distinction made by M. Madhava Prasad (1998: 50–51), the diaspora reads the scene as narrative (that is, receives a pre-given message) while the homeland reads the text as cinema (reproduces meaning).

THE COMPULSION TO REPEAT

Subhash Ghai's *Pardes* (Another land, 1997) is another "coming-of-age NRI film," as Shah Rukh Khan has called it (*Times of India,* January 24, 1999, Sunday section, 6). Like *DDLJ* it too allows for the momentary disavowal of crucial social indices, thereby placing value systems themselves in the realm of contestation. The story line of *Pardes* is simple: successful American businessman Kishori Lal (Amrish Puri) wants to arrange the marriage of his Indo-American son Rajiv to an Indian girl, Ganga. As he tells the girl's father, "In these trying times (in foreign lands), we desperately need daughters like your Ganga." The narrative itself plays on predictable motifs and character types. There are the dangerously Indophobic Rajiv of the Indian diaspora who before attempting to rape Ganga, declares, "Your India is nothing but a huge shithouse"; the Indophile and India-born Arjun (played by Shah Rukh Khan), who finally saves Ganga from inevitable destruction in the diaspora; the overzealous parents (of both Rajiv and Ganga); and Ganga herself, always the pure Indian like her name, the Indian untouched by diasporic values (although these values are always presented as forms of Western decadence already "pre-textualized" through Bombay Cinema), and so on. But even as the mise-en-scènes construct curiously premodern, pastoral India (about which Kishori Lal sings his paean "I love my India"), another modernity erupts through the grandmother's feminist voice. She speaks against woman as a commodity to be "auctioned" and defends Ganga's right to refuse to return to America against her will. "Why should you drink this poison? We women have suffered throughout history. Why should Ganga dislodge herself and move to a foreign land where there is no ocean for her?" she says. The grandmother's voice is again an important critique from within even as the film endorses the inviolability of the "Indian family structure" (Uberoi 1998: 312). In both *DDLJ* and *Pardes,* values and ideologies are contested (and become contestable) because diaspora offers a new space for these contestations to take place.

In Sanjay Leela Bhansali's *Hum Dil De Chuke Sanam* (I gave my heart away, my love, 1999), we get another narrative of return. There are two symmetrical journeys here: one young person, Sameer Rossellini (Salman Khan), a surname not unfamiliar to people who remember the Italian director's obsession with India in the 1950s, returns to India in search of culture (here music); another young man, Banraj (Ajay Devgan) takes his wife, Nandini (Aishwarya Rai), back to Italy to reunite her with her erstwhile lover. Although Italy is not cinematically Italy (it is Hungary, because as Bhansali confessed in a personal conversation, filming in Hungary didn't even cost half as much), the location of the diasporic hero (who is only part-Indian) in Italy plays on India's preeminent (Gandhi-Nehru) family, all of whom are either Italian (Sonia Gandhi) or part-Italian (her two children). In this respect Bhansali's film works on a very real consciousness about a family that has Italian genetic connections but which has been naturalized unproblematically as Indian.

In many ways *Hum Dil De Chuke Sanam* is a more complex film than either *DDLJ* or *Pardes* for the simple reason that the relay of tradition is located in the world of the young lovers themselves. There is no change of heart on the part of parents here as in *DDLJ*; the change occurs in the woman herself, who gradually falls in love with her husband so that in the end "arranged love marriage" is granted privilege over love marriage. Its acceptance by the liberated woman confirms the difficulty the form has with disruptions that affect the deep semantics of kinship. In the realm of scopic desire the symbology of the *maṅgalsūtra* (the auspicious thread tied by the bridegroom around his bride's neck) plays a decisive role. Nandini holds it in her hands as she returns to her husband even as the narrative is about to transgress the law that declares that marriages are inviolate.

What are the spectatorial investments in these films? Clearly there are at least two if not three or even four kinds of spectators we need to look at. There is the home crowd in the cinema halls looking for another *Masala* film in the current style but with a twist. This crowd perhaps does not want to buy the film's ideology, but the filmmakers believe that the foundationalist ideology of the India/Western divide is what they like. It probably uses the spectacle of a collective viewing even of the diasporic condition (however misrepresented it is) as a form of pleasure: the diaspora here is the desired Other. There are the diasporic home video viewers (largely homemakers and children) for whom the viewing is less "spectatorial" and more habitual. Here there is a collective diasporic solidarity of the kind discovered by Marie Gillespie in her analysis of the video-viewing culture of Indians in Southall. There is again the spectator as theorist who finds the exercise yet another stage in self-representation or misrepresentation by an apparatus that has been instrumental in keeping the homeland so firmly fixed in diasporic consciousness. And then there is the implied diasporic spectator, the subject to whom cinema returns, compulsively, his own absent desire (in a callous, threatening foreign nation-state) and for whom these texts relay an ideal homeland-diaspora narrative. This spectator is now such a crucial viewer of the Bollywood film that the aesthetics of diasporic representationalism is becoming internal to Bombay Cinema. So in a film such as *Kuch Kuch Hota Hai* (Sometimes things do happen, 1998), which is not specifically about the Indian diaspora, what is unusual is the film's self-conscious construction of the Indian diaspora as the ideal reader-spectator of the film. In this respect the heavy dependence of the film on North American/European landscapes (presented, of course, with no geographical specificity as the globe simply becomes an extension of India as Budapest may indeed stand for Rome) indicates the ease with which Bombay Cinema incorporates into its own representational practices landscapes with which only diasporas are largely familiar. *Kuch Kuch Hota Hai* raked in £1.2 million within five weeks in Britain, and in the San Francisco Bay Area it ran for six consecutive weeks. Some Bollywood stars work on this knowledge. Shah Rukh Khan makes regular visits to the North American Indian diaspora in particular, and Kajol has very popular North American home pages on the Internet. But there are two parallel points that should be made here. The first is that a Punjabi ethos (Sikh and Hindu) is displacing the old North Indian Hindi ethos of Bombay Cinema. It has been estimated that more than a million Punjabi speakers live abroad with a combined income equal to half the gross national product of the Punjab. The second is the way in which the diaspora (and presumed narratives about them) function as the ideal space for the Indian spectator as well. It is not that the diaspora is always the center of the narrative, but the experience of it functions as a site where, against all odds, Indian values are triumphantly maintained.

VIDEO CLIP: THE STAGED PERFORMANCE

Although there is a special payoff in the diaspora for films with diasporic themes, the element of Bombay Cinema that circulates most readily is not the film as a complete commodity (which requires concentrated viewing for some

Ajay Devgan and Aishwarya Rai in Sanjay Leela Bhansali's *Hum Dil De Chuke Sanam*, 1999. Husband and wife estranged in bed. Courtesy Bhansali Productions.

Aishwarya Rai and Salman Khan in Sanjay Leela Bhansali's *Hum Dil De Chuke Sanam*, 1999. Looking away from spectators. Courtesy Bhansali Productions.

three hours) but fragments from it. One of the points I have made in this chapter is that Indian cinema has incorporated the dance-hall and "clubbing" culture of diaspora youth into its own forms. This incorporation (which I argue is as much a response to diasporic demands as it is to a transnational urban culture within India itself) has been one of the more significant shifts in the old song-and-dance routines which, though also staged, had hitherto not been repackaged for consumption because video technology was not available then. In the film *Chahat* (Desire, 1996) a cabaret dance sequence is actually filmed (within the film) as a video clip and televised on cable TV. Here we get a self-reflexive allusion to the extent to which filmmakers themselves see the form as a marketable video clip. However, of the three video clips I discuss here—a wedding song from *DDLJ* and two from *English Babu Desi Mem* (The English gentleman and his Indian lady, 1995)—the wedding song has a slightly different focus in that it forthrightly confirms through the space of the elaborate Hindu wedding the ultimate longing (as Bombay Cinema sees it) of the diaspora. The second and third clips—referred to here as the Bollywood cabaret and the classic *mujrā*—function rather differently. The first (the Bollywood cabaret) is a re-projection of Western modern dance and song onto their own bodies. Let me explain. What we see here is a glamorized representation of music and dance that diasporic bodies perform among themselves. Their performances do not, except in very few instances, become part of a general musical mode of the nation-state. Here then is a double specularity. The diaspora sees in Western modern dance forms a lack that it wants desperately to correct. Bombay Cinema in turn plays on this lack and supplies it. The second kind of diasporic desire is offered through the classic form of the *mujrā* dance, originally the dance of the courtesan. The dramatic shift here is in the dancer herself who performs like a courtesan but isn't one. In fact as the heroine, she is presented as the virtuous Indian woman. In *English Babu Desi Mem* both these dances are performed by Sonali Bendre, who was also at the Vancouver concert of May 1996.

VIDEO CLIP ONE: THE WEDDING SONG

When we look back at the history of the circulation of the wedding video clip in the Indian diaspora the definitive wedding text will probably come from *Hum Aap Ke Hain Kaun* (1994). This film, based on the artistically more successful *Nadiya Ke Paar* (1982), set the tone for the wedding song as an autonomous, freestanding, "dramatic," endlessly reproducible fragment. The wedding song in *DDLJ* too can be taken out of the film and repackaged for use at weddings both at home and the diaspora. The song itself is sung by groups of men and women led by Raj (Shah Rukh Khan) and Simran (Kajol), respectively. The opening lines sung collectively by the groups is folkloric and mildly heteroglossic: "O women" (*he kuḍiyā*) cry the men; "O men" (*he muṇḍe*) cry the women. The male dancers wear black, the women a variety of colors. Then come the opening lines:

> Cover your body with henna
> Decorate your marriage carriage.
> To take you away fair maid
> Will come your own beloved.

We get an immediate cut to a girl, sitting down, elaborately dressed in green, who responds, softly, slowly:

> Make yourself pretty, but veil your face as well
> These words of desire, let them remain secret.

The camera alternates between the singing and dancing of men and women and then cuts either to single shots of men and women dancing together or Raj dancing with a veil on his head. The song-and-dance sequence comes to a somewhat dramatic end with the arrival of Simran's father who, initially, seems to be disturbed by the dance. Just when we think he is going to break into a lengthy speech about Indian values and Indian manhood, he sings a Manna Dey song to his wife (who had also been caught up in the dance routine): "o merī zohrā zabī, tujhe malūm nahīṁ tū abhī tak hai hasīṁ aur mai javān, tujh pe kurbān merī jān merī jān" (O my sweet Venus, you forget, you're still pretty and I young; I lay my life before you yet again). The dancers explode into action, dancing around the father and the mother.

VIDEO CLIP TWO: THE BOLLYWOOD CABARET

The wedding song is more likely to be a diegetic necessity in Bombay Cinema than any other song/dance sequence. The example I want to discuss now has little connection with the filmic narrative but it does work rather well as a form that "resignifies" what Dhareshwar and Niranjana, in their analysis of the song "Mukkaala Muqabla" (from the Tamil film *Kaadalan* [Loverboy]) have referred to as "'globalized' culture" (1996). Their point is that the modern autonomous song/dance sequence (which I have generically referred to as the video clip), although still primarily nondiegetic, can have both a synecdochic significance in terms of narrative structure and a global significance in terms of "high-tech audiovisual" internationalism. In the live performances of visiting Bombay stars in the diaspora the filmic video clip can be re-presented as a new form of multicultural, global culture, which is why Bollywood repackages them in this fashion. In matters of the staged performance, Bombay Cinema has therefore borrowed indiscriminately from every kind of dance, from Andrew Lloyd Webber musicals to Michael Jackson dance routines. In this video clip from *English Babu Desi Mem* a very suggestive Sonali Bendre does a double take on Liza Minnelli's dancing style in *Cabaret* (1972). The woman sings:

Love me honey honey, love me sweet
Kiss me honey honey kiss me sweet

The body language here is erotic. The woman lies in bed, her body covered in a sheet with her right leg exposed. She is seen throwing her hair back against a spray of water. She puts on her black stockings, then her gloves; she puts on red lipstick suggestively. The dance indeed demands a voyeuristic gaze as part of its own condition. The colors are bright red, blue, and green. The dancer swivels around on a chair with a top hat and completes the singing of the opening lines with "kar de merī life complete" (in this way make my life complete). As the band rock 'n' rolls, she slides onto the floor and breathes heavily. Vikram Mayur, the hero (once again played by Shah Rukh Khan), joins her and sings with her. Sonali Bendre changes suggestively into a leopard skin dress, then into a red "Arabian Nights" costume as she gyrates her body. The heavy, superimposed sounds of breathing continue. The dance comes to an end with the lights going off and Sonali taken away by a gang of hoodlums.

VIDEO CLIP THREE: THE CLASSIC *MUJRĀ*

The *mujrā* predates the modern dance routine. In fact the *mujrā* may be seen as the first video clip since, in cinema at any rate, *mujrā*s were relatively autonomous performances staged in front of men by court dancers, temple dancers, or courtesans. Classic *mujrā*s have appeared in *Anarkali* (1953), *Mughal-e-Azam* (1960), *Sahib Bibi Aur Ghulām* (1962), *Umrao Jaan* (1981), *Mandi* (The marketplace, 1983), and many other films. Raj Kapoor's last film, *Ram Teri Ganga Maili* (1985) also featured a *mujrā*, with considerable success. Unlike the modern dance, the *mujrā* was traditionally slow paced with the focus solely on the dancer. There were singers and musicians by the dancer's side, although the singing itself was often done by the dancer. In the new, jazzed-up version of the *mujrā* in *English Babu Desi Mem* the style modulates between the somber, slow movements of the woman dancer and the

Sonali Bendre in Praveen Nischol's *English Babu Desi Mem*. Dance as video clip. Courtesy Daasa Movies.

Sonali Bendre in Praveen Nischol's *English Babu Desi Mem*. Dance as video clip. Courtesy Daasa Movies.

much quicker pace of the men and women who dance with her. However, in this *mujrā* the tempo soon quickens, and Sonali dances as vigorously as the other men and women. What is the sequence here? Sonali sits in the center dressed in red, her face covered. Alongside her sit women dressed in black. As the camera zooms in to take a close-up, Sonali sings, "kaise mukhre se nazare haṭāūṁ kī tujh me hai rab dikhtā" (How can I turn my face away from you, for in you I see my Lord). The language is pure Urdu, but the sentiments combine Sufi and Hindu devotional metaphors of a woman seeing God in the face of her husband. In the context, however, this is also a huge conceit, as the men dancing vigorously are wearing pseudo Yasser Arafat headgear. Sonali's own dance and that of the women around her turn more and more into the dance of the Sufi dervishes, with the singing of the men rising to a crescendo. Intercuts to scenes at the airport draw the spectator's attention to the larger narrative into which the dance should be inserted. Sonali's dance reaches its frenzied height when she takes out a bottle of poison. At this point the villain lassoes the bottle, the dance stops, he slaps her.

THE LIMITS OF DIASPORIC DESIRE

Bombay Cinema consciously places standardized video clips progressively in response to the needs of an Indian diaspora for whom the culture of the homeland is mediated through Indian cinema. In these autonomous moments (often unrelated to the narrative diegesis of cinema), those cultural forms are celebrated that have a direct resonance in the diaspora. Wedding song and dance direct the diasporic gaze to the "ideal arranged love marriage" in some sense unlikely to be realized in the diaspora, where men and women have to negotiate between public notions of partners in marriage and private expectations (as seen in diasporic marriage columns in Indian newspapers such as *India Down Under* in Australia where homeland marital arrangements are presented as the norm). As to the Bollywood cabarets or modern-day *mujrās*, these become in part diasporic rememorations of an absence of self-representation in the domain of the popular in the nation-states themselves. So while Bombay Cinema incorporates these as an understandable component of diasporic desire, their reception has to be located in the unhappy, schizophrenic, cultural condition of the diaspora. In other words, they cannot be unproblematically incorporated into immediate diasporic needs. For instance, the fantasies of the wedding video clip are not always replicated in the diaspora, as the at times harsh conditions of work, labor, and interpersonal relations conflict with those fantasies. As I have said before, Bombay Cinema's reprojection of its own (mis)readings of the diaspora elides some cruel diasporic realities. Marriages celebrated on the Bombay filmic model of the video clips sometimes end in disaster. In Vancouver on April 5, 1996 (which also happened to be a Good Friday), Mark Chahal killed his estranged wife and eight relatives on a wedding day in the family. Photo albums of the would-be wedding day and those of Mark Chahal's own wedding several years before bear uncanny resemblance to the wedding video clips of Bombay Cinema. In Saskatoon a couple whose marriage had been celebrated on Canadian TV as an example of (East) Indian "arranged love marriage" was thrust into the public eye again when the wife fatally stabbed the husband in Baltimore a year later (*National Post*, April 13, 1999). In citing these examples I do not wish to make unproblematic connections between film and the real world, or to belittle the enormity of these tragedies, and certainly not to suggest that weddings that duplicate the verve and enthusiasm of their imaginary Bombay counterparts end up in disaster.

On the contrary, what I want to suggest is that these tragedies demonstrate that filmic representations of love (and marriage) between the diasporic girl and the *desī* boy (or vice versa) cannot, within their entertainment structure, so much as suggest the darker side of the diasporic dream. Disasters around marriage (in Vancouver, in Saskatoon/Baltimore) signal diasporic social and sexual histories that act as historical counternarratives (in the total diasporic unconscious) to Bombay Cinema's construction of the diaspora.

What Bombay Cinema keeps representing is never the diasporic Other but its own and India's (mis)reading of the diaspora. Part of this "misreading" reflects a center-periphery understanding of the homeland-diaspora nexus in which the diaspora becomes sites of permissible (but controlled) transgressions while the homeland is the crucible of timeless dharmik virtues. To make this clear I want to refer to two films very quickly here. The first film is *Jurm* (Offense, 1990) in which a woman (Sangeeta Bijlani) kept in protective custody has a brief sexual relationship with a married police inspector. However, this liaison does not destroy the marriage of the inspector (Vinod Khanna) and his wife (Meenakshi Sheshadri) because the woman in question is from New York. The dharmik sexual ethics that underpins Bombay Cinema may undergo a "regulated transgression" provided that the transgressor is not directly (or organically) linked to the culture. The diasporic woman, in this respect, enables the cinema to do two things: to extend sexual desire in cinema even as illicit sexual relationships are inadmissible in the culture and to play off a presumed diasporic sexual freedom against a "proper" homeland sexual decorum. This reading of diasporic sexual freedom is given a more extended treatment in the second film, *Judaii* (Separation, 1997). Here an

Indian woman from New York (an NRI) buys the husband of a woman who desires wealth and luxury and is willing to part with her husband for them. What begins as a purely mechanical divorce (a legalized separation, hence the title of the film) in the end leads to the transfer of the husband's (Raj/Anil Kapoor's) feelings from his estranged wife (Kajal/Sridevi) to the woman from the diaspora (Janhvi/Urmila Matondkar). However, the transfer of feelings also triggers the "return" of love from Sridevi to Anil Kapoor. The scene is then set for the classic dharmik binomial: the oaths of the original marriage against the equally legitimate but purchased oaths of the second. In this struggle the Hindu Marriage Act is on the side of the diasporic Urmila Matondkar, but the eternal dharmik law, the sanctity of the Hindu marriage ritual, is on the side of Sridevi. What happens next? The diasporic body confesses her error—I shouldn't have bought off your husband, I am the outsider, I have erred and so on—and returns her husband to the rightful dharmik wife. "The divorce papers are already with my lawyers," she says as she boards a plane to New York. There are layers and layers of meaning here, but unpacking only two or three of these layers should suffice to clarify my point. The first is the value-laden opposition between diaspora and homeland: the diaspora is gaudy, exhibitionist (the autonomous video clips are dream events staged in the diaspora), and selfish; the homeland is simple and selfless although it is the homeland wife who encourages the divorce for the sake of wealth. The second is the sacrifice that the diaspora must make—a sacrifice of her own desire—so as to not destroy homeland dharma. And finally, the diaspora returns pregnant with the homeland husband's child—a gift to the unauthentic diaspora. Clearly this is the obvious surface narrative. The critical narrative lies in the contradictions exposed at the level of *discours* even as the *histoire* reaffirms the grand narrative of dharma—the homeland wife who sells her husband, the homeland wife who wants both wealth and love, a generic framework that allows characters to parody the seeming high seriousness of Indian marriage transactions, materialism as a homeland problem, and so on. In *Judaii*, then, the homeland-diaspora nexus is used in a much more critical fashion even as the film continues to rework Bombay Cinema's uneasy readings of the diaspora stereotype. Although in the conflict of desire what triumphs is the narrative of the father, not of the diasporic child, it gets progressively clear as we read key films of the last decade of the millennium that diaspora is in many ways a re-projection of what the homeland has repressed.

In the end, Bombay Cinema simply replicates its own restless form. The Bombay film comes "pre-textualized," it comes with its own ideology, its own apparatuses of production. The resilience of Bombay Cinema has been so strong and its representationalism so distinctive that it may make a claim to be a fifth variety of realism to be added to Fredric Jameson's four different accounts of realism: experimental-oppositional, Hollywood, documentary, and the photographic-ontological (1990: 197). So when it feeds the diaspora its (the diaspora's) own narratives—narratives that supposedly grow out of felt diasporic experiences—it ends up replicating its own form. There is nothing distinctively diasporic about *DDLJ* or *Pardes* apart from a narrative diegesis that locates the texts in the idea of global migration. In this respect the Bombay diasporic film cannot have the same value as Srinivas Krishna's *Masala* and Hanif Kureishi's *My Son the Fanatic*, films that explore contradictions and social tensions within diasporas. But the attraction of the Bombay diasporic cinema may well be linked to what Marie Gillespie observed was the diaspora's (mistaken) belief that Bombay Cinema represents the "real" India. By extension it also represents if not the real diaspora at least those perennial values that a diaspora should aspire toward, and desire. What we need to address, finally, is Bombay Cinema's own complicity in both pandering to the diaspora and in constructing an imaginary diaspora for the people of the diaspora themselves. Already clusters of maple leaves (the Canadian national symbol) mark off transitions in *Mohabbatein* (see publicity poster of this film, [Fig. 25]) and *Fiza*'s actors' publicity stills are framed by a maple leaf! Apart from its growing economic power (which means that the market for Bombay films about diasporas will continue to expand), the diaspora is no longer simply pockets of culturally ossified people "out there." Diaspora consciousness is now internal to spectatorial desire within India, and essential too to Bombay Cinema's new global aesthetics, which means that, in however mediatized form, diasporas will constitute one of the key elements of Bombay Cinema. Which takes me to a final statement: a study of Bombay Cinema will no longer be complete without a theory of diasporic desire because this cinema is now global in a specifically diasporic sense.

Filmography

Aadharshila, "Foundation Stone," 1982, prod.: Ashok Ahuja, dir.: Ashok Ahuja.

Aadmi, "Man," 1939, prod.: Prabhat Studios, dir.: V. Shantaram.

Aag, "Desire," 1948, prod.: Raj Kapoor, dir.: Raj Kapoor.

Aag Aur Daag, "Fire and Blemish," 1970, prod.: Swaran Singh, dir.: A. Salaam.

Aag Ka Dariya, "A Ravine of Fire," 1953, prod.: Roop K. Shorey, dir.: Roop K. Shorey.

Aag Hi Aag, "Nothing but Fire," 1987, prod.: Vishal Deep Int., dir.: Shibu Mitra.

Aah, "Sighs from the Heart," 1953, prod.: Raj Kapoor, dir.: Raja Nawathe.

Aaj Ka Arjun, "The Modern Arjun," 1990, prod.: K. C. Bokadia, dir.: K. C. Bokadia.

Aan, "Vow," 1952, prod.: Mehboob Khan, dir.: Mehboob Khan.

Aashiqui, "Courtship," 1990, prod.: Gulshan Kumar, dir.: Mahesh Bhatt.

Ab Insaf Hoga, "Justice Time," 1994, prod.: Vinod Shah, dir.: Harish Shah.

Achhut Kanya, "The Untouchable Girl," 1936, prod.: Bombay Talkies, dir.: Franz Osten.

Agneepath, "The Path of Fire," 1990, prod.: Yash Johar, dir.: Mukul S. Anand.

Alaap, "The Dialogue," 1977, prod.: N. C. Sippy and Hrishikesh Mukherji, dir.: Hrishikesh Mukherji.

Aladin Aur Uska Jadavi Chirag, "Aladdin and the Wonderful Lamp," 1952, prod.: Basant Pictures, dir.: Homi Wadia.

Alam Ara, "World-adorning,"1931, prod.: Imperial Film Company, dir.: Ardeshir Irani.

Alibaba Aur Uske Chalis Chor, "Alibaba and the Forty Thieves," 1954, prod.: Basant Pictures, dir.: Homi Wadia.

Amar, "Forever," 1954, prod.: Mehboob Khan, dir.: Mehboob Khan.

Amar Akbar Anthony, 1977, prod.: Manmohan Desai, dir.: Manmohan Desai.

Amar Prem, "Love Eternal," 1971, prod.: Shakti Samanta, dir.: Shakti Samanta.

Amardeep, "Eternal Flame," 1979, prod.: K. Balajee, dir.: K. Vijayan and R. Krishnamurthy.

Anand, "Joy," 1970, prod.: N. C. Sippy, dir.: Hrishikesh Mukherji.

Anarkali, 1928, prod.: Imperial Films, dir.: R. S. Choudhary.

Anarkali, 1953, prod.: Filmistan, dir.: Nandlal Jaswantlal.

Andaz, "Style," 1949, prod.: Mehboob Khan, dir.: Mehboob Khan.

Andhaa Kaanoon, "Blind Justice," 1983, prod.: A. Purnachandra Rao, dir.: T. Rama Rao.

Anjam, "The Consequence," 1994, prod.: Ritu Rawail, dir.: Rahu Rawail.

Ankur, "The Seedling," 1974, prod.: Mohan J. Bijlani, dir.: Shyam Benegal.

Anmol Ghadi, "A Priceless Watch,"1946, prod.: Mehboob Khan, dir.: Mehboob Khan.

Apna Desh, "My Country," 1972, prod.: A. V. Subramaniam and T. M. Kittu, dir.: Jambu.

Aradhana, "The Worship," 1969, prod.: Shakti Films, dir.: Shakti Samanta.

Arth, "Substance," 1983, prod.: Kuljit Pal, dir.: Mahesh Bhatt.

Astitva, "My Being," 2000, prod.: Friend India and Ashvami Films, dir.: Mahesh Manjrekar

Aurat, "Woman," 1940, prod.: National Studios, dir.: Mehboob Khan.

Avtaar, "Reincarnation," 1983, prod.: Mohan Kumar, dir.: Mohan Kumar.

Awara, "The Vagabond," 1951, prod.: Raj Kapoor, dir.: Raj Kapoor.

Ayodhya Ka Raja, "The King of Ayodhya," 1932, prod.: Prabhat Studios, dir.: V. Shantaram.

Baazigar, "The Conjurer," 1993, prod.: Ganesh Jain, dir.: Abbas-Mustan.

Babul, "Childhood Home," 1950, prod. Sunny Art Productions, dir.: S. U. Sunny.

Baghdad Ka Chor, "Thief of Baghdad," 1934, prod.: Paramount Studios, dir.: D. N. Madhok.

Baghdad Ka Chor, "Thief of Baghdad," 1946, prod.: Mohan Pictures, dir.: N. Vakil.

Baghdad Ka Chor, "Thief of Baghdad," 1955, prod.: M. Chitra, dir.: Shreeram.

Baiju Bawra, 1952, prod.: Prakash Studios, dir.: Vijay Bhatt.

Balmaa, "Beloved," 1993, prod.: Suresh Grover, dir.: Lawrence D'Souza.

Bambai Ka Babu, "A Gentleman of Bombay," 1960, prod.: Naya Films, dir.: Raj Khosla.

Bandini, "The Caged," 1963, prod: Bimal Roy, dir.: Bimal Roy.

Baradari, "Intimate Relations," 1955, prod.: K. Amarnath, dir.: K. Amarnath.

Barsaat, "Monsoon," 1949, prod.: Raj Kapoor, dir.: Raj Kapoor.

Battu's Bioscope, 1998, prod.: Besta-Film and E Motion Pictures, dir.: Andrzej Fidyk.

Baware Nain, "Romantic Gaze," 1950, prod.: Ambitious Pictures, dir.: Kidar Sharma.

Bees Saal Baad, "Twenty Years On," 1962, prod.: Geetanjali Pictures, dir.: Biren Naug.

Bhaji on the Beach, 1995, prod.: Nadine Marsh-Edwards, dir.: Gurinder Chadha.

Bilwamangal, 1932, prod.: Madan Theatres, dir.: Fram Madan.

Bobby, 1973, prod.: Raj Kapoor, dir.: Raj Kapoor.

Bombay, 1995. prod.: S. Sriram, dir.: Mani Rathnam.

Bombay Boys, 1998, prod.: Kaizad Gustad, dir.: Kaizad Gustad.

Chahat, "Desire," 1996, prod.: Robin Bhatt and Viral Lakhia, dir.: Mahesh Bhatt.

Chalti Ka Naam Gadi, "That Which Goes Is Life," 1958, prod.: K. S. Pictures, dir.: Satyen Bose.

Chandidas, 1934, prod.: New Theatres, dir.: Nitin Bose.

Chasme Buddoor, "Bewitched," 1981, prod.: Gul Anand, dir.: Sai Paranjpye.

Chhalia, "The Trickster," 1960, prod.: Subhash Pictures, dir.: Manmohan Desai.

Chupke Chupke, "Silently, Silently," 1975, prod.: N.C. Sippy and Hrishikesh Mukherji, dir.: Hrishikesh Mukherji.

Coolie, 1983, prod.: Ketan Desai, dir.: Manmohan Desai and Prayag Raj.

Daag, "Stain," 1952, prod.: Mars and Movies, dir.: Amiya Chakraborty.

Deedar, "Vision," 1951, prod.: Filmkar, dir.: Nitin Bose.

Deewana, "Hopelessly in Love," 1992, prod.: Guddu Dhanoa, Lalit Kapoor, and Raju Kothari, dir.: Raj Kanwar.

Deewar, "The Wall," 1975, prod.: Gulshan Rai, dir.: Yash Chopra.

Desperately Seeking Helen, 1998, prod.: David Wilson, dir.: Eisha Marjara.

Devdas, 1935, prod.: New Theatres, dir.: P. C. Barua.

Devdas, 1955, prod.: Bimal Roy, dir.: Bimal Roy.

Dharamveer, 1977, prod.: Subhash Desai, dir.: Manmohan Desai.

Dharti Ke Lal, "Children of the Earth," 1946, prod.: Indian People's Association, dir.: K. A. Abbas.

Dil, "Love," 1990, prod.: Indra Kumar and Ashok Thakeria, dir.: Indra Kumar.

Dil Deke Dekho, "Give Your Heart Away," 1959, prod.: Filmlaya, dir.: Nazir Hussain.

Dil Diya Dard Liya, "The Pains of Love," 1966, prod.: Kay Productions, dir.: A. R. Kardar.

Dil Ek Mandir, "The Heart Is a Temple," 1963, prod.: Chitralaya, dir.: Sridhar.

Dil Se, "With Love," 1998, prod.: Mani Rathnam, dir.: Mani Rathnam.

Dil To Pagal Hai, "The Heart Is a Wild Thing," 1997, prod.: Yash Chopra, dir.: Yash Chopra.

Dilwale Dulhania Le Jayenge, "Lovers Win

Brides," 1995, prod.: Yash Chopra, dir.: Aditya Chopra.

Do Anjane, "Two Strangers, " 1976, prod.: Navjeevan Films, dir.: Dulal Guha.

Do Ankhen Barah Hath, "A Pair of Eyes and a Dozen Hands," 1957, prod.: Rajkamal Studios, dir.: V. Shantaram.

Do Aur Do Paanch, "Two and Two Make Five," 1980, prod.: C. Dandayuthapani, dir.: Rajesh Kumar.

Do Bigha Zamin, "Two Acres of Land," 1953, prod.: Bimal Roy, dir.: Bimal Roy.

Dostana, "Bonding," 1980, prod.: Yash Johar, dir.: Raj Khosla.

Drohi, "The Traitor," 1992, prod.: Boney Kapoor, dir.: Ram Gopal.

Dulhe Raja, "My Bridgeroom, My Prince," 1998, prod.: Harmesh Malhotra, dir.: Harmesh Malhotra.

Duvidha, "Confusion," 1979, prod.: Mani Kaul, dir.: Mani Kaul.

Earth, 1999, prod.: David Hamilton and Jhamu Sughand, dir.: Deepa Mehta.

Elan, "A Declaration," 1947, prod.: Mehboob Khan, dir.: Mehboob Khan.

English Babu Desi Mem, "The English Gentleman and His Indian Lady," 1995, prod.: Praveen Nischol, dir.: Praveen Nischol.

Faraar, "The Flight," 1975, prod.: Alankar Chitra, dir.: Shankar Mukerji.

Fiza, 2000, prod.: Javed Siddiqi, dir.: Khalid Mohamed.

Gaman, "Departure," 1979, prod.: Muzaffar Ali, dir.: Muzaffar Ali.

Gangaa Jamuna Saraswathi, 1988, prod.: S. Ramanathan, dir.: Manmohan Desai.

Ganga Ki Saugandh, "I Swear on the Ganges," 1978, prod.: Sultan Productions, dir.: Sultan Ahmed.

Garam Hawa, "Torrid Winds," 1973, prod.: Absivani Isan Arya, dir.: M. S. Sathyu.

Geet Gaya Patthro Ne, "The Stones Also Sang," 1964, prod.: V. Shantaram, dir.: V. Shantaram.

The Great Gambler, 1979, prod.: C.V.K. Sastry, dir.: Shakti Samanta.

Guide, 1965, prod.: Navketan, dir.: Vijay Anand.

Gul Bakavali, 1932, prod.: Saroj M. dir.: A. P. Kapoor.

Gunga Jamna, 1961, prod.: Citizen Films, dir.: Nitin Bose.

Hare Rama Hare Krishna, 1971, prod.: Dev Anand, dir.: Dev Anand.

Hatimtai, 1956, prod.: Basant Pictures, dir.: Homi Wadia.

Hind Kesari, "The Lion of India," 1935, prod.: Wadia Movietone, dir.: Homi Wadia.

House No 44, 1955, prod.: Navketan, dir.: M. K. Burman.

Hum, "The Collective," 1991, prod.: Romesh Sharma, dir.: Mukul S. Anand.

Hum Aap Ke Hain Kaun, "Who Am I to You?" 1994, prod.: Kamal Kumar Barjatya, Raj Kumar Barjatya, Ajit Kumar Barjatya, dir.: Sooraj R. Barjatya.

Humayun, 1945, prod.: Mehboob Khan, dir.: Mehboob Khan.

Hum Dil De Chuke Sanam, "I Gave My Heart Away, My Love," 1999, prod.: Sanjay Leela Bhansali, dir.: Sanjay Leela Bhansali.

Hum Ek Hain, "All for One," 1946, prod.: Prabhat Pictures, dir.: Santoshi.

Husn Ka Chor, "The Thief of Love," 1953, prod.: Basant Pictures, dir.: Homi Wadia.

Insaniyat, "Humanity," 1994, prod.: Tito, dir.: Tony.

Jaadugar, "The Magician," 1989, prod.: Prakash Mehra, dir.: Prakash Mehra.

Jaal, "The Net," 1952, prod.: Filmarts, dir.: Guru Dutt.

Jagte Raho, "Stay Awake!" 1956, prod.: Raj Kapoor, dir.: Sombhu Mitra and Amit Mitra.

Jai Santoshi Maa. "Hail Mother Santoshi," 1975, prod.: Satram Rohara, dir.: Vijay Sharma.

Jalsaghar, "The Music Room," 1958, prod. Satyajit Ray, dir.: Satyajit Ray.

Jeevan Sangram, "A Struggle for Freedom," 1974, prod.: P. Rajbans Khanna, dir.: P. Rajbans Khanna.

Jeewan Naiya, "The Boat of Life," 1936, prod.: Sagar, dir.: S. Badami.

Jhanak Jhanak Payal Baje, "The Anklet Makes Music," 1955, prod.: Rajkamal Kalamandir, dir.: V. Shantaram.

Jis Desh Men Ganga Behti Hai, "Where Flows the Ganges," 1960, prod.: Raj Kapoor, dir.: Raj Kapoor.

Jogan, "The Female Ascetic," 1950, prod.: Ranjit Studios, dir.: Kidar Sharma.

Judaii, "Separation," 1997, prod.: Boney Kapoor and Surinder Kapoor, dir.: Raj Kanwar.

Jurm, "Offense," 1990, prod.: Mahesh Bhatt,
   dir.: Mahesh Bhatt.

Kaagaz Ke Phool, "Paper Flowers," 1959, prod.:
   Guru Dutt, dir.: Guru Dutt.
Kabhi Haan Kabhi Naa, "Sometimes Yes,
   Sometimes No," 1993, prod.: Vikram
   Malhotra, dir.: Kundan Shah.
Kala Bazar, "Black Market," 1960, prod.:
   Navketan, dir.: Vijay Anand.
Kanhaiya, 1959, prod.: S. P. Pictures, dir.: S.
   N. Tripathi.
Kanoon, "The Law," 1960, prod.: B R Films,
   dir.: B. R. Chopra.
Karz, "Debt," 1980, prod.: Jagjit Khorana &
   Akhtar, dir.: Subhash Ghai.
Khalnayak, "The Antihero," 1993, prod.:
   Subhash Ghai, dir.: Subhash Ghai.
Khamoshi, "Silence," 1969, prod.: Geetanjali,
   dir.: Asit Sen.
Khoon Khoon, "Murder! Murder!" 1973,
   prod.: F. C. Mehra, dir.: Mohammad
   Hussain.
Khuddar, "Shreds," 1982, prod.: F.K. Rattonsey
   and Anwar Ali, dir.: Ravi Tandon.
Kismet, "Fate," 1943, prod.: Bombay Talkies,
   dir.: Gyan Mukerji.
Koyla, "Burning Coal," 1998, prod.: Rakesh
   Roshan, dir.: Rakesh Roshan.
Krantiveer, "The Heroic Revolutionary," 1994,
   prod.: Mehul Kumar, dir.: Mehul Kumar.
Kuch Kuch Hota Hai, "Sometimes Things Do
   Happen," 1998, prod.: Yash Johar, dir.:
   Karan Johar.

Laawaris, "The Orphan,"1981, prod.: Prakash
   Mehra, dir.: Prakash Mehra.
Lagaan, "Land Tax," 2001, prod.: Aamir Khan,
   dir.: Ashutosh Gowariker.
Lajwanti, "The Chaste Wife," 1958, prod.: De
   Luxe Films, dir.: Narendra Suri.
Lamhe, "The Moment," 1991, prod.: Yash
   Chopra, dir.: Yash Chopra.

Madhumati, 1958, prod.: Bimal Roy, dir.:
   Bimal Roy.
Madhuri, 1928, prod.: Imperial, dir.: R. S.
   Choudhry.
Mahabharat, 1965, prod.: A. G. Films, dir.:
   Babubhai Mistry.
Mahal, "The Mansion," 1949, prod.: Bombay
   Talkies, dir.: Kamal Amrohi.
Maharaja, 1998, prod.: Navchitr Productions,
   dir.: Anil Sharma.

Mai Azaad Hoon, "Freedom," 1989, prod.:
   Habib Nadiawala, dir.: Tinu Anand.
Main Tulsi Tere Aangan Ki, "I'm the Holy Basil
   of Your Garden," 1978, prod.: Raj Khosla,
   dir.: Raj Khosla.
Maine Pyar Kiya, "Yes, I've Fallen in Love,"
   1989, prod.: Tarachand Barjatya, dir.:
   Sooraj Barjatya.
Major Saab, "The Major," 1998, prod.:
   Amitabh Bachchan Corporation, dir.:
   Virinder Raj Anand.
Mandi, "The Marketplace," 1983, prod.: Freni
   Variava and Lalit Bijlan, dir.: Shyam
   Benegal.
Masala, 1991, prod.: Srinivas Krishna, dir.:
   Srinivas Krishna.
Mast Kalander, "The Carefree," 1991, prod.:
   Rahul Rawail, dir.: Rahul Rawail.
Maya Bazar, "The Bazaar of Illusion," 1932,
   prod.: Sagar, dir.: Nanubhai Vakil.
Maya Darpan, "The Mirror of Illusion," 1972,
   prod.: Kumar Shahani, dir.: Kumar Shahani.
Mela, "The Fair," 1948, prod.: Wadia Films,
   dir.: S. U. Sunny.
Mera Naam Joker, "The Joker," 1970, prod.:
   Raj Kapoor, dir.: Raj Kapoor.
Milan, "The Meeting," 1946, prod.: Bombay
   Talkies, dir.: Nitin Bose.
Mission Kashmir, 2000, prod.: Vir Chopra, dir.:
   Vidhu Vinod Chopra.
Mohabat Ke Ansu, "The Tears of Love," 1932,
   prod.: New Theatres, dir.: P. Atorthy.
Mohabbatein, "Varieties of Love," 2000, prod.:
   Yash Chopra, dir.: Aditya Chopra.
Mother India, 1938, prod.: Ardeshir Irani, dir.:
   Gunjal.
Mother India, 1957, prod.: Mehboob Khan,
   dir.: Mehboob Khan.
Mr. India, 1987, prod.: Boney Kapoor, dir.:
   Shekhar Kapoor.
Mr. Sampat, 1952, prod.: Gemini, dir.: S. S.
   Vasan.
Mughal-e-Azam, 1960, "The Great Mughal,"
   prod.: Sterling Investment Corporation,
   dir.: K. Asif.
Muqaddar Ka Sikander, "Blessed by Destiny,"
   1978, prod.: Prakash Mehra, dir.: Prakash
   Mehra.

Nadiya Ke Paar, "Beyond the River," 1948,
   prod.: Fimistan Studios, dir.: Kishore Sahu.
Nadiya Ke Paar, "Beyond the River," 1982,
   prod.: Tarachand Barjatya, dir.: Govind
   Moonis.

Nal Damayanti, 1945, prod.: Janak Pictures, dir.: Kumar Sen Samarth.

Namak Halaal, "The Ungrateful," 1982, prod.: Satyendra Pal, dir.: Prakash Mehra.

Naseeb, "Good Fortune," 1981, prod.: Manmohan Desai, dir.: Manmohan Desai.

Naseeb, "Destiny," 1997, prod.: Vinay Kumar Sinha, dir.: Kirti Kumar.

Nastik, "The Atheist," 1954, prod.: Filmistan, dir.: I. S. Johar.

Nau Do Gyarah, "The Con Artist," 1957, prod.: Navketan, dir.: Vijay Anand.

Nausherwan-E-Dil, 1957, prod.: Minerva, dir.: Sohrab Modi.

Nazrana, "A Gift of Love," 1961, prod.: Venus Pictures, dir.: Sridhar.

1942 A Love Story, 1994, prod.: Vidhu Vinod Chopra, dir.: Vidhu Vinod Chopra.

Pahali Nazar, "The First Encounter," 1945, prod.: Mazhar Art, dir.: Mazhar Khan.

Pakeezah, "The Pure One,"1971, prod.: Kamal Amrohi, dir.: Kamal Amrohi.

Pardes, "Another Land," 1997, prod.: Subhash Ghai, dir.: Subhash Ghai.

Patita, "The Fallen One," 1953, prod.: Mars and Movies, dir.: Amiya Chakrabarty.

Phir Bhi Dil Hai Hindustani, "After All, the Heart Is Indian," 2000, prod.: Aziz Mirza, dir.: Aziz Mirza.

Phool Bane Angaray, "The Anger of the Meek," 1991, prod.: K. C. Bokadia, dir.: K. C. Bokadia.

President, 1937, prod.: New Theatres, dir.: Nitin Bose.

Purab Aur Pachhim, "East and West," 1970, prod.: Manoj Kumar, dir.: Manoj Kumar.

Purana Mandir, "The Ancient Temple," 1984, prod.: Kanta Ramsay, dir.: Tulsi Ramsay.

Pyaasa, "The Thirsty One," 1957, prod. Guru Dutt, dir.: Guru Dutt.

Qayamat Se Qayamat Tak, "From Judgment Day to Judgment Day," 1988, prod.: Nasir Hussain, dir.: Mansoor Khan.

Raja, 1995, prod.: Indra Kumar & Ashok Thakeria, dir.: Indra Kumar.

Raja Harishchandra, 1913, prod.: Phalke & Company, dir.: D. G. Phalke.

Raju Ban Gaya Gentleman, "Gentleman Raju," 1997, prod.: G. P. Sippy, dir.: Aziz Mirza.

Ram Lakhan, "Ram and Lakshman," 1989, prod.: Ashok Ghai, dir.: Subhash Ghai.

Ram Rajya, "The Kingdom of Rama," 1943, prod.: Prakash Pictures, dir.: Vijay Bhatt.

Ram Teri Ganga Maili, "Rama Your Ganges Is Dirty," 1985, prod.: Randhir Kapoor, dir.: Raj Kapoor.

Rambaan, "Rama's Arrow," 1948, prod.: Prakash Pictures, dir.: Vijay Bhatt.

Rattan, "Invaluable Jewel," 1944, prod.: Jamini Dewan, dir.: M. Sadiq.

Roja, "The Fast," 1993, prod.: Babubhai Shah & Fatehchand B. Shah, dir.: Mani Rathnam.

Saat Hindustani, "Seven Indians," 1969, prod.: Naya Sansar, dir.: K. A. Abbas.

Saaz, "A Gift of Song," 1996, prod.: Sai Paranjpye, dir.: Sai Paranjpye.

Sadhna, 1958, prod.: B. R. Films, dir.: B. R. Chopra.

Sahib Bibi Aur Ghulam, "King, Queen, Knave," 1962, prod.: Guru Dutt, dir.: Abrar Alvi.

Sampoorna Ramayana, "The Extant Ramayana," 1961, prod.: Basant Pictures, dir.: Babubhai Mistry.

Samrat, "The Emperor, " 1954, prod.: Filmistan, dir.: Najam Naqvi.

Sangam, "The Confluence," 1964, prod.: Raj Kapoor, dir.: Raj Kapoor.

Sangdil, "Against Love," 1952, prod.: Talwar Films, dir.: T. C. Talwar.

Sant Tukaram, 1936, prod.: Prabhat Film Company, dir.: V. Damle and S. Fattelal.

Satyam Shivam Sundaram, 1978, prod.: Raj Kapoor, dir.: Raj Kapoor.

Sau Saal Baad, "A Hundred Years On," 1989, prod.: Yogesh Chhabra, dir.: M. Bhakri.

Shaan, "Grandeur," 1980, prod.: G. P. Sippy, dir.: Ramesh Sippy.

Shabistan, 1951, prod.: Filmistan, dir.: B. Mitra.

Shabnam, "Dew," 1949, prod.: Filmistan, dir.: B. Mitra.

Shakti, 1982, prod.: Mushir-Riaz, dir.: Ramesh Sippy.

Shakuntala, 1943, prod.: Rajkamal Kalamandir, dir.: V. Shantaram.

Sharaabi, "The Drunkard," 1984, prod.: Satyendra Pal, dir.: Prakash Mehra.

Sharada, 1957, prod.: Prasad Productions, dir.: L. V. Prasad.

Shikari, "The Prowler," 2000, prod.: G. Kishnani, dir.: N. Chandra.

Sholay, "Flames," 1975, prod.: G. P. Sippy, dir.: Ramesh Sippy.

Shree 420, "Mr. 420,"1955, prod.: Raj Kapoor, dir.: Raj Kapoor.

Silsila, "Continuity," 1981, prod.: Yash Chopra, dir.: Yash Chopra.

Soldier, 1998, prod.: Tips Films, dir.: Abbas-Mustan.

Sujata, "The Well-Born," 1959, prod.: Bimal Roy, dir.: Bimal Roy.

Swami, 1977, prod.: Jaya Chakravarty, dir.: Basu Chakravarty.

Taxi Driver, 1954, prod.: Navketan, dir.: Chetan Anand.

Thakshak, "The Serpent," 1999, prod.: Govind Nihalani, dir.: Govind Nihalani.

Toofan, "The Storm," 1989, prod.: Manmohan Desai, dir.: Ketan Desai.

Toofan Aur Diya, "The Storm and the Lamp," 1956, prod.: Rajkamal Kalamandir, dir.: Prabhat Kumar.

Tumsa Nahin Dekha, "No One Like You," 1957, prod.: Filmistan, dir.: Nazir Hussain.

Udan Khatola, "The Flying Machine," 1955, prod.: Sunny Art Productions, dir.: S. U. Sunny.

Umrao Jaan, 1981, prod.: Muzaffar Ali, dir.: Muzaffar Ali.

Upkar, "Good Deeds," 1967, prod.: Vishal Pictures, dir.: Manoj Kumar.

Vaastav, "Reality," 1999, prod.: Adishakti Films, dir.: Mahesh Manjrekar.

Veer Abhimanyu, "Valiant Abhimanyu," 1931, prod.: Sagar, dir.: Prafulla Ghosh.

Vidyapati, 1937, prod.: New Theatres, dir.: Debaki Bose.

Vikramaditya, 1945, prod.: Prakash Pictures, dir.: Vijay Bhatt.

Zameer, "The Heart," 1975, prod.: B. R. Chopra, dir.: Ravi Chopra.

Zanjeer, "The Chain," 1973, prod.: Prakash Mehra, dir.: Prakash Mehra.

Zarina, 1932, prod.: Sagar, dir.: Ezra Mir.

Bibliography

Abbas, K. A. 1940. "Barua, Bose, Shantaram."
Filmindia (June): 52–56.

———. 1977. *I Am Not an Island: An Experiment in Autobiography*. New Delhi: Vikas.

———. 1985. *Movie* (March): 99.

Ahmad, Jalal Al-e. 1982. *Plagued by the West* [*Gharbzadegi*]. Trans. Paul Sprachman. New York: Caravan Books.

Ahmed, Akbar S. 1992. "Bombay Films: The Cinema As Metaphor for Indian Society and Politics." *Modern Asian Studies* 26.2: 289–320.

Althusser, Louis. 1984. *Essay on Ideology*. London: Verso.

Anderson, Benedict. 1991. *Imagined Communities*. London: Verso.

———. 1994. "Exodus." *Critical Inquiry* 20.2: 314–327.

Andrews, C. F. 1939. *The True India*. London: George Allen and Unwin.

Appadurai, Arjun. 1996. *Modernity at Large. Cultural Dimensions of Globalization*. Minneapolis: University of Minnesota Press.

Aravamudan, Srinivas. 1989. "Being God's Postman Is No Fun, Yaar: Salman Rushdie's *The Satanic Verses*." *Diacritics* 19.2: 3–20.

Archer, Mildred. 1979. *India and British Portraiture 1770–1825*. London: Sotheby Parke Bernet.

Arnold, Alison. 1988. "Popular Film Songs in India: A Case of Mass-Market Musical Eclecticism." *Popular Music* 7. 2: 177–188.

Arora, V. N. 1986. "Popular Songs in Hindi Films." *Journal of Popular Culture*. 20.2: 143–166.

Asian Television Network (ATN) Canada. 1999. October.

Asiaweek. 1994. "The Mob in the Movies." Cover essay, July 27.

Australian, 2000. December 18: 6.

Azmi, Shabana. 1983. Interview. In *Indian Cinema Superbazaar*, ed. Aruna Vasudev and Philippe Lenglet. Delhi: Vikas. 145–156.

Babb, Lawrence A., and Susan S. Wadley, eds. 1995. *Media and the Transformation of Religion in South Asia*. Philadelphia: University of Pennsylvania Press.

Baghdadi, Rafique, and Rajiv Rao. 1995. *Talking Films*. New Delhi: HarperCollins.

Bailey, G. M. 1989. "On the De-construction of Culture in Indian Literature: A Tentative Response to Vijay Mishra's Article." *South Asia*. New Series. 12.1: 85–102.

Bakhtin, Mikhail M. 1981. *The Dialogic Imagination*. Trans. Caryl Emerson and Michael Holquist. Austin: University of Texas Press.

———. 1968. *Rabelais and His World*. Trans. Hélène Iswolsky. Cambridge, MA: MIT Press.

Balibar, Etienne, and Immanuel Wallerstein. 1991. *Race, Nation, Class*. London: Verso.

Banerjee, Haimanti. 1985. *Ritwik Kumar Ghatak*. Pune: National Film Archive of India.

Barnouw, Erik, and S. Krishnaswamy. 1980. *Indian Film*. New York: Oxford University Press.

Barthes, Roland. 1975. *S/Z*. Trans. Richard Howard. London: Jonathan Cape.

———. 1977. *Image-Music-Text*. London: Fontana.

Baudry, Jean-Louis, 1992. "The Apparatus: Metaphysical Approaches to the Impression of Reality in Cinema." In *Film Theory and Criticism*, ed. Gerald Mast, Marshall Cohen, and Leo Braudy. New York: Oxford University Press. 690–707.

Bazin, André. 1971. *What Is Cinema?* Trans. Hugh Gray. Berkeley: University of California Press. 2 vols.

Bellour, Raymond. 1975. "The Unattainable Text," trans. D. Matias. *Screen* 16.3: 19–27.

———. 1976. "To Analyze, To Segment." *Quarterly Review of Film Studies*. 1.3: 331–353.

———. 1979. "Cine-Repetitions." *Screen* 20.2: 69–92.

———. 1985. "Analysis in Flames." *Diacritics* 15.1: 54–56.

Benegal, Shyam. 1983. Interview. In *Indian Cinema Superbazaar*. Ed. Aruna Vasudev and Philippe Lenglet. Delhi: Vikas. 157–171.

Benjamin, Walter. 1973. *Illuminations*. Ed. and intr. Hannah Arendt. Trans. Harry Zohn. London: Collins/Fontana Books.

———. 1979. "Edward Fuchs, Collector and Historian." *One Way Street and Other Writings*. Trans. Edmund Jephcott and Kingsley Shorter. Intr. Susan Sontag. London: NLB.

Bergstrom, Janet. 1988. "Alternation, Segmentation, Hypnosis: Interview with Raymond Bellour—An Excerpt." In *Feminism and Film Theory*, ed. Constance Penley. 186–195.

Bhabha, Homi. 1994. *The Location of Culture*. London and New York: Routledge.

Bhaumika, Somesvara. 1995. *Indian Cinema Colonial Contours*. Calcutta: Papyrus.

Bhimani, Harish. 1995. *In Search of Lata Mangeshkar*. New Delhi: HarperCollins.

Binford, Mira Reym. 1983. "The New Cinema of India." *Quarterly Review of Film Studies* 8.4: 47–67.

Booth, Gregory D. 1995. "Traditional Content and Narrative Structure in Hindi Commercial Cinema." *Asian Folklore Studies* 54.2: 169–190.

Bordwell, David. 1985. *Narration in the Fiction Film*. London: Methuen.

———. 1991. *Making Meaning. Inference and Rhetoric in the Interpretation of Cinema*. Cambridge, MA: Harvard University Press.

Bourdieu, Pierre. 1993. *The Field of Cultural Production*. Ed. and intr. Randal Johnson. New York: Columbia University Press.

Boyarin, Daniel, and Jonathan Boyarin. 1993. "Diaspora: Generation and the Ground of Jewish Identity." *Critical Inquiry* 19.4: 693–725.

Branigan, Edward. 1984. *Point of View in the Cinema. A Theory of Narration and Subjectivity in Classical Film*. Amsterdam: Mouton Publishers.

———. 1992. *Narrative Comprehension and Film*. London and New York: Routledge.

Bratton, Jacky, Jim Cook, and Christine Gledhill, eds. 1994. *Melodrama. Stage Picture Screen*. London: British Film Institute.

Brecht, Bertolt. 1974. "The Epic Theatre and Its Difficulties." *Brecht on Theatre*. Ed. and trans. John Willett. London: Eyre Methuen. 22–24.

Brooks, Peter. 1982. *The Melodramatic Imagination. Balzac, Henry James, Melodrama, and the Mode of Excess*. New York and London: Yale University Press.

———. 1988. *The Mahābhārata*. Program brochure for the Boya Quarry performance, Perth.

———. 1994. "Melodrama, Body, Revolution." In *Melodrama. Stage Picture Screen*, ed. Jacky Brattan, Kim Cook, and Christine Gledhill. London: British Institute. 11–24.

Butalia, Urvashi. 1995. "Abduction and Abandonment." *Index on Censorship* 24.4: 81–88.

———. 2000. "Community, State, and Gender: Some Reflections on the Partition of India." In *Inventing Boundaries*, ed. Mushirul Hasan. New Delhi: Oxford University Press. 178–207.

Cameron, Bailey. 1992. "What the Story Is: An Interview with Srinivas Krishna." *Cineaction* 28: 38–47.

Caughie, John, ed. 1981. *Theories of*

Authorship: A Reader. London: Routledge and Kegan Paul.

Chakravarty, Sumita, S. 1993. *National Identity in Indian Popular Cinema 1947–1987*. Austin: University of Texas Press.

Chandrasekhar, K. 1988. "The Amitabh Persona: An Interpretation." *Deep Focus* 1.3: 52–57.

Chatterjee, Gayatri. 1992. *Awara*. Delhi: Wiley Eastern.

Chow, Rey. 1995. *Primitive Passions. Visuality, Sexuality, Ethnography and Contemporary Chinese Cinema*. New York: Columbia University Press.

———. 1998. *Ethics after Idealism*. Bloomington: University of Indiana Press.

Cineblitz. 1982. April.

Clifford, James. 1994. "Diasporas." *Cultural Anthropology* 9.3: 302–338.

Coulson, Michael, trans. 1981. *Three Sanskrit Plays*. Harmondsworth: Penguin.

Crawford, Larry. 1985. "Monstrous Criticism: Finding, Citing—Analyzing Film." *Diacritics* 15.1: 60–70.

Das, Veena. 1980. "The Mythological Film and Its Framework of Meaning: An Analysis of *Jai Santoshi Ma*." *India International Centre Quarterly* 8.1: 43–56.

———. 1996. "Language and Body: Transactions in the Construction of Pain." *Daedalus* 125.1: 67–91.

Das Gupta, Chidananda. 1981. *Talking about Films*. Delhi: Orient Longman.

———. 1988. "The Painted Face of Politics: The Actor-Politicians of South India." In *Cinema and Cultural Identity*, ed. Wimal Dissanayake. Lanham, MD: University Press of America. 127–147.

———. 1991. *The Painted Face. Studies in India's Popular Cinema*. Delhi: Roli Books.

Dasgupta, Shamita Das. 1996. "Feminist Consciousness in Women-Centered Hindi Films." *Journal of Popular Culture* 30.1: 173–189.

Deleuze, Gilles. 1986. *Cinema I: The Movement Image*. Trans. Hugh Tomlinson and Barbara Habberjam. Minneapolis: University of Minnesota Press.

Dhareshwar, Vivek, and Tejaswini Niranjana. 1996. "Kaadalan and the Politics of Resignification: Fashion, Violence, and the Body." *Journal of Arts and Ideas* 29: 5–26.

Dhondy, Farukh. 1985. "Keeping Faith: Indian Film and Its World." *Daedalus* 114.4: 125–140.

Dissanayake Wimal, ed. 1993. *Melodrama and Asian Cinema*. New York: Cambridge University Press.

———, ed. 1996. *Narratives of Agency: Self-Making in China, India and Japan*. Minneapolis: University of Minnesota Press.

Doane, Mary Ann. 1988. "Woman's Stake: Filming the Female Body." In *Feminism and Film Theory*, ed. Constance Penley. New York: Routledge. 216–228.

Dumézil, Georges. 1973. *The Destiny of a King*. Trans. Alf Hiltebeitel. Chicago: University of Chicago Press.

Dumont, Louis. 1960. "World Renunciation in Indian Religions." *Contributions to Indian Sociology* 4: 33–62.

Dwyer, Rachel. 2000. *All You Want Is Money, All You Need Is Love: Sex and Romance in Modern India*. London: Cassell.

Dyer, Richard. 1979. *Stars*. London: British Film Institute.

Eagleton, Terry. 1976. *Criticism and Ideology*. London: New Left Books.

———. 1981. *Walter Benjamin or towards a Revolutionary Criticism*. London: Verso Editions and NLB.

Edmonton Journal. 1999. March 8: C3.

Eliot, T. S. 1951. "Tradition and Individual Talent." *Selected Essays*. London: Faber and Faber. 13–22.

Ellis, John. 1982. *Visible Fictions: Cinema, Television, Video*. London: Routledge and Kegan Paul.

Elsaesser, Thomas. 1989. *New German Cinema. A History*. London: Macmillan.

Elsaesser, Thomas (with Adam Baker), eds. 1991. *Early Cinema. Space Frame Narrative*. London: BFI Publishing.

Emilsen, William W. 1987. "Gandhi and Mayo's 'Mother India.'" *South Asia*. New Series. 10.1: 69–81.

Fanon, Frantz. 1990. *The Wretched of the Earth*. Trans. Constance Farrington. Harmondsworth: Penguin Books.

Filmfare. 1973. June 1: 35.

Filmfare. 1978. November 16–30: 20–25.

Filmfare. 1980. February 1–15: 17–21.

Filmfare. 1982. September 1–15.

Filmfare. 1982. October 16–31: 61.

Filmfare. 1982. November 16–30: 71.

Filmfare. 1982. December 16–31: 36–45.

Filmfare. 1983. March 1–15: 36–37.

Filmfare. 1984. October 1–15: 22–23.

Filmfare. 1984. July 16–31: 48–55.

Filmfare. 1984. November 16–30: 8–15.

Filmfare. 1990. December.

Filmfare. 2001. April.

Foucault, Michel. 1978. *The Archaeology of Knowledge.* Trans. A. M. Sheridan Smith. London: Tavistock.

———. 1980. "What Is an Author?" In *Textual Strategies,* ed. J. V. Harari. London: Methuen. 141–160.

Friedman, Yohanan. 2000. "The Attitude of the *Jam'iyyati-i 'Ulama-i Hind* to the Indian National Movement and the Establishment of Pakistan." In *Inventing Boundaries,* ed. Mushirul Hasan. New Delhi: Oxford University Press. 157–177.

g. 1991. January.

Ganguly, Keya. 1996. "Carnal Knowledge: Visuality and the Modern in 'Charulata.'" *Camera Obscura* 37: 157–186.

Garga, B. D. 1984. "Achūt Kanyā." *Movie* [India] (September): 93–99.

George, T. J. S. 1994. *The Life and Times of Nargis.* New Delhi: Indus/HarperCollins.

Gerow, Edwin. 1971. *A Glossary of Indian Figures of Speech.* The Hague: Mouton.

Ghadially, Rehana, ed. 1988. *Women in Indian Society.* New Delhi: Sage.

Ghatak, Ritwik. 1987. *Cinema and I.* Calcutta: Ritwik Memorial Trust.

Ghosh, Amitav. 1989. "The Diaspora in Indian Culture." *Public Culture* 2: 73–78.

Gillespie, Marie. 1989. "Technology and Tradition: Audio-Visual Culture among South Asian Families in West London." *Cultural Studies* 3: 226–239.

———. 1995. *Television, Ethnicity, and Cultural Change.* London: Routledge.

Gilroy, Paul. 1993. *The Black Atlantic. Modernity, and Double Consciousness.* Cambridge, MA: Harvard University Press.

Gledhill, Christine, ed. 1991. *Stardom. Industry of Desire.* London: Routledge.

Gledhill, Christine, and Linda Williams, eds. 2000. *Reinventing Film Studies.* London: Arnold.

Goel, Sita Ram. 1993. *Hindu Temples. What Happened to Them?* New Delhi: Voice of India.

Goethe, Johann Wolfgang von. 1774/1795. *The Sorrows of Werther: A German Story.* Trans. Richard Graves. London: T. Osborne and S. Griffin.

Gopalan, Lalitha. 1997. "Avenging Women in Indian Cinema." *Screen* 38.1: 42–59.

Grundmann, Roy. 1994. "Where Is This Place Called Home?" *Cinemaya* 23: 22–27.

Habermas, Jürgen. 1991. *The Structural Transformation of the Public Sphere.* Trans. Thomas Bereger with the assistance of Frederick Lawrence. Cambridge, MA: MIT Press.

Hansen, Kathryn. 1992. *Ground of Play: The Nautankī Theater in North India.* Berkeley: University of California Press.

Hartman, Geoffrey H. 1971. *Wordsworth's Poetry 1787–1814.* New Haven, CT: Yale University Press.

Hasan, Mushirul, ed. 2000. *Inventing Boundaries. Gender, Politics, and the Partition of India.* New Delhi: Oxford University Press.

Heath, Stephen. 1981. *Questions of Cinema.* London: Macmillan.

Heckel, Angelika. 1989. "*Rasa*: The Audience and the Stage." *Journal of Arts and Ideas* 17–18: 33–42.

Hegel, G. W. F. 1975. *The Philosophy of Fine Art.* Ed. and trans. F. P. B. Osmaston. New York: Hacker Art Books. 4 vols.

———. 1977. *Phenomenology of Spirit.* Trans. A. V. Miller. Oxford: Clarendon Press.

Henderson, Brian. 1980. *A Critique of Film Theory.* New York: E. P. Dutton.

Hillstrom, Laurie Collier, ed. 1997. *International Directory of Films and Filmmakers—2: Directors,* 3rd ed. Detroit: St. James Press.

Hiltebeitel, Alf. 1976. *The Ritual of Battle: Krishna in the "Mahābhārata."* Ithaca, NY: Cornell University Press.

Hindustan Times. 2000. August 29: City Section.

The Illustrated Weekly of India. 1987. November 8–14.

The Illustrated Weekly of India. 1988. July 17–23.

The Illustrated Weekly of India. 1990. December 29–30.

The Illustrated Weekly of India. 1991. February 9–10.

India 1982. 1982. New Delhi: Government of India Publications Division.

India Today. 1988. May 31.
India Today. 1990. July 15: 94–96.
India Today. 1992. December 31.
India Today. 1993. September 15.
Indian Movie News. 1976. December.

Jameson, Fredric. 1986. "Third World
Literature in the Era of Multinational
Capitalism." *Social Text* 15: 65–88.
———. 1990. *Signatures of the Visible.* New
York: Routledge.
———. 1995. *The Geopolitical Aesthetic.
Cinema of Space in the World System.*
Bloomington and Indianapolis: University
of Indiana Press; London: BFI Publishing.
Jī-Stār. 1993. August 31.
John, Mary E. 1996. *Discrepant Dislocations.*
Berkeley: University of California Press.

Kabir, Nasreen Munni. 1997. *Guru Dutt. A
Life in Cinema.* Delhi: Oxford University
Press.
Kajri, Jain. 1998. "When the Gods Go to
Market: The Ritual Management of Desire
in Indian 'Bazaar Art.'" *Communal/Plural*
6.2: 187–204.
Kakar, Sudhir. 1980. "The Ties That Bind:
Family Relationships in the Mythology of
Hindi Cinema." *India International Centre
Quarterly* 8.1: 11–21.
———. 1981. *The Inner World: A Psycho-ana-
lytic Study of Childhood and Society in
India.* Delhi: Oxford University Press.
———. 1990. *Intimate Relations: Exploring
Indian Sexuality.* Delhi: Penguin.
Kalidasa, 1981. *Śakuntalā.* In *Three Sanskrit
Plays.* Trans. Michael Coulson.
Harmondsworth: Penguin. 35–61.
Kaplan, E. Ann. 1988. *Women and Film: Both
Sides of the Camera.* New York: Routledge.
———. 1997. *Looking for the Other:
Feminism, Film, and the Imperial Gaze.*
New York: Routledge.
Kapur, Anuradha, 1988. "Thinking about
Tradition: The Ramlila at Ramnagar."
Journal of Arts and Ideas 16: 5–32.
———. 1993. "The Representation of Gods
and Heroes: Parsi Mythological Drama of
the Early Twentieth Century." *Journal of
Arts and Ideas* 23–24: 85–107.
Kapur, Geeta. 1987. "Mythic Material in
Indian Cinema." *Journal of Arts and Ideas*
14–15: 79–108.
———. 1989. "Ravi Varma: Representational

Dilemmas of a Nineteenth Century
Painter." *Journal of Arts and Ideas* 17–18:
59–80.
Kasbekar, Asha. 1996. "An Introduction to
Indian Cinema." In *An Introduction to Film
Studies,* ed. Jill Nelmes. London:
Routledge. 381–415.
Kazmi, Fareeduddin. 1998. "How Angry Is the
Angry Young Man? 'Rebellion' in
Conventional Hindi Films." In *The Secret
Politics of Our Desires,* ed. Ashis Nandy.
London: Zed. 134–155.
Khopkar, Arun. 1985. *Gurudatt: tīn aṁkīvya
trāsdt.* Hindi trans. Nishkant Thakar.
Madhya Pradesh Film Development
Corporation.
Kodkani, Jayant. 1987. "Notes on Story-telling
in Indian Cinema." *Deep Focus* 1.1: 33–37.
Kolar-Panov, Dona. 1997. *Video, War, and the
Diasporic Imagination.* New York:
Routledge.
Kosambi, D. D. 1962. *Myth and Reality:
Studies in the Formation of Indian Culture.*
Bombay: Popular Prakashan.
Kosambi, D. D., and V. V. Gokhale, eds.
1957. *The Subhāṣitaratnakoṣa.* Comp.
Vidyākara. Cambridge, MA: Harvard
University Press.

Lacan, Jacques. 1977. *Écrits.* Trans. Alan
Sheridan. London: Tavistock.
Ladha, Yasmin. 1992. "Letter to Mira Nair."
Rungh 1.3: 37–38.
Lane-Poole, Stanley. [1903] 1970. *Medieval
India under Mohammedan Rule (A.D.
712–1764).* New York: Haskell House.
Lefèbvre, Henri. 1991. *The Production of Space.*
Trans. Donald Nicholson Smith. London:
Blackwell.
Lord, Albert B. 1960. *The Singer of the Tales.*
Cambridge, MA: Harvard University Press.
Lukács, Georg. 1971. *The Theory of the Novel.*
Trans. Anna Bostock. London: Merlin.
Lutgendorf, Philip. 1995. "All in the (Raghu)
Family: A Video Epic in Cultural Context."
In *Media and the Transformation of Religion
in South Asia,* ed. Lawrence A. Babb and
Susan S. Wadley. Philadelphia: University
of Pennsylvania Press. 217–253.
Lyon, Elisabeth. 1988. "The Cinema of Lol V.
Stein." In *Feminism and Film Theory,* ed.
Constance Penley. New York: Routledge.
244–273.
Lyotard, Jean-François. 1986. *The Postmodern*

Condition: A Report on Knowledge. Trans. Geoff Bennington and Brian Massumi. Manchester: Manchester University Press.
———. 1988. *The Differend. Phrases in Dispute.* Trans. Georges Van Den Abbeele. Manchester: Manchester University Press.

Mādhurī. 1982. October 29.

Maitra, Parbodh. 1995. *One Hundred Years of Cinema.* Calcutta: Nandan.

Majumdar, R. C. 1970. *Historiography of Modern India.* Delhi: Asia Publishing House.

Manekar, Purnima. 1999. *Screening Culture, Viewing Politics: An Ethnography of Television, Womanhood and Nation in Postcolonial India.* Durham, NC: Duke University Press.

Manto, S. H. 1984. *Mīnābāzār* [in Hindi, 1962]. Delhi: Rajkamal Paperbacks.

———. 1986. "Khol Do." In S. H. Manto, *Thaṇḍā Gośt.* New Delhi: Star Publications.

———. 1998. *Stars from Another Sky. The Bombay Film World of the 1940s.* Trans. Khalid Hasan. New Delhi: Penguin.

Manuel, Peter. 1993. *Cassette Culture. Popular Music and Technology in North India.* Chicago: University of Chicago Press.

Marcus, Scott. 1992. "Recycling Indian Film-Songs: Popular Music As a Source for North Indian Folk Musicians." *Asian Music: Journal of the Society for Asian Music* 24.1: 101–110.

Mast, Gerald, Marshall Cohen, and Leo Braudy, eds. 1992. *Film Theory and Criticism: Introductory Readings.* 4th ed. New York: Oxford University Press.

Māyāpurī. 1993. August 19.

Mayo, Katherine. 1925. *The Isles of Fear.* London: Faber and Gwyer.

———. 1927. *Mother India.* London: Jonathan Cape.

Mazumdar, Ranjani. 2000. "From Subjectification to Schizophrenia: The 'Angry Man' and the 'Psychotic' Hero of Bombay Cinema." In *Making Meaning in Indian Cinema,* ed. Ravi Vasudevan. New Delhi: Oxford University Press. 238–264.

Mehta, Monika. 1999. "A Banal Enquiry: Film Censorship and Sexuality in Bombay Cinema." Paper presented at the South Asian Popular Culture Conference. University of Victoria, BC, Canada. April 22–24.

Menon, Ritu, and Kamla Bhasin. 1993. "Abducted Women, the State, and Questions of Honour: Reflections on Post-Partition India." *COSAW Bulletin* 8.3–4: 30–36.

———. 2000. "Recovery, Rupture, Resistance: The Indian State and the Abduction of Women during Partition." In *Inventing Boundaries,* ed. Mushirul Hasan. New Delhi: Oxford University Press. 208–235.

Metz, Christian. 1974. *Language and Cinema.* Trans. Donna Jean Umiker-Sebeok. The Hague and Paris: Mouton.

———. 1982. *Psychoanalysis and Cinema: The Imaginary Signifier.* Trans. Celia Britton et al. Bloomington: University of Indiana Press.

Miller, Don. 1993. "Masque, Temple, and Crypt." Paper presented at the After Ayodhya: the BJP and the Indian Political System Conference. Curtin University of Technology. July 4–8.

Mishra, Vijay. 1985. "Towards a Theoretical Critique of Bombay Cinema." *Screen* 26.3–4: 133–146.

———. 1987. "David Shulman and the Laughter of South Indian Kings and Clowns." *South Asia.* New Series. 10.1: 83–88.

———. 1989. "The Centre Cannot Hold: Bailey, Indian Culture, and the Sublime." *South Asia.* New Series. 12.1: 103–114.

———. 1991. "The Great Indian Epic and Peter Brook." In *Peter Brook and "The Mahābhārata,"* ed. David Williams. London and New York: Routledge. 195–205.

———. 1992. "Decentering History: Some Versions of Bombay Cinema." *East-West Film Journal* 6.1: 111–155.

———. 1994. *The Gothic Sublime.* Albany: State University of New York Press.

———. 1996a. "Postcolonial Racism." *Meanjin* 55.2: 346–357.

———. 1996b. "The Diasporic Imaginary: Theorizing the Indian Diaspora." *Textual Practice* 10.3: 421–447.

———. 1998. *Devotional Poetics and the Indian Sublime.* Albany: State University of New York Press.

Mishra, Vijay, Peter Jeffery, and Brian Shoesmith. 1989. "The Actor As Parallel Text in Bombay Cinema." *Quarterly Review of Film and Video* 2: 49–67.

Mittal, Ashok. 1995. *Cinema Industry in India. Pricing and Taxation*. New Delhi: Indus.

Monier-Williams, M. 1976. *Sanskrit-English Dictionary*. New Delhi: Munshiram Manoharlal.

Movie. 1982. September: 25–33.

Movie. 1982. October: 17; 81–83.

Movie. 1982. October: 16–21.

Movie. 1983. September: 2–3; 38–48.

Movie. 1983. November: 34–38.

Movie. 1984. January.

Movie. 1984. September: 41; 48–49.

Movie. 1985. March: 99.

Movie. 1985. April: 26–32, 35.

Movie. 1985. April: 26–28.

Mukherjee, Bharati. 1989. *Jasmine*. New York: Grove Weidenfeld.

Mukherjee, Meenakshi. 1995. "The HAHK Phenomenon: Appeal of Permanence and Stability." *Times of India*. May 27.

Mulvey, Laura. 1988a. "Visual Pleasure and Narrative Cinema." In *Feminism and Film Theory*, ed. Constance Penley. New York: Routledge. 57–69.

———. 1988b. "After Thoughts on 'Visual Pleasure and Narrative Cinema' inspired by *Duel in the Sun*." In *Feminism and Film Theory*, ed. Constance Penley. New York: Routledge. 69–79.

Naficy, Hamid, ed. 1999. *Home, Exile, Media, and the Politics of Place*. New York: Routledge.

Naipaul, V. S. 1961. *A House for Mr. Biswas*. London: André Deutsch.

———. 1990. *India: A Million Mutinies Now*. London: Heinemann.

Nandakumar, R. 1995. "Raja Ravi Varma in the Realm of the Public." *Journal of Arts and Ideas* 27–28: 41–56.

Nandy, Ashis. 1980. "The Popular Hindi Film: Ideology and First Principles." *India International Centre Quarterly* 8.1: 89–96.

———. 1995. *The Savage Freud and Other Essays on Possible and Retrievable Selves*. Princeton, NJ: Princeton University Press.

———, ed. 1998. *The Secret Politics of Our Desires: Innocence, Culpability, and Indian Popular Cinema*. London: Zed.

———. 1998. "Indian Popular Cinema As a Slum's Eye View of Politics." In *The Secret Politics of Our Desires*, ed. Ashis Nandy. London: Zed. 1–18.

Narayan, R. K. 1988. *The Guide*. Harmondsworth: Penguin.

Nayar, Sheila J. 1997. "The Values of Fantasy: Indian Popular Cinema through Western Scripts." *Journal of Popular Culture* 31.1: 73–90.

Nichols, Bill. 1981. *Ideology and the Image. Social Representation in the Cinema and Other Media*. Bloomington: University of Indiana Press.

Nowell-Smith, Geoffrey, ed. 1996. *The Oxford History of World Cinema*. Oxford: Oxford University Press.

O'Flaherty, Wendy Doniger. 1980. *Women, Androgynes, and Other Mythical Beasts*. Chicago: University of Chicago Press.

Pandey, Gyan. 1992. "In Defence of the Fragment: Writing about Hindu-Muslim Riots in India Today." *Representations* 37: 27–55.

Parekh, Bhikhu. 1997. "South Asians in Britain." *History Today* (September): 65–68.

Patel, Baburao. 1940. "*Aadmi*." *Filmindia* (October): 37–40.

Pavarala, Vinod. 1999. "Studying Television Audiences: Problems and Possibilities." *Journal of Arts and Ideas* 32–33: 95–106.

Pendakur, Manjunath. 1989. "New Cultural Technologies and the Fading Glitter of Indian Cinema." *Quarterly Review of Film and Video* 11.3: 69–87.

Pendakur, Manjunath and Radha Subramanyam. 1996. "India. Part I: Indian Cinema Beyond National Boundaries." In *New Patterns in Global Television*, ed. John Sinclair, Elizabeth Jacka, and Stuart Cunningham. New York: Oxford University Press. 67–82.

Penley, Constance, ed. 1988. *Feminism and Film Theory*. New York: Routledge.

———, ed. 1988. Introduction to *Feminism and Film Theory*. New York: Routledge. 1–24.

Pines, Jim, and Paul Willemen, eds. 1989. *Questions of Third Cinema*. London: BFI Publishing.

Poduval, Satish. 1999. "The Possible Histories of Indian Television." *Journal of Arts and Ideas* 32–33: 107–118.

Pollock, Sheldon. 1993. "Rāmāyaṇa and Political Imagination in India." *Journal of Asian Studies* 52.2: 261–297.

Prasad, M. Madhava. 1998. *Ideology of the*

Hindi Film: A Historical Reconstruction. Delhi: Oxford University Press.

———. 1999. "Television and the National Culture." *Journal of Arts and Ideas* 32–33: 119–129.

Pritchett, Frances W. 1995. "The World of *Amar Chitra Katha.*" In *Media and the Transformation of Religion in South Asia*, ed. Lawrence A. Babb and Susan S. Wadley. Philadelphia: University of Pennsylvania Press. 76–106.

Purohit, Vinayak. 1990. *Some Aspects of Sociology of Indian Films and Profile of the Hindi Hit Movie: 1951–1989.* Bombay: Indian Institute of Social Research.

Radhakrishnan, R. 1996. *Diasporic Mediations. Between Home and Location.* Minneapolis: University of Minnesota Press.

Radhakrishnan S., trans. and ed. 1963. *The Bhagavadgītā.* London: George Allen and Unwin.

Rai, Amit. 1994. "An American Raj in Filmistan: Images of Elvis in Indian Films." *Screen* 35.1: 51–77.

Raina, M. L. 1986. "'I'm All Right Jack': Packaged Pleasures of the Middle Cinema." *Journal of Popular Culture* 20.2: 131–141.

Rajadhyaksha, Ashish. 1985a. "Art in Indian Cinema." In *Seventy Years of Indian Cinema (1913–1983)*, ed. R. M. Ramachandran. Bombay: Cinema India International. 224–236.

———. 1985b. "Filmotsav '84 (2)." *Framework* 25: 104–108.

———. 1986. "Neo-traditionalism: Film As Popular Art in India." *Framework* 32–33: 20–67.

———. 1987. "The Phalke Era: Conflict of Traditional Form and Modern Technology." *Journal of Arts and Ideas* 14–15: 47–77.

———. 1993. "The Epic Melodrama: Themes of Nationality in Indian Cinema." *Journal of Arts and Ideas* 25–26: 55–70.

———. 1996a. "Strange Attractions." *Sight and Sound* 6.8: 28–31.

———. 1996b. "Indian Cinema: Origins to Independence." In *The Oxford History of World Cinema*, ed. Geoffrey Nowell-Smith. Oxford: Oxford University Press. 398–409.

———. 1999. "The Judgement: Re-forming the 'Public.'" *Journal of Arts and Ideas* 32–33: 131–150.

———. 2000. "Viewership and Democracy in the Cinema." In *Making Meaning in Indian Cinema*, ed. Ravi Vasudevan. New Delhi: Oxford University Press. 267–296.

Rajadhyaksha, Ashish, and Paul Willemen. 1999. *Encyclopaedia of Indian Cinema.* London: British Film Institute; Delhi: Oxford University Press. 2nd revised ed.

Rajan, Rajeswari Sunder. 1993. *Real and Imagined Women: Gender, Culture, and Postcolonialism.* London and New York: Routledge.

Ramachandran, R. M., ed. 1985. *Seventy Years of Indian Cinema (1913–1983).* Bombay: Cinema India International.

The Rāmāyaṇa of Vālmīki. Vol. 1., Bālakāṇḍa. 1984. Trans. Robert P. Goldman. Princeton, NJ: Princeton University Press.

Rangoonwalla, Firoze. 1973. *Guru Dutt 1925–1965.* Poona: National Film Archives of India.

———. 1982. *Indian Cinema: Past and Present.* Delhi: Clarion.

Ray, Satyajit. 1983. *Our Films, Their Films.* Calcutta: Orient Longman.

Reuben, Bunny. 1988. *Raj Kapoor. The Fabulous Showman.* Bombay: N. F. D. C. Publication.

———. 1999. *Mehboob … India's DeMille.* New Delhi: HarperCollins.

Richmond, Farley P., Darius L. Swan, and Phillip B. Zarrilli, eds. 1990. *Indian Theater. Traditions of Performance.* Honolulu: University of Hawaii Press.

Rodowick, D. N. 1985. "The Figure and the Text." *Diacritics* 15.1: 34–50.

Rosen, Philip, ed. 1986. *Narrative, Apparatus, Ideology. A Film Theory Reader.* New York: Columbia University Press.

Rosenthal, A. M. 1957. "The Future in Retrospect. 'Mother India' Thirty Years After." *Foreign Affairs* 35.4: 621–632.

Roy, Parama. 1998. *Indian Traffic. Identities in Question in Colonial and Postcolonial India.* Berkeley: University of California Press.

Rushdie, Salman. 1981. *Midnight's Children.* London: Jonathan Cape.

———. 1983. *Shame.* London: Jonathan Cape.

———. 1988. *The Satanic Verses.* London: Viking.

———. 1991. *Imaginary Homelands.* London: Granta.

———. 1995. *The Moor's Last Sigh.* London: Jonathan Cape.

Sahai, Malti. 1987. "Raj Kapoor and the Indianization of Charlie Chaplin." *East-West Film Journal* 2.1: 62–76.

Said, Edward. 1985. *Orientalism*. Harmondsworth: Penguin.

———. 1985. "Orientalism Reconsidered." *Race and Class* 27: 1–15.

Sarris, Andrew. 1992. "Notes on the Auteur Theory in 1962." In *Film Theory and Criticism*, ed. Gerald Mast, Marshall Cohen, and Leo Braudy. New York: Oxford University Press. 585–588.

Savarkar, V. D. 1989. *Essentials of Hindutva*. Bombay: Veer Savarkar Prakashan.

Schiele, Nicole. 1999. "Chronicles of a Virtual Traveller." Unpublished paper. University of Alberta, Canada.

Sen, Amartya. 1997. "Indian Traditions and the Western Imagination." *Daedalus* 126.2: 1–26.

Sequeira, Isaac. 1986. "The Carnival in Goa." *Journal of Popular Culture* 20.2: 167–173.

Shah, Panna. 1981. *The Indian Film*. Westport, CT: Greenwood.

Shahani, Kumar. 1985. "The Saint Poets of Prabhat." In *Seventy Years of Indian Cinema (1913–1983)*, ed. R. M. Ramachandran. Bombay: Cinema India International. 197–202.

———. 1986. "Dossier: Kumar Shahani." *Framework* 30/31: 68–111.

Sharma, Y. D., K. M. Srivastava, S. P. Gupta, et al. 1992. *Ramajanma Bhumi: Ayodhya. New Archaeological Discoveries*. New Delhi: Historians' Forum.

Shohat, Ella, and Robert Stam. 1994. *Unthinking Eurocentrism. Multiculturalism and the Media*. New York: Routledge.

Shulman, David D. 1985. *The King and the Clown in South Indian Myth and Poetry*. Princeton, NJ: Princeton University Press.

Siegel, Lee. 1978. *Sacred and Profane Dimensions of Love in Indian Traditions As Exemplified in the 'Gītagovinda' of Jayadeva*. Delhi: Oxford University Press.

Silverman, Kaja. 1988. *The Acoustic Mirror. The Female Voice in Psychoanalysis and Cinema*. Bloomington: University of Indiana Press.

Sinclair, John, Elizabeth Jacka, and Stuart Cunningham, eds. 1996. *New Patterns in Global Television*. New York: Oxford University Press.

Singh, Anup. 1991. "Notes before Filmmaking." *Journal of Arts and Ideas* 20–21: 21–25.

Singh, Bikram. 1968. "Achut Kanya—A Gem from the Past." *Filmfare* (July 19): 43, 55.

———. 1983. "The Commercial Reality Disturbed." In *Indian Cinema Superbazaar*, ed. Aruna Vasudev and Philippe Lenglet. Delhi: Vikas. 28–32.

Singh, Sujala. 1995. "The Epic (on) Tube: Plumbing the Depths of History. A Paradigm for Viewing the TV Serialization on the *Mahābhārata*." *Quarterly Review of Film and Video* 16.1: 77–101.

Smith, Anna Marie. 1994. "The Imaginary Inclusion of the Assimilable Good Homosexual: The British New Right's Representations of Sexuality and Race." *Diacritics* 24.2–3: 58–70.

Spear, Percival. *Modern India 1740–1947*. Oxford: Clarendon Press.

Srinivas, S. V. 1996. "Devotion and Defiance in Fan Activity." *Journal of Arts and Ideas* 29: 66–83.

———. 1999. "Fans, Families, and Censorship: The *Alluda Majaka* Controversy." *Journal of Arts and Ideas*. 32–33: 9–34.

Srivastava, Sanjay. 2002. "The Idea of Lata Mangeshkar: Speculations of Voice, Masculinity and the Post-colonial Condition." In *Politics of Innocence and Culpability in Indian Cinema*, ed. Ashis Nandy and Vinay Lal. Delhi: Oxford University Press.

Srivatsan, R. 1993. "Cartier-Bresson and the Birth of Modern India." *Journal of Arts and Ideas* 25–26: 37–53.

Star and Style. 1969. May: 30.

Star and Style. 1970. February: 6.

Star and Style. 1970. May: 33.

Star and Style. 1973. June: 35.

Steiner, Wendy. 1995. *The Scandal of Pleasure*. Chicago: University of Chicago Press.

Subramanyam, Radha. 1996. "Class, Caste, Performance in 'Subaltern' Feminist Film Theory and Praxis: An Analysis of *Rudaali*." *Cinema Journal* 35.3: 34–51.

Sukthankar, V. S. 1957. *On the Meaning of the Mahābhārata*. Bombay: Asiatic Society of Bombay.

Sukthankar, V. S., et al., eds. 1944–1959. *The Mahābhārata*. Poona: Bhandarkar Institute. [Poona Critical Edition]

Sutcliffe, William. 1997. *Are You Experienced?* Harmondsworth: Penguin.

Tharoor, Shashi. 1994. *Show Business*. London: Picador.

Thomas, Rosie. 1985. "Indian Cinema: Pleasures and Popularity." *Screen* 26.3–4: 116–131.

———. 1989. "Sanctity and Scandal: The Mythologization of Mother India." *Quarterly Review of Film and Video* 2: 11–30.

Thomas, Rosie, et al. 1983. *Cinema Cinema*. Channel 4 UK Television production. London.

Time. 1991. April 8.

Time. 1997. June 2: 76–77.

The Times of India. 1984. July 32–33.

The Times of India. 1999. January 24.

The Times of India. 1999. April 16.

The Times of India. 2000. September 24.

Tulsidasa, 1947. *Rāmacaritamānasa*, ed. S. N. Chaube. Gorakhpur: Gita Press.

Uberoi, Patricia. 1998. "The Diaspora Comes Home: Disciplining Desire in *DDLJ*." *Contributions to Indian Sociology* (n.s.) 32.2: 305–336.

Vaidyanathan, T. G. 1996. *Hours in the Dark: Essays on Cinema*. Delhi: Oxford University Press.

Valicha, Kishore. 1988. *The Moving Image: A Study of Indian Cinema*. Bombay: Orient Longman.

Van Buitenen, J. A. B., trans. 1973. *The Mahābhārata I. The Book of the Beginning*. Chicago: University of Chicago Press.

Vasudev, Aruna. 1978. *Liberty and Licence in the Indian Cinema*. Delhi: Vikas.

———. 1986. *The New Indian Cinema*. Delhi: Macmillan.

———. ed. 1995. *Frames of Mind. Reflections on Indian Cinema*. Delhi: UBSPD.

Vasudev, Aruna, and Philippe Lenglet, eds. 1983. *Indian Cinema Superbazaar*. Delhi: Vikas.

Vasudevan, Ravi, S. 1989. "The Melodramatic Mode and the Commercial Hindi Cinema." *Screen* 30.3: 29–50.

———. 1990. "Indian Commercial Cinema." *Screen* 31.4: 446–453.

———. 1995a. "'You Cannot Live in Society—and Ignore It': Nationhood and Female Modernity in *Andaz*." *Contributions to Indian Sociology* (n.s.) 29.1 & 2: 83–108.

———. 1995b. "Addressing the Spectator of a 'Third World' National Cinema: The Bombay 'Social' Film of the 1940s and 1950s." *Screen* 36.4: 305–324.

———. 1996a. "Bombay and Its Public." *Journal of Arts and Ideas* 29: 45–65.

———. 1996b. "Shifting Codes, Dissolving Identities. The Hindi Social Film of the 1950s As Popular Culture." *Third Text* 34: 59–77.

———. 2000a. *Making Meaning in Indian Cinema*. New Delhi: Oxford University Press.

———. 2000b. "National Pasts and Futures: Indian Cinema." *Screen* 41.1: 119–125.

———. 2000c. "The Politics of Cultural Address in a 'Transitional' Cinema: A Case Study of Indian Popular Cinema." In *Reinventing Film Studies*, ed. Christine Gledhill and Linda Williams. London: Arnold. 130–164.

Virdi, Jyotika. 1999. "Reverence, Rape—and Then Revenge: Popular Hindi Cinema's 'Woman's Film.'" *Screen*. 40.1: 17–37.

Viveshvar, Acharya, ed. 1960. *Mammaṭācarya Kāvyaprakāśa*. Varanasi: Jnanamandal Limited. 4.29.

Williams, David, ed. 1991. *Peter Brook and The Mahābhārata*. London and New York: Routledge.

Wollen, Peter. 1969. *Signs and Meaning in the Cinema*. Revised edition 1972. London: Secker and Warburg.

———. 1982. *Readings and Writings. Semiotic Counter-Strategies*. London: Verso.

———. 1992. "The Auteur Theory." In *Film Theory and Criticism*, ed. Gerald Mast, Marshall Cohen, and Leo Brandy. New York: Oxford University Press. 589–605.

Wright, Will. 1975. *Six Guns and Society. A Structural Study of the Western*. Berkeley: University of California Press.

Young, Robert J. C. 1995. *Colonial Desire. Hybridity in Theory, Culture, and Race*. London: Routledge.

Žižek, Slavoj. 1989. *The Sublime Object of Ideology*. London: Verso.

———. 1997a. "Multiculturalism, or, the Cultural Logic of Multinational Capitalism." *New Left Review* 225: 28–51.

———. 1997b. *The Plague of Fantasies*. London: Verso.

Index

Dyer, General 230
Dyer, Richard 126, 147, 156

Earth 211
Eisenstein, Sergei 81
Elan 66
Eliade, Mircea 120
Ellis, John 126, 147, 156
English Babu Desi Mem 250, 262, 264–6

Fanon, Frantz 86
Fanzines: and the construction of the star
    129–44; in English 129–39; in Hindi 130
Fairbanks, Douglas Sr. 126
Faraar 135
Fattelal, Sheikh 21, 22, 23
Fellini, Federico 91, 115
Fidyk, Andrzej 33, 98
Fiji: Aah in 105; cable TV in 240–1; cinema in
    x; fragment society x; popularity of
    Bollywood 240; racialization in 236; the-
    atres in xi
Fiza 37, 86, 146, 218, 233, 269
Flynn, Errol 126
Ford, John 91
Foucault, Michel 4
Frankenstein 49
Freud, Sigmund 4, 50, 94, 95

Gaji, Baejnath xi
Gandhi, Indira 62, 81, 128, 144, 146
Gandhi, Mahatma 18, 46, 67,73, 83, 84, 107,
    137, 160, 174, 176
Gandhi, Rajiv 140, 144, 145, 146
Gandhi, Sonia 259
Gangaa Jamuna Saraswathi 145
Ganga Ki Saugandh 137
Garam Hawa 209
Garroni, Emilio 157
George, T. J. S. 63
Ghai, Subhash 224, 226, 258
Ghatak, Ritwik 56
Ghori, Mohammed 206
Gigi 157, 158
Gillespie, Marie 245–7, 260, 269
Goel, Sita Ram 209
Goethe, Wolfgang von 17, 25
Good Earth, The 66
Gopalan, Lalitha 65

Gorky, Maxim 66
Gothic, The: and the uncanny 50; as literary
    genre 49–50, 52
Gothic, The Indian 49–59; and reincarnation
    51; and the supernatural 55
Govil, Arun 220–1
Govinda xv, xix, 5, 138
Great Gambler, The 135
Griffith, D.W. 68
Grover, Gulshan xvii
Guide 46–8, 97
Guide, The 44–6
Gul Bakavali xi
Gunga Jamna 81
Gupta, Dilip 57
Gustad, Kaizad xvii

Hartman, Geoffrey 120
Hasan, Mushirul 210
Hatimtai xii
Hattangadi, Shekhar 137, 138
Hawks, Howard 91
Heath, Stephen 92, 93
Hegel, G. W. F. 212
Hind Kesari xi, 126
Hindutva 213
Hiralal xvi
Hitchcock, Alfred 96
Hollywood Cinema 126, 269; and realist fic-
    tion 35
House for Mr. Biswas, A 236
House No. 44 97
Hublikar, Shanta: as Kesar in Aadmi 21–3
Hum xv, 127, 130, 132, 136, 137, 145
Hum Aap Ke Hain Kaun 7, 10, 66, 146, 218,
    240, 251, 262
Humayun 66, 217
Hum Dil De Chuke Sanam 259, 261
Hum Ek Hain xiii
Husnbanu 166
Husn Ka Chor 126
Hussain, Nazir 63

Ibrahim, Dawood 86
Imperial Film Company 17
Indian television 2–3
Indiana Jones and the Temple of Doom 245
Insaniyat 222, 227–9
Irani, Ardeshir 68